CHRONICLE OF THE
TRUTH COMMISSION

Foreword by
Archbishop Desmond Tutu

CHRONICLE OF THE
TRUTH COMMISSION

*A journey through the past and present
- into the future of South Africa*

PIET MEIRING

WIPF & STOCK · Eugene, Oregon

Wipf and Stock Publishers
199 W 8th Ave, Suite 3
Eugene, OR 97401

Chronicle of the Truth Commission
A Journey Through the Past and Present - Into the Future of South Africa
By Meiring, Pieter and Tutu, Desmond
Copyright©1999 by Meiring, Pieter
ISBN 13: 948-1-62564-714-6
Publication date 2/25/2014
Previously published by Carpe Diem Press, 1999

INDEX

FOREWORD

After the Truth and Reconciliation Commission had been appointed by President Nelson Mandela, it became its task to nominate and appoint 17 persons who would become members of the Human Rights Violations and the Reparation and Rehabilitation Committees. We were very careful to ensure the broadest possible representativeness in those we nominated, taking into account gender, race, geography, political, cultural, linguistic, etc. factors. We were particularly concerned that we would have someone from the Afrikaner Community who would strengthen the input from that grouping that would be provided by the two Afrikaner Commissioners – Wynand Malan and Chris de Jager. (The latter subsequently resigned as a Commissioner but stayed on as an Amnesty Committee member.)

I suggested Professor Piet Meiring as someone I believed had very considerable credibility and influence within a very important part of our South African society. He would bring important insights about the thinking, perspectives and concerns of the Afrikaner community, speaking as he would from well within that community. After all, he was a leading NGK theologian, being Professor in the Theology faculty of a former Afrikaans University and a leading light in that church's hierarchy and leadership élite, being at the time we would approach him, Moderator of one of its regional synods.

Had we been intent on being one-eyed and biased in favour of the ANC and seeking to engage in a witch-hunt against the former regime and Afrikaners as has been the accusation of some, then it is odd that we should have been at such pains to find a representative from that community who would share authentically the viewpoint of his people. It would have been pointless to look for a token appointee since most people would have seen through such a sham. I had known Professor Meiring as a person of considerable integrity and someone who had broad ecumenical interests. We were glad when he accepted our invitation. We have been wonderfully enriched by his fervent spirituality, his warm humanity and compassion and his zeal for justice, freedom and reconciliation informed by a sharp theological intellect.

Professor Meiring has done a superb job in speaking about the TRC and commending it to the Afrikaner community. He has used his regular column in *Beeld*, the leading Afrikaans daily in Gauteng, to very good effect in this regard.

We have not been disappointed by his outstanding contributions to our work. Our expectations have been more than met and it is such a person who has produced this reflection on the work of the TRC. He has, not surprisingly, used a motif that has resonance for Afrikaners – the motif of the *trek*. The TRC's work is refracted through the prism of the trek and an Afrikaner has provided the commentary. It is noteworthy that this will be the second book published on the TRC. Is it some coincidence that both books are by Afrikaners? I hope, so fervently, that my Afrikaner fellow-South Africans will be moved by Piet Meiring to see the TRC as a remarkable tool to enable us South Africans to come to terms with our horrendous past as efficaciously as possible – that we will be moved to confess, to forgive and be forgiven, responding to the extraordinary magnanimity of victims – black and white – and to be reconciled so that we can be healed. The world is looking on in amazement as we seek to become more and more the rainbow people of God revelling in and celebrating our God-given diversity of language, culture, ethnicity and religion. And the world is wondering, "if it can happen in post-apartheid South Africa, can't it happen here in Rwanda, Northern Ireland, Bosnia, Sri Lanka, et al?"

And we shall succeed in our bold experiment for the sake of God and for the sake of God's world, and a Piet Meiring will have made a telling contribution to that success.

– Archbishop Desmond Tutu –

CHAPTER 1
THE GREAT TREK TO THE PAST

16 JANUARY 1996: WHEN THE TELEPHONE RANG ...

"Hello, Piet, Desmond speaking. Are you sitting down ... ?"

On that Thursday afternoon, I was working peacefully in my office when the telephone rang. The academic year at the University of Pretoria would start in earnest within a week or so and the theological students would begin to arrive. It was my responsibility to see to it that all the necessary arrangements in the Science of Religion and Missiology Department had been made. Inundated as I was by the course material, minutes and correspondence to be dealt with that same afternoon, the Truth and Reconciliation Commission was the last thing on my mind. It was true that the appointment of the TRC and the immense task to be borne by the commissioners, had received a great deal of attention from the press and on the air. But I was not involved – and secretly grateful for that. Like many South Africans I held my breath when we did talk about the work of the Truth Commission. Where would this process lead? What shocking truths would be unearthed? Would our country and its people survive the work of the TRC?

"As you probably know, the TRC was granted the right to appoint a number of committee members besides the seventeen commissioners who have been appointed," Archbishop Desmond Tutu continued. "The idea is to make the TRC as representative of the South African community as possible. It concerns us that there is not a single representative from the Afrikaans churches on the TRC. That is why I am calling you. Your name was circulated among all the interested parties and was found acceptable."

I listened, my heart in my mouth. With his characteristic chuckle the archbishop continued. "Piet, you know of course that I am the archbishop of Cape Town and that I am allowed to speak on behalf of God. Well, the Lord says you must come ... but you have three days to decide!"

In this way I departed on a journey which would change my life once and for all. As the South African nation, too, departed on a journey, an epic journey back into the past, and onwards to the new future, a great trek which would leave none of the inhabitants of the country unaffected. For the next two and a half years the Truth Commission would be on everybody's lips. Newspapers and the radio would report daily on the work of the commission and the faces of hundreds of victims and offenders would appear on millions of television screens night after night.

◆ ◆ ◆

There was a long and vehement debate on the establishment of the Truth and Reconciliation Commission. For many days and nights the multiparty conference which had to guide the transition of the old South Africa to the new South Africa during the first months of 1994, struggled with the problem: what do we do with the unpaid account of the past, with the thousands of victims who had to suffer acutely for decades – and with the unknown number of offenders who were guilty of grossly violating human rights? How on earth will we get a reliable picture of what had happened in our country during the past thirty years – the so-called years of apartheid? How do we go about laying the first building stones of reconciliation?

Various possibilities had been considered.

On one side of the scale there was the option of a Nuremberg Trial. As the Allies, after the Second World War, took the German war criminals to court and sentenced them – some to death, others to imprisonment for life – the worst offenders in our country – politicians, members of the Defence Force and the Police who were guilty of gross violations of human rights – could be brought to justice. The death penalty no longer existed in South Africa, but life sentences could be passed. However, this possibility was rejected very soon. The circumstances at that time in Germany and today in South Africa cannot be compared, historians explained. A trial of the Nuremberg type implied that one group would be the indisputable conquerors, while the other party would be the definite losers. And this was not the case in South Africa where, after years of combat, the various parties all decided together to lay down arms, to negotiate a political solution together. Besides, a Nuremberg Trial would not be practical. The costs of court proceedings over many years would be astronomical. Above all, this would not lead to reconciliation in this country. On the contrary, new martyrs would be created, new wounds inflicted, which would take ages to heal.

On the opposite side of the scale, there was a possibility of proclaiming general amnesty, of closing the books as was the case in the neighbouring countries of Zambia, Zimbabwe and Namibia during their attainment of independence, to attempt to forgive and forget. But, experts had warned, this would also not be the ideal solution. It would mean a slap in the faces of the many victims and their families, as if their pain and suffering in the past was not that acute, as if it could be easily brushed away. Besides, this would not work: one cannot sweep the ghosts of the past under the carpet and pretend that they do not exist. Unsettled matters, long-standing injustices and reproaches have a way of returning, of growing with the passing of the years. This, some argued, is what is currently happening in our neighbouring countries. An easy general amnesty was not the answer. It would be much better to face the past squarely, to put the truth on the table – however hard it might be. "Of course we have to close the books," Archbishop Tutu declared on television. "But the books must first be opened – before they can be closed for the last time."

The solution had to be found somewhere in the middle, between the Nuremberg model and the model of general amnesty. A process had to be developed to attend to the needs of victims as much as to those of the offenders. On the eve of the elections of 14 April 1994, late in the afternoon, the so-called sunset clause was accepted by the various parties of the Multiparty Conference: a *Truth and Reconciliation Commission* would be established, comprising three committees, each with its own agenda: a *Committee on Human Rights Violations* which would afford the thousands of victims in the country the opportunity to relate their stories, to put a hitherto unwritten chapter of our history on the table. In the same way the *Committee on Amnesty* would have to make it possible for the many offenders – of all sides of the spectrum, white, as well as black – to approach the TRC, also with their stories and testimonies to eventually apply for amnesty. Thirdly, provision had to be made for a *Committee on Reparation and Rehabilitation* to pay particular attention to the needs of the victims, to prepare proposals for remuneration and reparation.

The establishment of a South African Truth and Reconciliation Commission was not totally unique. During the past twenty years (1974-1994) nineteen similar commissions had been operating in sixteen countries in all: in Latin America, in countries such as Chile, Argentina, Brazil, Bolivia and El Salvadore; in Africa, in Uganda, Chad, Ethiopia, Rwanda; as well as in Europe, with the unification of East and West Germany.

Some of these commissions had been convened by international organisations such as the United Nations, others by local government bodies or sometimes by non-government organisations (NGOs). Some of these commissions did good work and produced extensive reports, as those of the Chilean Commission. Others never functioned well.

What distinguished the work of the South African TRC from the other commissions were, among other things, the following:

◆ The establishment of the TRC was as democratic as possible, with as many people as possible participating.
◆ The commissioners were appointed from various interest groups by means of a process which was as democratic and transparent as possible.
◆ The establishment, objectives and methods of the commission were based upon an act accepted by Parliament.
◆ The press and the public had full access to the hearings.
◆ The commission was granted the authority to subpoena people and to confiscate documents.
◆ The commission was granted the power to grant amnesty to offenders.
◆ Not only the names of victims, but also those of the violators of human rights would be made known.

◆ ◆ ◆

Shortly after the inauguration of the new president, Nelson Mandela, the writing of the act commenced. During July 1995 the Minister of Justice, Mr Dullah Omar, submitted the bill to the South African Parliament. On 19 July 1995, the Promotion of National Unity and Reconciliation Act, 1995 (Act No 34 of 1995) was accepted by Parliament with a great majority and just as much anticipation.

The National Party voted in favour of the Act – despite the warning by the party leader, Mr FW de Klerk, that the TRC should not degenerate into a witch-hunt. Also General Constand Viljoen from the Freedom Front, had objections – and requested the president to extend the cut-off date from December 1993 until the inauguration of the new president on 10 May 1994. The Inkatha Freedom Party, who raised serious objections against the Act, voted against the legislation.

The long Preamble to the Act based on the final clause of the Interim Constitution, is moving, almost poetic. At that time Kader Asmal, who had to submit the text of the final clause for approval, succeeded in enlisting the help of a number of persons, among whom the distinguished Afrikaans novelist, André Brink – in compiling the wording. Nothing could be more inspiring:

"SINCE the Constitution of the Republic of South Africa, 1993 (Act No 200 of 1993), provides a historic bridge between the past of a deeply divided society characterised by strife, conflict, untold suffering and injustice, and a future founded on the recognition of human rights, democracy and peaceful co-existence for all South Africans, irrespective of colour, race, class, belief or sex;

AND SINCE it is deemed necessary to establish the truth in relation to past events as well as the motives for and circumstances in which gross violations of human rights have occurred, and to make the findings known in order to prevent repetition of such acts in future;

AND SINCE the Constitution states that the pursuit of national unity, the well-being of all South African citizens and peace require reconciliation between the people of South Africa and the reconstruction of society;

AND SINCE the Constitution states that there is a need for understanding but not for vengeance, a need for reparation but not for retaliation, a need for *ubuntu* but not for victimization;

AND SINCE the Constitution states that in order to advance such reconciliation and reconstruction amnesty shall be granted in respect of acts, omissions and offences associated with political objectives committed in the course of the conflicts of the past;

AND SINCE the Constitution provides that Parliament shall under the Constitution adopt a law which determines a firm cut-off date, which shall be a date after 8 October 1990 and before the cut-off date envisaged in the Constitution, and providing for the mechanisms, criteria and procedures, including tribunals, if any, through which such amnesty shall be dealt with;

– BE IT THEREFORE ENACTED by the Parliament of the Republic of South Africa ..."

The aims of the Truth and Reconciliation Commission, as Minister Omar explained in his address to Parliament, were to promote national unity and reconciliation in South Africa, in a spirit of understanding which transcends the conflicts and divisions of the past by:

◆ establishing as complete a picture as possible of the causes, nature and extent of the gross violations of human rights which were committed during the period from 1 March 1960 to the cut-off date including the antecedents, circumstances, factors and context of such violations, as well as the perspectives of the victims and the motives and perspectives of the persons responsible for the commission of the violations, by conducting investigations and holding hearings;

◆ facilitating the granting of amnesty to persons who make full disclosure of all the relevant facts relating to acts associated with a political objective and comply with the requirements of this Act;

◆ establishing and making known the fate or whereabouts of victims and by restoring the human and civil dignity of such victims by granting them the opportunity to relate their own accounts of the violations of which they are the victims, and by recommending reparation measures in respect of them;

◆ compiling a report providing as comprehensive an account as possible of the activities and findings of the Commission ... and which contains recommendations of measures to prevent the future violations of human rights;

"We are very much in earnest in intending to leave the past behind, to heal the wounds of the past, to forgive, but not forget, to build a future founded on respect for human rights," Dullah Omar said. "We must embark on the Great Trek away from the past, through our period of transition and into a new future."

13 FEBRUARY 1996: THE TREK BEGINS

In Cape Town the newly furnished office of the TRC in Adderley Street was a hive of activity. It was the day of the official opening of the Truth and Reconciliation Commission. Very appropriately, it would take place in the Saint George's Cathedral, the cathedral of the chairperson of the TRC. From the regional offices in Johannesburg, Durban and East London, the seventeen commissioners, together with eleven committee members, travelled to the Cape. On this occasion our spouses were allowed to accompany us. "They will have to sacrifice a great deal and will have to get on without their husbands and wives for long periods of time," the deputy chairperson, Alex Boraine, explained. "This once we can spoil them a little."

During a luncheon at one o'clock, the members of the TRC had the opportunity to get better acquainted. Definitely an interesting and diverse group, black and brown and white and Indian, old and (reasonably) young, jurists and ministers, writers, academics, ex-prisoners, doctors and psychologists, activists and parliamentarians, people who, in the past, had been on different sides of the struggle, representatives of wellnigh all religions in the country, Christian, Jewish, Muslim and Hindu. The rainbow nation on a smaller scale!

The three judges, Hassen Mall, Andrew Wilson and Bernard Ngoepe, who would serve on the Committee on Amnesty with Advocates Chris de Jager and Sisi Khampepe, were there. Also the people of the Committee on Human Rights Violations: Desmond Tutu and Alex Boraine,

The comment of Zapiro, famous English cartoonist, on the news that the Truth Commission had started its work.

Yasmin Sooka, Wynand Malan, Mary Burton, Bongani Finca, Richard Lyster, Fazel Randera, Dumisa Ntsebeza, Denzil Potgieter, Pumla Gobode-Madikizela, Joyce Seroke, Hugh Lewin, Russel Ally and Ilan Lax. Thirdly, there were the members of the Reparation and Rehabilitation Committee, the committee on which I myself would serve for more than two years: Hlengiwe Mkhize, Wendy Orr, Khoza Mgojo, Mapule Ramashala, Glenda Wildschut, Piet Meiring, Tom Manthata, Mcibisi Xundu and Smangele Mgwaza.

The three of us who were Afrikaners on the TRC, Chris de Jager (former Member of Parliament for the Conservative Party and Freedom Front, founder member of the AWB), Wynand Malan (well-known "liberal" National Party Member of Parliament, who later on found his way to the Democratic Party) and myself (minister of the NG Kerk – Dutch Reformed Church – who became professor at the Theological Faculty of the University of Pretoria), derived pleasure from telling everybody who wanted to listen – and those who did not want to listen – that all three of us were ex-students of the University of Pretoria. More so, that we had been in the same hostel, in Sonop.

◆ ◆ ◆

When the service was about to start, the cathedral was already packed. People came from far and wide, victims and well-wishers, choirs and women in uniform, ambassadors and politicians, members of the press from all over the world. We sang and prayed, we lit candles of reconciliation. After the TRC commissioners had been sworn in solemnly, each received an olive branch.

The whole audience was requested to stand when Barney Beck from the Western Cape Peace Centre read a moving litany from the heart of the Quaker tradition, in Afrikaans. Loosely translated, it reads as follows:

Before You, in anguish and shame, we bring the polars of our
society – oppressor and oppressed, victim and offender,
and we pray for an end to the alienation,
for healing and reparation.

Congregation: Hear our prayer.

We looked into the eyes of our children and were overwhelmed.
We looked into the eyes of our parents and were dejected.
We looked into each other's eyes and turned away.

Congregation: We desire peace.

Merciful God, we confess that we never believed what had happened.
We tried to escape from reality.
We never really listened or heard.
We allowed a wedge to be driven between us.
Forgive us.
We pray for forgiveness.

Congregation: Hear us by your grace.

President Mandela talked solemnly about the Commission and its mandate. Politicians who wanted to suppress the past were making a big mistake, he said. Ordinary South Africans were determined that everything had to be disclosed, to ensure that the mistakes of the past would never be repeated. "The choice we have is not whether we should disclose the past, but how it will be done. It must be done in such a way that reconciliation and peace are promoted." When looking back, he continued, one realizes that every one of us was a victim, that the whole South African nation had suffered. The process of healing which had been set in motion, was likewise intended for everybody, for individuals, families and communities. Above all, it was intended for the whole nation, the nation who had to find healing and deliverance in the process that we were facing.

"I am not really known as a man of few words," Desmond Tutu declared at the end of the ceremony, "but the service, the prayers, leave me speechless!"

However, the service also had its tense moments – to an extent already an adumbration of what lay ahead of us in the months to come.

Firstly, Deputy President F W de Klerk did not appear to take his seat in the front, next to President Nelson Mandela. Why not? was the question on many lips. Was he withdrawing his support of the process? The explanation came later from Mr de Klerk's office: he was informed of the service in the cathedral too late!

Secondly, Mrs Winnie Madikizela-Mandela was there as well, dressed charmingly, bodyguard and all. She had already been separated from her husband. The divorce would follow shortly. But she took the seat intended for the deputy president, in the front row, a few seats from the president. The president did not once look in her direction. But when the service had come to an end and Mr Mandela left the cathedral a few minutes earlier than the rest of the audience, Winnie Mandela, uninvited, got up and accompanied him to wave to the crowd outside the church. This would not be the last time that she made her appearance at the TRC in an unorthodox way.

After the service, my wife Inza, and I, chatted to Tim du Plessis, deputy editor of the *Beeld*, on the steps of the cathedral: about the service, about President Mandela's words, Tutu's reaction and about the moving Afrikaans prayer. It was clear that the TRC, and also the whole nation of South Africa, had embarked on a vital journey, a great trek through the history of our country. Where would this trek eventually lead? What experiences awaited us all? How many casualties would there be along the road? What would be the role of the press – Tim's newspaper and all the other newspapers in our country – in this process? There were more questions than answers.

29 FEBRUARY 1996: HEAVY WEATHER

We very soon realized that the TRC would make heavy weather. In the Johannesburg office on the tenth floor of the Sanlam Centre – the '*Boere* Carlton' as it is locally referred to – the commissioners and committee members gathered daily. Plans and administrative arrangements had to be made and staff members appointed. Above all, the Promotion of National Unity and Reconciliation Act, with all the instructions for the work of the three committees, had to be studied closely.

As for the work of the Reparation and Rehabilitation Committee, the first trial run was a meeting in KwaZulu-Natal which already took place on 7 February, a few days before the official opening of the TRC in Cape Town. In the vicinity of Port Shepstone, there were, over a very long period of time, reports of unrest and violence. Long-standing disputes, some which lasted for decades, flared up again. Several victims of the ANC and the Inkatha Freedom Party, as well as other political groupings, wished to be heard by members of the Truth Commission. The question on everybody's lips was: what would the TRC do to alleviate the fate of the victims and their families?

Under heavy police escort, the TRC members travelled from Durban to Port Shepstone. During the first weeks the TRC, as well as the security people who had to protect them, were rather nervous. No disaster should befall the commissioners! There was a medley of victims, interested persons and members of the press in the hall. For hours on end they debated and asked questions – questions to which, I am afraid, the TRC did not have all the answers. The process had scarcely begun, needs still had to be identified and a policy formulated.

Where the TRC often, during the months to come, had to endure criticism from the Afrikaner ranks, the first blows came from the opposite side of the political spectrum. During the Port Shepstone gathering, Father Cosmas Desmond, former priest and anti-apartheid campaigner who participated as PAC candidate in the 1994 elections, asked scathing questions. Some of these questions he repeated a week or so later in the Johannesburg newspaper, *The Star* (29 February 1996): one of the criteria for appointment of the commissioners was that they should not have a high political profile, Cosmas Desmond expostulated. One could understand that there should be a place for Desmond Tutu, "John the Baptist to Mandela's Messiah". But what was Alex Boraine, who was part of the illegitimate apartheid parliament in the old South Africa, doing on the TRC? It was not sufficient to say that Boraine and some of his associates had been in the seats of the opposition. They were part of an illegitimate and unfair system, a system which they now, as judges, had to judge. And the members of the committees, where did they come from? And the "over-representation of religious bodies"? And the "Christian" – better phrased "Western" – way in which the process was undertaken? Was it fair and effective? It was as clear as daylight that the Reparation and Rehabilitation Committee had disappointed the Catholic Father that day in Port Shepstone.

While we, rather concerned, sat in the Johannesburg office discussing Cosmas Desmond's article, Yasmin Sooka remarked, "This is only the tip of the iceberg. There are several persons, especially from the ranks of AZAPO and the PAC, of the former Black Consciousness Movement, who are just as dissatisfied. We will still have a lot to do with them. In the Eastern Cape the families of Steve Biko, Matthew Goniwe and quite a large number of other activists had already expressed their dissatisfaction concerning the TRC Act. The process was perpetrator-friendly, they said. The perpetrators who applied for amnesty, and received it, would receive full absolution of all their actions. Irrespective of whether they had committed forty murders! No criminal or civil action can be taken against them. And the victims, what will there be for them? As good as nothing! The family members cannot even subpoena the perpetrators for compensation. The TRC, so they said, took the bread from the mouths of the widows and orphans!"

"We will have to get started with our proposals on what can be done to alleviate the fate of the victims and their families," Hlengiwe Mkhize, chairperson of the Reparation and Rehabilitation Committee, remarked. "It is our only defence against the criticism of Cosmas Desmond and the others. We will have to show clearly, by what we negotiate for the thousands of men, women and children who were subjected to gross violations of human rights, that we really care about these people, that the TRC process is profoundly victim-friendly."

1 MARCH 1996: THE NG KERK (DUTCH REFORMED CHURCH) MAKES ITS VOICE HEARD

It was clear that the Nederduitse Gereformeerde Kerk, perhaps more than any other denomination in the country, would be involved in the work of the TRC during the months to come. In the eyes of many people, within and outside the Republic, this church was the church of apartheid, "the National Party at prayer", which not only established the theological infrastructure for the apartheid system, but also the church where several politicians and public service officials, members of the Police and Defence Force, the enforcers of the apartheid policy, worshipped on Sundays. Developments in the church, also the arduous process during which the NG Kerk took leave of apartheid, were of great importance to the TRC.

The NG Kerk, on its part, took thorough notice of the work of the TRC. Already at the end of 1995 the General Synodal Commission took a number of decisions in which the church promised its support and intercession by prayer, but also directed the serious request that the TRC would act fairly to all sides. The church even went further by naming seven candidates to be appointed as commissioners. It was quite a disappointment that none of these seven made the grade. The fact that I later became involved in the TRC, although not as official representative of the church, was to some extent a consolation.

In an open letter to *Die Kerkbode* (9/10 February 1996), the official mouthpiece of the NG Kerk, a group of forty-six ministers and professors of the church promised their support to the TRC. The letter read that the time had come for the NG Kerk to reach out to others, to work together in the process of the search for truth and reconciliation. "The issues under discussion in the TRC," wrote the forty-six, "namely truth, confession of guilt, restitution, compassion with the fate of victims, reconciliation, etc, are all issues that closely concern the church. These are central themes of the Gospel and should characterise the life of the church. A church which loves Christ lives by, and for, these issues. Moreover, the church knows that the truth does not threaten but liberate; that reconciliation does not work in a self-destructive but enriching manner; that contrariwise lies enslave and, together with impenitence and pride, destroy life."

The church, by definition, should have taken the lead in the search for truth and reconciliation, but now that the TRC had been set in motion, the church should provide its enthusiastic, critical and whole-hearted co-operation. Victims, as well as perpetrators, who would find their way to the TRC in the months to come, deserved the empathy and support of the church.

"The NG Kerk has already at many occasions confessed its guilt with regard to the establishment and maintenance of the apartheid system. We have also confessed that serious misdemeanours systematically and regularly took place against people's basic rights and human dignity. We are now facing the test to convert these confessions into actions. One of these actions is to sincerely support the Truth Commission and the issues that this commission strives for. Any impeachment or avoid-ance of the matter can seriously harm the moral foundations of our life as a church and community for years to come. Without insight into the deep ambivalences of the past of the NG Kerk and those of the society served by this church, we cannot begin to understand ourselves. With-out this insight the church remains impervious to change and revival. To expose the past now, is to build, faithfully, a new future. We trust that the church will have the courage and humility to accept this diffi-cult task." The letter concluded on a very serious note: "In this we may not let the members of the church down."

In *Die Kerkbode* of 1 March it was reported that the moderature of the General Synod, had visited the offices of the TRC in Cape Town. A full and enthusiastic account was given of the interview that they had conducted with Archbishop Tutu. Tutu, from his side, requested that the Truth Commission be afforded the opportunity to prove itself and to show that it was sincere in its intentions to deal with victims as well as perpetrators fairly and sensibly. "The Commission does not wish to instigate a witch-hunt, but to afford South Africans of all convictions the opportunity to close the book of the past."

From the side of the NG Kerk, the Moderator, Rev Freek Swanepoel, together with his colleagues, reconfirmed that they wished to support the work of the TRC and that they would regularly intercede by prayer for the TRC. They added: "The NG Kerk will also make its voice heard if, in the opinion of the church, the Commission performs its work justly and equitably – and if not."

In his comments on the events, the editor of *Die Kerkbode* added: "It will be a traumatic time for all of us, but, if undertaken correctly, it can also be a time of purging, a catharsis which can eventually heal our torn community. It appeared from the conversation that Archbishop

Tutu comprehends the formidability of the task and how easy it would be to achieve exactly the opposite of what he intended. It is indeed extremely difficult to observe the recent history objectively and to determine the 'truth' of yesterday from today's perspective."

Exactly how difficult it would be to depart on this journey through the past, would not only be experienced by the members of the NG Kerk in the months to come. Every South African would be confronted with the past.

16-19 APRIL 1996: EAST LONDON – THE VERY FIRST HUMAN RIGHTS VIOLATIONS HEARING

People from far and wide flocked to the East London City Hall. The first human rights violations hearing would commence. Victims and their families started to arrive on the previous day, together with journalists and camera crews. In the office of the TRC in Oxford Street, Archbishop Tutu, who would act as chairperson, discussed the proceedings for the next four days with his colleagues.

There was enough to report on. In all four of the regional offices of the TRC, in Cape Town, Johannesburg, Durban and East London, arrangements for similar hearings had been made in March. Every office would follow its own programme. Prototeams had already visited several cities and towns to make contact with victims, to assist them in completing the necessary forms. Information meetings had been held everywhere. In the company of Fazel Randera, the Head of the Johannesburg office, Wynand Malan, Tom Manthata, Russel Ally, Hugh Lewin and Joyce Seroke, I had to meet audiences in the remote corners of the four northern provinces, from Potchefstroom and Klerksdorp and Zeerust to Pietersburg and Louis Trichardt and Messina, from Thohoyandou in Venda to Giyani, capital of the former Gazankulu. In Mpumalanga various cities and towns had been visited: Nelspruit, Witbank, Standerton, Volksrust and Balfour. Everywhere we were confronted with the same questions: What will the TRC really achieve? Is it not merely a witchhunt of one group against the other – Blacks (actually the ANC) against Whites (the apartheid regime)? How fair would the process proceed? Wouldn't the evidence to be disclosed cause a wave of hatred in the community?

Furthermore: the East London session would commence on a somewhat cloudy note. Yasmin Sooka's predictions of a week or two ago came true. On 15 April, a week before the session would start, the newspapers announced that the families of a number of notable victims – Griffiths Mxenge, Steve Biko and Fabian Ribeiro – had submitted an application at the Constitutional Court to invalidate the whole Act according to which the TRC had been established. Their argument was that by granting amnesty to the guilty, justice would not be done to those who had been murdered or their relatives. And they were not the only ones. Even earlier, on 5 April, the outspoken president of the SA Prisoners Organisation for Human Rights (SAPOHR), Golden Miles Bhudu, sent a strongly worded letter to Archbishop Tutu, expressing his serious misgivings about the whole TRC process, especially the offer of amnesty to perpetrators of the former apartheid regime.

There were, therefore, several questions which needed answers, more than one urgent problem which had to be solved. Procedures for dealing with the victims would be determined and tested for the first time.

◆　◆　◆

In the course of four days the victims, altogether thirty-three men and women, one after the other, came forward to testify in East London. Twenty-seven incidents of gross violations of human rights would be scrutinised. Victims and their relatives, commissioners and committee members, journalists, camera crews, crowds of interested persons – the majority of them black, with a few Whites scattered in between – crowded into the city hall.

Every morning at nine Archbishop Tutu, followed by the TRC members who would be present at that day's hearing, stepped into the hall. Behind them, the group of victims who would testify that day, followed. After a candle, symbol of reconciliation which would burn every day, had been lit by Tutu, the deputy chairperson, Alex Boraine, invited the victims one by one to come forward, take the oath and tell their stories. With each witness two or three persons took their places on the platform: a relative or friend, sometimes a minister who had known the family for years, as well as an official "supporter" (briefer) who would guide the victim through the process. By placing a hand on the shoulder for comfort, often with a tissue to stop the tears, the briefer who had regular contact with the victims and their families in the preceding weeks, played a most important role.

On the first day the proceedings started off on a somewhat formal note. Neither the chairperson and his colleagues, nor the witnesses or the audience, knew exactly what lay ahead. Gradually, however, the proceedings became more informal. There was no alternative, the dramatic events that were taking place, the emotions that were roused, could not be handled in a juridically correct, hyperformal tone. The witnesses were allowed to testify in the language of their choice. Headphones, with simultaneous translations in English and Xhosa, were made available to everybody for this purpose.

Of the thirty-three witnesses who were given a turn to speak, eight used the opportunity to talk about themselves, to relate the gross violations of human rights that had been committed against them personally. The rest of the witnesses spoke about their relatives, their spouses who had been killed, of children, friends or a brother who had been murdered or disappeared. The story of Singqokwana Malgas, one of the first in the Eastern Cape to die in police custody, took the audience far back into the past, to the early sixties. Other stories, the majority, came from the era of 1980-1992.

First of all, the most well-known, notorious cases came up for discussion: those of the abduction of the Pepco Three, the murder of the Cradock Four and the attacks on the Highgate Hotel and the King William's Town Golf Club. Later on the stories of lesser-known, half forgotten victims such as Billy Kohl and Mandisa Mbovane were also related. The victims had fought under different colours: ANC, PAC, AZAPO, SRC and Cosas. Others had no political affiliation, had landed in the cross-fire as innocent bystanders. The majority of the offenders who were debunked, came from the ranks of the Police and Defence Force, although accusing fingers also pointed to members of Apla, the ANC and the Ciskeian Defence Force.

Drama, high-strung emotion, was the order of the day. When it was the turn of Mrs Nomonde Calata, the wife of Fort Calata, one of the Cradock Four who had been abducted and murdered in June 1985, to speak, her grief overwhelmed her. She ran short of words and uttered a long, agonizing cry. A shocked silence descended on the hall. The chairperson adjourned the hearing for ten minutes to give Mrs Calata and her briefer the opportunity to go outside for a respite. How would Tutu and his colleagues deal with this, many a person wondered. When Mrs Calata was led into the hall again, Tutu surprised each and everyone by doing what had never been done before, but would be repeated frequently later during similar situations – by requesting the audience to stand up and sing a hymn. He himself intoned the moving words of

Senzeni na ("What have we done?"). The members of the press and camera crew joined in. Then the hearing could proceed.

◆ ◆ ◆

Was everything worth it? I asked myself when, after one of the morning sessions, I walked outside.

What one of the Xhosa women – one of the unknown, practically forgotten witnesses, had to say in the hall just now did not only move the archbishop to tears, but left everyone of us with a lump in the throat. With effort she put the tale on the table: of how she, years ago, sent her fourteen-year-old son to the shop to buy bread. There was unrest in the township and somewhere along the way it must have happened that the boy landed in the cross-fire. For some reason the Security Police arrested the wounded child and subjected him to brutal torture. Two days later, the mother who, panic-stricken, fumbled about to find out what had happened to her son, saw, on her neighbours' television set during the eight o'clock news, the boy being pulled down from a *bakkie* (open vehicle) by his ankles, how he was being dragged across the tarmac.

It was difficult for the old mother to relate how the police eventually gave her an address where she could find her son. When she arrived there, it was the mortuary. With her own hands she had to prepare her son's body – with the bullet wounds, a gaping wound on the back of his head, the burn marks where he was tortured – for the funeral. One could have heard a pin drop in the hall.

My lunch in my hand, I encountered the woman in the midst of a small group of victims.

"Madam, please tell me," I asked, "you have come such a long way, over so many years, with your story. Yesterday you had to travel such a long distance to come here. All of us saw how difficult it was for you to tell the story of your son in front of all the people. Please tell me: was it worth it?"

The tear marks were still on her cheeks. But when she raised her head and smiled, it was like the dawn breaking:

"Oh yes, Sir, absolutely! It was difficult to talk about all these things. But tonight, for the first time in sixteen years, I think I will be able to sleep through the night. Maybe tonight I will sleep soundly without having nightmares!"

◆ ◆ ◆

It was important to keep a record of the requests of the victims. It had to be done, because the Reparation and Rehabilitation Committee was instructed to listen attentively, research the needs and fate of the victims and their families, in order to eventually formulate suitable and practicable recommendations for compensation.

The victims produced a humble list of needs:

Nearly everybody wanted information, wanted to know what had happened to them or their loved ones, and why. Others requested that photographs and other personal possessions confiscated at the time, should be returned, or that the mortal remains of a husband or a child be brought home for reinterment. Some requested gravestones, which they could not afford at the time of death. Mrs Mgwinya requested the TRC to assist her in returning the cutlery and chairs that she borrowed from her neighbour the day when she lost all her possessions. Twelve witnesses requested help to keep their children at school. Others raised the point of medical care and housing, or talked about the need for a special day of reconciliation in the country. The strangest, and saddest, request came from Mrs Mhlawuli who wanted her husband's hand, which was severed by the police at the time and kept as deterrent in a bottle of formalin, to be returned to the family. They wanted to bury it.

Were the victims and their families willing to forgive the offenders, the abductors and torturers? Was reconciliation really possible? Witnesses were not unanimous about this matter. Some showed a nearly unbelievable magnanimity – people such as Beth Savage – to forgive unconditionally those who treated them cruelly. Others – such as Karl Weber and Mrs Kondile – raised the question: shouldn't justice be done, the guilty ones be brought to book before forgiveness and reconciliation can become a reality? This problem would long still be mulled over in the months to come.

◆ ◆ ◆

Speaking about Beth Savage: her testimony was one of the most moving heard during the whole TRC process. When she related her story, of how she and her friends attended the annual Christmas party at the Golf Club in King William's Town (28 November 1992), everybody straightened up in their chairs. While they had been chatting cheerfully,

Beth related, she became aware of something which sounded like fire-crackers. When she swung around to look what was happening, she saw that a man wearing a balaclava on his head, with an AK 47 in his hand, was shooting at her and her friends. Hand-grenades were thrown. Before she blacked out, she saw her friends falling around her. Beth was taken to a hospital in Bloemfontein by helicopter, where she remained in the intensive care unit for a month. Open-heart surgery followed. She also had a large part of her intestines removed. A lot of shrapnel could never be removed from her body, so much that (in her own words) "all the bells ring when I go through the airport!"

Beth's life, as well as that of the members of her family, would never be the same again. Her husband and children were still struggling to cope with the trauma. Her father, who had been against apartheid all his life, sat by her bedside for days on end. Over and over he muttered through his tears, "You know, I can't believe what has happened!" He went into a very deep depression. Six months before Beth would testify in East London, her father, a broken man, died. Two months later her mother passed away.

And still, Beth testified, not everything was bad. What had happened to her, had wonderfully enriched her. It had made her grow. "It has given me the ability to relate to other people who may be going through trauma."

When one of the TRC members asked Beth Savage how she now felt about the perpetrators, she answered quietly, "It is a difficult question. But truthfully, my honest feeling is: 'there, but for the grace of God, go I'. I do not know how I would have reacted, if I were one of them (the freedom fighters). It is all I can say. I think it is marvellous that we can have a Truth Commission. To be able to get everything off your chest brings healing ... I hope that everybody will experience this healing. You know, there are people present here who wrestle with endless more problems than I am."

When questioned further, about what the TRC could do for her, Beth's reaction was, "I have often said this: what I really want, is to meet the man who threw the hand-grenade. I would want to do it in a spirit of forgiveness, in the hope that he, for whatever reason, will also forgive me ... "

Archbishop Tutu was greatly moved: "Thank you very much! All I can say is, what a wonderful country this is! We really have extraordinary people. Yesterday I declared that I was proud to be black, for the way in which black people have endured the hardships they encountered. And now we have another such example (a white example)! I think this predicts a wonderful future for our country. We thank you for the attitude of forgiveness that you have shown and pray that everybody who hears you, and sees you, will say, "We have indeed an astonishing country, with extraordinary people, of all races!"

◆ ◆ ◆

When I boarded the plane back to Johannesburg, there was much to reflect upon. How could one ever forget all these testimonies – that of Beth Savage, together with the rest? With a feeling of sorrow I made a note of the question raised by a black minister, who, one morning before the hearing commenced, rose to address the people around him.

"There must be a mistake somewhere," he said. "I brought nearly my whole congregation along to be here today. They had to come and listen to what the victims say. They wanted to stretch out their hands to all the white people of East London, to forgive them, to be reconciled with them." Waving his hand over the people in the city hall, over the many black people and the small group of white people. "But I see nearly no white people to talk to today. There is nobody with whom we can be reconciled. Where are they?"

But everything had not yet been lost. A day or so after the hearing Desmond Tutu provided me with a copy of an English letter that he received, which was written following on the East London hearing. He did not want to reveal the name of the white author without his or her permission. The letter, with a poem attached, reads as follows in the original English:

"As an ordinary member of the public I would like you to know that I have been intensely moved and inspired by the testimonies heard at the T and R Commission in East   London last week. My pain and inspiration come from the awesome, horrific and humbling stories, and the extraordinary forgiveness of those wounded people. We are all wounded. I wrote a poem to try and understand what all this means, and I would like you to know that there are many people out there, who FEEL with those people. The pain belongs to us all. Thank you, all of you, for your own humility, and for helping us towards healing.

TOWARDS HEALING

The world is wet.
Blood and pain seep into our listening,
into our wounded souls.
The sound of your sobbing is my own weeping,
your wet handkerchief, my pillow
for a past so exhausted
it cannot rest, not yet.
Speak, weep, look, listen for us all,
oh people of the silent, hidden past,
let your stories scatter seeds
into our lonely, frightened winds;
sow more
until the stillness of this land can soften,
can dare to hope and smile and sing,
until the ghosts can dance unshackled,
until our lives can know your sorrows,
and be healed.

29 APRIL-3 MAY 1996: THE JOHANNESBURG HEARING – "THIS WON'T WORK!"

"No, this won't work!," the chairperson declared. "We really cannot start like this!" The first human rights violations hearing in the central business district of Johannesburg, in the building of the Central Methodist Church, did indeed start out in a curious way.

A great deal of effort was made at the Johannesburg office to get everything in order. As in the other three regions of the country, where they worked equally hard on the hearings to be held, the local team, too, laboured for weeks. TRC personnel spent long hours in black, and also in white, residential areas. Information meetings were held, victims assisted in completing their statements. Local congregations and welfare organisations were visited. Would they be able to provide aid in counselling victims and their families? Lists had to be checked. The programme needed to be balanced, in order that victims of all sides of the struggle could appear on the platform. Everybody needed to see that the TRC was acting fairly and was unprejudiced in the execution of its task.

A delicate matter which caused rather severe differences in the Johannesburg office, was how the proceedings should be opened. The Johannesburg hearing would be an important display window for the TRC. Nearly the full diplomatic corps had informed us that they would be there, as well as several cabinet ministers and senior officials. Foreign guests came from far and wide. A day before, members of the press from all over the world had staked their claim on the gallery and in the press room. Fazel Randera, the head of the office, and some of the jurists with him, seriously felt that the East London hearing – as well as other TRC functions recently – proceeded altogether too 'religiously'. The many prayers and hymns did not belong in a juridical process. That the archbishop was wearing his official dress, bishop's cross and all – they could do nothing about. But a TRC hearing was a juridical act and not a service in the Saint George's Cathedral in Cape Town! If the ceremony should start solemnly, why not a half minute of silence and meditation, as is the practice in Parliament these days?

In the vestry of the Methodist Church, early in the morning of Day Number One, Tutu discussed the issue with the local TRC members. "Very well," he agreed, "it is your hearing. I will do as you ask. We will only have a moment of silence before we proceed."

When the clock struck nine the witnesses and their families were escorted into the crowded hall. Tutu followed with his colleagues. Chairperson shook hands with the victims one by one. Then he proceeded to the platform where he took his seat. He asked for half a minute of silence. The first witness was brought to the table and sworn in.

But Tutu could not get under way. He sat down. He moved his papers from side to side. Visibly uncomfortable, he looked at the victims, at the audience in the hall. "No, this won't work! We really cannot start like this," he said over the loudspeakers. "People, close your eyes so that we can pray!" A long, earnest prayer followed – to Christ, who is the Truth, and to the Holy Spirit who had to lead us that day. After closing with "Amen", Tutu rubbed his hands together and informed the audience with a disarming smile, "There ... now we are ready to proceed!"

Fazel Randera and his supporters good-naturedly gave up. From then on, every day would be opened and adjourned properly.

◆ ◆ ◆

The Johannesburg hearing evoked great interest. Night after night the images of the victims appeared on millions of television screens.

The first face was that of the elderly Mrs Moleseng Anna Tiro, mother of the well-known student leader Abraham Tiro, who came all the way from Zeerust to tell the tale of the murder of her son. Abraham Tiro was one of the most prominent and eloquent student activists of the seventies. At the University of the North he joined SASO (South African Students Organisation) and soon stood out as a razor-sharp critic of the "white domination of black universities". When Tiro had been pointed out as one of the most dangerous student leaders in the country by the Schlebusch Commission, which investigated unrest among black students, he decided to flee across the border to Botswana.

With tears in her voice the old mother related how her son, on a Friday afternoon, took a parcel bomb out of the mail-box at his house in Gaborone. When he opened it in the dining room, the bomb exploded in his face. "There were people outside who heard the sound of the explosion, but they did not go to see what had happened." Only the next morning a little boy who had to deliver a message at the house, discovered the gruesome scene. Abraham Tiro's face was utterly mutilated. On Sunday 3 February 1974 there was a knock at Mrs Tiro's door. It was the police of Gaborone who had come to tell her.

The view of the Johannesburg newspaper *The Star* of the process: white and black sheep are separated.

Shortly after Mrs Tiro, it was Lorraine Lenkoe's turn to tell about the murder of her father, James Lenkoe. He had already died in 1967 in political custody after being imprisoned for 180 days without a hearing, according to the legislation of that time. Lorraine was only a little girl aged two. But to this day their family suffers the consequences of that terrible day.

◆ ◆ ◆

Just after lunch, on the first day, there was a surprise. After somebody had whispered into his ear, the chairperson, in turn, said something to the deputy chairperson and then left the hall hurriedly. Ten minutes later, while a certain Mr George Dube was delivering his testimony, the front door opened and President Nelson Mandela, followed by Tutu and the presidential bodyguard, entered the hall. 'Madiba magic' was the order of the day! In unison the crowd rose and applauded the president. With a broad smile Mr Mandela came to shake hands with everyone of us at the table and exchanged a few words with each. Showing great interest, he then sat down in a chair placed at the front of the hall by one of the TRC members. His face serious, the president listened.

Ironically – and to the embarrassment of many – George Dube was one of the first black victims of the ANC, who narrated in great detail how badly the ANC functionaries had treated him – after he had skipped the country to join the organisation. They had denounced him (wrongly, he declared) as a spy. He, together with a number of prisoners, had been exposed to hardship and humiliation of all sorts in Mozambique, in Tanzania and Angola. Without circumlocution he told about his experiences in the Quibashi prison, of how some of his friends had died, how he himself had frequently been tortured.

His face solemn, the president of South Africa – also the president of the ANC – sat and listened to the long story. When at last George Dube had finished, Mr Mandela's hour was up. He got up and left the hall, to return to Pretoria.

◆ ◆ ◆

"*Salaam aleikum*, Auntie Hawa," Fazel Randera welcomed Mrs Hawa Timol on the Tuesday morning in the witness box. On her typed statement, next to the paragraphs containing her story about her son, Ahmed,

I wrote the following note on this day: *It is a moving sight! The small elderly women who looks much older than her 76 years struggles with her headphones. Her two sons have to help her. She asks whether she could testify in Gujurati. She wipes her tears. She looks very frail … and very brave. When she first starts talking, it is like a tap being opened.*

During October 1971 the police had raided 115 homes and offices across the country, mostly belonging to Indians, ostensibly in search of information and documents relating to banned organisations – especially the Indian Congress Party. Seven persons had been arrested, among whom the 30-year-old Roodepoort school teacher, Ahmed Timol, and his brother, Mohammed. On 28 October Mrs Hawa Timol received news from the police that her son Ahmed had committed suicide by jumping from the tenth floor of the Police Head Office, John Vorster Square. This had been on the fifth day of his detention.

During the week before the news of Ahmed's death reached the Timol family, they had often been visited by the police. They, as well as their neighbours, had been intimidated in many ways. Their questions about Ahmed and his brother had been ignored. "I was so frightened that I even said to one of the policemen that perhaps he should go home and speak to his wife to find out what it is like to bring up a child and not knowing the whereabouts of that child! I remember saying to this policeman, 'If my body had a zip, you could unzip me and see how I ache inside.'"

Her voice breaking at times, Auntie Hawa continued: "On the Wednesday evening, my husband and son had gone to the mosque for evening prayers. During this time three policemen … entered my house. One of them pushed me into a seat and then proceeded to tell me that my son Ahmed had tried to escape by jumping from the tenth floor of John Vorster Square and that I was to tell my husband that his body was lying in the Hillbrow Government Mortuary … I was crying and screaming so much that the neighbours thought I was being arrested!"

On the Friday of the funeral as is customary in Islamic tradition, Ahmed's body was brought to the house after it had been washed and bathed at the mosque. When Mrs Timol, after the body had been returned, wanted to see her son's face, which was covered, friends and relatives tried to prevent her. "But I insisted that I wanted to see my son for the last time. Nothing could have prepared me for what I saw. His face was disfigured and one of his eyes appeared to have come out of the socket. There were bruises and marks on his face and other people who also saw the rest of his body remarked on all the injuries that they had seen. His nails had been ripped out and the coffin was smeared with blood."

Mrs Timol related that she had not for one moment believed that her son had committed suicide. It was impossible for him to have jumped through the window by himself! However, during an inquest, Magistrate J. J. de Villiers accepted the testimony of the police. Timol was a confessed communist, he said, and party members were expected to commit suicide rather than betray the party. The bruises on his body had been caused prior to his detention, it was found – contradicting the testimony of prominent pathologist, Dr Jonathan Gluckman. In 1981 Mrs Timol's husband, who had never recovered from the shock, died a broken man.

Ahmed's brother, Mohammed, who had only been released months after the events, came to support his mother: "She has been living through the death of Ahmed every day for 25 years."

◆ ◆ ◆

The Timol family was not the only Indian family who had suffered intensely. Earlier on that Tuesday morning, Mrs Rokaya Salojee testified that her husband, Suluman – 'Babla' his friends called him – had died in a similar way. The 32-year-old Salojee worked as an attorney's clerk when he, as a result of his activities as member of the Transvaal Indian Congress as well as the ANC, had been arrested. On 9 September 1964 he, according to police witnesses, had plunged from the seventh floor office of the security police in Grays Building in Johannesburg. From the clothes that were returned to the family afterwards, it was clear that Babla, before his death, had been badly tortured. "The clothing there in the bag was covered in blood. I actually did not know what colour it was, because it had gone hard and black already ... I want to know what happened to Babla ... His torturers must be brought to book."

"Babla was the fourth person to die in detention after the first state of emergency was introduced in 1960," commissioner, Yasmin Sooka noted during the hearing. "By 1990, 78 000 people had been detained, of whom 73 died. Inquest courts found 33 of these deaths were suicides. Of these, five detainees allegedly jumped from buildings."

◆ ◆ ◆

This week during the hearing, two white women also took their places in the witness box. Their stories about the two men in their lives were just as shocking.

Elizabeth Floyd, friend of the prominent Johannesburg doctor and trade unionist, Neil Aggett, came to tell how Aggett had been arrested by the Security Police in November 1981 and taken to John Vorster Square where he was interrogated for sixty hours (between 28 and 31 January). He was assaulted and tortured, placed in solitary confinement. Fellow detainees who had seen him in passing noticed a visible physical deterioration. A few hours before his death, they saw that there was blood on his forehead and that he was walking with enormous difficulty, like an extremely ill man.

Dr Neil Agget had committed suicide by hanging himself in his cell, the magistrate found during the inquest. "However, the point was," Ms Floyd argued, "if Neil was not detained he wouldn't have died. Everyone is sceptical about the so-called suicide in detention. He never left the tenth floor of John Vorster Square. He never saw anyone except his interrogators ... "

Maggie Friedman, friend of David Webster, senior lecturer in Social Anthropology at the University of the Witwatersrand, well-known activist and advocate of human rights, related how the two of them went on an outing with their dogs on 1 May 1989, a public holiday. On the way they stopped at a nursery to buy plants for the garden.

"David was driving. He parked the car at the side of the road outside our house. David was first out of the car and went to the back to open the canopy to let out the dogs. I got out more slowly on the passenger side. As I got out, I heard a car moving slowly down the street. It seemed to backfire as it passed us and then I was aware of it accelerating away. I then became aware of David staggering. He said to me that he had been shot with a shotgun and I should call an ambulance. He then fell on the pavement where he lost consciousness and died in my arms about half an hour later."

After the death of Dr Webster various investigations had been conducted, Maggie Friedman related. Among them was the Harms Commission, who, according to her, ignored important evidence and did not do justice to David Webster. Clearly, there were many questions left unanswered. It was her serious wish that the TRC would use the powers to its disposal to obtain all the necessary information. "I believe that David Webster's murder was ordered and planned from within state structures, that many employees of the state in many of its institutions were involved or have knowledge of this assassination, that state resources were used in its execution and that the state apparatus has been used and manipulated in such a fashion as to prevent its exposure."

Maggie Friedman's wish came true during the following months. At many applications for amnesty hearings, as well as other hearings, the name of Dr Webster was mentioned. Would the TRC be able to unravel the whole truth before closing its term?

◆ ◆ ◆

It became all too clear during the Johannesburg hearing that the battle that raged these past decades claimed victims from all sectors of the community. It was often perfectly innocent persons, men, women, children, who landed in the cross-fire.

Johan Smit, a Pretorian, came to relate such an incident.

"During the December holiday of 1985, my father, mother and child, Cornio, were on holiday in Durban. Two days before Christmas they went to the Sanlam Shopping Centre in Amanzimtoti to do some shopping, when a bomb exploded there. It took place in the morning.

"My uncle called us ... First he only said there was an accident. Later on he called again to say it was serious. We had to go to Durban. Only when we arrived in Durban did we find out our child was dead! He was killed nearly instantaneously ... I heard at the hospital that there was a bomb explosion. When I heard that my child was dead, I did not believe it. I wanted to see him myself first.

"The next morning we went to identify our child's body. My wife and father had to convince me that it was my child. My mother was also admitted to hospital. She still has trouble with her feet. There is still shrapnel in her body which they cannot remove.

"Directly after the bomb explosion I said we had to stop our nonsense, that we had to negotiate with the ANC. We sat together, thinking that we would not like it to be oppressed like that. People flayed me because of what I said. The only one who called me to congratulate me, was Dr Alex Boraine. People could not understand. They thought I was a traitor. There are some who believe it to this day. We are not really interested in who planned the explosion. I also do not want to know. What is over, is over.

"Reversed racism must not be applied in our country in future. We must forget all about the colour of our skins. Therefore, affirmative action is dangerous. All of us are only South Africans.

"Our child was eight years old when this happened. The rest of my family does not feel the way I do. Neither does my wife. I know that when you are in the army, you have to follow commands. You do what you are told to.

"My wife feels that it is a comfort that the person who planted the bomb has been hanged."

Andrew Zondo, an ANC member, was sentenced to death, and executed, for his part in the bomb explosion. He declared in court that he had been so outraged about an attack by the SA Police in Lesotho, during which Jackie Quinn, amongst others, was killed, that he agreed immediately when his commander in Durban ordered him to plant a bomb. In extenuation it was alleged that he did try to give a warning, but that he could not get to a telephone in time.

◆ ◆ ◆

The bomb explosion in Church Street, Pretoria, on 20 May 1983 attracted a good deal of attention. I myself remember how shocked the people were. It was Pentecost and in our congregation, Lynnwood Ridge, as in most congregations of the NG Kerk, the faithful attended church that night. One of my colleagues, the Rev Kobus Bezuidenhout, escaped death by inches. Moments before the bomb exploded, he walked down Church Street. In our church, prayers of thanksgiving went up.

But not everybody was so fortunate. Two of them made their appearance in the witness box in Johannesburg.

First, P F Botha, a staff officer in the SA Defence Force, told us how he, on that ill-fated day when 19 people died and 219 were injured, had been flung into a restaurant by the force of the explosion. Thirteen years later he was still troubled by the multiple injuries sustained during the explosion.

After that, Marina Geldenhuys, 31 years of age, took her place in the witness box.

"In one moment, one flash, my youth was gone," she started. In a voice breaking with emotion she continued to tell what had happened to her as an eighteen-year-old girl: "I had just left the Nedbank Building, the South African Air Force Headquarters where I worked ... It was approximately a quarter past four in the afternoon. Just when I stepped onto the sidewalk, the bomb exploded. My colleague, Paula Francke, was with me.

"Both of us were blown into the air. We landed right inside a shop. People rushed in to assist ... I was taken to the H F Verwoerd Hospital, where I was operated on immediately ... I was unconscious for the next three days. I remained in hospital for four weeks. For five months I could not go to work." Marina Geldenhuys' hearing was affected permanently. She sustained deep wounds in her legs. She had to undergo several skin transplants. She sustained internal injuries and, to this day, she does not have the full use of her thumbs. Her face carries the scars of the explosion. There were still operations to be done on Marina. Above all, there was the emotional damage to cope with.

Smiling sadly, Marina looked at the panelists, "I had just finished school when it all happened. My dream was to become a beauty consultant one day. Now, I have scars on my face, my whole body. I can never be a beautician ... My dream was shattered ... "

When one of the TRC members asked about her political background, Marina answered, "I can't really say I was politically aware at that stage. We didn't really know what was right and what was wrong. We were confused. But having listened to the testimonies of other victims yesterday and today, I think I can grasp something of the frustration that black people had to experience during those years in our country."

The Church Street bomb was not an isolated incident. During the eighties, the ANC's armed resistance escalated. During only one year (1982), for example, twenty-nine instances of sabotage, two assassinations, and one armed attack, could reasonably be attributed to the ANC. The most alarming of all these actions was the explosion of four explosive devices at the Koeberg Nuclear Power Station in December 1982.

◆ ◆ ◆

Another one of the casual victims of whom his mother came to tell, was the young pupil from Soweto, Mbuyisa Makhubu. While his name would not be known to most people, his face – the face of a young boy who picked up in his arms the first child victim of the 1976 rebellion, Hector Petersen – would be familiar to millions throughout the world. The photograph of the crying boy with the dying child in his arms had appeared in virtually every newspaper on earth. This photograph had been etched on a metal plate which hangs on the wall of the Hector Petersen Memorial in Soweto.

Today his mother still did not know what had happened to him.

Mrs Makhubu approached the Truth Commission to seek help in tracing her son. "His sin was to pick up a fallen child. He was not a hero. He did what was natural in our tradition when he saw Hector Petersen falling down."

"June 16," she added, "changed our lives." From the minute Mbuyisa was photographed holding the child in his arms, he became a target to the police. He was molested and harassed. Finally he decided to leave the country, first living as an exile in Botswana and later Nigeria. In Nigeria he became ill. Eventually, he was reported missing. Nobody ever heard of him again.

IN MEMORY OF HECTOR PETERSON AND ALL OTHER YOUNG HEROES AND HEROINES OF OUR STRUGGLE WHO LAID DOWN THEIR LIVES FOR FREEDOM, PEACE AND DEMOCRACY

The first child victim of the 1976 rebellion, Hector Petersen

"Always around June 16, the papers and TV want to be sensational. But what is news to them is pain to me."

Mrs Makhubu ended on a passionate note: "I came here as a last hope to find my child. I want to speak to somebody who has seen him, somebody who knows."

◆   ◆   ◆

Another mother who came to talk about her son, was Mrs Hester Grobbelaar from Krugersdorp. Her son was a member of a far-right student organisation who helped to disrupt the occasion when Nelson Mandela came to address the students at the University of Pretoria. The man who would later become president, had to leave the campus without being able to deliver his speech.

Emotions ran so high after that, related Hester Grobbelaar, that her son decided to leave Pretoria. She was convinced that her son's own comrades turned their backs on him, that they were responsible for his being shot dead.

"I have decided to testify," Mrs Grobbelaar said, "so that people can see that this sort of thing did not only happen to people of other races, but also to white people. I feel upset and hope that the truth will eventually come out. I want answers to many questions. Who were the murderers? Why did they kill my son? It is our right to know what happened in our own country."

◆ ◆ ◆

And, lastly, there was the mother and her daughter-in-law, Catherine Mlangeni and Seipati Mlangeni, who related the events of the ill-fated day when Bheki Mlangeni, well-known lawyer and activist, met his end in a shocking way. If Bheki had not been so successful in his work, collecting information on the hit squads of the security police for the Harms Commission, he would probably still be alive today.

His mother and wife wept bitterly when they told their story. Of how dedicated he had been in his work. How he, when his mother tried to persuade him to stop his dangerous work, answered, "I am living to help people; this is the work I want to do." Both women testified how he cared for them, to what extent their future expectations revolved around him. "One day I will lift you out of poverty," he promised his mother. "He was so thoughtful, he did not even mind washing his daughter's underwear," Seipati added. "He showed me more than love. He was also like a brother and friend!"

Although he was on study leave, Bheki visited the office – where he picked up the fatal parcel. The parcel had apparently been intended for Dirk Coetzee, former Vlakplaas operator who in the meantime started working with the ANC abroad. The parcel had not been delivered and was returned to the sender, given falsely as Bheki Mlangeni.

That night, after returning from the cinema – ironically enough they saw a political thriller, *Reversal of Fortune* – Bheki wanted to open the parcel. Inside was a portable cassette recorder with headphones, plus an audio cassette marked: *Hit Squads: new evidence.* Mlangeni had previously discussed these cases with Coetzee and he apparently wanted to hear what the recording was about.

"I was getting undressed for bed," Seipati related, "and I said, 'Why don't you connect it to the hi-fi, so I can also listen ... ?'"

But Bheki had already donned the headphones and put the cassette into the machine. The next moment there was a loud bang, like a gun-shot. Seipati saw her husband's lifeless body slump to the ground. The explosive device had served its awful purpose.

In blind panic Seipati ran outside. When the elderly Catherine Mlangeni entered the house, against the advice of friends and neighbours who were drawn by the blast, she found her son, "in pieces ... pieces of him, brains, splattered all over the room."

Moved, she looked at the audience: "That was the end of Bheki." For Seipati, who had been married only two months before, it was the end of her dreams.

Wally Mbhele, experienced black journalist, later remarked, "Even the most hardened journalists battled to suppress their tears."

Heads nodded sympathetically in the hall when Mrs Mlangeni ad-dressed the commissioners: "The murderers of my son must be found and prosecuted! I understand that Eugene de Kock is asking for am-nesty from you. I oppose that! He knew that people would die when he sent those explosives. Today I am a widow. I feel like an outcast be-cause of a person who is asking for pardon. How can you kill defence-less people – and seek amnesty thereafter?"

Archbishop Tutu pointed out in his answer that many bad things had happened in the past, that many people shared her pain. "But," he added, "if you want to oppose an amnesty application, you can do that. You are not obliged to forgive ... "

◆ ◆ ◆

Back in the office the next Monday morning, we deliberated for a long time.

The Johannesburg hearing had been a great success, was the gen-eral feeling. A great deal of important evidence had come out. How would we process this evidence? What would we eventually do with it?

That the Committee on Amnesty, which would start within a few days with their public sessions, would encounter many problems and also a great deal of emotion, became clear during the hearing. Catherine Mlangeni, who was sceptical about the easy granting of amnesty to offenders who caused so much grief in people's lives, talked on behalf of many others. Besides, we were still awaiting the verdict of the Constitutional Court, following the complaint of the Mxenge, Biko and Ribeiro families who questioned the whole process of the TRC.

Another, very difficult question was: to what extent could one accept the testimonies of the hundreds of victims who had already made their submissions in writing, as well as those of the group who delivered their testimonies in public? As one journalist put it rather crudely: "Do you really swallow everything you are told?"

Shortly before the hearing, the well-known Johannesburg advocate, the man who for years defended ANC accused in court, George Bizos, advised the local TRC members on their task. After explaining the exact legal procedures to be applied by us, he warned, "You may find it strange that I am telling you this. But you must take into account that even the most serious and honest of all witnesses suffer from that human frailty, the weakness of exaggeration." Now we could experience the wisdom of his words.

"Our investigative teams will have to work day and night," Wynand Malan and his co-jurists on the commission summed up the position. "They will have to find the necessary corroborating material. Only when they have found proper corroborative evidence for every single submission, will we be able to make a verdict." And so it happened. Throughout the next two years the Johannesburg investigative team – as too, those at the other regional offices – travelled across the country, first led by André Steenkamp, then by Fanie Kilian. Police records were requisitioned, hospital reports perused, radio and television programmes replayed, newspaper articles and reports combed, books read, eye-witnesses interrogated. The instruction was to find two or three pieces of corroborative evidence for every story received from each victim and family member. Only then would it be possible to reach a verdict. Untested testimonies were not acceptable to the TRC. There was too much at stake.

A growing concern was the prevalent absence of Whites at the hearings. Small groups, Afrikaans and English-speaking persons, did come. Some enterprising teachers conveyed school children. But the East London cry sounded in my ears all the time: where are the people with whom we want to reconcile? It was undisputable that all the TRC-personnel – especially Wynand Malan, Chris de Jager and I – would have to reach out to the white community with even more vigour.

But we also had reason for merriment. Following the hearing of the past week, an unknown person, pseudonym and all, sent the following piece of craftiness to the TRC office – referring to the serious way in which Desmond Tutu saw to it that every witness took the prescribed oath properly:

TOOTH COMMISSION, OR K9

THE SWEARING IN:
I BISHOP DESMOND (DENTIST) TU TUTH DO HEREBY SWEAR TO UPHOLD THE TOOTH, THE WHOLE TOOTH AND NOTHING BUT THE TOOTH. I APPOINT THE TOOTH FAIRY TO BE THE JUDGE OF RIGHT AND WRONG AND TO ENSURE THAT THERE IS NO FALSE TOOTH. THE MISSION SHALL BE TO STOP PEOPLE LYING THROUGH THEIR EYE TOOTH, IF NECESSARY TO DRILL THE TOOTH OUT, AND TO USE OUR WISDOM TOO(TH). WE SHALL DISCONTINUE THE USE OF COLGATE AS WE NOW WISH NOT ONLY THE WHITE TOOTH, NO FALSE TOOTH BUT THE REAL TOOTH, AND NOTHING BUT THE TOOTH.
SO HELP ME BITE!

20-21 MAY 1996: PHOKENG – THE FIRST AMNESTY HEARING

Nothing was to go wrong. The place and the time, as well as the case to be heard, had been chosen with great care. The eyes of South Africa and the world – above all the eyes of the outspoken critics of the process of amnesty – were on Phokeng.

A small distance from Rustenburg in the North West Province, in Phokeng, lived the Bafokeng tribe. They were an independent group of people, proud of their tradition and, unlike many black communities in the vicinity of Rustenburg, not at all poor. Mining had been taking place in their tribal area for many years, which offered a stable income to the captain and the tribal authority, as well as the rest of the Bafokeng people.

Years ago President Lucas Mangope, president of Bophuthatswana, dismissed the popular Bafokeng chief, Molotlegi, from his post and appointed one of his confidants in his place. From the first day Glad Mokgatle was a hated figure. The more he tried to enforce his authority, the more resistance grew against him. One day two hot-headed young men from the tribe, Boy Diale and Christopher Makgale, confronted the chief in his office. They threatened him in several ways and later even abducted him. After attacking him, Diale and Makgale decided to kill him. If they did not do it, they debated, he would report them to the police. Anyhow, they were sure that the whole Bafokeng tribe would welcome it.

The two young men were later arrested and sentenced to death. When the death penalty in the country was abolished, the sentence was changed to life imprisonment. When the offer of amnesty was announced, Diale and Makgale were among the first to apply.

Nearly the whole Bafokeng tribe crowded into the large auditorium, built from the tribe's own funds.

◆ ◆ ◆

Before Judge Hassen Mall, chairperson of the Amnesty Committee, and his two colleagues, Judges Andrew Wilson and Bernard Ngoepe, together with the two advocates, Chris de Jager and Sisi Khampepe, could take their places in the hall, a lot had to happen first ...

Not only the Amnesty Committee, but all the commissioners and committee members, exerted themselves weeks before to study the sections of the Act applying to amnesty. Several meetings and workshops had been held. On two occasions, in Johannesburg and in Cape Town, Professor Carl Norgaard, well-known Danish jurist – who formerly played an important role in establishing the criteria for amnesty accepted by the Chilean Truth Commission – participated in the discussions. He and his wife, also a jurist, travelled to South Africa specially for this purpose.

The Norgaard principles were also included in the South African TRC Act. In short, it amounted to the fact that amnesty would be granted to offenders provided that they were willing to make a full disclosure of the relevant facts in regard to the action for which they requested amnesty. The context and the motive for the action, too, had to be taken into consideration. If the offender could indicate that he had been executing an order in committing the act, or that he did it in terms of the military battle, or even that he had some political motive for the action, he could be granted amnesty. The offer of amnesty was surprisingly open and generous. No criminal case could then be instituted against the perpetrator, not for that particular offense. Civil claims, too, could no longer be instituted. The offender who was granted amnesty would leave the court-room as free as a bird. It was not made a condition that the applicant had to show remorse for his actions, or that he had to express his regret to those whom he had wronged. For many of us – for me as well – this stipulation appeared peculiar. The least one would expect from an offender was to say, "I am sorry!" However, Judge Mall placed it into perspective: "It is very good that there is no such require- ment in the Act. Because how can one read a man's heart? How will one ever really know whether he has sincere regrets, or whether he is just saying the right words? Such a condition would force some people to be dishonest."

The first series of applications for amnesty nearly all came from pris- oners, very frequently from ordinary criminals who did not qualify at all, but – understandably – wanted to take a chance. Ingenious motives of all sorts were contrived: bank robbers who carried away thousands of rands, because they really wanted to hand the money over to a political party to help cover the electoral expenses!

But the case of Diale and Makgale was different. According to ju- rists, who discussed the case from all sides, they stood a good chance of receiving amnesty.

◆ ◆ ◆

Chris de Jager, who did not want anything to go wrong during the Phokeng hearing, accompanied Tom Manthata and me to Phokeng weeks before. We had to hold an information meeting and Chris wanted to see for himself what was happening in the community before the amnesty hearing was due to start. After the gathering we dined with the acting chief, a quite formidable lady – to talk everything through once more.

To Tom and me, members of the Reparation and Rehabilitation Com- mittee, it was just as important that everything would proceed smoothly. The Reparation and Rehabilitation Committee, after all, was instructed to support and counsel the victims and their family members, also those who would attend the amnesty hearings. A question that was heavily debated among us, was whether perpetrators were also entitled to counselling. The process already offered them so much. Did we have to support and comfort them as well? However, the more we talked, the more the conviction grew: yes, we had a responsibility towards the offenders and their families. Some of the perpetrators could also be regarded as victims, it was felt. That went for their families too. Many wives and children never had an inkling of what the men were doing. Many of them were so shocked about the revelations that they indeed needed professional help. Moreover, if the end goal of the TRC process was reconciliation in the country, we had no choice: we had to do everything in our power to help the perpetrators take their places in the community again.

But Diale and Makgale did not really need the Reparation and Rehabilitation Committee's support. The whole community was gathered in the hall and supported them loudly.

◆ ◆ ◆

For two days Judge Mall and his colleagues listened to the tale of the two young men. Several questions were asked, legal points raised. When Boy Diale and Christopher Makgale related how they had abducted the chief, one could hear a pin drop in the hall. In no uncertain terms these two offenders, provided a blow by blow description to how they murdered Glad Mokgatle. It was clear that they did not feel much remorse. They had done the Bafokeng tribe a favour! It was equally clear that most of the people in the hall agreed.

When the hearing was nearly over, something happened about which we would talk for a long time to come, something which warmed the cockles of one's heart. Very unexpectedly the son of the murdered Chief Mokgatle sent an urgent message to the chairperson. Would it be possible for him to get a turn to speak? He had something on his mind. When Judge Mall agreed, the young man got onto the platform. He turned to Diale and Makgale, and to the crowd in front of him.

"Today I stand before you as the son of the man whom you murdered. I have been listening since yesterday how you did it and why you did it. I think I am beginning to understand why you hated him so. These past years our family has been living under a cloud because of everything that happened. Now I would like to stretch out my hands to you and ask your forgiveness for what my father did to you. Please forgive us! And, if you desire my and my family's forgiveness, we would be happy to give it."

When the young man embraced the two murderers, a loud applause broke out. Somebody started to sing a song of praise, and all the people in the hall joined in.

The first amnesty hearing, which started out with so many questions, ended on a positive note.

◆   ◆   ◆

The first chapter of the story had been written. The first part of the great trek through the past of our country, was behind us. On the whole, it went reasonably well. The first decisions had been taken, the first procedures accepted. Mistakes had been made, too, but these would hopefully be corrected in the months to come. That the next stretch would proceed much faster, that higher demands would be made, we could already guess.

At the time a film version of Ariel Dorfman's drama *Death and the Maiden*, which deals with the Chilean Truth Commission, was broadcast on SA Television. The following lines from it lingered in my head as we embarked on the next lap of our journey:

How are we to keep the past alive
without becoming its prisoner?
How are we to forget it
without being in danger of repeating it in the future?

CHAPTER 2

VIA DOLOROSA

JULY 1996: THE SECOND PART OF THE JOURNEY

The second stage of the trek started out on a merry note. The small group of TRC members who, on that day, travelled to the official residence of the president in Pretoria to hand over the first interim report of the Truth Commission to President Mandela, was overwhelmed with hospitality. There was much to eat and drink. And the president was his charming self. With every one of us he had a chat, asking about the work of the Truth Commission.

The first interim report of the Truth Commission handed over to President Mandela

In those days the newspapers were crammed with news about the relationship that was developing between the president and Mrs Graca Machel, widow of the former Head of State of Mozambique. There was plenty of time for banter, and around the table Archbishop Tutu congratulated the president, teasing him good-naturedly. In turn, the president poked fun at the chairperson of the TRC who, after the first six months, had already decided that the Commission would not finish in time; who, after six months' work, already requested six months' postponement. Was that how the church taught its archbishops to plan?

During a photo session the president entertained us with one anecdote after the other, of how he, with his Robben Island background, had to learn how to make the stately official residence, Mahlambandlopfu, his home. His course, his 'long walk to freedom' was remarkable. But what about the other victims in this country, the thousands of men and women and children, who each had to find their own way through a dark past?

How would the Truth Commission fare on its great trek, throughout the country, throughout the past with its pain and suffering, with the injustices and the struggle, the blood and tears?

For the Truth Commission, for the victims and their families, for the offenders, in truth for everybody in the country, the second shift was no less than a *via dolorosa*, a road of suffering.

◆ ◆ ◆

Throughout the next six months TRC teams would depart in all four directions of the wind, to hold information meetings and to meet victims. And, especially, to hold hearings. Eventually, when the December holidays started, it was reported that 57 hearings had been held: 45 human rights violations hearings and 12 amnesty hearings.

Amidst wide media interest the TRC teams departed to organise hearings in the large South African cities – in Johannesburg and Pretoria, Cape Town, Port Elizabeth, East London, Durban, Pietermaritzburg and Bloemfontein. Other teams departed to the provincial capitals where groups of victims awaited them: in Pietersburg, Mmabatho, Nelspruit and Bisho. In the large mining towns of the country – Welkom and Klerksdorp – hearings took place. In KwaZulu-Natal, in Empangeni, Port Shepstone and Newcastle, many wondered if – in the midst of the ANC-Inkatha battle – it was safe enough to attend the hearings, and then decided to come after all. In the large black residential areas of Gauteng, in Soweto and Alexandra, Sebokeng and Boipatong, witnesses came to tell their stories of mass murders and violence. In Moutse, on the far side of Pretoria, men and women queued up to be heard.

In Uitenhage, in the Eastern Cape, as well as in Umtata and Queenstown, posters along the streets publicized TRC hearings. In the Southern Cape, George was the appropriate place. In two Boland towns, in the Paarl and in Worcester, commissioners and committee members listened to the experiences of farm labourers and business people, pastors and activists. In two towns along the Orange River, situated hundreds of kilometres from each other, Aliwal North and Upington, victims and relatives came forward. One TRC trek departed to three Karoo towns, Beaufort West, Hanover and De Aar to hold hearings. Another went to the Highveld, to swear in witnesses in Kroonstad and Potchefstroom. In the remote rural areas, in Thohoyando, victims whom the world had apparently forgotten, came to put their stories on the table.

A wide variety of people came to testify. Some of them were high-profile persons whose stories were already known. Newspaper articles, sometimes books, had been written about their experiences. Films and television programmes were made about some of them. However, most of them were quite ordinary, often half-forgotten men and women, some-times children. To me it often felt as if I, together with my colleagues on the TRC, had the painful, but also the incredibly wonderful privilege to, as it were, have a giant photo-album of the history of our country before us. From all regions a stream of people came, representatives from all communities, black, white, brown, to stick the photographs of their experiences into the album – some with the glue of their tears. By December 1996, 6 000 victims had already submitted their statements to the TRC. Some 1 200 appeared during public hearings.

But speaking of tears, for many South Africans who watched the TRC broadcasts on television, the crying faces seemed strange and dis-turbing. Some were annoyed. Very soon the TRC, because of the many tissues used by witnesses and relatives, was nicknamed "the Kleenex Commission". But for all that, the tears were important. For most vic-tims their testimonies before the TRC was a cathartic experience, the tears that flowed were healing tears. For several who struggled alone for years with their sorrow and pain, often with great frustration, it was all they needed: to be heard for once. One man, one morning dur-ing the Soweto hearing, spoke on behalf of thousands: "When the of-ficer tortured me at that time in John Vorster Square, he laughed at me: 'You can scream your head off, nobody will ever hear you!' He was wrong. Today there are people who hear me ... "

9 JULY 1996: TUTU AT THE WOMEN'S MEMORIAL

For Afrikaners the revelations which were reported day after day in the newspapers, as well as on the radio and television, were painful. In a very special sense of the word the second shift of the Truth Commission was for them also a *via dolorosa*, a road of suffering.

Because I was a pastor, I was invited to speak to congregations throughout our country virtually every Sunday, sometimes also during the week – to preach about forgiveness and reconciliation, and to answer questions to the TRC. The concerns raised nearly every time in every congregation, reflected the questions in my own heart: was it really possible that all these actrocities could have happened? Is everything true? How should we cope with it? We never knew, at any rate not everything. To which extent are we, nevertheless, guilty? Eventually also: was it necessary to rake up all the unpleasantness, particularly now in the midst of this difficult period of transition? Sometimes the discussions were painful, at other times vehement.

On 9 July a large photograph of Archbishop Tutu appeared on the centre page of the Johannesburg newspaper, *Beeld*. A few days previously he, as chairperson of the TRC, visited the Women's Memorial in Bloemfontein. It is a rather striking photograph: Desmond Tutu in his episcopal dress, in front of the statue of the two women with a dying child. If there could only have been a Truth Commission after the Boer War, Tutu remarked on more than one occasion, if there could only have been an opportunity at which all the pain and injustice of that war – everything that had been done to the women and children in the concentration camps – could be faced and talked through, how different would the political history of South Africa have been. But the books remained closed, and for more than half a century the Afrikaner and Englishman continued to fight the war. Ghosts that are not buried, will continue to haunt one!

While we, a week later, were in the car on our way to a gathering in Pietersburg, Tom Manthata and I discussed the picture: Tutu at the Women's Memorial. Tom, ex-activist, one of the Committee of Ten who ruled Soweto with a rod of iron during the seventies, was my guide to the black community. In Soweto nearly everybody knew him. What an experience it was to walk with him through the streets! But his tracks lay also in the Northern Province. During the struggle he travelled from one small town to another to gain support for the ANC. He knew everybody and where everything happened.

But this time, in the car, Tom wanted to talk about the Afrikaners.

"We often told each other that, of all people, the *Boere* had to understand our struggle. They fought long enough against the English, to attain their own independence. The Afrikaners had experienced what it means to go into exile, to be in prison for the sake of their ideals of freedom. It is ironic that it was the Afrikaners, in particular, who established apartheid, who made us suffer so much hardship."

After a while Tim spoke again. Two days earlier Tom and I met a number of Afrikaners in Warmbaths, in the rectory of one of the local NG Kerk ministers. It was a pleasant meeting, with coffee and *koeksisters*, but Tom was nevertheless concerned. "It bothers me that the Truth Commission does not succeed in communicating properly with the majority of Afrikaners. The people whom we talked to yesterday, are good and nice people. But I do feel that they remain somewhat aloof, as if they do not really appreciate the necessity of the process."

In Pietersburg Tom's suspicion was confirmed: a hall full of black people, a small group of Indians and Coloureds. But the white people, Afrikaners and the English, would not fill two rows of chairs. My feeling, which I shared with Tom, was: it was not that they merely did not want to come. It was difficult for them to come, difficult to have to face the mirror of the past.

Nevertheless, it would be to the advantage of the whole country if the white people did participate in the process. There was a press cutting among my Pietersburg papers in which Beyers Naudé, a while ago, in Durban, made a serious plea that Whites who, in the past, had participated in political violence, who had been guilty of gross violations of human rights, should come forward. The "thundering silence" of the large group of offenders was shocking! But besides the perpetrators, it was vital for Afrikaners who were not guilty of gross violations of human rights, to identify with the process. They owed it to the victims, as well as to themselves to come and listen, Naude said.

Some Afrikaners did appear at the violations of human rights hearings, to listen to what was said and also to tell their own stories. Their testimonies had a definite impact. When a young theological student from Bloemfontein related during one of the hearings how his whole life had changed the day when he had hit a land-mine while driving his father's *bakkie*, it opened the eyes of many black South Africans: there were indeed victims on the 'other' side too.

However, several tales that needed to be told, were unfortunately never heard: farms that had been attacked, lives that had been taken. The TRC process was definitely hampered by the unwillingness of some to come and testify. In Messina and Louis Trichardt I had to phone a number of victims. "We need to hear about your experiences. What happened to you must be shared with the nation," I tried to explain. However, they were reluctant to testify. "Rather not," was a typical reaction. "Let the black people go and cry their hearts out. It is not our style ... we attempt in our own way to make peace with the past."

22 JULY 1996: VISITING THE *BROEDERBOND*

The conversation about the Afrikaners and the Truth Commission was continued a few days later, when Wynand Malan and I were invited to the Head Office of the Afrikaner-Broederbond (AB). For me, who stood far beyond the line of the Broederbond my whole life, it was an interesting experience to step through the front door of *Die Eike*. For Wynand Malan, who had been a leading brother earlier in his life, before he resigned from the AB, it was familiar terrain. Boet Schoeman and his colleagues on the Executive Board of the AB welcomed us cordially.

During the conversation Wynand and I did our best to explain the TRC process and to answer the many questions that were raised. It was clear that the perception was already growing that the TRC was one-sided, that a number of commissioners had their knives into the Afrikaner and his traditions. However, it was important to me that the Afrikaner community should seize the opportunity offered by the TRC to embark on the journey through our shared past, to the future that awaited us all. The Broederbond should consider making a formal submission before the TRC, Wynand and I emphasised. The AB's perspective on the community all these years, the information that they alone could provide – also on the AB's own influence and activities – would be crucial for the writing of the final report.

We took the parting words of Dr Gerrit Viljoen, ex-academic and ex-politician, seriously, to the point that Wynand and I relayed them in a memorandum to the chairperson and deputy chairperson of the TRC: "You will have to improve your communication. We readily accept your word that the TRC wishes to act fairly and impartially. But the perception of the people – fed by what they read daily in the press and hear on the radio and television – is different. Our people experience the Truth Commission as a witch-hunt!" One of his colleagues added, "It feels as though you have already found all of us guilty – and surely not everybody was guilty of all these misdemeanours."

While we sat talking about all these things, the first victims and their families started to arrive at the large Catholic Regina Mundi Church in Soweto, a half-hour journey by car from *Die Eike*. That same morning the Soweto hearing would commence.

22-26 JULY 1996: THE SOWETO HEARING (1) – ASPECTS OF PAIN

People reacted differently to their pain – to the road of suffering on which the TRC took all of us. Of this the Soweto hearing was an object lesson.

That first morning of the hearing, early, just before the first witness was sworn in, Archbishop Tutu made an opening speech. It was of symbolic importance that the hearing would be held in Soweto. So much of what had taken place in the history of South Africa, above all, the 'black' history of the country, had taken place in this large black city. Some of these historic tales and episodes would be under discussion during the days to come.

But, before this happened, Tutu declared, he first wanted to read out a letter. The letter sent to the TRC by a white minister from the NG Kerk, made a powerful impression on the audience. I wished that the brothers at *Die Eike* – that all Afrikaners – could hear it.

As a result of all the things that happened in our country during the past years, the minister wrote about his own personal *via dolorosa*:

"I am 33 years of age, born in South Africa ... My mother is a good person, who, as far as she could, tried to do right by her fellow-man. But she was also a child of her times. I talk to her about the things that happened during the past decades and then I hear my grandmother's words like a refrain: 'But we did not know anything about it.' For me it is the most difficult thing to believe, to cope with and to accept. Then I know that in my family's life there is a dark spot and it looks like a black hand stretching out for help. Then I cry about what has happened, although I can change nothing of it. Then, introspectively, I seek to understand, how is it possible that nobody simply knew? How is it possible that so few did something about it? How is it possible that, many times, I also merely looked on? Then I wonder how it is possible to live with all that guilt and shame in my heart? I do not know what to say and what to do.

"I apologize for this. I am sorry about all the pain and sorrow. I do not say this easily. I say it with a heart which is breaking and with tears in my eyes. Then I ask, forgive me for the times that I looked the other way, the times that I remained silent, the times that I walked away. God knows, without your forgiveness, I, and others like me, cannot go on. It lies too heavily and painfully upon me and then I know that your hurt and your pain are even greater than mine. But I ask you, my brothers and sisters in Christ, forgive me.

"May God give you mercy, wisdom and strength for your activities. May He envelop you in his love so that you can endure listening to the horrors that were committed."

◆ ◆ ◆

A statement that we received a few weeks later, which I wish to quote here, came from an English-speaking woman from one of the northern suburbs of Johannesburg. Her submission showed how painful the road could be for a white woman. She was not a minister, but, interestingly enough, a person who played a leading role in the Presbyterian Church. At a public meeting in the central business district, Lesley Morgan poured out her heart:

"I am 47 years old. I am a middle-aged, middle class South African housewife, an elder in my congregation, a wife, a mother, a nursing sister ... I grew up with all the advantages and opportunities afforded me because I was white. I was oblivious of the fact that there were so many people around me who were not as privileged as I was, not because I was unfeeling, but because I was unaware. I became aware by the time I reached high school and can remember heated discussions in classrooms ...

"When I was in my twenties, I had many friends at university, including young people who were arrested and harassed by security policemen. It filled me with anger, but also with helplessness ...

"By the late 70's and early 80's I was married, with a young family. Although I was fully aware of the dreadful things that were happening all around me, fear paralysed me. I was no activist. I was afraid of being arrested, afraid of being detained without trial, afraid of being tortured or killed. I do not even have the excuse of not knowing. I was well aware of what was happening. I read the Black Sash publications and knew the terrible consequences of the apartheid laws ... God forgive me, I did nothing to speak out against these obscene laws.

"The TRC hearings on gross human rights violations have devastated me! I have watched them on television and read about them in the press and in magazines and they have made me weep with anger and horror. There is a strong feeling of denial ... I don't want to believe those things ... There is a sense of complicity, a terrible feeling of failure. I remember a quotation I read many years ago. It disturbed me then, it haunts me now: 'It is sufficient for evil to prosper that good men do nothing' ... "

It bothered her that she did not attend the TRC hearings: "I started talking about it in my community and discussing it with my friends. I started asking myself why I have not attended. I know it is causing great pain amongst the black community. I cannot imagine how it must feel to bear your pain and suffering so openly and publicly. I can imagine what it must feel like to stretch out your hand in an attempt to forgive and reconcile and have no-one there to grasp it ...

"It is not denial that keeps me away, it is a deep and overwhelming sense of shame ... I find it almost impossible to look you in the face ... "

Following on a gathering that she attended, scarcely a week before, Lesley Morgan continued:

"If you had asked me a week ago about my faith, I would have said to you that I was of strong faith, that I believe in God as Creator ... in Jesus Christ as my Saviour ... That because of my faith, I have tried to do the best I can, that I have treated all people as human beings, that I have tried to follow the teachings of the Scriptures ... I have always loved God with all my heart ... I have not always been successful with loving one another ...

"I am of the Reformed tradition. We are not given to Pentecostal or Charismatic experiences. On Wednesday, I was driving to a conference on the eradication of poverty ... For the first time in my life I truly heard the voice of Christ. In all the years I ignored the cries of the oppressed ... In my fear and concern for my own safety, like Peter before me, I denied my Lord. Like Peter, the realisation of that denial has filled me with unbearable sorrow. The realisation that my faith is so small, so selfish, so empty, has broken me ... I profess to be a follower of Christ, but have been unwilling to go where He has led me ... It would be so much easier to blame apartheid for all of it. The truth is, I made my own choices ... I will not run away from what is happening ...

"Finally, I need to say one last thing ... the hardest part ... It is so hopelessly inadequate to make right what has happened, so puny in the face of such suffering and I am overwhelmed at my temerity in even offering it, but it is all I have to give – I'm sorry!"

After Lesley had finished talking, there was a a moment of total silence. Then applause broke out. Somebody intoned a song. Women from Soweto and Alexandra, from everywhere, stepped forward to embrace the white, English-speaking, middle-aged housewife from the northern suburbs and to ensure her that her plea, her apology had been accepted.

22-26 JULY 1996: THE SOWETO HEARING (2)
– THE DAY THE CHILDREN REBELLED

Back to the Soweto hearing.

On the road of South Africa, 16 June 1976 will always stand out as one of the most important landmarks, the day when the youth of Soweto rebelled. The process which was started would irrevocably change the political and social landscape of South Africa. One witness after the other came to talk about that day, and the days that followed. The pain spared nobody.

Two black women, both journalists, each got a turn to speak. Sophie Tema, who was attached to the black newspaper *The World* in 1976, related how excited and exuberant the children were that gathered that day in Soweto. They would hold a demonstration. When the procession arrived in Orlando West, the police was already there. "The children provoked the police, like children would do. Some children threw small stones to the police. It angered the police and they started to shoot at the children."

Sophie Tema testified that she never heard any warning from the side of the police. After she and her driver, Stanley, had taken a wounded boy to the clinic, they returned. They saw a girl "with grief on her face" running down the street. Next to her, was a young man who carried a wounded boy in his arms. The boy's name was Hector Petersen. The driver loaded the young people in his car to take them to the clinic. She, Sophie, ran after them. "Arriving at the clinic, the doctor told me it was too late – Hector had been shot in the throat."

Ms Nomavenda Mathiane who was attached to the magazine *True Love* at that time, related that the doctor, Abu-Baker Asvat, the 'people's doctor' as he was called in Soweto, was always ready to help. Nomavenda was in Dr Asvat's consulting room when a group of wounded school children stormed in. The children knew that they were safe there, that the doctor would not give them away to the police. While the doctor was busy dealing with the more serious cases, a few women who were in the consulting room, helped to get the fine shot out of the children's wounds.

Christina Buthelezi, permanently paralysed after having been shot in the back on 16 June, also came to tell her story. In 1976 she was a standard seven pupil. She did not even know that there would be a demonstration that day. But when she arrived at school and saw what was happening, she joined the procession. Together with the other children, she "became very angry" when she heard about the death of Hector Petersen.

After the demonstration, she went to collect her school books which she had left at her aunt's house. On her way back, she encountered a police convoy. "They shot randomly, and I was hit. I lost consciousness." In hospital the police came to interrogate her. They thought that she was Antoinette Sithole, Hector Peterson's sister. What she came to ask from the Truth Commission was whether she could get a wheelchair and medical treatment.

Johannes Dube was also in the witness-box. He came to relate how he, a standard eight pupil, walked down the street on the same day. Police in camouflage uniforms shot at him. It was the last day that he would be able to see – he had been blind ever since. He had dreams of becoming a teacher, he said. But now, it would never happen.

However, it was not only the children who were traumatised that day, Leonard Mosala declared during the hearing. Also the people who shot at them, would not be able to forget what happened. Mr Mosala, who had been a member of the Civic Council, who had worked with the government at the time, testified how he had heard a young policeman shouting to the women in the street to "please get out of the way" because he did not want to shoot them. Shortly after the incident Leonard Mosala severed connections with the Civic Council, as he no longer believed that co-operation with the government would help to change things. Later, as one of the Commission of Ten who had been appointed by the people of Soweto themselves, he personally experienced what it meant to rebel against the government. He and his wife were arrested and tortured. During that time he was working for the IBM company who put pressure on a number of embassies to take up the case of Leonard and his wife with the Government. The then Minister of Justice, Mr Jimmy Kruger, released Mosala from prison and apologized to him personally.

Looking back, one realized that 16 June 1976 had been one of the most important dates in our history, Leonard Mosala said. "The moment when the State unchained its power against the unarmed black children, the children grabbed the initiative for the struggle from their parents' hands. At the same time the parents were shocked into active support of the children. They no longer questioned the children's actions. In a way which had never been equalled before, the old and the young joined hands in the struggle against oppression and brutality ... "

◆ ◆ ◆

Who was responsible for the demonstration on 16 June? Murphy Morobe – currently a senior government official – was in 1976 one of the student leaders who had made the arrangements. He and his colleagues in the Black Consciousness Movement wanted "to teach black people to be proud". Shortly before 16 June the South African Students Movement formed an action committee to reflect on how to alleviate the smouldering tension and unrest in Soweto. The committee, Morobe related, did plan the demonstration which took place on 16 June, "but violence was not part of their plans".

According to Murphy Morobe the police that day in Orlando West set a dog on the singing children. The children killed the dog. The police then started shooting at the children. "Most of the policemen", the former member of the city council testified, "were black. They followed the orders of a white commander. I think that group of policemen still have a lot to explain."

◆ ◆ ◆

In the past, much had been written about the death of the well-known Dr Melville Edelstein on that ill-fated day. The photograph of his mutilated body, in a street of Soweto, deeply shocked South Africans. Dr Edelstein had devoted his whole life to Soweto. He took his work as sociologist in the service of the Western Administration Board extremely seriously.

"My dad loved the people of Soweto nearly as much as he loved his family," Janet Goldblatt testified before the TRC. Dr Edelstein took her and her sister, Shana, to school the morning before work. "He never came back," Mrs Goldblatt added. Later that day he was found dead after being dragged from his car and beaten to death with spades.

"We heard later that he had already been on his way out of Soweto when, worried about a woman who worked with him, he turned back." Her father, she said, was a wonderful person who cared for the under-privileged. He was a campaigner for better education and he had per-sonally initiated a special project to help disabled black people. His thesis at that time dealt with the question: How do young black people think?

Dr Edelstein never felt unsafe in Soweto. But the week before his death he told his wife that he "had a bad feeling about the state of mind of the students".

Nothing would ever bring her father back, Shana Goldblatt came to say. But the family wanted to know what exactly had happened on that day. If anybody had any information, they were requested to come for-ward. "I would like for a monument or something like that to be erected on the place where he died. He was part of the struggle and loved the people of Soweto."

◆ ◆ ◆

A last witness: the elderly Mr Elliot Ndlovu, who was principal at a primary school in Soweto during the 1976 riots. He came to tell about his son Hastings, who was shot dead on 16 June. His closing remark made the audience straighten up in their chairs. The day was not only a day of grief and pain, he said, but also a day of triumph. "Even those of us who have lost loved ones, believed that the school children were doing the right thing. The tree of freedom was watered with blood … "

24 JULY 1996: BACK TO THE CAPE, BACK TO THE NG KERK

While the Soweto hearing was still in session, I had to fly to the Cape. Mary Burton, Wilhelm Verwoerd and Pumla Gobode-Madikizela had ar-ranged an appointment with the moderature of the Western and South-ern Cape Synod and I had to accompany them. The TRC did not want to lose the support of the Afrikaans community – neither that of the Afrikaans churches – and needed advice. Dr Frits Gaum, the moderator, and his colleagues spoke quite frankly. They once again assured the Truth Commission of their co-operation and intercession by prayer. They promised readily to provide aid with counselling and pastoral care of victims and offenders. But they were still concerned about the fairness of the process. "You will have to make a better effort of assuring and convincing people that the TRC will not degenerate into a witch-hunt," was the general feeling.

With the events of the last few days – the Soweto hearing which was currently in progress – on our minds, we had a number of requests from the side of the TRC as well. Wouldn't the NG Kerk, as well as the other churches in the country, be willing to accept ownership of the process? Who would be better able to guide the nation on the way of truth, forgiveness and reconciliation, than the churches themselves? At that time it had already become evident that not only the large number of *victims* who came forward needed pastoral counselling, but especially also the *perpetrators* and their families. Would the church bear its responsibility? The most important of it all was that the church, at this time, would support all its *members*, who had also been immersed in a crisis, who came to face the mirror of our history, who were startled by what they saw. Would the church lead its members on the difficult road of confession and reconciliation?

21 AUGUST 1996: WHO ARE THE GUILTY ONES?

"The things that had happened are horrible. One cannot believe one's eyes and ears, when listening to the victims. One asks oneself: is this the country where I lived these past years? Is this what our people did to others?" There was general agreement with the elder's words.

I was invited that night to a parish meeting in Randfontein, on the West Rand. As it happened often during the past months in several congregations, they wanted to talk about the Truth Commission. What gave the discussion on that particular Wednesday evening, an extra urgency, was the TRC hearing in Sebokeng, which was widely broadcast in the past week. In Sebokeng and the nearby Boipatong, some of the most serious human rights violations of all over the past years took place. Young people were arrested, women raped, men came to tell about atrocious methods of torture. The community was divided: activists had died, but also members of the city councils and their families, by means of the cruel necklace method. Gangs ruled the streets during the night, with the permission and co-operation of certain members of the police, some victims alleged. People were thrown from moving trains.

Above all, there were the reports of one massacre after the other in Sebokeng and Boipatong. Nobody knew exactly how many people had died. Not even now. In addition, the revelations of the most recent amnesty hearings alarmed the brothers and sisters.

"We did not know!" Like many Germans after the Second World War, when the cruelties of the Nazis became public knowledge, we struggled with the problem of our guilt on that Wednesday evening in the church hall in Randfontein. As was the case with many South Africans night after night when they watched the next episode of the TRC on television. "We really did not know! Can we be guilty of the misdeeds of a small group of criminals? I have not been a member of the Security Police. My husband did not work at Vlakplaas! To tell the truth, my parents taught me years ago to have respect for other people – also for black people."

◆ ◆ ◆

In 1946 just after the end of the Second World War, Karl Jaspers, the German philosopher, delivered a famous lecture at the University of Heidelberg in which he tried to answer the question: "Who is guilty?". He had reason to write about these things. Because he was married to a woman of Jewish background, he (and she) escaped the German death camps by inches. From his analysis of what guilt meant in the German context, we could learn valuable lessons.

South Africa was not Germany and what had happened in Nazi-Germany during the thirties and forties, was not exactly similar to what had happened during the apartheid years in South Africa. However, his four categories of guilt were also of interest to us.

Firstly, Jaspers said, they had to contend with *criminal guilt*. In Germany there was a group of people, politicians, SS officers, and others, who were directly involved in gross violations of human rights. They were charged during the Nuremberg trials with specific crimes, and duly sentenced. The same applied to our country, where several people on all sides of the struggle were guilty of specific offences. Their guilt was not difficult to indicate. In many cases it was proclaimed from the house-tops. Many of these people indeed applied for amnesty.

Secondly, there was *political guilt*. Through the years there were millions of Germans who voted for Hitler and the Nazi Party, who supported their policies, who enthusiastically cheered the Führer in the streets, who had to accept political responsibility. As was the case in our country. The National Party, who had accepted and implemented apartheid as policy, did not come into office by itself. With every election held in this country hundreds of thousands of white people – the people who had suffrage – sounded a resounding "Yes" at the polls. In many different ways we gave our approval to the apartheid policy. And of this we are guilty.

The third category, according to Jaspers, was that of *moral guilt*, the reverse side of political guilt. This was the guilt of people in Germany – and here in South Africa – who had allowed themselves to be misled, who enjoyed the benefits of a very unfair system, and did not object to it. There were very few white South Africans who could say with a clear conscience today that they did not know *anything*. Closer to the truth would be: I knew about certain things, but I pretended to be ignorant; in many newspapers from time to time articles appeared, but I chose not to take it seriously; I knew that people were being treated unfairly, but I did not want to become involved; my conscience urged me to talk, but I was afraid and kept quiet.

Mercifully, there was also a fourth category. Jaspers called it *metaphysical guilt*. This concerned our communal guilt. All people, standing before God, are equally guilty. "Before God not only a few, or many, or even the majority, are guilty," Jaspers explained, "but everybody!" Collectively we were carrying the guilt of mankind on our shoulders! Knowing this made one humble, less prone to judge others. Because who of us could guarantee that we, if we found ourselves in the same circumstances and were subjected to the same influences as, for example, the SS soldiers, would have acted differently? Some of the young Germans who were guilty of gross offences came from the best homes in the country, Jaspers said. The knowledge that all of us were guilty made it possible for us to forgive each other.

I remembered an anecdote from our Johannesburg office, which I could convey to the people in Roodepoort, that illustrated Jasper's last point. Jan Luuks was a senior detective from Holland who had been seconded by the Netherlands Government to the TRC to assist us in our investigations. He was Head of Security at the Soesdijk Palace, where the royal family of the Netherlands stayed. The tale that Jan told us, however, did not concern Queen Beatrix, but a group of students from the United States.

During the 1950s a number of Criminology students from two American Universities, Yale and Stanford, were given permission to undertake a unique roleplay experiment in a newly restored prison. A group of senior students were divided into two groups. One half would be prisoners and were locked in the cells. The other half were made guards with the instruction to supervise the prisoners for the next week. Already on the first day, the lecturer received complaints. The "warders" started to maltreat the "inmates". At the end of the second day the lecturer had to terminate the whole experiment! The "guards" had ill-treated the "prisoners", their own classmates, to such an extent that they were in danger of sustaining serious injuries. The lesson was clear Jan Luuks said, one should never be too sure of oneself, that one would not, in similar circumstances, lay your hands on others.

◆ ◆ ◆

"But what do I do with *my* guilt?" a Randfontein woman asked, quite upset. "Must I go and confess before Archbishop Tutu?" The answer is simple, our group told each other that evening. In the first place it was *God*, who, through his Spirit, worked inside us, who had to convince us of our guilt. And in this conviction we had to go to Him, empty our hearts before Him. We had, in the first place, to reconcile with God. But then, Jesus taught us, one should also reach out to one's *fellow*-man. If you have wronged someone, you must also confess to that person and ask for forgiveness. You must correct what you have done wrong. You must be reconciled with God and your fellow-man. In this regard the Sermon on the Mount is very clear: *"Therefore, if you are offering your gift at the altar and there remember that your brother has something against you, leave your gift there in front of the altar. First go and be reconciled to your brother; then come and offer your gift."* (Matt. 5:23, 24)

The TRC was not our confessional box, but it was one important forum where we could reach out to each other, where the things that were to be said, could be said, where we could learn to listen and understand, where the tears of healing could flow.

I only returned to my house in Pretoria very late that night. Exhausted. But nevertheless with a feeling in my heart that the few of us, that evening, had achieved something. There were still many questions, but there was also a new understanding of the rough road, our Afrikaners' own *via dolorosa*, which lay ahead.

22 AUGUST 1996: WHAT ABOUT THE ENGLISH?

The next morning Hugh Lewin and I discussed the conversation of the previous evening. Teatime in the TRC office was quite informal. We were often too busy for chit-chat, and then everybody would take their cup of tea or coffee to their offices. But not today. Hugh was interested in the Roodepoort discussion, and in Karl Jaspers' categories of guilt.

"You are worried about the Afrikaners," Hugh remarked. "I am worried about the English! I think I have more problems with my compatriots than you have with yours. Everybody does not feel the same as Lesley Morgan. You Afrikaners at least talk about the Truth Commission. You are in favour of or against it. You have strong feelings about the matter. But many English-speaking persons continue their lives as if these things do not affect them at all. It was, after all, not they who had instituted apartheid. They are not *Boere* or Nationalists! And still they benefited from the process just as much ... "

"Well," I remembered, "when I was a student in the sixties, the story went the round of the university that English-speaking South Africans reacted rather typically every time when an election was held. In their hearts they supported the United Party. To impress their colleagues, they voted Progressive. And the night after the election they secretly thanked God that the National Party had won again!"

"We will have to work hard to guide the English-speaking people on the way of truth and reconciliation," Hugh closed the conversation. "Believe me, it is a painful process to our people as well, even though we do not easily admit it. It is not easy to face the mirror of the past."

3 SEPTEMBER 1996: APOLOGY FOR THE MURDER OF PIET RETIEF

By the end of August various political parties had made their first submissions to the TRC. The Afrikaner Volksfront, the National Party and the ANC each presented bulky reports. These reports would be studied carefully over the next few months, so that when the parties would be called in for their second appearance, a meaningful discussion could be held about the contents.

The fact that Dr Mangosuthu Buthelezi, the leader of the Inkatha Freedom Party, also put in an appearance at the TRC, was regarded as a breakthrough. Buthelezi and the IFP had expressed criticism about the work of the Truth Commission. When the Act that had to make provision for the introduction of the TRC served before Parliament in 1995, the IFP voted against the promulgation of the Act. What would Buthelezi, who served as the Minister of Internal Affairs in the national Cabinet, be able to tell the TRC?

From the word go Buthelezi had the full attention of the journalists present. "This morning, during my quiet time I chanced upon a wonderful hymn that is exactly right for today's events. I would like to sing it to you." The leader of the IFP began singing in a resonant voice. Tutu joined him in song: "Just as I am, without one plea, I come before the Lamb of God ... "

Before Buthelezi gave Dr Ben Ngubane the opportunity to submit the lengthy IFP report – five hundred pages – he touched upon a few matters that weighed heavily upon him.

First, he had a word for Afrikaners: "I want to apologize to my Afrikaner brothers for the murder of Piet Retief and his men, committed in the previous century by Dingane."

Secondly he wanted to say something about the violence in South Africa, and about the role the IFP played in the violence: "I reject violence! Sometimes it happens that the IFP members are drawn into violence against their will ... I tell South Africa I am sorry about it. Even if I did not orchestrate one single act of violence, I know that I carry the final responsibility. The buck stops here!" On behalf of his supporters Buthelezi apologized to everyone who had been hurt in the process, also for the pain he had inflicted on the ANC leadership. "I really hope that the apology to Mr Nelson Mandela and others that I carry in my heart, will also be expressed as simply, and in public, by him and others, as I have just done."

Which does not mean that the IFP leader did not have an axe to grind with the ANC! Buthelezi continued, and in no uncertain terms accused the ANC of breaking its promise to invite international negotiators to our country. The ANC had also plotted against the IFP – as the report would indicate – against which the IFP objected in the strongest terms.

When Dr Ngubane began reading substantial portions of the long report, the audience sank back in their chairs. He was at it for three hours! A *Beeld* reporter remarked impishly that one of the TRC commissioners had been the first to nod off. Tutu had to give him a nudge in the ribs.

5 SEPTEMBER 1996: WHY, LORD?

During the hearing of the Truth Commission in Nelspruit various witnesses came forward – persons from different communities, black as well as white – to tell their tales.

When Mr Johan Roos, who was residing temporarily in Botswana, began talking, many persons in the audience listened, their faces buried in their hands.

On the evening of 27 August 1976, Johan Roos said, he and his family attended church in Nelspruit. There they heard the shocking news that a landmine explosion had occurred earlier that day on one of the farms in the district, and that a number of people had died. Little did Johan and his family know what events would await them that very same evening.

After the service, Johan and his wife Marietjie, drove home in two cars. Marietjie had their three children with her. On the dirt road near their home Johan suddenly saw flames shooting out from underneath his wife's car. The car was flung into the air. Pieces of metal, dust and soil flew through the air. "I said, 'Why, Lord?'" When he reached her, his wife was still seated in the car. "Parts of her feet were gone. She moaned, 'Where are my legs, why does it hurt so much?'"

Their eight-year-old son, Jaco, was unconscious in the back seat of the car. Johan Roos lifted his other two frightened children out of the wreck and sought assistance from a neighbour. Back at the car he knelt at Marietjie's side. "Don't lose heart", he tried to comfort her. "The Lord will carry us through." In hospital Marietjie Roos' right leg was amputated below the knee. Her left leg was crushed. Her throat was ripped open.

"I knew that a piece of her shin was still in the wreck. I went looking for it so that I could bury it. Instead I found a piece of my son's forehead. I found parts of his brain on the seat. I picked everything up, put it in a tissue, wrapped it and went to bury it at my house. After such an experience, how can one ever be normal again?"

Three days after the attack Marietjie Roos died. "My son was getting convulsions, so badly that four sisters, my father and I had to battle to hold him down on the hospital bed. They had to give him morphine. We had the privilege of having him home for Christmas. But he was no longer the child I knew. He did not enquire after his mother. He did not recognize me as his father."

When the boy died "after seven months of hell and suffering", he weighed a pitiful 15 kilograms, as against the 35 kilograms before the attack.

"My daughter – she was five at the time – never cried. She still does not cry today. My son Johan, who was fifteen months old at the time, adjusted better to the changes in his life. He is a happy child, but I don't know how he will develop later on.

"What kind of monsters decided that these things had to be done, I do not know. I am asking the party responsible to stand up, and to my face, tell me why he did it ... "

Before leaving the witness stand, Johan Roos asked whether he could offer a prayer. Deeply moved, the commissioners listened how the bereaved father entrusted South Africa, her people and especially the work of the Truth Commission to the Lord, how he pleaded with God to bring peace in the new South Africa.

◆ ◆ ◆

Yet another victim who had a turn to speak at the Nelspruit hearing was Mr Dirk van Eck.

In 1985 Dirk van Eck and his family went on holiday in the Messina district, visiting Koos de Nyschen and his wife. On 15 December, at four o'clock in the afternoon, the two families went on a game drive. The pickup truck was packed.

"At about five o'clock I heard an enormous explosion. There was a surge of intense heat and I felt that we were flying through the air and then we hit the ground. All around me were flames and dust. I held my son, Erick, eighteen months old, in my arms. He was still alive, but I don't think he realized what had happened. My friend Koos de Nyschen lay with his face against the steering wheel. He was covered with blood and his hair was burning.

"I was unable to open the door at my side. I tried to kick it open. I failed to do so and crept through the window, although there were still burning flames, lifted my child out of the pickup and put him down in the road. Koos had in the meantime come round; I also helped him out, through my window. His scalp had been torn loose and hung over his face. I tied our handkerchiefs together and bandaged his wound.

"I then went looking for other survivors. When I reached the back of the vehicle, now a total wreck, I found Mrs Theo de Nyschen; she was burning. I smothered the flames with my hands and helped her lie down flat in the road. Her arms and hands were severely burnt. The lower part of her body was bleeding.

"I searched for other survivors but found my wife and Mrs Marie de Nyschen lying dead close to one another. They lay in the bushes about six metres behind the pickup truck. Both of my wife's legs had been blown off. I was shocked by her death and the condition she was in.

"I looked further on and about ten metres to the north I found my young daughter, Nelmarie, eight years old, and Carla de Nyschen, ten years old, lying dead. Both had been burnt so badly that they were pitch-black.

"I tried to find my son Ignatius Michael, two and a half years old. I couldn't find him at all. I later learnt that the Police had found his tiny foot about a hundred metres from that point.

"One of Koos's daughters, Grizelle, came walking out of the veld. She was about eight years old. It was obvious that she was in a severe state of shock. She was blackened by the dust or soot. She had a cut on her nose. I took her to her father and she sat down beside him. I realized that some of the survivors' lives might be in danger and ran to the homestead about eight kilometres from there to summon help.

"I had great difficulty talking to the Police – I discovered that I had sustained a hearing problem as a result of the explosion. Fortunately, they managed to understand my message. I took my vehicle and rushed back to the scene, with the necessary medical equipment that I could scrape together. On my arrival the local commando members were already on the scene and they had already been applying first aid.

"By nine o'clock the field ambulance of the Defence Force arrived. As they feared further landmines, they drove through the veld. It was a shocking sight to see how Mrs Theo de Nyschen had to cling to the stretcher with severely burnt hands, so that she wouldn't fall off in the ambulance. We only reached the hospital in Messina at about twelve o' clock at night, where the injured were treated. They decided to transfer us to the Pietersburg Hospital. We were taken by Dakota to Pietersburg ... My son Erick and I were discharged the next day. Mr Koos de Nyschen, his wife, Theo and their daughter Grizelle remained in hospital.

"About a week later – after the funeral – I began suffering from back-ache. The doctor took X-rays and informed me that the five lower back vertebrae had been severely damaged. He alleged that if I was not careful I would be confined to a wheelchair within five years. The psychological damage, however, was the worst. I had lost my wife and two children, who were in the prime of their lives, as well as members of my best friend's family. This was caused by a cowardly and criminal deed which had been committed by members of the ANC, as I later heard. I suffered from insomnia. As soon as I fell asleep, the gruesome scene kept replaying in my mind. After all these years I still experience it at times, especially now the Truth Commission is opening up old sores."

At the time of the landmine explosion, Dirk van Eck was a prosperous farmer who employed five white and some nine hundred black workers. Since the events, however, he had to devote himself full-time to looking after his son, who was in a state of shock and missed his mother terribly. His farming and business interests went into a decline. He was later sequestrated, and lived, as he put it, "from alms until my father-in-law helped me get a place to stay."

Dirk van Eck testified that the two men who had set the landmine had been caught and sentenced to death in 1988. In 1991 the sentence was commuted to nineteen years' imprisonment. However, they were released shortly afterwards and in December 1993 they received "awards for bravery" from the ANC. "I have a problem with how one manages to see the bravery", he concluded his testimony.

6 SEPTEMBER 1996: "WE ARE NOT GOING TO MAKE IT ... "

I was quite dejected when I entered my office that morning. It was going to be one of *those* days. The traffic was impossible, the trip from Pretoria to Johannesburg took more than two hours. And the whole time, over the radio, the topics discussed concerned murder and violence, corruption and crime in our country. People called in. Some were angry, others frightened or discouraged. Fine words about peace and reconciliation were not welcome. "Fazel", I told our office boss, "I don't know whether we are going to make it. People's attitudes, the negative spirit dominating our country, keep me awake at night. What chance do we at the Truth Commission have of succeeding if all these things are happening in South Africa?"

Fazel responded in his quiet way: "That may be true, Piet. But can you think of a more necessary time to be engaged in this work?"

9-11 SEPTEMBER 1996: RECONCILIATION IN BISHO

On 7 September 1992 the fragile transitional process in South Africa nearly broke down when a group of Ciskeian soldiers fired at a disorderly group of protestors. The ANC insisted that, despite the tense situation in the former Ciskei, it would hold a big meeting in Bisho. Brandishing banners and placards, they marched through the streets of Bisho. When a group of protestors, led by Mr Ronnie Kasrils, broke away from the rest of the ANC group, the Ciskeian soldiers fired at them. In the ensuing chaos 28 people died, while more than 200 were injured. According to eye-witnesses shots were fired at Ronnie Kasrils and also at Cyril Ramaphosa. In the Goldstone Commission's report the action of the Ciskeian soldiers was sharply criticized, while the ANC also came under fire.

Four years later, from 9 to 11 September 1996, the TRC created a special opportunity at which the "Bisho massacre" could be scrutinized. All the parties were present: Ronnie Kasrils and Cyril Ramaphosa, former cabinet minister Pik Botha, as well as two senior officers, General Marius Oelshig, Head of the Ciskei Army, and the head of staff operations, Horst Schobergsberger.

The comments of a number of senior journalists who attended the hearing were as revealing as the facts that came to light. For them the testimonies of the three days proved that the TRC was succeeding in its mandate. The journalists' words were like music to the Truth Commission, as it regularly had to endure criticism: "The fact that the TRC succeeded in bringing together perpetrators and victims during the hearing, largely ensured that a basis was laid for reconciliation", wrote the political correspondent of the *Sowetan*, Mzimsi Ngudle. "Except for the fact that Oupa Gqozo did not give testimony and that Pik Botha denied that the South African government did not have the political will to prevent the bloodbath, we just about received a full picture of what had happened in the three terrible days. The trial clearly showed that one needed both the testimony of the victims as well as that of the offenders if you wanted to achieve real reconciliation."

Ross Colvin of *Sapa* regarded the trial as the best he had ever attended. "It was important that so many high-profile persons appeared in public to give account ... " The reporter of the *Daily Despatch*, Eric Naki, wrote that the fact that the TRC succeeded in getting both the offenders and the victims on one stage, was an indication of the influence and power of the TRC. This illustrated the fact that the TRC, with a few exceptions, were being accepted by both sides of the conflict. "So far the spotlight has fallen, virtually without exception, on the Police. Now this has at last happened with the Defence Force ... " The commissioners and committee members needed the feather in their cap, as despondency and fatigue were beginning to overwhelm them. The pace was fast and demanding.

13 SEPTEMBER 1996: IF THE ROAD BECOMES TOO MUCH FOR THE COMMISSIONERS, WHAT THEN?

In the plane on my way to Stellenbosch, where I was invited to conduct the morning service in the Mother Church, I read the September issue of The Evangelical Alliance of South Africa (TEASA's) *Truth and Reconciliation Prayer Bulletin*. It was heartwarming. Traditionally the English-speaking Gospel Churches in our country did not wish to become involved in socio-political issues. The fear of 'social gospel' was just too great! But with Moss Nthla as the new, energetic secretary of TEASA at the helm, several Evangelical churches and parachurch organisations committed themselves to the process of truth and reconciliation. Moss was a regular visitor to the Gauteng TRC office, attended several of our conferences and workshops, and often brought some of his colleagues along.

In the bulletin Michael Cassidy, one of the influential evangelical leaders, spoke enthusiastically of the work of the TRC: "I believe the TRC can, with the help of the Lord, stand as a landmark ... not only of our nation but of the rest of the world ... If it is to succeed, it will tax the moral and spiritual resources of our nation to the utmost."

Moss Nthla wanted even more. In addition to the moral and spiritual resources, he also wanted to give evangelicals an opportunity to muster their financial resources. TEASA announced that the organisation was collecting one million rand. The money would be made available to the TRC to help victims, especially those who suffered financially, who could not hold out much longer.

◆ ◆ ◆

On the front page of TEASA's bulletin a second article appeared which I also read with interest – and in the plane discussed with my wife who, too, was invited to Stellenbosch. The heading appeared in capital letters:

TRC TAKES ITS TOLL ON COMMISSIONERS

"The commissioners are assigned the pastoral task of hearing victims of human rights violations telling their stories, often in tearful and vivid detail. As though it happened just yesterday. How do they cope? Theirs is not a nine-to-five job. They carry the horror stories home with them and can't sleep well at night. All find the task overwhelming and traumatic."

To prove his point the editor had questioned a number of commissioners and committee members. From their answers it was clear that also the TRC people were travelling along their own *via dolorosa* during these months of hearings.

Three examples will suffice:

Hlengiwe Mkhize (chairperson of the Reparation and Rehabilitation Committee, Johannesburg): "Each story opens a wound further and further. At a certain point it becomes difficult and you start feeling tense and uneasy ... "

Russel Ally (member of the Human Rights Violations Committee, Johannesburg): "The testimonies have a cumulative impact. It builds and builds until at the end of the hearing you feel emotionally and physically shattered ... It was not possible for anyone before the TRC to capture the cruelty."

Bongani Finca (Methodist preacher, member of the Human Rights Violations Committee, East London): "It is difficult to hold back tears while we listen. We go home and are haunted by their pain. We thought we knew about it, but there was so much we did not know ... "

Not only the commissioners and committee members suffered. Also the other members of the staff – the statement takers who moved through the country, the helpers and briefers during the hearings, the translators and researchers – had a hard time of it. Sleeplessness, nightmares, depression, were the order of the day.

Frank Mohape, one of the Johannesburg statement takers once told how he was sitting in a room, assisting three victims with their submissions. They were the only suvivors. The rest of the family had been wiped out. While Frank sat writing, he observed that the chair on which he sat was riddled with bullet-holes. "When I looked around me, I also saw the bullet marks on the walls, on many pieces of furniture. Suddenly I realized: these people have been living in these desperate circumstances all these years, in poverty. And tonight I return to my hotel room, to my clean sheets and a warm meal. There was precious little that I could do to help them." Angry and confused about his own role in the process, Frank returned to the hotel that night. He went to sit in the bar ... and tried to forget.

At one stage the TRC, concerned about the well-being of its staff, decided to appoint a full-time psychologist. Thulani Grenville-Grey came from England. His father was a white churchman, advisor of the bishop of Johannesburg, his mother a black woman. For the sake of their marriage they had to leave the country. Mixed marriages were, in the sixties, a transgression of the law. Thulani with his friendly smile, his love for the saxophone and his luxurious dreadlocks, made himself at home quickly. His weekly therapy sessions were popular among commissioners and members of the staff.

Thulani had to help the TRC staff to understand and cope with their own reactions. They encountered some of the most horrible violations of human rights on earth – and they had to learn how to deal with it emotionally. "The TRC people reacted in different ways," Thulani said. "Like sponges they absorbed the sorrow, pain and aggression of others. Many of them started to show the classic symptoms of post-trauraumatic stress. It was important for them to attend the weekly sessions, in order to talk through their feelings and experiences."

On more than one occasion the translators who were involved for weeks on end in the hearings, came to Grenville-Grey to ask help. They, in a certain sense, suffered most. While they, in the first person, translated the stories, they also identified with the emotions of the victims. One evening during the eight o'clock news, the cameraman turned his camera away from the witness to the face of one of the translators. She sat in one of the booths, translating, with tears running down her cheeks.

"The translating", Dr Theo du Plessis from the University of the Free State who was the co-ordinator of the translating service, admitted during a newspaper interview, "had a 'helluva' effect on every one of us! Not only when one was busy, but especially when one tried to relax at night." If, during that day of the hearing, stories of children who suffered were discussed, it was twice as bad: "I myself am a father and at one or two occasions, when parents testified about what had happened to their children, I burst into tears and cried."

Also journalists reported to Thulani. The exposure that they had, the pressure to report on it every day, to interpret to the readers and listeners what happened, nearly became too much for them. Many became ill. Others requested special leave, just to restore their balance. Ross Colvin, who worked for SAPA, said, "I have had enough of listening to stories of death, torture, poisoning, of all the bodies that were burnt. I was busy with the most disturbing work you can imagine ... Sometimes I thought my feelings had become deadened. That nothing that people could say would affect me any longer ... And then somebody told another story that affected me horribly." Headaches, sleeplessness, low blood pressure caused this journalist to want to stop writing.

When, during one of the amnesty hearings, a few security policemen related how, next to the stake where they were burning the bodies of their victims, they stood at their own fire, barbequing meat, it was just too much for black journalist Thapelo Mokushane. It made him physically ill, he said later. Over and over, images of what had happened flashed through his mind at the most unexpected times. "In order to keep my job, I constantly had to fight my own emotions!"

That Thulani Grenville-Grey, psychologist, had important work to do, was evident.

◆ ◆ ◆

Also in this regard Desmond Tutu had some advice. He often spoke appreciatively of Thulani's work. But as pastor and spiritual father, he offered his own advice to everybody who landed on their own personal *via dolorosa*.

"We must watch over and take care of each other," he liked to repeat. "Make sure that you keep your bonds with your husbands and wives, with your children, strong. Their interest and love and encouragement will make it possible for you to keep going." That this worked, we could see from the relationship between him and his wife, Leah. Countless times when things progressed at an extra quick pace and caused a great deal of tension – when the Archbishop was confronted with almost inhuman demands – Leah, unobtrusively and always with a friendly smile on her face, appeared. One could then see how Tutu was revived. When Leah was nearby, he got his second wind.

Tutu's own example also illustrated how we had to be each other's family. A note, a friendly embrace, a word of appreciation, a card, an e-mail message on your screen, a bouquet of flowers if there was illness in the family – in many ways he supported his colleagues. I was present at one occasion when he made a very distinguished and influential lady who phoned from England wait a couple of minutes – to pray over a second telephone for Janis Grobbelaar who had to be in theatre within a few moments for major heart surgery. Once when I arrived at the office only after nine – I had to participate in an early breakfast pro-gramme on the radio – the telephonist said breathlessly, "The arch-bishop has already phoned you three times this morning. He wants you urgently. You must call him in the Cape immediately!" Rather concerned I obeyed. What did I do wrong? Lavinia Brown, Tutu's secretary, made me wonder even more. "It is good that you have phoned. The arch has been looking for you the whole morning!" However, when she had put me through, Tutu said with laughter in his voice, "I say! Piet, I have already phoned you three times this morning ... It is urgent. It just couldn't wait. I wanted to thank you for the work you are doing ... " How many others he encouraged in the same way during those months, I wondered, still holding the receiver in my hand.

"Above all you must hold on to God, you must take your faith seri-ously," was Tutu's final bit of advice. And in this regard, too, he suited the action to the word. During the afternoons, between one and two when the others went out to lunch, Tutu disappeared. It was an open secret what he did. Somewhere in a quiet room, Tutu would withdraw. He wanted to pray. He wanted to talk to God. "If I do not remain close to God, I will never be able to proceed with my work," he liked to say. "And the same applies to you!" Once, during the Sebokeng hearing, I walked to the platform during the lunch hour to fetch my papers. In one of the translator booths, I saw the purple-clad figure of the arch-bishop, sideways, leaning with his shoulder against the glass window, his eyes closed. In that large complex, it was the only place where he could find a quiet spot to pray.

18-19 SEPTEMBER 1996: *"BOSBERAAD"* (BUSH SUMMIT) AT THE LORD CHARLES HOTEL

It was time for the TRC trek to pause, to come to a halt for a moment. Eight months lay behind us, and it was necessary to look back, before we could resume our strenuous trek forward.

Early that morning, on Wednesday 18 September, the commissioners and committee members gathered in one of the conference halls of the Lord Charles Hotel, just outside Somerset West. Before it was Alex Boraine's turn to inaugurate the agenda for the day, Professor John de Gruchy, church historian at the University of Cape Town was requested to lead us in meditation.

Instead of the traditional Scripture reading and prayer, John de Gruchy made us listen to the Polish composer Henryk Gorecki's Third Symphony. The third movement contained a poignant folk song, in which a Polish mother, like numerous women of her day, grieved about her son who had died in the Polish rebellion.

With the long series of hearings behind us, the hundreds of victims who came to relate their painful stories, Gorecki's song acquired a new significance. The little Polish woman at the Oder River sang on behalf of the mothers of all victims – also those in Soweto and Sebokeng, Cape Town and Bisho:

Where has he gone
My dearest son?
Killed by the harsh enemy, perhaps,
In the rebellion.
You bad people,
In the name of the Holy God,
Tell me why you killed
My dear son.

Never more
Will I have his protection,
Even if I weep
My old eyes away,
Or if my bitter tears
Were to make another Oder

They would not bring back
My son to life.

He lies in the grave
I know not where
Though I ask people
Everywhere
Perhaps the poor boy
Lies in a rough trench
Instead of lying, as he might,
In a warm bed.

Sing for him,
Little song-birds of God,
For his mother
Cannot find him.
And God's little flowers
May you bloom all around
So that my son
May sleep happy.

"There are varying views," Alex Boraine had his turn, "as to where the Commission is after a concentrated period of eight months. There are those who feel, with justification, that we have achieved an enormous amount in a short space of time; others, however, feel almost a sense of crisis when they consider the limited time available and the overwhelming demands on the Commission to deliver in terms of the objectives and functions as set out in the Act."

After giving a brief survey of the hearings, of the victims who came to the TRC, of the political parties who came to testify, of the new information that surfaced in the event of the hearings, Deputy Chairperson Boraine continued:

"Hearings are imperative but in an important sense they are a means to an end. Catharsis, healing, restoration of dignity of survivors, did occur, but the fervent plea of survivors has been to know who was responsible for their suffering ... We haven't begun to move towards establishing accountability. In other words, we have been successful in encouraging survivors to come forward, but we need to develop a clear strategy to encourage or compel perpetrators to tell their side of the conflict."

Everybody realized that the amnesty process, in the months to come, would demand a great deal of attention. The same applied to the work of the Reparation and Rehabilitation Committee. There were numerous victims who were living in desperate circumstances. There were old people, and those who were ill, who could not wait much longer. Something drastic had to be done – and soon – to help them.

"We would do well to keep in mind that essentially the Commission is not about the past; it is directed towards the future and seeks to make possible a human rights culture which does not exist in South Africa today. In order to prepare for such a future, in order to ensure that we are never again trapped in the pattern of human rights violations of the past, we have to deal with that past, but our emphasis is on the future. Thus, our recommendations have to take account of what needs to happen in South Africa so that we are not trapped by the past but that we have successfully overcome it; we are not paralysed by it but are free to build a society of decency, of compassion and of mutual respect. It is never too early to begin thinking of these terms."

In other words: there was work to be done, enough for everybody!

5 OCTOBER 1996: VISITING THE COMFORTER

October 1996 was, in a special sense, the month of the churches. While the hearings and amnesty sessions continued non-stop, various churches made their voices heard.

Firstly, there was the news that Bishop Modise, leader of the International Pentecostal Church, had made a special award to Tutu and the Truth Commission. The prize would be handed over with great ceremony on Saturday 5 October at the huge church centre, at Zuurbekom, halfway to Potchefstroom.

The International Pentecostal Church was one of the large, black independent churches in our country with – according to their own calculations – one million members. Whether this is true, I would not know, but in the church, as large as an aeroplane hangar, twenty thousand people were present to attend the festivities that day. Choirs sang, functionaries marched in colourful uniforms. Eventually the bishop, called by his followers 'The Comforter', appeared on the podium. Tutu was with him, and they were both greeted with cheers. For the TRC it was important that one of the large independent churches would in this way identify with the work of the Truth Commission. If future closer relationships and reconciliation in the country were to be discussed, all the role players should be willing to report for the conversation.

The representatives of the TRC received seats of honour on the podium and were asked to rise when the document – together with a large silver trophy – was handed to the archbishop.

Bishop J S Modise read the words:

Star of Silo Award

In recognition of the
Truth and Reconciliation Commission,
in their strive in pursuing the Doctrines of Love
Caring and Understanding amongst
people who hurt each other and view each other as enemies.
In the quest for forgiveness and for people
to find each other as practised by the Truth and Reconciliation
Commission.
The Star of Silo
is hereby bestowed upon the Commission
in terms of the teachings of the Comforter that
who even serves a person unknown serves God,
and that you will never see God with your naked eyes,
but will always see a person before you.

With love and showers of blessings

Comforter: J S Modise

1996/10/05
Zuurbekom, Gauteng, South Africa

It was a joyful occasion, with many speeches and a great deal of singing. At one stage one of Modise's elders, apparently afraid that Tutu had received too much honour and that his own bishop was making a poor showing in comparison, came forward. After every phrase of praise about what Tutu and the TRC did, he called out, "Yes, but do you know everything The Comforter did?" and then related one miracle after the other. Should somebody have held count, the result of the contest of compliments at the end of a long day would be a good fifty-fifty!

15 OCTOBER 1996: A CONFESSION IN THE PAARL

When the TRC office in the Cape invited me to participate in the human rights violations hearing to be held in the Paarl, I immediately accepted. Not only for me, but for many people in the country the three-day hearing in the beautiful Boland town in the shade of the Afrikaans Language Monument, was of particular significance.

There was much to talk about. In the local museum there was a special display where past events were portrayed: the shocking Poqo murders which had been committed years ago, injustices at the farms, children who had disappeared, men and women who had been arrested and never returned. And the sorrow did not only come from one side. During the trial Mrs McGregor came to tell about her son, Wallace. As a national serviceman he, a cheerful young man, went to the frontier ... to return to the Paarl in a coffin. What was it all about?, Mrs McGregor wanted to know. "For what exactly did my son — and several others with him — die? Was it a just war that he had fought? Or was it to maintain an unfair system, a system which did horrible things to people?"

However, what I was certain would remain in my memory for years to come, was the conduct of two Stellenbosch ministers who, on behalf of the NG Kerk Presbytery of Stellenbosch came to make a statement. That they would come, we had already known. The news that the Presbytery of Stellenbosch, which represented all the congregations in and around the town, had decided to make their own submission before the TRC, was widely spread. While the debate was carried on country-wide in numerous synodal areas — about the question of whether the NG Kerk owed it to the country and also to the TRC to 'confess' — this Presbytery took the lead. That the confession came from Stellenbosch in particular — the town which played such a great role in the life of the church, where the theological seminary had been erected, where generations of leaders had been fostered at the University, the birthplace of Afrikaner nationalism — was of historic and symbolic significance.

The hall was crammed, the press present in full strength, when Professor Bethel Muller and Rev Jan Marais walked to the podium.

"An exceptional moment," Tutu whispered to me. Then he turned to the audience: "It is remarkable that of all churches it is the NG Kerk, in particular, who comes to the Truth Commission first. It is appropriate, because the church has played an important role in society in the past. But I hope that many churches will follow this example." For the two theologians Tutu had a special word: "Your behaviour fills one with humility. Thank you that you have come. I feel like rejoicing!"

Just like the TRC, the Presbytery wanted to make a contribution towards the process of healing and reconciliation, the statement began. Therefore, the Presbytery wanted to tell the story of Stellenbosch, as they saw it:

The NG Kerk had been active for more than three hundred years in Stellenbosch. The congregation of Stellenbosch had been established in 1686 and since then a number of congregations grew from this congregation. As the Church of Christ it was important for them to live in obedience to the Bible as the Word of God. They were a part of the Reformed tradition that Jesus Christ is the Lord of all lords and that the sovereignty of God, therefore, had to be proclaimed in every aspect of the community. They, therefore, believe that the Church of Christ has to be, in every situation, a witness of the truth, justice, reconciliation and love.

"In looking back, we realise that there have been times in the history of Stellenbosch when we as a Presbytery (and also as separate congregations) either failed wholesale or made only the most timid of efforts to fulfil the prophetic responsibility the Lord has given us. We think especially of the past forty years during which the official policy of apartheid radically impaired the human dignity of people all around us and resulted in gross violations of human rights. Within the borders of our Presbytery, there were those who actively developed and defended the ideological framework by which these violations and actions were justified.

"At times, standpoints and decisions taken within this Presbytery itself functioned within this ideological framework.

"There were voices among our own ranks and within our church that condemned apartheid and sought to call our church to its senses and who witnessed against injustice within society. However, the testimony and the protest of many of these people were, time and again, suppressed or ignored, also from within our own ranks. Others were maligned and some were even personally wronged ...

"Various factors contributed to this lack of a strong, unified witness from within our Presbytery. The nationalist ideology deeply influenced the way in which local Christians thought and read the Bible. This made us insensitive to the injustice and suffering inflicted by the policy of apartheid on those living around us. Other factors which aggravated the situation were the privileged position occupied by most members of our church and the fact that apartheid increasingly isolated people from each other's lives and experiences.

"As a result of the growing ecumenical isolation and the lack of meaningful church unity, we became deaf to the protest and the cries for help by many of our brothers and sisters in faith. Many church members and church ministers therefore often uncritically accepted that, because many of them were also members of our church, political leaders could be trusted to do what is right. This further reinforced the widespread belief that apartheid or separate development was truly in the best interest of all groups in the country. Misinformation and a lack of exposure to other people's suffering are other factors that contributed to this omission.

"We cannot and do not want to deny that behind such factors there often was a large measure of selfishness and unwillingness to listen sincerely to God's word and to fellow-Christians. The result has been that we in Stellenbosch did not speak out enough against injustice in our society: did not speak out enough against racist attitudes among our church members; did not speak out enough against the violation of people's rights and human dignity.

"During the Soweto riots of 1976 and the countrywide unrest that followed, general decisions were taken concerning the situation in the country, but very little protest was made against the gross violations of people's rights taking place at that time.

"When forced removals were carried out in our town, when people were forced to leave their historic neighbourhoods and had to resettle elsewhere, little or no protest was voiced by the Presbytery. These removals constituted a violation of human rights, which invariably went hand in hand with severe personal trauma, financial loss and social disruption. Tragically, as a result of the great separation brought about in South Africa by apartheid, we of the Presbytery often were not even aware of this suffering.

"Over many years, people of our town [were] shut out from important decision-making positions simply because of the colour of their skin. More decisions were made about them than with them. Also in the church and amongst individual Christians there was often insensitivity as to how grievously people's human dignity was violated in these and many other ways ... "

They went on to say that it was this insensitivity and the ideologies arising from it, that had caused total incomprehension in 1982 among so many members of the congregation of their Presbytery, for the cries from the hearts of their brothers and sisters in the former Dutch Reformed Missionary Church, by the mouth of the Confession of Belhar.

They stated that in the late sixties, however, positive attempts had been made to bridge the gap between them and the other members of the NG Kerk family locally. That the initiative (including the establishment of a Combined Presbytery of Stellenbosch) failed, despite good progress that had been made, was something for which they were at least co-responsible.

"Eventually we did begin to see the error of our ways. And this is why the Lord brought us to these insights. That is why, in a formal resolution adopted in 1985, the Presbytery confessed our guilt for our actions during the apartheid era. Now that the work of the Truth and Reconciliation Commission is confronting us once again with the pain and grief endured by fellow-citizens and fellow-believers under the previous political dispensation, we feel the need to confess our guilt once again before God and before people. We feel the need to make this confession specifically at this session of the Truth and Reconciliation Commission, because it is here that people from our vicinity are sharing the pain and grief that they have to live through.

"We confess that we kept silent at times when we should have spoken out clearly in testimony. We confess that although we did at times try to protest against the unjust treatment of people, we often did so only with great timidity and circumspection. We did at times offer critisism, but we often, in doing so, were not prepared to speak out against the system itself. What is more, we often gave way to the opposition we encountered. At the very times when we should have continued to speak out clearly for the truth and against injustice, we grew tired and gave up protesting.

"Today we confess these things anew before the many people of Stellenbosch and surrounding areas who suffered injustice because of that. We confess these things before the youth and the children of our own church and our own congregations who feel that through our actions we have failed them ... "

They proceeded by saying that the fact that God, despite everything, did not abandon them, gave them hope for the future. Therefore, they wanted to testify, in conclusion, that they honestly believed that God could bring about true forgiveness, reconciliation and healing in South Africa, that God would be able to use them, in future, as instruments of reconciliation, despite their many mistakes and failures of the past. They declared that they, therefore, committed themselves to seek, together with fellow faithful members of other churches, constantly the will of God for the whole community.

They further wanted to testify like the Prophet Micah, that the God whom we serve, would also in South Africa, give us the grace that swords would become ploughshares, that spears would become pruning-hooks and that people would start living together in peace and reconciliation. For this, they would pray constantly.

When the two Stellenbosch *dominees* had finished their statement, you could hear a pin drop in the hall. Professor Muller, retired clergyman, who for years had trained ministers at the theological seminary, had something more to say: "I am one of the old folks. What is stated in the statement, also applies to me. I never physically hit somebody or committed murder or dragged them to prison! But the Bible says that if I allowed something, I am co-responsible. Then I am guilty before the Higher Justice. And before you. I ask you to forgive me – all of us."

The younger minister, Jan Marais added, "The young people with whom I am concerned, ask me: how is it possible that such things could have happened in a country of so many Christians? There are some of them who say: it is too painful. I can't remain in this country! Then I say to them: there is a future for us in this country. But our future must be founded on the truth of the past. The Word of God teaches us that the truth makes us free!"

The archbishop was visibly moved.

"I am sure that I express the feelings of everybody in the hall if I say how thankful I am to God for what has happened here today. I am deeply humbled. But this is what the grace of God does with a person. If you, like Isaiah, the prophet, experience how guilty and full of shame you are standing before God, you also experience how God comes to join you in the fire, as it happened with Daniel's three friends ! The God of glory is also the God of the Cross ... You are here today as wounded menders, the kind of menders that God can use for his purpose.

"I think God has a wonderful sense of humour. He looks down and says to us: But what did you think? This is *my* world! Everything will turn out well!"

What struck Tutu – and most of us with him – was that the ministers did not try to rationalise, that they did not balance their confession with a "Yes, but ... " They did not yield to any temptation to remind the audience of all the good things that the church had done throughout the years. The result was that Tutu then did it. He told the people in the hall that the NG Kerk was not only guilty of apartheid, but that the church had done good things as well, things that could serve as an example to the other churches in the country.

"Afrikaners are interesting people," he concluded. "They are not very subtle. You know exactly where you stand with them. If once they have turned around, if they have taken leave of the mistakes of the past, one can enter the future with them, confidently!"

16 OCTOBER 1996: GOOD NEWS FROM THE EASTERN CAPE

A day after the confession of the Stellenbosch ministers, there was another bit of good news. On 16 October John Allen, press representative of the TRC, issued the following press statement:

STATEMENT OF ARCHBISHOP TUTU FOLLOWING THE DECISION OF THE NG KERK TO CALL ON ITS MEMBERS TO TESTIFY BEFORE THE TRC

We are delighted! Thank God for the way in which the NG Kerk in the Eastern Cape has reacted to God's grace.

Already since 1980 I repeatedly said that without the contribution of the NG Kerk we would never have been able to achieve justice and reconciliation in South Africa. It is especially of great importance that the call has come from the Eastern Cape where so many instances of human rights violations took place.

I hope that the NG Kerk countrywide – as well as all the other churches – will follow this outstanding example. The NG Kerk is going to make an exceptional contribution towards reconciliation in our country.

23-25 OCTOBER 1996: THE FIRE OF RECONCILIATION – IN THE WORLD TRADE CENTRE

A week later Tutu's wish was fulfilled. A great number of church leaders – from within and outside the Republic – gathered in the World Trade Centre, in Kempton Park. In the building where the representatives to the Multiparty Conference two years ago agreed on the guidelines for the Truth and Reconciliation Commission, the churches would confer for three days. Shortly after the 1994 elections, the South African Council of Churces (SACC) played an important part in drafting the necessary legislation. At the beginning when the TRC had departed on its first lap, the SACC was there to advise and pray together. But now ten months had passed. The trek was in full swing. What would the role of the churches be on the way ahead?

In his opening statement the president, Bishop Dwane, made a serious plea for the churches to become involved, especially in the process of healing. Above all, this was the contribution that Christians could make. "I am sometimes concerned that the political parties in our country will want to exploit the work of the Commission for their own purposes. This must not happen!" Dwane concluded, "We must proceed on our set course. I have much hope for the future."

After him, it was the turn of Senator Valli Moosa, chairperson of the Parliamentary Committee on Juctice, to speak. "Our greatest dilemma," he said, "is how we can alleviate the immense pain and anger, the memories that people carry with them. We must look further than the individual pain of the victims: we must allay the collective guilt of the society. Our greatest responsibility is not towards the generations behind us, but to the generations before us, to far in the future. We dare not fail them!" That the churches – like also the other faith communities in the country – had an irreplaceable role to play in this regard was evident.

Finally it was Tutu's turn to speak. He started with an anecdote:

"During the Olympic Games in Atlanta a group of people, at an underground station, crowded around me. They wanted signatures. Suddenly a stout American women forced her way through them. She pressed a piece of paper into my hand and demanded: 'I also want your signature!' When she walked away, I clearly heard her asking one of the bystanders, 'Tell me, who exactly is that little man? What does he do?'"

After the laughter had subsided, the chairperson of the TRC continued, "This is what I came to ask the churches today. 'Who exactly are you? What do you do?'" If we are the Church of Christ, we should know what is expected of us. When it concerns truth, justice, forgiveness and reconciliation, the church cannot help but be involved, Tutu explained. These are thoroughly religious concepts, just like the process is a thoroughly religious process.

On the possibility of reconciliation, Tutu spoke with enthusiasm.

"I have often felt inclined to say to God, 'You have placed wonderful people in South Africa!' In the Paarl an old man came to the TRC, bearing the scars of his suffering, just to say, 'I forgive those who did this to me'. In King William's Town a woman, the shrapnel still in her body, related how the pain had enriched her life. In Bisho four generals appeared before the people, to talk about the genocide. 'We gave the order to shoot. We are guilty. But we are also infinitely sorry about what happened. We ask you to forgive us.' And what did the crowd do? They applauded and cheered the generals loudly! In the Paarl two ministers of the NG Kerk appeared. Not a word of self-justification – only a humble confession. Where are the other churches? I asked. They have just as much to confess as the Afrikaans church! Did you hear about the reconciliation at Phokeng? I repeat, what an unbelievable country, what unbelievable people! God is inconceivably good to us ... "

After Desmond Tutu gave the conference a bird's-eye view of the work of the TRC, he concluded by saying that he wanted to talk theology with the church people.

"You must take the great theological truths, the things that you take from the Scriptures, very seriously. You must highlight them for the members of your congregation. *Firstly*: you must take the doctrine of original sin seriously. This sin lives in each of us. We will have to avoid making yesterday's oppressed tomorrow's oppressor. *Secondly*: you must proclaim the grace of God. It is appropriate for each of us, while looking at the offences of the past, to say, 'There but for the grace of God go I.' We dare not revel in the embarrassment of others. Who says we would have acted differently? *Lastly*: the Bible teaches us not to judge. We dare not send somebody to hell! People *can* change. People *can* start over. This is exactly what the Gospel is about."

◆ ◆ ◆

For three days we conferred. Input came from all sides, also from foreign speakers who travelled here specially for this purpose. On the contribution that churches could make to counsel the victims and their families, much was said. On the churches' responsibility with regard to the perpetrators, on how they could be brought back into society, a warm debate ensued. Also on remuneration, on the rehabilitation of victims and communities, the churches could contribute a great deal of input. On symbolic processes to help the country to cope with its memories, to keep its ideals alive, interesting proposals were made.

And then, on the last day, a reconciliation service was held. I will not easily forget this occasion. That day, I experienced something of the inconceivable of which Tutu liked to speak.

The liturgy for the service was prepared exquisitely. The elderly black minister who conducted the service, asked the two hundred delegates to rise for prayer:

"Oh Father, purify our hearts through your Holy Spirit. Burn down the walls of separation between us. Purify us through your Word, purify our hearts, test our faith, banish the fear from our hearts. Allow us to discover each other's warmth. Help us to dispel the ghosts of the past ... "

After his solemn prayer the minister invited all the representatives to the front. Before the podium the flame which he had just lit, burnt brightly. In two long rows the men and women walked to the front. In pairs they, when they came to the fire, moved their hands over the flames. As a gesture of reconciliation they embraced each other.

Reconciliation? There was much talk about it, but how difficult was it to achieve reconciliation?, I was thinking while moving slowly forward. Did the churches really have a solution for the country? It was easy to talk, to hold conferences. But to truly, unconditionally, reach out to each other ...

How difficult it was for ministers who came from different backgrounds to open their hearts to each other, I personally experienced thirteen years before. I was on study leave, in England, collecting material for a publication on Marxism and the churches in Africa. In the early eighties everybody was all too aware of the fate of Christians in Mozambique, Angola, Ethiopia, and a group of other countries where communist governments ruled. The Marxist undertones in many ANC utterances – which were often reported in the press – concerned many South Africans. "You must go and talk to Michael Lapsley," the secretary of the British Council of Churches said one day, and arranged an appointment straight off.

It was a strange experience, that day in London, to talk to Father Lapsley, the exiled Anglican priest about whom the newspapers had so much to say, the man who had fled from South Africa before the Security Police. With enthusiasm Lapsley, radical liberation theologian, talked about Marxism that day. I, trained in the Reformed tradition, could scarcely believe my ears.

As far as I can remember we accepted each other's integrity. But in our hearts we were miles removed from one another. "How is it possible that Christians who serve the same God, who read the same Bible, can land in such different camps?" I asked myself when we greeted and each went his own way.

My way led home, to my congregation in Pretoria. Michael Lapsley's way led to Zimbabwe where he continued the struggle together with his ANC comrades. One morning, during April 1990, it was front page news: a letter bomb had exploded in Harare in the hands of the notorious Father Lapsley. He did not die, but he would be disfigured for the rest of his life. Both his hands had been ripped to shreds. He had lost one eye and was deaf in one ear. My heart went out to him at the time – but we were not any closer. With his radical standpoints, Lapsley was, as far as I was concerned, in the camp of the enemy. I would probably never see him again ...

Still lost in thought I found myself at the front of the row. It was my turn to walk to the flame together with the person at the front of the other row, where we would warm our hands together and embrace one another as brothers.

I stretched out my two hands, he his two stainless steel hooks. When I looked up, it was into the smile of Father Lapsley. After thirteen years, over the precipice of our differences, we could embrace each other. At the cross of Christ the impossible became true, two ministers could experience that the things that bound us together were infinitely more than those that kept us apart. Naturally we still had many things to discuss. We still differed on a number of issues. But at the fire of reconciliation we discovered one another's warmth. We had started to dispel the ghosts of the past.

"Father, enlighten our path with your fire," the prayer of the elderly minister led us back to our pews. "Set our hearts alight. Help us to build new fires diligently."

26 OCTOBER 1996: FRUSTRATION IN MAMELODI

Everybody was not equally pleased with the work of the Truth Commission. One of our responsibilities – especially those of us who were attached to the Reparation and Rehabilitation Committee – was to speak to groups of victims in various parts of the country.

One Saturday afternoon, Tom Manthata and I went to Mamelodi, the black residential area east of Pretoria, to meet a number of families. The Khulumani Organisation who regularly brought groups of victims in different centres of Gauteng together to deliberate on their prob-

lems, had asked us to come. *Khulumani* means 'let us talk together' –
and that was exactly what we did that afternoon.

Nearly all the people to whom we talked in the community centre of
Mamelodi were either victims, or family members of victims, of the so-
called Mamelodi massacre and of the KwaNdebele riots which claimed
the lives of a large number of young people.

The group was impatient with the TRC. The Commission had been
working for the best part of a year and their circumstances had not
changed one bit. They heard about reparation and rehabilitation, but
nothing had reached them as yet. Tom and I tried our best to explain to
them how slowly the process worked: surveys had to be made, information processed, proposals formulated, and only then, finally, money
could be paid out, or other forms of assitance be assigned. The audience was not impressed!

Most of them were older people who were dependent on their children, and now that their sons had been taken away from them, there
was nobody to take care of them. At the time of our visit to Mamelodi
there was a rent boycott in progress and feelings were running high.
The authorities had threatened to remove people who failed to pay,
from their houses. The police had already started doing it. "Nothing
has changed," one of the women sighed. "We are back in the old days!"
"If the Truth Commission is serious about reconciliation, they must go
and negotiate with the city council about the rent boycott," another
added. "Can't Archbishop Tutu do something for us?"

The frustration of the Mamelodi families was also our frustration. In
the TRC Act the Commission was granted the right to – in cases of
urgent need where the victims or their dependents were very old or ill,
or if they lived in desperate circumstances – provide interim help. We
had talked for a long time about the application of urgent interim reparation and made a number of plans, but the programme struggled to
get off the ground. What did happen, was that victims who came to
hearings and who were in dire straits, could be helped on an *ad hoc*
basis. Here and there new wheelchairs had been found, patients could
be sent for specialist treatment. Help was provided with exhumations
and reinterment. But this was merely a drop in the ocean.

Money was indeed found. The Swiss Government had made available
a large amount for interim help, but the procedures for applying the
money often tripped us up. One of the great embarrassments which
the Johannesburg office had to face, was in this regard. After the first
amount had been used up, the Swiss Government let us know that they

wanted to make yet another grant. A Swiss television team travelled to Johannesburg especially to make a film about how the money had been applied and which families had benefited from it. With the television film the Swiss Parliament could be easily persuaded to give more.

At the office we provided the film team with names of a number of grateful people who already had been helped. They would be able to make a beautiful, inspiring recording, we thought.

Later that afternoon the team returned. Pale. Frightened to death. Shortly after they started walking around in the streets of Soweto in search of the houses and families whom they wanted to film, they related, they were confronted and robbed by a group of criminals. They had lost everything: their purses, their expensive cameras, everything they had with them. The only comfort was that they themselves had not been injured, that their lives were spared.

It speaks volumes that the Swiss, in spite of what had happened, allocated money once again!

The frustration of the people of Mamelodi would appear in many places in the country. As the amnesty process progressed and articles appeared in newspapers of perpetrators who, in spite of everything they had done, were granted amnesty, victims started to wonder whether the Eastern Cape families who had made the TRC out as perpetrator-friendly, hadn't been right. It became all the more clear and urgent to us at the office – and for Tom and me that Saturday in Mamelodi – that the TRC would have to balance the generous amnesty offer with a dynamic reparation programme.

28-30 OCTOBER 1996: THE ALEXANDRA HEARING – HUGH LEWIN SPEAKS

In the Johannesburg office Hugh Lewin was a much sought-after person. He did not only play an important role on the Committee on Human Rights Violations. He was also a bright academic and researcher, a popular speaker. And Hugh did not repeat hearsay. He himself had been in prison for years. As a young student at the University of the Witwatersrand, in the sixties, he joined an ANC cell and became involved in their illegal activities. He was arrested and sentenced to many years in prison. In the maximum security division of the Pretoria Prison, in Potgieter Street, Hugh – the son of a clergyman – was locked up together with a small group of political prisoners, among hardened criminals, even persons condemned to death. The result was that Hugh had a particular empathy with victims who told about their experiences in prison. In addition, Hugh was a poet who could convey with sensitivity what he had seen.

During the Alexandra hearing several witnesses had told their stories. Hugh Lewin reported as follows:

One witness
has a dark suit and waistcoat and a glove on his hand
to help with his arthritis – and a stick.
Thirty years before he didn't need a stick
to stir the streets, him and the other kids.
They picked him up, he said
and roughed him up a bit in Alex
before taking him to Pretoria
    – Kompol, the big house, their house.
    With the warrens of offices like cells
    In corridors where they do what they want –
and they start giving him the treatment,
pausing only to bring in another pick-up
(looking dazed) to watch,
while they batter him, and batter him, and batter him.
But I was lucky, he said, I shat myself
and they said: *Yussus, maar die kaffer't gekak en – vat hom weg –
hy stink.*
They started instead on the spectator. He is from Cape Town.
His name is Looksmart. By morning he's dead.

Another witness
tells how she heard about her teenage son;
how he'd been passing in the street with friends
when a passing hippo shot him
    – no sense to it, no reason –
then they collect him, she said, still alive
and batter his head against a rock.
Twenty years later, tall and high-pitched,
she spits fury
    red-hot.
Maybe, she says, crumpling into her pain,

he'd still be there
if they hadn't hit his head against the rock.

Three witnesses together –
grannies, with *doeks* and darting eyes –
take it in turns to weep
as they tell of their children across the border in the safety
of Gaborone.
So many details: of the cars they took to get there,
the scenery along the way, all the details.
The soldiers, they explain, shot anything that moved
and raked the cupboard (where the overnight visitor hid)
tore even the cupboard to pieces, pieces, to pieces.
There was this large white sheet at the funeral, she said,
with all the names listed – and his wasn't there
    wasn't there
    wasn't there
but there, right at the bottom ... ah, Joseph.

Afterwards, the hall echoes
with the laughter of kids on the square outside
and we sit
wondering about these lists of bodies
    and mortuaries and more mortuaries
    and coffins, coffins, coffins
    bones, bones
and the glistening eyes of their mothers
    and survivors,
The evening shadows ring with the sounds of the children
and you have to think of tomorrow
    and tomorrow
    and tomorrow.

30 OCTOBER 1996: NO AND YES

During the meeting of the General Synodal Commission of the NG Kerk held in Pretoria on 29 and 30 October, the contribution of the church to the TRC process was once again discussed. Previous decisions about co-operation and intercession in prayer and critical counselling were reconfirmed. But on whether the church had to make an official submission to the TRC, as the Stellenbosch ministers did, the brothers were seriously divided. With a majority of three votes it was decided *not* to submit such an official confession to the TRC on behalf of the NG Kerk, countrywide. It would cause too much of a disturbance among members who were seriously divided about the TRC.

I was disappointed and sad.

A few days later there was some comfort: the Synod of the Western and Southern Cape had decided to make a submission. They would like to submit to the TRC the tale of the NG Kerk's involvement in society – especially about what had happened in the Western and Southern Cape. Rev Christo Alheit, secretary of Synod, had told the brothers, "The Western Cape moderature believes that the TRC offers a unique opportunity to testify, that must be utilized."

4 NOVEMBER 1996: AFRIKANER REACTION (1)

It was not only the people of Mamelodi and Alexandra who started to express their frustration – even their anger. It was also not only those attending synodal meetings who made their voices heard. From the Western Transvaal I received, a few days later, the following letter, addressed to me personally:

"We detest the TRC and its methods. It is only Afrikaners who must confess, while daily our people are murdered, raped and robbed by savages, and no word is spoken against it and no action is taken to protect us. This is not violation of human rights. We will protect ourselves.

"We must confess before a godless government's creation. They do not believe in the True Trinity. You are playing judge and want to bring reconciliation. With whom?

"You must also go and confess your sins at the right place.

"It is nice to receive such a fat cheque, while people suffering from hunger and unemployment is the order of the day."

5 NOVEMBER 1996: AFRIKANER REACTION (2)

The next day I received a friendlier – be it also critical – reaction. Leon Malan, prominent businessman from Clarens, in the Free State, saw to it that the congregation invited me to conduct a service. "Seeing that you and Inza will be coming anyway," Leon explained over the telephone, "we hoped that you would be willing to talk to a group of Afrikaners about the Truth Commission. We are wondering about many things, and you will have to come and answer our questions."

That Saturday evening my wife and I went with the Malans to the farm of the Farrells, just outside the town. The large reception room of Paul Farrell, in his time National MP for Bethlehem, was crammed. Fifty-odd guests from across the two districts, Clarens and Bethlehem, were there. Among the Afrikaners were a few specially invited English friends. A number of questions were directed at me. Criticism was uttered. Everything in a very good spirit. There were indeed a few guests who, as it appeared to me, seemed positive and supported the TRC. The majority, however, had misgivings. Couldn't we just forgive and forget, and close the books once and for all? I put the Boer War argument on the table. If there had been something like the TRC after 1902, if all the misery of the camps, all the injustices of the battle, the things that had happened in the Eastern Free State, too, could have been talked through thoroughly after the war, things in our land would have proceeded differently. Not everybody in the room was convinced! The perception of a one-sided process, a witch-hunt, lay heavily in the room.

Over the meal – such an overwhelmingly delicious meal as one could find only in the Free State – the discussion was continued: "I accept what you are saying," the host emphasised. "But you will have to work very hard to convince the Afrikaners that the process is fair. It feels to us as if every white person, every Afrikaner, is placed in the dock."

4 DECEMBER 1996: VISITING *RAPPORT* AND *BEELD*

Something had to be done to improve the perceptions of the average Afrikaner of the Truth Commission. But what? John Allen, press representative of the TRC, and I often talked about our concerns in this regard. Shouldn't we arrange for Archbishop Tutu to meet the editors of the leading Afrikaans newspapers? Maybe they would be able to solve some of the most important problems and misconceptions over a cup of tea. When I talked this over with Izak de Villiers from the Sunday newspaper *Rapport* months before, he was not enthusiastic. He did not like the Truth Commission, its chairperson or its methods. However, when I came across Izak de Villiers at a church function during November in Pretoria, he agreed: he would receive Tutu in his editorial office.

On 4 December Desmond Tutu would be in Johannesburg. I made two appointments: with the editor of *Rapport* for morning tea, and with the editor of *Beeld* for lunch.

The conversation with *Rapport* did not – to put it mildly – live up to expectations. From the start Izak de Villiers was on the attack. He made it very clear that he did not trust the TRC process, that it was nothing other than a political onslaught on the Afrikaner and his history. Of course many wrong things had happened in the past, Izak said. But what we now faced, was apartheid in reverse. The archbishop tried to explain. As often in the past, he repeated his hope that the Afrikaners would play a decisive role in the future of the country. The Afrikaans newspapers – *Rapport* – would be able to do much in cultivating a positive view, to guide Afrikaners on the way of truth and reconciliation. The archbishop was concerned about *Rapport's* reporting which – to his opinion – was one-sided.

The conversation dragged. Also when I tried to convince Izak and his sub-editor, Z B du Toit, that the Afrikaners – together with their fellow South Africans – had departed on one of the most important journeys in their existence. If we did not grab this historic moment, if we did not guide our people on the trek – throughout the past and into the future – we were doing them an injustice.

When Izak de Villiers at one stage admonished Tutu that everything in the past was not really that bad, that apartheid also had a good side, the conversation became more heated. "Let me tell you what apartheid did to me and my family," Tutu answered. And he did! He told us about his childhood, how much hardship they suffered as a family, how humiliating it was to be a black person in South Africa – until he, for the first time in his life, in 1994, could participate in a democratic election, when he, for the first time, as a reasonably old man could vote!

"I have known Tutu for many years," John Allen remarked to me when we left the building. "And in all these years I have only seen him angry once. Today was the second time."

◆ ◆ ◆

The visit to *Beeld* was a salve for our wounds.

In front of the building a secretary awaited us with a friendly smile, to escort us in the lift to the office of the editor. Over a companionable lunch Johan de Wet, Tim du Plessis and other staff at *Beeld* started talking. They had high appreciation for the TRC – but they also wanted to raise a number of questions. But their whole attitude was so positive, they felt themselves so involved in the process of transition in our country, that the chairperson of the Truth Commission listened with special interest to what they had to say. He ensured *Beeld* of his great appreciation for their fair and positive reporting – and added that any criticism of certain aspects of the TRC by *Beeld* was studied with equal seriousness. With the coffee at the end of the meal, Johan de Wet presented Tutu with a humorous, framed cartoon of himself, which had recently appeared in the newspaper. John Allen and I had to be satisfied with a beautiful calendar each. We were.

On our way back, the three of us in the car talked about the experiences of that day. We had heard very clearly two voices from the ranks of the Afrikaans press. It was evident that we would have to deal with those two different perspectives, those two sounds from the circle of Afrikaners.

Little could we guess what was to follow in the months to come ...

31 DECEMBER 1996: I HAVE FOUND PEACE

The first year in the life of the TRC had come to an end. It had been a difficult year. The second trek to be travelled – by everyone of us, the TRC, the victims, the perpetrators, the whole country – was in many ways a *via dolorosa*. Few of us had completed the journey, untouched. But by the grace of God we completed this stretch with a sense of gratitude, with a new understanding of what forgiveness and reconciliation meant.

On New Year's Eve, 31 December 1996, Mahlomola Isaac Tlale died.

Two months before, on 28 October, he was the very first witness to step on to the platform at the hearing in Alexandra, Johannesburg, to tell his story. He made an unforgettable impression, 83 years old, smartly clad in a new suit, bolt upright, walking-stick in his hand. For fifty years, he said, he had been a member of the ANC. In 1963 five men arrived in three cars to arrest him. In Pretoria he was interrogated and tortured with a plastic bag over his head. He was found guilty of a charge of sabotage and sent to Robben Island for twelve years. When he was finally released, he was banned to Qua-Qua. It took years before he was allowed to return to his loved ones in Alexandra.

"Since 1965 I have been a sick man," Mr Tlale said. "I suffer from high blood pressure and already had a heart attack. I lay in hospital for a long time. I have suffered. I have suffered. I have suffered ... "

And then, on the last day of the year, the old man died. At his funeral the priest related how Mahlomola Tlale one day told him about his bitterness. He was *really* embittered. "If I have to die today," Tlale had said, "and if I arrive in Heaven, and come across the perpetrators who had done me so much wrong, I will say to God: I am in the wrong place. Please send me to Hell!"

But, the priest continued, when Tlale came home from the hearing in Alexandra, he was a totally different person. His bitterness was gone. He went to talk to the priest: "If I have to die now and I arrive in Heaven, I will be able to forgive the perpetrators who did me wrong. I have found peace. I am reconciled."

On New Year's Eve, at the end of his painful journey, the elderly Mahlomola Tlale died in peace.

CHAPTER 3

ON MOUNTAINS AND IN VALLEYS

On mountains and in valleys,
and everywhere is God
Wherever we may wander
God is always there!

"Op berge en in dale" (On mountains and in valleys) was, according to historians, one of the most loved songs of the Voortrekkers on their way into the interior. The words rang out during evenings at the camp fire, after the umpteenth expedition over the mountains into the interior or through the valleys which waited beyond the mountains. At every height on the road, as well as at many lows they knew: God is here. His grace carries us through!

This is a hymn which the TRC – and South Africa – needed just as much. On its next trek through the past, the Truth Commission had to deal with countless mountains and valleys, with several highs and lows.

In January 1997 the TRC departed on a rough road. The journey had become more and more complicated. There was often criticism from outside. Within our own ranks, there was, from time to time, tension. There were heights – many of them. But there were definitely also lows. Mistakes were made. Set-backs were endured. Above all, early in the new year, Desmond Tutu, chairperson of the TRC, was diagnosed with cancer.

10 JANUARY 1997: THE REFORMED CHURCHES SAY NO

When it became time for the synod of the Gereformeerde Kerke van Suid Afrika (the Reformed Church of South Africa), the denomination to which former President F W de Klerk belonged, to meet in Potchefstroom, there was a feeling of expectation – for some rather a feeling of concern. The Reformed Church (RCSA) is the smallest of the three Afrikaans churches in the country, with approximately 125 000 members. But through the years this church, especially in Afrikaner ranks, played an important role. The decision made in Potchefstroom, when the Truth Commission would be discussed, would be of great importance.

Prior to the meeting of Synod the editor of *Beeld* (10 January 1997) devoted an editorial to the coming discussions. The RCSA, he remarked, took pride in the fact that the church had never, *officially*, tried to justify apartheid in Biblical forms. This does them credit. But did they ever judge apartheid as *unbiblical?* And if they did, at what level of church life did they do it? Of course it would be difficult for the church to appear before the TRC, even to make a written submission. Many congregants would be shocked to the core! But the RCSA could not disassosiate herself from the process of truth and reconciliation. "The whole country is going through the painful, disconcerting process of placing the past under the spotlight ... and the RCSA would commit a historic mistake if she excused herself from the process." Now was the time for a clear statement, for a courageous Biblical testimony.

When Synod met, in Potchefstroom, the delegates had to decide on a proposal prepared by one of the regional synods, to decide on whether the RCSA should accept accountability for the establishment as well as the practice of apartheid. Some delegates objected to the discussion, using a technical argument: the proposal did not specify precisely *which* past RCSA decisions were in contention.

The chairperson of Synod, Dr Jan Visser, took a strong stance: "We are living in a country which has become infested by a guilt psychosis," he argued. "The church should be careful in this climate, not to lose its bearings." As a member of the RCSA he did not feel any responsibility at all for the horrors committed in the name of apartheid.

A number of speakers, however, pleaded with the church, not to miss the historic opportunity to rid itself of its apartheid past. And if Synod was unsure about which past pronouncements needed to be looked at, a comprehensive list existed! Weeks before Synod commenced, a former RCSA minister, Dr Theuns Eloff, published a full account of all the 'apartheid resolutions and directives' taken by the church, since 1948.

Synod, however, decided *not* to make a submission to the TRC, much to the chagrin of many members. The editor of *Beeld* expressed the feelings of many: "The RCSA did let the opportunity pass to give guidance, in a clear voice, about the apartheid past. The delegates got stuck in rules of procedure, and other technical arguments, which resulted in the larger picture being overlooked." It may be true, he continued, that many in the RCSA did not know about all the atrocities, but then it would be time to confess their ignorance and negligence – not to be submerged in feelings of guilt, but to be liberated by the truth!

A few days after Synod had come to an end, I received a telephone call from Professor Bennie van der Walt, from the Potchefstroom University. "Piet," he said, "a number of RCSA members are very disappointed by the decision. We are planning to do something about it – maybe submit a confession of our own. You will hear from us."

16 JANUARY 1997: TUTU HAS CANCER!

The news report on the air on Thursday evening 16 January, made everybody in the country – also the TRC members – straighten up in their chairs: Tutu had cancer!

The next morning, in the Johannesburg office, we, after getting over our initial shock and grief, talked about the implications of Desmond Tutu's illness for the TRC process. How ill was he? Would he be able to continue his work? The past year Tutu had proved himself the heart and soul of the process, he had been accepted by the public to such an extent as the embodiment of the TRC, that one could not imagine that we could continue without him.

While we were still talking, an e-mail note from Alex Boraine, together with the press statement from John Allen appeared on our screens:

FROM: Dr Alex Boraine

Dear Colleagues

I am very distressed to give you further news concerning Archbishop Tutu's health. This time the news is not good. Subsequent to further tests, as the attached press statement indicates, definite cancer of the prostate has been found. Because of who he is and what he means to us, I know you will want to be informed before you hear about it or read about it in the media.

I know also that you will be as concerned as I am and will remember him, Leah and the family in your prayers and thoughts.

◆ ◆ ◆

FROM: John Allen

STATEMENT FROM THE TRUTH AND RECONCILIATION COMMISSION

Doctors have discovered cancer in Archbishop Desmond Tutu's prostate gland but will take some weeks to establish how serious it is and whether it has spread beyond the prostate.

This has been revealed by test results which became available after the release last night of a statement on Archbishop Tutu's condition. (The statement indicated that no malignancy had been discovered in initial tests.)

The initial procedure carried out by the specialists who treated the Archbishop on Wednesday involved a simple biopsy. An examination of tissue from the periphery of the prostate by microscope revealed no sign of cancer. The Archbishop's urologist then proceeded with a full prostate operation and removed the bulk of the prostate.

Further tests were carried out on the removed tissue. The results of these tests have indicated a definite cancer of the prostate but further tests will be needed to determine its extent and its seriousness. There is nothing to suggest cancer outside the prostate at this stage but only tests will determine this accurately.

The urologist does not believe it helpful to become involved in speculative comment about the prognosis or the implications of results received so far. Bulletins will be issued when further test results become available.

◆ ◆ ◆

Endless telephone calls came in the rest of the day. Everybody wanted to know how the archbishop was. It struck me in the weeks and months to come how many people who were very critical before, enquired about Tutu's health. Letters and faxes came pouring in from everywhere, from within, as well as outside the Republic, also from people who belonged to other faiths. It was evident that "the arch" had obtained a special place in the hearts of millions.

◆ ◆ ◆

TO: Archbishop Tutu
FROM: Piet Meiring

Dear Archbishop Desmond and Leah

For all of us at the TRC – as well as millions of people in our country and also from abroad – it was a great shock to hear that you have been admitted to hospital and also for longer than was initially intended. May the good Father grant that you will recover quickly and completely – and that you will soon be ready for all the work that is waiting.

Of course you are aware of how much we pray for you in these days. What you, maybe, do not realise, is how many prayers are coming from the within the circle of Afrikaans Christians. You have succeeded in touching to the hearts of many of our people. To give one example: last week Joyce Seroke and I went to a meeting of thirty-odd NG Kerk ministers on the East Rand. We had been rather concerned that they were negative towards the work of the TRC. They were not. On the contrary, they were surprisingly positive – especially about your role in the process. With great seriousness you and Leah were entrusted to God's care. The ministers told God (as if He didn't know it!) that the TRC will never succeed without their chairperson.

Last week the moderature of the Eastern Transvaal Synod gathered in Pretoria. They asked me, on behalf of Synod and all the congregations in Synod, to wish you all the best.

Personally I would like to, once again, express my sincere appreciation and gratitude to you for your example and your love ... When you persuaded me to serve on the TRC, I agreed, on the one hand, because I believed that the process of truth and reconciliation is important and essential in our country, but on the other hand (I have to confess) the opportunity to work under your wings for two years, was something I could not resist.

My wife and children are right behind me when I say: we pray for you both, daily. May God grant that you will become stronger and healthier every day. And may Leah receive the strength to take care of you and support you. May the peace of God which is beyond our understanding, be with you.

21 JANUARY 1997: THE TRC DIVIDED

Tutu's illness was not the only set-back. All along the streets of Johannesburg posters of *The Citizen* broadcast: *TRC divided over the race issue.*

I could not wait to open the newspaper. With growing concern I, when I arrived in my office, began to read:

CAPE TOWN. – "Differing backgrounds and a staff structure which placed Whites in key posts and Black employees on the 'lower rung' were the causes of distrust among many Truth Commission employees", a senior official said yesterday. "There are racial tensions but the problem with the commission is mainly its composition – it puts lawyers and priests together. People come from different backgrounds, there is an inherent distrust", the official said. "The formation of the commission had thrown together former Black activists with members of the 'White liberal intelligentsia,'" he said. "Some of the commission's intentions were good, bringing in unemployed people without skills to give them jobs. But if they can't cope they will feel marginalised."

According to the article a white liberal clique was in control of the work programme of the TRC – namely in Durban, where white members of the Commission allegedly marginalised the head of the office, Dr Khoza Mgojo, in many decisions that were taken. Hlengiwe Mkhize, chairperson of the Reparation and Rehabilitation Committee was approached by the newspaper for comment. She said she believed it was important for the commission to take into account the different backgrounds of its employees. "Some people have been seriously undermined for half their lives and not taken seriously. Any practice which triggers off those feelings may cause anger that is difficult to contain. One should actually have expected a degree of racial tension in the ranks of the TRC."

The Star's comment on the news that there was discord within the TRC

The next morning Dumisa Ntsebeza and Alex Boraine made themselves heard from the Cape. It was true that there was tension in the ranks of the TRC. "It would be surprising if there was not a degree of suspicion among staff members," Dumisa, head of the investigative unit, admitted. But there was no evidence that racial tensions had reached crisis proportions. Boraine added that "it would be surprising if there were no tensions in the Commission, which was a microcosm of South Africa." "This country has not suddenly become paradise island," Dumisa expostulated further. There were still many unequalities to be corrected, not only with regard to racial issues, but especially also regarding the position of women. And it was to the credit of the TRC that there had as yet been no real crisis!

However, when a similar article appeared in the *Natal Witness*, which reported on the alleged tension in the Durban Office, the Natal members of the TRC reacted vehemently. Khoza Mgojo said in a press statement that he strongly denies these allegations and for the record "we wish to state that of the twelve participants in this meeting, only three are 'white'. There is certainly no feeling within the region that anybody is sidelined ... these allegations ... are very harmful to the work of the TRC" – and to Dr Mgojo personally. We have no racial tensions in this office, which is truly a miracle considering that we emanate from such an incredibly socially destructive history."

Tom Manthata, Barbara Watson (National Co-ordinator of the Reparation and Rehabilitation Committee) and I sat in my office discussing the allegations. Was there an element of truth in them? It was certainly true that the commissioners and committee members came from different communities. That was how it was intended – that as many communities as possible would be represented, that people with a wide variety of views and experiences, people who were selected from several religious communities and occupational groups would serve on the TRC. In the meetings, during discussions, everybody was allowed, even encouraged, to express their own standpoints. Naturally people would sometimes differ. Several of the TRC members were individuals with strong personalities who did not like to be contradicted! Sometimes we had to work under a lot of pressure. And when tension runs high, people easily tread on each other's corns.

There was, from time to time, a feeling among some of the staff members – the secretaries, the researchers, the statement takers and the investigating team – that the commissioners and committee members did not have enough sympathy with them, that they held themselves aloof. One of our briefers, Fikile Mlotshwa, named the corridor where the commissioners and committee members had their offices, 'Commissioner Street' (Johannesburg's main street), while the rest of the personnel lived in 'shanty town'!

But it was my contention, and also that of Tom and Barbara, that things actually proceeded remarkably smoothly. As the months progressed, we obtained more appreciation for each other, we were able to learn from and to enrich each other. Tom and I experienced it ourselves. He was an ANC activist, a man with a formidable reputation, ex-prisoner of Robben Island, one of the Committee of Ten who ruled Soweto in the seventies. I was a white Afrikaner, a minister of the NG Kerk, part of the privileged community who plucked the fruits of apartheid over the years. But on the Truth Commission we got to know each other, we became blood-brothers. He introduced me to Soweto and its people. And I could take Tom to my people, to visit Afrikaners, experience their hospitality, to hear how their hearts were beating.

And Barbara Watson, daughter of a white father and black mother, charming, but also fiery advocate of women's and children's rights, worked constantly, daily, on the (alleged) chauvinism displayed by Tom and me.

I experienced the same with the rest of the staff. Admittedly, the first month or two, I rather had the feeling that some of the TRC members watched me 'with a wooden eye', as though they first wanted to make sure with whom they were dealing. During that time everybody spoke English to me. But soon they relaxed. Some of the young secretaries started to call me "*Oom* (Uncle) Piet" – and the name stuck, to the point where even Desmond Tutu and Alex Boraine started to use it. In the corridors my colleagues chatted with me in Afrikaans. And when we were joined by one of the 'exiles' whose Afrikaans was rusty, the reaction usually was: "No man! You are in South Africa now. You must learn to speak Afrikaans." It warmed my heart to see that this was also true of my two fellow-Afrikaners. Wynand Malan, with his legal background and sharp intellect, was often the centre of heated debates, but was always allowed to speak his mind. And when Chris de Jager, founder member of the AWB, conservative politician, walked down the corridor to discuss something with his fellow-advocate on the Amnesty Committee, Sisi Khampepe, you could deduce from the cheerful greetings the special place he obtained in the hearts of the people of Commissioner Street.

◆ ◆ ◆

It would definitely be an overstatement to speak of racial tension, of a commission that was close to exploding. To talk about a 'white liberal clique' who wielded the sceptre under the command of Alex Boraine while the chairperson was ill, was unfair.

The newspaper reports, however, did upset Tutu. On 22 January the archbishop summoned John Allen to the hospital to dictate a press statement right there from his hospital bed:

"Newspaper reports on the alleged marginalisation of black members of the TRC have forced me into doing something which I should not be doing, which is issuing a statement from my sick-bed.

"Firstly, all major decisions are taken by the full Commission. Most commissioners are black. Most members of each of the three constituent committees of the TRC are black. The chairpersons of each of the committees, as well as the Chief Executive Officer, are black.

"Secondly, the suggestion from anonymous sources in the Commission that it is run by a clique of liberals is insulting to me and I take very strong umbrage.

"The implication is that I am almost a token chairperson who is not in control. Anyone who knows me is aware that I am not a person to be manipulated by cliques. Dr Alex Boraine consults closely with me on what he is doing. He does not take decisions other than those delegated to him without discussing them with me.

"What is more, when we were appointing a Chief Executive Officer last year, Dr Boraine was quite insistent that a suitably qualified black person should be appointed.

"It is sad that anonymous individuals are not using the existing channels laid down in the TRC to resolve grievances because it undermines the tremendously committed and conscientious work being done by staff, committee members and commissioners."

◆ ◆ ◆

It was during that time that Dudu Chili, one of our briefers, neatly cut me down to size. In the tearoom somebody wanted to hear my point of view on a matter. Modestly I demurred, "Not at all, I would rather keep my mouth shut. We 'white liberals' must tread cautiously."

"What are you talking about?" Dudu answered. "You are not a 'white liberal'. You are our white 'conservative'! Go ahead."

27 JANUARY 1997: VISITORS FROM RWANDA

Dr Faustin Ntezilyayo, Minister of Justice and leader of the Rwandan delegation to the TRC, was visibly irritated with my question. His eyes flashed when he answered me ...

The visit of a high-profile delegation from Rwanda to our Johannesburg office, caused quite a few ripples. At the invitation of the Rwandan Government a group of TRC members had visited this war-racked country a few months ago (5-8 October 1996). The Government wanted to learn from the South African experience and wanted to hold discussions on dealing with victims and the process of amnesty in particular. Alex Boraine became ill just before the visit and requested Hlengiwe Mkhize to lead the TRC delegation. She and her fellow-travellers brought the most upsetting and gruesome reports with them when they returned.

Near Nyamate, Thulani Grenville-Grey related, they were taken to a church where one of the worst mass murders in the battle between the Hutus and the Tutsis took place. The hundreds of bodies had not been buried, but were left in the church as they were, to serve as deterrent, as a macabre 'monument' for the people of that country. "The whole floor of the church, the rows, between the pews, before the pulpit, were scattered with skeletons – still in their tattered clothing. We had to walk on the pews to avoid stepping on the dead. Once my foot slipped. The skeleton under my shoes broke like dried wood." However, what had upset him most of all, what gave him nightmares, was the group of small children who played on the grass outside. "Here and there a skeleton was still lying under the trees, but the children unconcernedly ran among the dead, as if it was the most common sight."

This all induced us to listen with attention when it was Dr Ntezilyayo's turn to speak. He spoke about the three bloody months (February – April 1994), when more than a million Rwandan inhabitants had lost their lives. "The worst of this story," the minister emphasised, "is that these people had not been decimated in large groups with machine guns, or by bombs which rained from the sky, but that they were hacked to death with pangas. Neighbours stormed into each other's houses. Men, women and children were hacked one by one. In our country there are half a million people with blood on their hands!"

After Faustin Ntezilyayo and his colleagues had painted this sombre picture, a long discussion followed. How does a society deal with so much misery? How should the victims be counselled? What about the children? Above all, how should the cases of the thousands of perpetrators – of whom large numbers were already detained in overcrowded prisons – be dealt with? The Rwandan inhabitants criticised the TRC's process of amnesty. The 'easy' pardon for perpetrators who step forward to confess their guilt, would not work in their country. Amnesty could indeed be considered, but total pardon could never be granted. Amnesty, as they saw it, could mean that sentences could be reduced, that the death penalty in certain cases could, for example, be replaced with long-term imprisonment, or that the number of years imposed to a perpetrator, be reduced. But total forgiveness, to release the perpetrators summarily, that would be too much to ask.

It was during the debate that I had asked my question. I thought it was not such a dumb question! Rwanda, according to all the handbooks, was one of the most 'Christian' countries in Africa. According to recent statistics, 85% of the people belonged to some church or other. "While all these things happened in Rwanda," I asked, "what was the role of the churches? With so many faithful in the country they should somehow have made a difference? Did the churches contribute towards reconciliation?"

"The churches!" the minister exploded. "They did not play any role. No, it is worse than that. The Christians were part of the problem! Some of the ministers and priests and even nuns were just as guilty as all the rest. They also had blood on their hands. In some churches it happened that the priest allowed refugees to seek cover inside the building, just to lock the doors and fetch the soldiers with their rifles and pangas. In some churches men and women and children were decimated at the pulpits and altars. Christians who had been neighbours for years, Tutsis and Hutus, attacked each other."

Late that afternoon, after all the talking, we went to a Johannesburg restaurant for something to eat. I found myself sitting opposite the Minister of Justice. By that time he had calmed down. But he had not forgotten my question. While we waited for the waiter to serve our hors-d'oevre, he looked at me with an arch smile. "It was you who asked the question about the churches, wasn't it? I have one for you, too: South Africa, so I hear, is also one of the most 'Christian' countries in Africa. There are millions of Christians in the country. We see churches everywhere. Please tell me, in all the things that happened in your past, all the things unearthed by the TRC, did the Christians play any role? Did the churches really take the need of the people seriously, help the people to reconcile? Moreover, with the problems you are facing today, does it matter that there are Christians in South Africa?"

That question would be ringing in my ears for a long time.

10 FEBRUARY 1997: A SOCIETY IN TRAUMA; UNDERSTANDING ASKED

"Does it matter that there are Christians in South Africa?"

The annual opening of the Theological Faculty at the University of Stellenbosch is an important day on the church calender. Pastors came from far and wide to hold conferences. The 1997 Conference would deal with Truth and Reconciliation, with the role that churches could be expected to play in this regard. Two of the local lecturers, Professor Hannes Olivier, well-known expert on the Old Testament and Dr Jan Botha, expert on the New Testament, explained in an interesting and inspiring way how important the concepts of truth, forgiveness and reconciliation figured in the Bible, that no faithful person could withdraw himself or herself from the process of promoting truth and reconciliation.

Then I had to speak, about the challenges offered by the truth and reconciliation process to the churches, especially the NG Kerk in South Africa. I could think of no more appropriate opening than the words of Faustin Ntezilyayo from Rwanda. Informing the conference on the visit by the delegation from Central Africa, I relayed the minister's question to the audience: "Do the churches in our country make a difference? Does it really matter that there are Christians in South Africa?"

Everybody would admit that the NG Kerk had a prophetic calling to shed the light of the Word on our society, to explain the meaning of truth, justice, forgiveness and reconciliation in our circumstances. All agreed that the church had to be a living example of its message, a community where love and healing are experienced by all. The pertinent question, however, remained: was the NG Kerk able to guide its members on the way of truth and reconciliation and were they doing it?

After just more than a year it was clear that the TRC process did not leave anyone in the country untouched. The majority of *black* South Africans were, with a few exceptions, positive about the work of the commission. Naturally it was difficult, sometimes shocking, to listen to all the disclosures. But it was *their* stories, *their* sorrow, which were brought to light, and for this they were grateful. At long last they received acknowledgement of all the injustice and pain which lay behind them. For them the TRC was a healing process.

But for the majority of *white* South Africans the process was a nightmare. "I no longer listen to the news," several remarked to me. "If I see the logo of the TRC on the screen, I switch off the television. I can no longer endure the crying faces, the unpleasantness that is dished up!" Letters sent to the TRC, or appearing in the correspondence columns of the newspapers, confirmed this. The upsetting reports and the underlying implication that white South Africans were responsible for most of these things, were just too much for them. To many the process was extremely traumatic. The question remained: could the NG Kerk, as well as the other churches in the country, support its members on this road?

◆ ◆ ◆

Ministers are expected to give pastoral support and counselling to their members when the latter are in extreme need, when they land in an existential crisis. For this purpose theological students – also at the theological seminary – are introduced to the works of the American therapist Elizabeth Kübler-Ross. She is regarded worldwide as one of the great authorities in the field of trauma counselling. Since the TRC process had started, the idea began forming in my head: did the things written by Kübler-Ross with regard to her work among *individuals* who experienced serious trauma, not also apply to *groups* of people who found themselves in similar circumstances?

According to Kübler-Ross, the process during which somebody who faces an existential crisis – for example, when a doctor diagnoses a terminal illness, or when a person sits at the deathbed of a child, or is confronted with the final breaking down of his or her marriage – has to come to terms with his or her trauma, progresses through a number of stages. Different defence mechanisms are applied. For the therapist to support the patient, or for the minister to help his congregant, it is important to determine which stage the person is experiencing, which defence mechanism is being applied. Only when this has been accomplished, the person can be helped. What applied to individuals, so it seemed to me, also applied to groups – in this case Afrikaners and the English during the TRC process.

The first stage is *denial*. The patient simply does not accept what the doctor says. The news is just too bad. It cannot be true! A second opinion is sought. And even if the second opinion confirms the diagnosis, the patient still refuses to accept it. The same applies to the mother who is sitting at her child's bedside, or the woman who finds herself at her minister's door with the divorce order in her hand: I simply do not believe it!

Wasn't this what was happening in our country? The alarming news that cropped up via the TRC process, the possibility that some of 'our people' were responsible for the gross violation of human rights, was just too much. The first reaction of countless South Africans was: this isn't true! I do not believe it! "It is untested evidence," more than one told me, "it is a distortion of the facts, everything is gross exaggeration". The natural reaction of many was simply to switch off their television sets or their radios. They did not want to hear the news. During the conference of the SA Council of Churches, at the end of 1996, a German theologian, Geiko Müller-Fahrenholz, described the way in which several Germans after the Second World War reacted to the disclosure of the crimes committed by the Nazis. Denial was in their case also the first defence mechanism. Denial, he explained, usually had two aspects: a moral and a psychological aspect. Some of the Nazis were just not able morally to acknowledge that they were guilty. What they did, did not seem wrong to them, it was for the sake of their fatherland that they had committed these crimes. However, for others it is psychologically impossible to acknowledge that they were involved in misdeeds. If they confessed their guilt to themselves – and to society – their whole existence would collapse. Instinctively they refused to accept their accountability. They were just not able to. Was this also the case in South Africa?

The second stage – that is to say, defence mechanism – is *anger*. When the patient, or the woman who has been wronged, is confronted with the bad news, he or she reacts with aggression, sometimes even anger. Often the doctor or a spouse must suffer for it. Sometimes God, who allows these things in one's life, is the target of his or her indignation.

"Shouldn't we have expected it," I asked my audience, "that several of our members would react with anger to the disclosures of the TRC?" The aggression of many Whites, the reaction of some politicians, the countless irritated letters in newspapers, many of the hot-tempered telephone calls we received at the office, were to be expected, even understandable.

The third stage is that of *negotiation and rationalisation*. If denial no longer helps and when the anger has died down, the patient starts to negotiate – with the doctor, with his or her spouse, especially with God. If God would just bring healing, if my child could only be spared, if my marriage could only be saved, I will dedicate my whole life to Him. Or, if negotiation fails, the patient starts to rationalise his or her position. Maybe things are not really that bad; the symptoms may be explained in various ways.

This is what happened in our country. Negotiation and rationalisation took place about the human rights violations in the past, the cruelties that cropped up. Especially rationalisation! "Of course one is ashamed of the things that happened, but you must remember we were confronted with a 'total onslaught'. Communism was a substantial danger in the sixties and seventies. We had to fight it in various ways. Even though many wrong things happened, our intentions were usually not that bad." A second argument often used, was: "Were the things that happened in our country really so unique? Doesn't every country, every government, have its own 'dirty tricks department'? And what about the liberation movements – weren't they also guilty of human rights violations?" It was clear that numerous South Africans used this defence mechanism.

The fourth stage is a *deep depression*. The patient, the person who experiences trauma, has tried everything: denial, anger, negotiation – without any success. Tired and helpless, they end up in the depths of despair. The patient, the woman who has been wronged, withdraws from everything and everybody. All bonds are severed, even with those closest to them. They no longer want to see their husbands or wives. They turn their backs on God. Lonely and desolate, they are ready to surrender.

In this way many people in our country have sunk into a depression, a total despondency. They cannot go further. Some emigrate to foreign countries because they see no hope for this country. Others emigrate to the inside, they withdraw from society. Interestingly enough, Kübler-Ross does not see this fourth stage as negative, but as potentially creative: stripped of all external things, of all false securities, the person is ready to start anew. When the person has passed through the crucible of affliction, the pure gold appears.

Therefore the last stage is a very positive one: the phase of *acceptance*. Finally the person who was immersed in an existential crisis, who moved through one phase to the other, reaches the mature stage where he or she has faced the crisis, has come to terms with his or her reactions and learned from them. The person learned to accept, and found peace. Whatever lies ahead, the person would now be able to face it, with equanimity. The illness, the approaching death or the pending divorce, is accepted. The future can be entered into with confidence.

Mercifully there were numerous examples of this: South Africans arriving at the point of acceptance and peace after going through the deep trauma of the truth and reconciliation process.

My plea before the audience of the theological seminary was that the church should guide its members on the rough road, through all the defence mechanisms and stages, to the point of acceptance and of making peace with the past, of stretching hands out to each other, of real forgiveness and reconciliation. It should be possible for us as ministers, was my contention, because we are on the road *together*, we ourselves had to learn to find our way through the phases of denial and anger, of rationalising and depression. Not from the heights, but as fellow-travellers, as persons who are also wounded, we could embark on the journey together.

The question was: did we want to? Was the church ready to accept the challenge?

◆ ◆ ◆

One touching answer which came from the audience, during the ensuing discussion, was that of the prominent emeritus professor Dawid de Villiers. While looking around at his colleagues and former students in the auditorium, *"Heilige Dawid"* (Saint Dawid), who had trained the students for years in practical theology, as well as in pastoral counselling, said, "We can no longer afford to play games. The NG Kerk has an enormous responsibility to guide our people in this time. We cannot let go of their hands. I urgently appeal to you to accept the challenge. I am an old man, my time is short. But I who lived in the paradise time of apartheid, implore you, my younger brothers: Do something! Put the history of my church before the feet of the Truth Commission, before it is too late, before the new millennium comes."

17-19 FEBRUARY 1997: THREE REMARKABLE DAYS AT OUDTSHOORN

During January and February all three committees of the TRC were urgently planning their programme for the next year. The Human Rights Violations Committee planned hearings in several parts of the country. The Amnesty Committee was inundated with a stack of applications. The Reparation and Rehabilitation Committee decided on an experiment: the searchlight would be focussed on one specific community in

South Africa – which had been acutely traumatised in the past – to attempt to understand their circumstances, what lived in the hearts of the people and what the TRC could, if need be, recommend to provide in their deepest needs.

Bag and baggage the Reparation and Rehabilitation Committee arrived at Oudtshoorn. The town was after all not only famous for its ostrich palaces and fertile farms, for the impressive Cango Caves, or the Little Karoo Arts Festival which annually attracted thousands of visitors. Oudtshoorn was also the town where tension between racial groups in the past often boiled over. In many submissions before the TRC, this was mentioned: the political separation, the conservatism of Whites in the town who insisted that Oudtshoorn had to be part of a future Afrikaner nation state, and the protest of many inhabitants of Bridgton, the Coloured residential area just outside the town, who wanted to prevent this at all costs. If there was one town that could serve as guinea-pig for the Reparation and Rehabilitation Committee, it was Oudtshoorn.

First we deliberated with a group of representatives from the community. The stormy history of what had happened in and around this Karoo town during the period 1960-1994, was discussed. Those who were not in the know, were referred to a special exhibition of the history of the town, which had been opened by Alex Boraine. On Tuesday evening, 18 February, a church service was held in the Uniting Reformed Church in Bridgton. Hundreds of congregation members, from different denominations, were present. Each of the three ministers on the Reparation and Rehabilitation Committee received a task: Khoza Mgojo delivered the sermon, Mcibisi Xundu had to pray and I had to explain the work of the TRC. The comment of Thulani Grenville-Grey, the TRC's psychologist from England who understood little Afrikaans, on my attempt was kindly: "I didn't understand a word of what you said, but I like the way in which you said it!"

The next morning, 19 February, we had breakfast early. After that, the Reparation and Rehabilitation Committee departed in two kombis to the black township of Bongolethu. Hlengiwe Mkhize had convinced us that, before listening to the stories from the black community, we first had to meet some of the people face to face. We had to see how they were living. With an hour and a half at our disposal we drove through the streets of Bongolethu. Here and there we stopped and talked to the somewhat surprised people. Many of them, also those who were already on their way to the hall, were not quite certain how to deal with this invasion by the TRC! However, with great dignity the people spoke to us and even invited us into their homes. Mapule Ramashala and a few others accepted the invitation eagerly. I looked at my watch – it was twenty minutes to nine – and decided that we would be hopelessly late. Fortunately I was the driver of one of the kombis and whether my passengers wanted to or not, I took the road through the winding paths of Bongolethu. The hearing would start at nine o'clock in the hall of the College of Education, and how would it appear if the TRC members allowed the mayor and the rest of the town to wait?

At nine o'clock the hall was crammed. More than five hundred people came together to listen and to talk, about everything that had happened in the town and district. Representatives of several interest groups appeared: women, youth leaders, local journalists, the churches, victims and their families. Every group had something special to tell, but everybody was insistent that something had to be done *now* to alleviate the need of the community. "The people," Mapule Ramashala (who arrived a full hour late, but with a broad smile and a basket full of stories collected by her and her fellow passengers in the kombi) later remarked to the press, "are not willing to wait any longer. They want action. They do not want to wait until one day when the president will relay the TRC's recommendations to the nation. They themselves will take care that reparation starts at Oudtshoorn, immediately!"

Personal involvement of the local community, which often posed a problem to the TRC, was no problem at Oudtshoorn. The *women* undertook to personally visit the victims and their families, in order to decide what could be done for them. "We want to raise a fund to help children of victims with their school funds," was one of their resolutions. For the *children*, the community had many plans: building a technikon, actions to ensure employment, better co-operation between schools, opportunities for white and brown and black children to meet. The *churches*, in the spirit of the times, announced that they would start an 'ecclesiastical Codesa' for the town. In Oudtshoorn, during the eighties, a small war raged on *journalistic terrain*, when the white inhabitants of the town, and the Coloureds, each had their own newspaper on the street. The Coloured editor of *Saamstaan* related the painful story of how his newspaper took punishment, how it had been banned eventually. This should never happen again, the meeting decided. What they needed was objective and extensive news covering. The mistakes of the past dared not be repeated. The community had to start thinking critically, they had to learn to come to terms with and deal with the consequences of the apartheid past. Would the press please, in future, fulfil their responsibilities!

As at many other TRC gatherings, there was unfortunately also a note of discord: among the many Coloured and Black inhabitants of Oudtshoorn, there was only a handful of Whites. What could be done to involve them? Pieter Fourie, Head Organiser of the Little Karoo Arts Festival which would start a few weeks later, attended our gathering. "The Festival," he comforted me over a cup of coffee that afternoon, "will afford us the opportunity to introduce the communities to each other and secure the ties between them. As a matter of fact, this is what we envisage when the festivities commence. The people of our town must learn to laugh together, have fun together, build a culture together." Little did we know then that the famous black singer, Miriam Makeba, who came to the festival as a gesture of reconciliation, would be greeted on stage with booing and empty beer cans.

On our way back to the airport, the Reparation and Rehabilitation Committee members chatted about the remarkable three days in the Karoo town. The experiment had succeeded, we felt. The people of Oudtshoorn – the majority at any rate – opened their hearts to us, shared their pain and their expectations with us. Plans had been made, dreams dreamt. Would it last? Would things really change? Would Oudtshoorn serve as example to the rest of the country? The future would tell. At any rate, we had much to report the following day when the TRC commissioners gathered for the regular monthly meeting in Cape Town.

20 FEBRUARY 1997: TUTU RETURNS TO OFFICE

When Archbishop Tutu entered the TRC Conference Room, everybody rose to applaud. Our chairperson was well! Well enough, at any rate, to proceed with his work.

"There is nothing that concentrates the mind so much as a bout with cancer," Tutu started. "My illness taught me some clear lessons. One of these lessons is that one is forced to distinguish between the *important* and *very important* things in one's life. What I want to ask you today, is: let us concentrate on the very important things ... "

For nearly two hours Archbishop Tutu, at the table, led the meeting. We could see that his operation and the treatment after the operation did not leave him unaffected. He looked smaller and frailer than a few weeks ago. But the fire was back in his eyes. The smile on his face, too. Later, when standing had tired him out, he sat down. But he had much to say.

The newspaper reports about the strife in the TRC concerned Tutu. This had to be discussed. Also the immense task that lay ahead. "Our task is a God-given calling," he said. "It is an honour and an exceptional privilege to be allowed to be busy with this work, to guide our young democracy on the road from war to peace, from chaos to order, from oppression to freedom, from hatred to love. The nation is holding their breath, waiting. The outside world looks in wonder and awe at what is happening. Throughout the world people are praying for the process. They believe that people in Germany and New Zealand, in Northern Ireland and Rwanda can learn from us. We dare not disappoint these people! Especially not the thousands of victims and their families. It is not important who we are, how esteemed people think us to be, that we appear in the limelight. What we can give, our duty to others, is important. Jesus Christ taught us that if you want to win your life, you must learn to sacrifice it ... "

"My cancer, although it is not terminal, started me thinking. One is reminded of one's own mortality! Of everything that has happened in my life, this is the one thing that I can be sure of: I am going to die. If today was my last day on earth, what would I like to do? What would be the last thing I want to do? These are the questions that we must ask ourselves, in the weeks and months to come."

On this serious note we went home.

11 MARCH 1997: TWO VILJOENS

MEMORANDUM

To: Archbishop Desmond Tutu
From: Piet Meiring
Re: Meeting with General Constand Viljoen and former Minister Gerrit Viljoen

The NG Kerk Waterkloof, Pretoria, invited me to talk about the work of the TRC during the morning and evening services the day before yesterday. Among the members of the congregation who attended both services, were Dr Gerrit Viljoen, former minister and chairperson of the Afrikaner Broederbond and General Constand Viljoen, former head of the Defence Force and leader of the Freedom Front Party in Parliament. Both participated in the discussion after the evening service – and although they asked critical questions, it was done in the friendliest of ways.

After the evening service I had a long conversation with General Viljoen, about the amnesty process in particular and the mass gathering of ex-Defence Force members that would be held in Pretoria at the end of the month. I have the strong impression that the general, at several places, interprets the TRC Act, as well as some of the procedures following in this regard, differently than we do. To my opinion he is unnecessarily concerned about quite a number of issues.

General Viljoen had already talked to Dr Boraine, but he agreed with me that it would probably be worth the trouble to clear up matters with you personally, especially before the meeting in Pretoria. "I would like to give the best possible advice to the officers and soldiers," he declared.

I offered to discuss the matter with you, to ask whether a meeting between you and the General could be arranged. The sooner, the better.

May I accept that your office will take up the matter with General Viljoen?

11 MARCH 1997: THE SA COUNCIL OF CHURCHES REQUESTS A "FAITH COMMUNITY" HEARING

Brigalia Bam, Secretary-General of the SA Council of Churches, was concerned that the faith community in the country was not doing enough to advance the process of truth and reconciliation. On 11 March the Central Committee of the Council would gather in Johannesburg, she told me over the telephone. I was to attend, to report on the work of the TRC, and to encourage the brothers and sisters to do their share.

It was an interesting meeting. The Minister for Safety and Security, Sydney Mufamadi, was first invited to talk about the security situation in our country. One after the other the church leaders expressed their concern about the growing violence and crime in South Africa.

The churches would do their part, was the consensus, but it was clear that the government had to take drastic steps.

And then it was the TRC's turn. There was much I could thank the church leaders for. The aid that we received from the churches – particularly at local level, where ministers and pastors and priests had the mammoth task of counselling victims and their families during the hearings – was great. The reaction to my question of whether a public gathering should be arranged during which all the churches, in fact all the faith communities in the country, should be invited to testify, was overwhelming. "It is not only the Afrikaans churches that have something to confess," Bishop Dwane, President of the SACC, emphasised. "Every church, every religious society has a story to tell. Everybody has something to confess. If the churches do not lead the country in this, who will?

10 APRIL 1997: TESTIMONY FROM THE GRAVE

STATEMENT BY DUMISA NTSEBEZA, HEAD OF THE TRC INVESTIGATIVE UNIT, CAPE TOWN, 10 APRIL.

Exhumations on a farm in the vicinity of Aliwal North, where the bodies of MK soldiers were allegedly buried secretly, were temporarily terminated when human bones – amongst others a human femur, dorsal vertebrae and ribs – had been found on the terrain.

A pathologist was summoned from Bloemfontein and only at his arrival would the exhumations be proceeded. Until now, we worked with mechanical spades, but we will proceed with the exhumation carefully, using ordinary spades.

Today's discovery was made just after we started to dig at another place. We had determined the exact location after discussions with the policeman who at the time transported the bodies to the farm, with the undertaker, as well as with farm labourers who know the area well.

Dogs brought specially from Durban were utilized to sniff out the place where the bones were found.

The soldiers whose bodies were looked for, were killed during two separate shooting incidents in the vicinity of Elliot, during August 1981. Investigators who had been appointed by Mr Tokyo Sexwale to investigate the death of his brother who was one of the murdered soldiers, confirmed the findings of our own investigative team, namely that four soldiers had secretly been buried on the farm at that time.

The Truth Commission will not reveal the names of the soldiers before the bodies have been found and positively identified, and the relatives have been informed.

13 APRIL 1997: BRIAN MITCHELL ASKS FORGIVENESS

This morning, when I checked the previous day's e-mail, I found on my computer screen the interesting description of Brian Mitchell's visit to the Trust Feeds community in KwaZulu-Natal, which took place some weeks before. The news was no longer fresh, but it was nice to see what a foreign journalist had made of it.

When Brian Mitchell walked into the Trust Feeds School Hall, an audience of three hundred awaited him. One song after the other followed before it was the ex-policeman's turn to speak.

"I understand that it is not easy to forgive," Mitchell, his mouth twitching nervously, started. "But I would still ask you to forgive me for everything that happened."

There was a great deal to forgive. Just more than eight years ago, three policemen, of which Mitchell was one, attacked a house in Trust Feeds. They were under the impression that a group of United Democratic Front officials, who were closely connected to the ANC, were in the house. They were wrong. The house was filled with people, men, women and children, holding a vigil the night before a funeral. When the policemen drove off, eleven bodies were lying on the floor, together with a great number of wounded people.

Brian Mitchell was arrested in 1992 and sentenced to death on eleven charges of murder. When the death penalty was abolished in 1994, the sentence was changed to 30 years' imprisonment. The Trust Feeds community was bitterly opposed to Mitchell's amnesty application. The fact that the Amnesty Committee, after thorough consideration of Mitchell's case, had found that his action was politically inspired, that it was part of a campaign against the ANC, stuck in the throats of the families of the victims. Mitchell's first attempts to meet people from Trust Feeds were firmly turned down. They did not want to have anything to do with him. And when the gathering had eventually been arranged, it was clear that there were many people who were not willing to forgive the policeman.

"I lost my husband on that terrible day in December 1988," Mavis Madondo called out in tears. "Now I have to struggle on my own with my children. I cannot send them to school. How can you help us?" An elderly woman, on crutches, as a result of the wounds that she had sustained that night, stood next to Mavis. Mothers in the hall comforted the two crying women and led them back to their seats.

The TRC commissioners who attended the gathering as facilitators, were secretly grateful that a strong protection unit, altogether 80 policemen and Defence Force officers, were present. Anything could happen. While one song after the other had been sung and several inhabitants of the town came forward to speak, Brian Mitchell, alone on a chair, sat in the front of the hall. Finally he rose and, using a loud-speaker, addressed the audience.

Simply, humbly, Mitchell thanked the Trust Feeds community that they were willing to meet him. He related how he, for a long time, had tried to create such an opportunity by means of intermediators, church groups and other institutions. He explained how he had become in-volved in various projects aimed at advancing the economical develop-ment of the town. He proceeded in telling how he had lost his job when colleagues heard about his dark past, how difficult it had become to maintain his own family.

After Mitchell had finished talking, many questions followed. It was clear that everybody was not satisfied. But the majority in the hall were willing to extend an olive branch to the ex-policeman.

Jabulisiwe Ngubane, who had lost both her mother and a few children in the attack, told journalists that it was her faith in God, the God who constantly forgives our sins, which had made it possible for her to reach out to Brian Mitchell: "It is not easy to forgive, but because he stepped forward to ask forgiveness, I have no choice. I must forgive him ... "

21 APRIL 1997: THE GOD OF SURPRISES

"One can see God's influence in what has happened tonight," Mcibisi Xundu, minister and committee member of the TRC said. He looked solemnly at Eric Taylor, former police officer who had applied for am-nesty for his part in the death of the Cradock Four. "It is God who has led you to take this step towards reconciliation. We realise that it must a painful process for you, but rest assured: we will try to understand, just as Jesus understands. We will listen with a positive attitude to what you have to say."

A few weeks ago nobody would have dreamt of this gathering.

Earlier this year, the moderature of the Eastern Cape Synod of the NG Kerk had decided to convene a special meeting to discuss the re-sponsibility of the church in regard to the process of amnesty – how the victims can be supported and how members of the church who applied for amnesty could be counselled.

After the meeting, a young minister, Charl Coetzee, came to talk to me. One of the members of his congregation, Eric Taylor, who had applied for amnesty, indicated that he would like to meet the families of the Cradock Four. He wanted to ask their forgiveness for what he had done to them.

"It is wonderful news," I answered. "But you will first have to make sure that Mr Taylor knows what he will be letting himself in for. Once he has taken the first step on the path of reconciliation and forgiveness, he will not be able to turn back. We, in the meantime, will talk to the families of Matthew Goniwe and Fort Calata and the others. We will have to hear whether they see their way clear for such a meeting." I held my breath. Would Eric Taylor, after discussing with his minister the full implication of what he wanted to do, still feel that he could meet the families of the victims? More than that: would the families of the Cradock Four be willing to talk to him? Mrs Goniwe had often made it clear that she was highly critical of the TRC process. Would she be willing to attend?

However, Charl Coetzee returned with the message: Eric Taylor knew what he was letting himself in for, how it could influence his application for amnesty. But, even against his lawyer's advice, he wanted to proceed.

In Cape Town Glenda Wildschut, who knew Mrs Goniwe well, started negotiating about the matter. In the Eastern Cape too, June Chrighton and Mcibisi Xundu – who had conducted the funeral of the Cradock Four – negotiated with the families. Mrs Goniwe informed us that it would for her personally, be very difficult to have to look into the eyes of the man who had murdered her husband and to forgive him. But it was not her decision, she said, the family in Cradock would have to speak the final word. The reaction of the people in Cradock, the Goniwe family and the others, warmed our hearts. They were willing to meet Eric Taylor, to come and listen to what he had to say.

In the meantime, Rev Coetzee became rather concerned. What would his church council and the members of his congregation think of his efforts? Not everybody approved of the TRC. Would they resent him for his involvement in the matter? One evening he informed his church council of his part in the Taylor saga. Their reaction was a great comfort. "You are doing the right thing, *Dominee* (Reverend). Go ahead! And if you need a venue, why not use our church hall? See it as our congregation's contribution to the process."

On Monday evening, 21 April 1997, the family members of the Cradock Four travelled from Cradock to the church hall of the NG Kerk of Port Elizabeth-Nooitgedacht. Charl Coetzee, Mcibisi Xundu and June Chrighton awaited them. So, too, Eric Taylor.

After Reverend Xundu had explained the purpose of the gathering, and added why it was sensible for the meeting to he held in Port Elizabeth rather than in Cradock where feelings still ran high about the deaths of the four activists, he gave Eric Taylor the floor.

It was a long evening. Taylor explained why he wanted to meet the families, what he wanted to say to them. "I am here in response to God's prompting," he declared, "and I fully believe that He has forgiven me. I also applied for amnesty and although it is not a certainty, amnesty may be granted. But amnesty is a technical matter and will do nothing towards reconciliation. I have realised that the only way to find peace, is to tell the families, wives, children, brothers and sisters that I am sorry for a lot that happened and to ask them if they can find strength through God to forgive."

The ex-policeman related the procedures that he and his colleagues usually followed, how they executed orders from the top structures. But he also related how he, after some time, started to question their actions. In 1989 he saw the film *Mississippi Burning* which made a deep impression on him. He then realised the wrongness of what they had done. Later he read President Mandela's biography. "It changed my heart! I wish I could have read it in 1985 ... "

An in-depth conversation followed. Taylor explained what had happened on that ill-fated day when Goniwe, Calata and the other activists were stopped by two cars and arrested. How he himself was involved in their deaths, how they were first knocked unconscious and then stabbed. The families wanted details. What did the police do to the men? Were they tortured? How did they die?

It was getting late. Eric Taylor looked at the people of Cradock. "Thank you very much for coming. I realise that there still are a lot of questions regarding the death of the four men ... But I came here to ask you to forgive me, if you can do that through the strength of God. Thank you for the opportunity and for being willing to see me. I hope that you will all eventually find peace in God."

The response was moving.

The wife of one of the activists said, "My prayer has always been to meet them (the perpetrators) so they could explain what they did and why. I prayed daily. Sometimes I got very angry. I feel they should take responsibility for caring for my children. I lost my job. I lost my husband, my friend, my children's father. I loved him. He loved his children. I was about to have a baby when he died. He wanted a girl. I wanted a boy. The day that he left I was supposed to go to the doctor. The last thing he said was, 'I want a girl, tell the doctor.' When she was born I couldn't even take her in my arms.

"My children were worried about my coming here today. They were worried I would cry ... We have learned to live with these things. I taught the children not to hate. My 15-year-old is full of anger still. Over the last eleven and a half years you have destroyed my life.

"But, thanks be to God that He has answered my prayers; that you have come to tell us these things, and to answer our questions. It is a relief."

One of the male relatives shook hands with Eric Taylor. "Thank you," he said. "I told God if He put you in front of me I would shake your hand. I appreciate what you have done here today. I am relieved ... but not yet fully."

Another man, also a family member, said, "We live because they died. We have agonised over the type of death they had. We thank you for your honesty. We will communicate what you have said to the other wives and family members. We thank God for your minister and pastor. We hope to speak to you again."

◆ ◆ ◆

Early the following morning Rev Charl Coetzee phoned me and told me excitedly what had happened, how the son of Matthew Goniwe walked up to Eric Taylor. His right arm was in plaster, but with his left arm he embraced the white policeman. "You murdered our father. But we forgive you!"

I immediately picked up the receiver to phone Archbishop Tutu in the Cape. He would be glad about the news. Before I could start, he told me! The Goniwe family had already called him from Cradock. "And," he continued, "Mrs Goniwe said next time she would also be there!"

When a while later I wanted to end the call and replace the receiver, Tutu stopped me. The receiver was nearly back on the hook when I heard him call, in Afrikaans, "Oh no, old chap, not so quick. First we are going to pray!"

I will not easily forget his prayer over the telephone line, he in Cape Town and I in Johannesburg: "O Lord, we thank You for being the God of surprises and for surprising us, every day, about what you do with your children, for working the miracle of reconciliation in our country, time after time. Thank you, thank you so much, that we may be in your service!"

Later Rev Charl Coetzee related that Archbishop Tutu had also phoned him that morning to thank him for his part in the process. He prayed with the young Afrikaans minister, too. Only Charl Coetzee reacted more appropriately than I did. Because, when Tutu said "Amen", Charl asked him, "Bishop Tutu, may I also pray for you? May I entrust you to God as well?"

Which he then did.

24 APRIL 1997: GENERAL MAGNUS MALAN AGREES TO TESTIFY

In all four regional offices of the TRC the news was received with great interest: General Magnus Malan, former Head of the Defence Force and Minister of Defence in the Government of President P W Botha, had agreed to testify before the TRC. However, the general was not planning to apply for amnesty or to apologise for his actions.

"I have decided to testify, because it appears that there is a total lack of military expertise in the Truth Commission when it comes to assessing the past actions of the South African Defence Force ... Blatant, untrue and unfair accusations are being made regarding the former SADF in an apparent vendetta ... I am not prepared to permit these incorrect perceptions to go unchallenged."

According to a report published by the press agent Reuters, Malan, after discussions with former President Botha, agreed to co-operate with the TRC. It might also be that the coming elections of 1999 had persuaded Malan to testify – as was the case with other colleagues from the ranks of the National Party who also agreed to come. One could expect that the final TRC report would become part of the election propaganda, Professor Jannie Gagiano, a political scientist at the University of Stellenbosch, declared, according to Reuters. "People are going to stand on platforms and pull out that report as if it was given to humanity by God ... " he said. The National Party, according to Gagiano, was not at all convinced of its guilt in applying apartheid. It was a pity that all these things had happened, was their attitude, but "that was the way the situation required us to act, and although some of us went overboard, much of what was done was in accordance with what was required," he said. General Malan would be able to put into perspective the conduct of the SA Defence Force, viewed against the total onslaught against the country during the eighties.

Be that as it may, Tutu and also Boraine were delighted about General Malan's resolution. As far as they were concerned, it was a break-through. Malan's conduct, they hoped, would pave the way for many other officers and soldiers to come forward with information or applications for amnesty.

25 APRIL 1997: FREEDOM DAY AT UPINGTON. DONKEYS AND ANGELS ... AND MANDELA

"Cut down to size" is the expression. This was exactly what happened to me on Freedom Day 1997.

I would be lying if I said I did not feel a little flattered when the invitation came. Freedom Day would be celebrated for the third time in our country. This time the Northern Cape would act as host. The national celebration would take place on Sunday, 25 April, on the banks of the Orange River, in Upington. President Mandela would be the guest of honour. The Afrikaans minister on the Truth Commission had been requested to conduct the public worship and to deliver the sermon before the president would speak.

Already the previous day Inza and I arrived in Upington. Rev Aubrey Beukes of the Uniting Reformed Church as well as chairperson of the Local Council of Churches, awaited us. Together we went to take a look at the Danie Kuys Stadium where the festivities would take place. He explained to us exactly which route the donkey-cart, on which the president would enter the stadium the next day, would follow. It was appropriate that it would be donkeys – it was not for nothing that on the town square of Upington stood a bronze statue of a donkey – to mark the role of the humble beast of burden in the development of this part of the world. Then we proceeded through the town along the bank of the river to the museum and lovely old missionary church, a national monument in itself, before he introduced us to some of the members of his congregation in the brown community.

As a result of everything we saw and heard that afternoon, I rewrote large parts of my sermon that night at the hotel. Such an opportunity comes only once in a lifetime, I explained to Inza, and in preparing the sermon I had to take note of the people's most heartfelt needs. The whole festival, Rev Beukes had warned me, would be broadcast directly, countrywide, on television. Which was enough to keep me busy, in the hotel room, for another hour or so.

At seven o'clock that Sunday morning the festivities commenced. Choirs and brass bands from all over the province appeared, from Upington and Keimoes, Kenhardt and Kimberley and Carnarvon – seventeen in total. Keeping an eye on my watch I later started to feel rather worried. The service was supposed to start at twenty minutes to ten, but at that time the choirs were still singing joyously. When the last Hallelujah reverberated there was little left of the three quarters of an hour allowed for the service. "It doesn't matter," Aubrey Beukes ensured me when we walked to the podium, together with the local spiritual leaders, "The organisers assured me that we have three quarters of an hour, and we will use that three quarters of an hour. Every minute was measured off. You have eighteen minutes to deliver the sermon. Use ît!" I was not totally convinced because the Air Force's liaison officer had warned me that the aeroplanes which would take off from Kimberley to participate in the ceremonial overflight after the public worship, would work strictly according to the clock. But if Aubrey Beukes was so convinced, who was I to argue?

After a few prayers and two parts from the Scriptures read in Afrikaans and English, it was my turn. As text I chose the moving words of Psalm 85 which, it seemed to me, had everything to say for our country and our time: "You showed favour to your land, O LORD; you restored the fortunes of Jacob. You forgave the iniquity of your people and covered all their sins ... I will listen to what God the Lord will say; he promises peace to his people, his saints ... Love and faithfulness meet together; righteousness and peace kiss each other. Truth springs forth from the earth, and righteousness looks down from heaven. The Lord will indeed give what is good, and our land will yield its harvest. Righteousness goes before him and prepares the way for his steps."

I wanted to stress that for the children of God, for all South Africans who loved and served Him, Psalm 85 contained wonderful promises, various images and perspectives to indicate to the farmers along the Orange River, as well as the people of the Northern Cape, all citizens of the country, the way we need to work together and to travel together. To conclude my message of truth and reconciliation I wanted to quote the beautiful poem of H A Fagan, the Afrikaner judge of long ago, with the title *Nkosi Sikelel' iAfrika*. This should move the crowd, I thought, the poem of the Afrikaner who many years ago foresaw the day when many nations would join hands, of how many voices would sing together in one large choir ...

But alas! I was scarcely at page two of the sermon when I heard a noise among the crowd on the pavilion. Half a page further, applause broke out here and there. Any minister's dream! Another paragraph further a general cheering went up from the crowd. Something like this had never before happened to me – or as far as I know, to any of my colleagues.

However, when I raised my head to look around, it was clear what was happening. Without my realising it, Kimberley's aeroplanes had arrived, and were flying low over the stadium. I was so engrossed in delivering my sermon that I didn't even hear them. From the belly of every aeroplane sky-divers jumped, a coloured line of smoke trailing behind each of them, dramatically, in the colours of the national flag.

When the last parachutist finally landed on the grass behind my pulpit and the crowd became a little quieter, Rev Beukes gestured to me: "Continue your sermon, only keep it short!"

With new fervour I proceeded. Two sentences further, a brass band fanfare at the entrance of the stadium made everybody – me in particular – jump. A few donkeys, carrying the premier and the mayor, followed by a simple donkey-cart conveying the President of South Africa, made their appearance, together with a guard of honour and some torch-bearers. The cheering was deafening. The national salute and the national anthem resounded ...

Aubrey Beukes and I looked at each other. The other clergymen agreed. The church was out! While, at the top of their voices, the crowd escorted President Mandela on his trip, taking a wide turn from the gate to his place of honour directly in front of the pavilion, we took our Bibles, took off our togas and sheepishly went to sit with our wives.

After the president's address, which was completed with much more success, it was time for lunch. On the steps on our way down from the pavilion, the words of an old coloured gentleman was a salve to my bruised ego, "Well, Reverend, you did not get much time to preach. But this is the first time in my life that I have seen a minister preaching the angels down from heaven – parachutes and all!"

28 APRIL 1997: ONE OF THE MURDERERS OF AMY BIEHL REQUESTS AMNESTY

Three days later one of the murderers of Amy Biehl, American exchange student, appeared before the Amnesty Committee in Cape Town – a sad reminder of the fact that not only South Africans were victims of the struggle, but that also foreigners landed in the cross-fire.

Amy Biehl, a bright young Fulbright scholar from Newport Beach, California, came to South Africa to do research about women's rights in the country. She also conducted voter education classes to help Blacks prepare for the coming elections. On 25 August 1993, after work, she drove a few black colleagues home to Guguletu, outside Cape Town. A stone-throwing mob pulled Amy from the car, shouting the anti-white slogan "One settler! One bullet!". They overpowered the American girl, beat her with bricks and stabbed her. Her black colleagues were roughed up by the attackers.

During their eleven-month trial the four youths, members of the youth wing of the PAC, argued that, in the early nineties, their movement had been involved in a military struggle against the apartheid regime, and against all Whites.

Clarence Makwetu, former PAC leader, remarked to the press that the 25-year-old Mongezi Manqina and his three friends deserved amnesty. Makwetu added that the apartheid regime had encouraged violence against Blacks. PAC members started to follow their own heads and, without consulting the party's leadership in Tanzania, chose their own victims, answering violence with violence. Mongezi was the first to apply for amnesty, but the applications of the three accomplices would follow soon. We learned that Amy's parents wanted to be present at the next hearing when the case would proceed. What would their reaction be? Would they be able to face their daughter's murderers? Could one ever forgive if something like this happened to your child?

4 MAY 1997: LESSONS FROM A JEWISH CEMETERY

One morning in Pretoria Judge Ralph Zulman stressed in a moving way that suffering was a universal phenomenon, that communities from all over the world had to learn how to live with their painful memories.

The twenty-seventh day of the Spring month, Nissan (in 1997 it fell on the 4th of May) Jews throughout the world gathered formally to remember the six million Jews who died during the Second World War. I was to represent the TRC at the annual Yom Hashua occasion held in the Jewish cemetery in Rebecca Street, Pretoria.

"Why do we gather? What point is there in raking up unpleasant memories?," Judge Zulman asked. Numerous people, also in our country, wrestle with this problem. As answer he quoted the words of the Jewish sculptor Ernest Ullman which appear on a memorial plaque displayed in the Yad Vashem Memorial Centre in Johannesburg:

"When I remember the dead, I am awed to have been saved. Is there not a feeling of guilt in all of us to be alive? Why were we singled out for this blessing? Were we better than those who died and were we more worthy that they to be spared the bitterness of the final sacrifice?

"We ask forgiveness from the dead for having failed them and abandoned them. We want to remember their suffering because it could perhaps have been our fate as well.

"To be spared, implies an obligation. It is the duty of the son to honour his parents and their memory – love will dictate his reverence. But more than that – is it not also the sacred obligation of the living to keep the flame alight, to carry the torch, to hand on the spirit of hope to others, so that it may not be extinguished, so that the last sighs of those who have perished be heard and preserved and not be lost forever in nothingness?"

One cannot simply close the books, forgive and forget, the judge stressed. On the contrary, one must remember, learn to come to terms with it. In a moving way he painted a picture of the suffering of his people during the thirties and forties. Also the South African Jewish community had been deeply affected. Moreover, the South African Jews were guilty too, because they could have done much more to reach out to their compatriots during the years of war.

"Hopefully the world will pay heed to the words of Martin Niemöller, German submarine commander in the First World War and an ardent German Nationalist who warmly welcomed Hitler's accession to power in 1933 but who, by 1935, had become completely disillusioned and openly defiant of Hitler ... " the judge said. Niemöller who later became a Protestant minister, was arrested in 1935 and had to remain for years in Nazi-camps and prisons. From the Moabit prison in 1937 he wrote:

"First they came for the Socialists and I did not speak out because I was not a Socialist. Then they came for the Trade Unionists and I did not speak out because I was not a Trade Unionist. Then they came for the Jews and I did not speak out because I was not a Jew. Then they came for me and there was no one left to speak for me."

The judge's last quotation, the words of the American Jewish philosopher, Hescher, made me reflect and wonder deeply, about myself and the community that I came from, the people closest to my heart, who suffered so much hardship in discounting the occurrences raked up by the Truth Commission this past year and a half:

"Indifference to evil is more insidious than evil itself; it is more universal, more contagious, more dangerous. A silent justification, it makes possible an evil erupting as an exception becoming the rule, and being in turn accepted."

6-8 MAY 1997: ZEERUST, RUSTENBURG AND MABOPANE: "HAAST TE ERG OM AAN TE HO-REN" (ALMOST TOO SHOCKING TO LISTEN TO)

The Truth Commission through the eyes of a Dutchman!

Jan van Butselaar, an old friend and fellow-student at the Free University of Amsterdam, where the both of us were enrolled for a doctorate in Theology, was visiting South Africa. No two ways about it, Jan and his wife, Marijke, had to accompany the TRC trek to the North West Province. As secretary of the Netherlands Missionary Council, Jan was following the TRC process with interest. I booked the Van Butselaars into the same hotels where we would stay. They would be able to follow the hearings in Zeerust, Rustenburg and Mabopane closely from the inside. Over dinners and at breakfast Jan tirelessly questioned the Commission. It was refreshing to hear his observations and comments.

Some weeks later Jan sent me a copy of an article that had appeared on the front page of *Centraal Weekblad*, a widely read opinion paper.

Under the title *Haast te erg om aan te horen*, Jan van Butselaar reported extensively on the work of the TRC. It was a traumatic experience for him to listen to the stories from Zeerust and Mabopane. What had happened to several political opponents of President Mangope in Bophuthatswana, greatly moved him:

"During one hearing in Zeerust ... one young man, twenty-three years of age, came to testify about an attack by the Bop Police on an anti-apartheid group, where the police took care to shoot the men below the belt. As a result, this young man's testicles had to be removed later.

"Women told stories about assault, of rape. One of them, Louisa Malebo, secretary of one of the opposition parties in Bop, was regularly hauled out of bed during the night and abused in the police cells. The audience – nearly exclusively black – were greatly moved by her heart-rending stories.

"The attitude of the Commission, who had to listen to so many tales of untold sorrow which are nearly too much for any person to cope with, was also very impressive. The prayer with which a local minister opened every hearing, was not merely a pro-forma request for God to grant the witnesses and the commission strength. They really needed it."

But especially the testimony of the Catholic bishop of Rustenburg, Bishop Kevin Dowling, deeply moved Van Butselaar. He reported extensively in this regard:

"Bishop Kevin Dowling, whose duties are partly in Bop, but who himself lives just outside this homeland, related how the leader of this homeland, Mangope, acted in regard to resistance by churches. The bishop was sharply criticised for allowing opposition groups, such as the ANC to gather in his church. When, during a protest demonstration, he attempted to release one of his priests who had been arrested, tear-gas was shot at him. A few months later, his church was blown up."

The Dutch theologian found it remarkable that Dowling did not yield to any temptation during the hearing to make party-political remarks. The church must be on the side of the oppressed, was his point of view. The bishop's love and his attitude of reconciliation made a great impression. With acclamation Jan van Butselaar quoted the words of Joyce Seroke, TRC committee member, to Dowling: "We will need churches and leaders of your calibre to achieve reconciliation in South Africa."

Jan concluded that "the Truth and Reconciliation Commission has developed a unique method of paving the way for reconciliation in the society. So unique, that it could hardly be applied in the conflict situations of other African countries ...

"But it seems too idealistic to expect that in December, when the work of the Commission would come to an end, reconciliation would have been attained in the torn society of South Africa. Some black voices even now are saying that more time will be needed. Some white voices still hope for a white 'homeland' in which they can continue the old dispensation.

"South Africa still has a long way to go to achieve true and total reconciliation. But the work of the Truth and Reconciliation Commission has indeed shown how the way could be made practicable. And this is, in a country with such a bitter history, truly a blessing."

10 MAY 1997: D-DAY FOR AMNESTY!

On the Saturday evening of 10 May it was D-day for all amnesty applications. Teams of workers in Cape Town, Johannesburg, Durban and East London worked until late that night to process the last applications which were delivered at the last moment.

A few days before, Tutu had made a serious appeal in the press and on the air. There were still numerous perpetrators on all sides of the political spectrum, who had to react! The cut-off date had already been extended once, from December 1996 to May 1997. However, this would be the final date.

"This appeal is coming from my heart," the archbishop said. " I appeal to all of you to come, to use this excellent opportunity offered to you. I appeal to political leaders ... Defence Force personnel ... to those who participated in the activities across the borders of this country ... to the self-defence units in the townships and the hostels ... to the men of the Civil Co-operation Bureau and Military Intelligence ... Please step forward. This is your opportunity to put the past behind you, to bring about your own healing, to help mend our beautiful country. Please come!"

At twelve o'clock on Saturday night there were nearly eight thousand applications for amnesty. Many did indeed use their last opportunity.

The Johannesburg office was a hive of activity. One of the volunteers who stayed until the end, later narrated with gusto: "Nompi had to man the telephone. Several applicants wanted to know how to fax their documents. One perpetrator informed us that he was at a party, couldn't the TRC send somebody to collect his application? Rather late that night a 'prominent name' entered the office, a concertina file containing 58 ANC applications in her arms. However, the real big one was still to come: Eugene de Kock. We knew that he wouldn't come personally. He was in prison! But would his legal representative arrive in time? Twenty minutes to twelve De Kock's advocate walked in at the door, but we were so busy attending to another group of latecomers that we did not recognise him immediately. However, his submission was bulky enough to convince us: here was a weighty matter. Just after twelve we locked the door. Finally we could relax. Somebody collected the files to lock them in the safe. Thanks to Jan Luuks and his helpers all the applications had been captured on computer. And then, consternation! Absent-mindedly I pulled the plug of the computer, with all the hours of work in the machine! I wanted to burst into tears, but Patrick (the office manager) comforted me: 'Never mind, I saved all of it exactly one minute ago!'"

With all the excitement, there was also a measure of concern: there were many perpetrators, especially from the Defence Force, who had not come, who deliberately chose not to make use of the amnesty offer. What would the reason be?

Whether the Amnesty Committee would be able to process all the applications, was an additional source of concern. The government would have to be requested urgently to augment the committee of five, otherwise the process would get bogged down.

12-13 MAY 1997: THE ANC MUST ANSWER STRAIGHT QUESTIONS

After most political parties in the country had made their submissions, already months before, the time had finally come for the most important political leaders of South Africa to appear before the Truth Commission for a second time, to answer specific questions. Preparations had been made for a long time, for what would take place during that week, for the specific "mountains and valleys" where this journey would take us. Work groups had been formed to study and weigh the first submissions, to highlight anything that was not clear and to formulate questions.

◆ ◆ ◆

Deputy President Thabo Mbeki led the ANC delegation. "We won the first round two-zero," Mbeki (referring to the first appearance of the ANC before the Commission in August 1996) said with a smile. "I hope that the TRC commissioners will allow us to win this round too."

However, when Hanif Vally, head of the TRC's legal desk – with the ANC's submission of 137 pages before him – started asking one penetrating question after the other, it appeared that the deputy president's wish would not be fulfilled that day.

In his report the ANC accepted responsibility for more than 500 incidents of violence committed between 1977 and 1989. However, they distanced themselves from 95 cases of violence against "soft targets" – amongst others attacks on shopping centres and restaurants. The ANC admitted that it might be possible that confusing statements by the leadership could have led some ANC members to believe that they did not have to worry about civilian victims. The ANC regretted these incidents.

The Church Street bomb explosion on 20 May 1983 which claimed the lives of nineteen Pretorians had, according to the ANC report, indeed been approved by the president of the movement, Mr Oliver Tambo. He regarded it as an attack on the Air Force Headquarters. The ANC also accepted responsibility for dozens of landmine explosions at different places in the country, which claimed the lives of more than twenty people and injured many, for attacks on police officials and black council members, as well as for hundreds of limpet mine explosions which caused great damages to state buildings.

Among the incidents of violence against soft targets, for which the ANC did not accept responsibility – but did admit that its members could have been responsible without the knowledge of the leaders – was a car bomb explosion in a shopping centre in Witbank during which two persons were killed and 42 injured (October 1988), a bomb explosion at the Witwatersrand Command, Johannesburg, in which twelve civilians had been killed, various explosions in Wimpy restaurants and a limpet mine explosion at a games arcade in Johannesburg in which ten people died (22 June 1988).

Hanif Vally questioned the ANC delegation in detail about the soft target attacks. Mr Mac Maharaj, Minister of Transport, explained that several persons who pretended to be ANC members, did not appear on their official list of the organisation. "It was extremely difficult for us to keep contact with ANC units inside the country from the neighbouring states," Mr Ronnie Kasrils, Deputy Minister of Defence, added. It could even be, speculated the ANC report, that some of the incidents were executed by the South African security forces to present the ANC in a bad light.

However, what was remarkable, ANC spokespersons declared, was that relatively few armed attacks took place in which civilians had died. The military wing of the Party, Umkhonto We Sizwe (MK), had the ability to kill thousands of men and women and children. It would have been easy, but even under the greatest provocation, this way had not been followed. "When compared to the policy directions and armed actions of other freedom parties in Africa and elsewhere, the degree of self-control by the ANC and MK was extraordinary." However, the ANC accepted collective accountability for all *bona fide* attacks by MK soldiers. The organisation expressed its regrets in regard to the death and injuries of civilian victims, and apologized to the families and relatives.

In the ANC report it was disclosed that the leadership had forbidden one of its units which planned the assassination of Dr Mangosuthu Buthelezi, leader of the IFP, to proceed with the plan. It was also brought to light that the former ANC president, Oliver Tambo, at one stage had sent a message to Winnie Madikizela-Mandela to persuade her to relinquish executions by means of the disapproved of necklace method.

Offences committed in some ANC camps abroad, also came under the spotlight. Certain commanders had definitely misused their positions and put pressure on young women for "sexual favours". "I think you understand what is meant by 'sexual favours'," Joe Modise, Minister of Defence, explained when penetrating questions were asked about the alleged violation of women's rights in the ANC. "This serious problem had caused the MK leadership to visit various camps and they instructed camp commanders to put a stop to it." However, the young men, isolated in military camps in enemy territory, often had a hard time. They could not go to neighbouring towns in search of young women. "The confinement of men and women led to these misdemeanours," Modise narrated.

One of the most thorny problems that landed on the table during the ANC hearing, was the names of a number of *izimpipi* – traitors, or spies, in the ANC – which appeared in the ANC report. "Only for the TRC" appeared on the document submitted with the report. "Please keep the names confidential," Mac Maharaj requested. These persons had made full confessions to the ANC and had already gone through a process of rehabilitation. "Many of them are leading normal lives." Alex Boraine answered that, although he could understand the request, the policy of the TRC was to be transparent. The names would have to be revealed. "We will decide when to make the list available," Tutu added. "But we have to be satisfied that there is enough evidence to support the allegations ... If there is a case to be made then we are bound to give the persons who are implicated 21 days notice – so that they can come and tell their side of the story."

14 MAY 1997: FORMER PRESIDENT F W DE KLERK APPEARS BEFORE THE TRC

Careful arrangements had been made for the appearance of the National Party before the TRC. I was part of the work group who had to study the National Party's first submission and identify follow-up questions. There was a great deal of appreciation for the contents of the report, especially for the description by the National Party of the various phases the party had to go through, from instituting the policy of apartheid to debunking the same policy half a century later. However, there were also a number of questions that we wanted to put to former President de Klerk and his colleagues. Archbishop Tutu wanted the occasion to start on a positive note. I had the task of helping to write the archbishop's opening address, in which he wanted to express his appreciation of the former president, for the important role that the latter had played these past years, for his part in the process of transition. The man who stood next to Nelson Mandela in Oslo to receive the Nobel prize for peace, had to be treated with deference and respect.

However, things worked out differently than we had hoped ...

In retrospect the National Party, as well as the TRC, was responsible for it. The fact that Mr de Klerk preferred to appear before the TRC *alone*, to answer all the questions personally, unlike the ANC delegation who appeared as a group the previous two days and dealt with the questions together, did not come across well. It is to be regretted that some of F W de Klerk's senior colleagues did not appear at the table with him. One man before a panel of commissioners appeared unfair. The TRC, on its part, thought that it would be a proper gesture to appoint a white member of the legal team, Glenn Goosen, to direct the questions to the former president. But unlike the previous days when Hanif Vally led the ANC hearing, Glenn Goosen with his scathing questions appeared hard-nosed and challenging. The Englishman with the Afrikaans surname visibly rubbed Mr de Klerk up the wrong way.

The commissioners started listening to Mr de Klerk with great anticipation – maybe too much anticipation. Would he be prepared to admit that he, and his government, did not only have to accept responsibility in general for the things that went wrong during his time of rule, but also had to accept political responsibility for the misdeeds of many perpetrators from the ranks of the security forces? In their application for amnesty many senior officers from the Police and Defence Force testified that they, according to their honest conviction, executed government policy, that they received instructions from "the top" for the deeds for which they requested amnesty. Would Mr de Klerk – and the National Party – back them?

Former President F W de Klerk

It was a huge disappointment when this did not happen. Mr de Klerk fervently apologised, as he did earlier (during the first NP submission in 1996) for the policy of apartheid and for the pain it had caused in the lives of many South Africans. But for assassinations committed by security forces, he accepted no responsibility. He had not been aware of it. His government never authorized these illegal actions, was his standpoint. "But the Security Police (who have applied for amnesty) told us they were carrying out the orders of their superiors," Glenn Goosen remarked. "During a meeting of the Government Security Council held on 12 May ... where Mr de Klerk was personally present, General Malan, Minister of Defence and Mr Louis le Grange, Minister of Police, were instructed to train people to exterminate terrorists, to use their own methods in this regard. Wouldn't reasonable members of the security forces interpret these instructions as a 'licence to kill?'" Goosen wanted to know.

However, De Klerk denied that it ever became government policy. There had been deliberate operations, exceptional methods had been used, people started to work covertly, spied on the enemy, states of emergency had been declared, people had been imprisoned without trial. But murder? A licence to kill? Definitely not!

Desmond Tutu's first reaction was one of shock. "I am devastated about what has happened with De Klerk." He added that nobody could deny the decisive role that de Klerk had played in 1990 with his brave initiatives. His place was ensured in the history of South Africa. But it devastated Tutu to see how he undermined his own credibility. According to Tutu it was not the actions of the Truth Commission which dissatisfied De Klerk, but the revelations made by people who requested amnesty. "We did not force these people. We cannot force anyone to apply for amnesty. They came voluntarily and it was their testimonies – as well as Mr de Klerk's reaction in this regard – that damaged his reputation."

The next day when asked in a press conference about De Klerk's testimony, Tutu was almost in tears. He said he could not understand how De Klerk could still insist that he had been unaware of apartheid atrocities, when delegations from Lawyers for Human Rights and the Black Sash, among many others, had told him of security force involvement in gross human rights abuses. "I myself had told De Klerk about allegations of security force involvement in the Boipatong massacre, after visiting survivors and hearing their stories ... There was an avalanche of information. To say he did not know ... I find that hard to understand.

"I have got to say that I sat there (at the hearing) ... I was close to tears ... I feel sorry for him ... I am devastated ... To make an impassioned apology ... and then to negate it ... All that is required is to say that 'we believed in this policy but it is a policy that brought about all of this suffering. It is a policy that killed people. Not by accident, deliberately. It was planned'."

The deputy chairperson, Alex Boraine, added that Mr de Klerk had contradicted himself when he first denied the NP had abandoned the security forces, and then distanced the party from gross human rights abuses perpetrated by them.

16 MAY 1997: THE FREEDOM FRONT: "WE ALL HAVE DIRTY HANDS"

There was less drama when General Constand Viljoen testified. Which did not mean that a few hard words were not spoken.

In his submission General Viljoen accused Mr F W de Klerk that he was power hungry. Therefore, during the process of negotiation, he and his party sacrificed that which was the creation of the NP – the right of self-determination. Mr de Klerk himself admitted, in London, that he and his party "had surrendered". The result was that the "ethnic Afrikaners" across the country felt betrayed and threatened.

During the election time, he testified, there were numerous people who had plans ready to resort to violence. "As far as capacity is concerned, we were in a position of power. But our people are not trigger-happy and aggressive and diligently looked for ways other than our own armed struggle." Everywhere in the country his supporters were ready to pay the highest price, Viljoen said, but he, as their leader, approached the matter rationally and thought of the devastating consequences that the Afrikaner suffered during the Boer War. Therefore he decided against a war – even though he disappointed several of his followers.

There was currently still pressure brought to bear on him by people who were frustrated about the little progress made with regard to self-determination. The frustration grew further as a result of the disparagement of the Afrikaans language and the threat to mother-tongue education in schools.

In regard to the conflict of the past, one had to accept that it was a political struggle which asked political responsibility of everybody who was involved. The excuse of the ANC that they first exhausted all other possibilities before joining the armed struggle, he did not accept readily. Also not the NP's excuse that their hands were clean, that the blame for what had happened had to be put at operator's level.

"In my opinion it is not that important to find out who the guiltiest party is, because nobody can really lay claim to clean hands. Why can't we agree that everyone of us has dirty hands? We have fought a war which was to have been prevented or at least terminated at a much earlier stage. And we fought a dirty war."

General Viljoen also admonished the Truth Commission to promote the reconciliation aspect of its instruction with more diligence. To date the conduct of the TRC led to polarisation between the population groups of our country. Several communities, also the Afrikaans community, were alienated by this process. When the TRC had finished its job, the Commission should proceed and seek ways in which to promote reconciliation. Organs in the ecclesiastical and civilian society should be involved in these reconciliation actions on a permanent basis. Viljoen ended his submission by once again, wholeheartedly, committing himself to the process of reconciliation.

❖ ❖ ❖

Throughout the next week the submissions of the political parties were the topic of conversation not only in the country, but also in the TRC offices. Every session was dissected. One point of view contradicted the other. Wynand Malan was bitterly unhappy about the way in which the TRC had dealt with Mr de Klerk and the National Party. In his private capacity he made a press statement, imploring both parties not to leave each other on the way ahead. Some of our black colleagues were even more upset than Tutu and Boraine. To their opinion Mr de Klerk had failed the process of truth and reconciliation which he himself had initiated.

It was clear that the final word on the role of the political parties – especially that of the National Party – had not been spoken.

20 MAY 1997: ATHLONE'S TROJAN HORSE

In October 1985 a Trojan horse rode into Athlone, a residential area in Cape Town. This was how the inhabitants of Athlone, as well as the general public, referred to the shocking incident when a group of policemen, hidden in some crates at the back of a truck, drove through their township. Feelings ran high that day. Suddenly stone-throwing broke out in the street. In a flash the policemen jumped from the crates and started firing at the people in the street – adults, as well as children. Some of the bullets cut through the houses in the street. When the firing ceased there were several wounded persons in the street, as well as in the houses in the vicinity. Three persons – a young man and two children – died.

The hall in Athlone to which the community flocked to commemorate the incident which happened nearly twelve years ago, was crammed. The emotion was raw. It was as if the incident had taken place just the other day. Relatives of the three families were there to tell their stories. Not one of the three who had died was involved in the stone-throwing, they testified indignantly. A photographer who was at the scene agreed. The police who hid on the back of the truck, jumped up and started shooting so quickly that they did not have a chance to identify the real stone-throwers. They just fired!

Mrs Zainab Ryklief, who herself was wounded on this ill-fated day, narrated how a group of children who came to hide in her house were outside just for a moment when the shooting started. She quickly called them inside and locked the door. In the confusion one of her own children was locked out. He hurriedly went to hide in the chicken-coop. When the chickens kicked up a noise he wrung their necks one by one to prevent his hiding place from being discovered by the police.

In the house there was chaos. One of the children, the sixteen-year-old Shaun Magmoed, died of his wounds on the bed. Next to him lay Mrs Ryklief's bosom friend, Mrs Amina Abrahams and her wounded children, Toyer (12 years old) and Ahsraf (6 years). Little Ahsraf was wounded so badly that he never fully recovered.

Zainab Ryklief testified that all the windows of her house had been shattered by the shots. Various pieces of crockery in the kitchen were broken. Her mattress was so saturated with blood that it could never be used again.

Mrs Abrahams narrated how a policeman kicked open the door of the house and stormed into the bedroom, a machine gun in his hand. He aimed the gun at her and her children. She remembered that she called for help, panic-stricken. However, a second policeman intervened. "Don't panic, Mama," he stopped her – and then called an ambulance. Policeman Number One dragged out from under a dressing-table, the ten-year-old Ismael Ryklief who was hiding there, wounded. His elder brother, Ghalieb, begged the policeman to leave the boy and to arrest him instead.

During the hearing Ismael related that the dying Shaun's last words were, "The battle must proceed!" One of the policemen pulled Shaun Ryklief's body from the bed and dragged it out of the house. At the step by the front door, his mother testified, his head jerked. The policeman remarked, "The pig is dead!"

Since then Mrs Zainab Ryklief had to undergo psychological treatment. "I have become like a child and can't endure any noise." Some of the other family members related how difficult it was to identify the bodies of the three victims, how difficult the police made it for them, how they were humiliated, when they asked that the bodies be returned for burial.

To forgive and forget would not be easy, declared some of the victims who had been wounded that day – one of them had been a child of eleven. Only when the those who were guilty had been brought to book, would they be able to make peace ...

However, it was not only in Athlone that children got hurt. Boys and girls were not only shot from the Trojan horse. How badly children and adults throughout the country took punishment, would be revealed three weeks later.

12 JUNE 1997: WHAT HAPPENED TO THE CHILDREN

We share with Ingrid Jonker that noble vision of the child who
wanted only to play in the sun, the child grown into a giant,
journeying over the whole world, without a pass.
... we share with her the knowledge that this succession of massacres
will not deny us our journey over the whole world –
free at last, at last free, perhaps the last to be free, but free at last.

Diana Scott began her testimony before the TRC with these words of Oliver Tambo on the front page of her submission on behalf of the National Children and Violence Trust. Months before, it had already been decided to devote a special session to the fate of children during the years of apartheid. Several submissions that had been made, statistics provided by various organisations, stated that children and young people took severe punishment. In the Johannesburg City Hall a large number of interested persons, parents and children were gathered. Welfare workers, journalists, politicians, came to listen. Ms Graca Machel was invited to open the proceedings. Not only because she was the president's companion. Her reputation as campaigner for children across the world – especially in war-racked countries – preceded her.

Stories and testimonies were brought up. Information documents, lists and tables crammed with statistics were distributed. Young children were not asked to tell their own stories. It would be traumatic for them. Others reported on their behalf. However, some were old enough to relate their own stories:

Nomande Ntabeni was 16 years old when she, in Soweto in 1976, had been shot in the stomach. Potlako Saboshego was seventeen when he, in Daveyton in 1984, had been arrested and severely tortured. He lost the use of one eye permanently.

Petrus Mokoena was 14 years old when he was taken to prison in the boot of a car. His face had been covered with a white cloth before he received electric shocks. For two days he had been tortured in various ways.

Fanie Guduka was 11 years old when the police picked him up in Alexandra in the rain. He was detained for days on end in a cell with hardened criminals.

A high school girl, her name was not revealed, was forced to take off her blouse. Electric wires were connected to her breasts. She was shocked several times and had to be admitted to hospital. Her breasts had been badly swollen. The scars were still visible.

They were the lucky ones. They were still alive.

Nixon Phiri (16 years old) was taken with a group of school children to the Welverdiend police station for questioning. Witnesses related how they were taken to a special room one by one. When it was Nixon's turn, his friends heard him screaming – and then there was silence. His interrogators left the room, locked the door behind them and continued their questioning in the room next door. Nixon never left the room again. He was dead. During the inquest, serious head wounds and bruises over his whole body were found.

During the years 1960-1989, 7 000 people died as a result of political violence. A quarter of them, altogether 1 750, were children under the age of 18. During these years, conservatively calculated, 12 000 children were seriously injured: by bullets, tear gas, rubber bullets or *sjamboks* (horsewhips). During the same time approximately 80 000 people were detained countrywide, of which 25 percent were children. One out of every eight were girls. These children had often been tortured: according to statistics, one out of every four.

During the years 1990-1994 when the plans to establish a new South Africa had been well advanced, the situation in regard to children was even worse. In black residential areas, on trains, in squatter camps, violence was still rampant. During these four years 14 000 died, double the figure in the previous thirty years (1960-1989)! During these four years 517 children died as a result of political violence. The number might be even higher, according to researchers. During the 91 massacres that took place after 1990, numerous children had been hit. One example was given: at Boipatong, on the night of 17 June 1992, 45 people died: 16 were women, 9 (among them two small babies) were children. Operations by the security forces were in that time responsible for the death of 43 children; 165 were seriously wounded. Vigilante action claimed another 449 lives of children. The hit squads had to answer for 17 children. Under bizarre circumstances 8 children were killed by so-called right-wing groups.

"The way in which a society treats its children, is the clearest reflection of its true character," one of the speakers quoted during the hearing. "The way in which children, especially black children were treated during the years of apartheid, is one of the darkest chapters of our history."

In South Africa, in the townships, children did not remain children very long. In the struggle for apartheid it was often the children who took the lead, and paid a high price for it.

"Children had to grow up very quickly," a social worker said. "I was amazed more than once about how quickly boys and girls became mature, how politicised they had become. There was no time for playing and running around, for carefree childhood. What was happening to their parents, the humiliation of their moms and dads, their powerlessness to change their circumstances, affected the children deeply – and radicalised them."

More than a million school children joined COSAS (Congress of South African Students) to the great irritation of the Security Police who had a vendetta with this organisation. In August 1985 COSAS was declared a banned organisation. Several of the leaders were arrested and locked up.

During the state of emergency in the country, things had happened that should have convinced the world that the South African society had become insane. Sometimes whole schools – teachers, children, some as young as seven years – were loaded into trucks to be charged with violation of emergency regulations. On 22 August 1985 more than 800 school children, among whom primary school children, had been arrested and detained for a night. 360 of them, among whom an eight-year-old child, were formally charged.

How would we deal with the scars sustained by the children? How could the young boys and girls who learned bad habits in prison, be rehabilitated? How would we reintegrate young activists who had become totally radicalised, in a normal society? How did one drive away the ghosts and nightmares causing children to lie awake at night, years after these things had happened to them? What sort of parents will these traumatised children turn out to be one day?

There were more questions than answers. Representatives from several human rights and children's rights organisations participated in the discussions. It was a hopeful sign that three young Afrikaners came on behalf of the *Junior Rapportryers* (a cultural organisation for young Afrikaners). Their submission made a particular impression.

Just before lunch a group of school children from Soweto staged a play which they had rehearsed many times – a portrayal of what had happened in a classroom on 16 June 1976. They were carried away by their own acting. The tears and screams of anguish, the songs and prayers, their political speeches, their words of comfort to each other and their parents, were so true and realistic that it made a shiver run down one's spine. That was how these children, who had not even been born that day, experienced Soweto Day.

Would we ever understand?

19 JUNE 1997: VISITING THREE FAMILIES IN SOWETO

"Piet, you must come accompany Joyce and me to Soweto today. The day after tomorrow the remains of the three young men that were exhumed in Aliwal North, are to be buried in Soweto. You remember, don't you? Tokyo Sexwale's brother and the other two. We must go and visit the families on behalf of the TRC."

It was always an exceptional experience to drive through Soweto with Tom Manthata and Joyce Seroke. It was their world and they knew every street corner. They could tell many stories of what had happened, and where. Tom once took me to the Hector Petersen Monument, to explain to me exactly what had happened on 16 June 1976 at the square where we stood. Joyce loved the area of the large Regina Mundi Church, where the women in the past held their services and arranged one demonstration after the other.

But this time it was not a sightseeing tour.

The news that the remains of the three young men who, sixteen years ago, greeted their parents to join the struggle and never returned, had been exhumed and positively identified, had spread like wildfire. The ANC arranged a mammoth funeral on 21 June, in a football stadium. Thousands were expected when the three young "heroes" – as the posters introduced them – would be buried in the heroes' acre of the Avalon Cemetery. Common African decency demanded that we should visit the family before the funeral.

The first visit was to the family of Thabiso Rakobo. In a humble small two-roomed house, one of thousands in the Mafulo township, Mrs Rakobo, Thabiso's mother awaited us. As always when a family was in mourning, all the furniture had been carried from the house. In the bedroom only the double-bed mattress lay on the floor. Mrs Rakobo lay on the mattress under a blanket, her friends and relatives gathered around her. After we had greeted each other, she haltingly started to tell her story of that fateful day, sixteen years ago, when Thabiso left. About her sorrow when he did not return with the other exiles. When she finally heard the news that her son was really dead, that he had died years ago in a battle with the Security Police in the former Transkei, but that his remains had been exhumed, her heart wanted to break. She was glad that the ANC took over the arrangements for the funeral. That her Thabiso would be buried in the heroes' acre, was a great consolation to the family. After we had tea and scones, and prayed together, we took our leave.

House number two, in Mdeni, where the parents of Anthony Sureboy Dali lived, was more stylish. Especially inside. "When Anthony left that day," his mother, Mrs Letitia Mangane, related, "he comforted me: 'It will only be for a short while, Mom, then I'll be back. I will get a job and make lots of money to make your house the most beautiful one the street. I will put wooden panels against the walls and buy large copper lights.' He had been shot dead before he could fulfil his promise, but I then decided that I would do it for my son's sake." Proudly Mrs Mangane pointed to the pine-wood panels, to the beautiful ceiling, to the heavy lamp and fan. "It took a long time and much money, but I am sure Dali would be satisfied."

While tea was served, Letitia Mangane rose to fetch a Mother's Day card which Dali gave her just before he left. On the card, actually a small book with beautiful photographs and poems, was written: "When the sun forgets to shine … " Inside were various words of comfort for somebody in need. "I wonder whether my son had a premonition? But this is all I have left of him, the card and his school photograph."

When Chris Hani at the time brought them the news that their son had died in a gun-fight with the police in the vicinity of Elliot, her world fell apart. But now that they had discovered his bones, she could lift her head once again.

The next day, Friday, the remains of her son would be returned home in a proper wooden coffin. "The coffin will be placed right here on the table. Here in this room we will sing and pray through the night. All the neighbours and family will come. We will drink tea and eat. And then we will bury Anthony. When I have buried his bones, I will be able to wash my hands. The young men lived together, fought together and died together. It is right for them to be buried together."

I had already been in the third house, in Dube, before, the residence of the elderly Mr and Mrs Sexwale. The parents of Tokyo Sexwale, then Premier of the Gauteng Province, received us cordially. On the wall in the sitting room were two photographs: one of the head of the house, in military uniform, during the First World War. The second was of young Lesetja, soldier of the struggle, who never returned home. For a long time we talked about the struggle of the past, of his son's part in the struggle. "Of course we are sad about Lesetja's death. But we are also proud of him. It is young people like him who paid for our country's freedom."

The Sexwale family were stalwart Catholics. The picture of Jesus against the wall and the small image of the Virgin Mary on the cupboard, made that clear. When the time came to sing and pray, Fikile Mlotshwa, one of the TRC staff members who accompanied us, started with a well-known Catholic hymn. Then the Afrikaans minister of the NG Kerk was allowed to entrust the family to God's care. Things had to be done the proper way!

On our way to the front door, Mr Sexwale showed us the photograph of his other son, Tokyo, against the wall in the porch. "Of this son of us we are even prouder! We are very grateful to God for him. Do you think I would have been able to live in such a beautiful house, that my wife and I would be doing so well, if he did not take care of us?"

19 JUNE 1997: THE MOTHER OF ALL FOLLIES

Dear Professor Meiring

After all the nonsense that you wrote in *Beeld* in the past concerning racial matters, etc. your column of 19 June, The mother of all follies, compels me to reprimand you.

As to the so-called "confession", we'll leave it at that, because by no means do I "as a Christian, struggle with it." You and others, for no reason, keep harping on all the so-called injustices, the suffering, etc, of apartheid against black people. I would just like to have a list of all these. I would also like you to tell me what we actually should have done or have failed to do. We conservative Christian Afrikaners, whose minds have not yet been contaminated with the liberalism, humanism, semi-communism and what else, are now becoming sick and tired of this feeling of guilt and other disparaging insults with which the so-called Afrikaner intelligentsia constantly pester us to break down our self-respect and will to fight.

I do not owe the Blacks anything and unfortunately Afrikaners like you allow your-selves to be misused as 'useful idiots' in making the Boer War's last phase succeed, namely Milner's ideal: To wipe out Afrikanerdom. Your wonderful Uncle Bey's history makes me seriously doubt his Christianity and therefore means one great zero to me.

Don't worry, I do not belong to some Klu-Klux Klan, but was born and raised in the NG Kerk, have been a member of the church council for years – 11 years ago I was even a member of your congregation in Lynnwood Ridge for a while. You are therefore one of the many notable apartheid critics whom I am asking these questions. Nobody has answered me as yet. Apparently they can't, or they are like Don Quixote who wants to storm the world and then suddenly discovers that his thin old horse won't make it.

You may disregard this letter if you want to, but very certainly Piet Meiring and his colleagues, like lost sheep will one day swallow every word against apartheid and their New Age mixture of races (which is a direct contradiction of God's order of Creation).

I am awaiting such a list, please.

Regards
Andries Loubser, Elsburg.

20 JUNE 1997: THE NATIONAL PARTY FORMALLY CHARGES THE TRC

What we feared the whole time, had happened. The National Party had officially charged the Truth Commission. Ever since the second appear-ance of Mr de Klerk before the TRC – and the disappointment with which the chairperson and deputy chairperson of the TRC reacted to his testimony – we speculated: would the NP really go so far as to drag the TRC to court?

The NP was apparently not satisfied with the course of events. Threat upon threat followed. And then on 20 June, the official summons came; The TRC had to appear in the Supreme Court. Tutu, Boraine and Dullah Omar, Minister of Justice under whose wings the TRC operated, were named co-respondents. The NP requested in the summons that the Supreme Court should instruct Archbishop Tutu to refrain from making any remarks which could damage the credibility and impartiality of the TRC. Secondly, it was requested that the court should discharge Alex Boraine as commissioner of the TRC, as he, in their opinion, acted contradictory to several stipulations in the TRC Act. The court should warn the whole TRC to act impartially and objectively.

Tutu's first reaction was: "This is not how we wanted to handle our differences. But if we are challenged, we must accept the challenge."

23 JUNE 1997: TEARS AND TOYI-TOYING ABOUT CHRIS HANI

When Tom Manthata and I arrived at the Benoni City Hall that Monday morning, the atmosphere was loaded. Four years after the assassination of the popular leader of the South African Communist Party, Chris Hani, the two assassins would appear before the Amnesty Committee. Tom and I had to attend the occasion on behalf of the Reparation and Rehabilitation Committee. We forced our way through the crowd, to report at the hall where the judges were deliberating. Winnie Madikizela-Mandela stood among a group of young people bearing posters screaming. *You have killed our leader. Today we want to hear the truth!* "I'll introduce you to her later," Tom promised. "It is high time that you get to know her."

Days before, the newspapers started to write about the amnesty hearing. What would Janusz Walus and Clive Derby-Lewis say? Would they ask forgiveness? Did Clive Derby-Lewis, the man who planned the assassination, and Janusz Walus who killed Hani on 10 April 1993 in the driveway to his house in Benoni with four shots, act in their own right, or were they part of a wider conspiracy? Spokesmen of the ANC-SACP Alliance were convinced that more people were involved in the assassination. "It is clear that there was a conspiracy and that people close to the former government were involved," Jeremy Cronin, leader of the SACP declared. "We want to know who they were!" What questions would George Bizos, the advocate for the Hani family, ask? What demands would he make? The press speculated about many possibilities.

Just before the two men were led into the hall, a short photo session for the press was arranged. Derby-Lewis and Walus had both been sentenced to death on 15 October 1993. Later the sentence was changed to imprisonment for life. During the past four years, the two men had not changed much. Walus still looked just like the photographs taken at the trial. A little tense, he took his place in front of the cameras, in his grey suit of which the arms were rather short. Derby-Lewis appeared quite relaxed. He had lost much weight. Not a hair was out of place, his moustache neatly clipped. In prison he kept himself fit. "I can easily do thirty chin-ups," he said excitedly. "It is clear that the adrenalin is pumping today," one of the journalists remarked. While a small group of Conservative Party supporters visited the two men in turn in the room, some of the women brought snacks. "What we did was an act of war," Derby-Lewis told the press. "We have left all that behind. But they must not expect us to apologise now."

When the two men, under heavy police escort, were led into the hall, they were booed by the majority. The audience was chanting and toyi-toying noisily. Together with other ANC functionaries, Mrs Limpho Hani, in a shocking-pink outfit, danced and sang. For Chris Hani's teenage daughter, Nomakwezi, everything became too much. Crying, she stormed out of the hall. Winnie Madikizela-Mandela saw it and hurried out after the girl to comfort her. In the middle of the hall Dr Ferdi Hartzenberg and a small group of CP supporters stared into space, their faces expressionless. A few rows before them Mrs Derby-Lewis sat. She talked to the people around her and shook her head about the toyi-toying.

Mrs Margaretha Vorster, eighty years old and an inhabitant of the Kruinhof home for the aged, came specially to support Derby-Lewis and Walus. While she was knitting peacefully, the little old lady unburdened her heart to Marga Ley, a Johannesburg journalist: "The noise does not intimidate me. The days of being afraid are over. One can never try to justify murder. But if Christ carried our sins, He will also forgive this sin. I am here to show Clive and all the others how I feel. I have just said hello to them. I squeezed their hands and gave them each a kiss. I am so glad that I could do it. You know, I voted yes in the referendum, but my eyes were opened during the negotiations."

Mrs Phyllis Mzame came from Daveyton, together with her colleagues in the ANC Women's League. She was also much older than seventy, but still had a spark in the eye and carried her years well. "Who gave these people the right to kill? This is what I want to know ... I came to listen to what they have to say. I am very sorry for Limpho Hani. The murderers must give all the information about who were involved. And then they must still be punished. I do not feel like forgiving them. Maybe if they have told everything, we must change our minds. We will have to listen and see ... "

Finally Matthews Phosa, Premier of the Mpumalanga Province, silenced the crowd. The amnesty hearing could commence. Tom and I took our seats at the back of the hall to listen.

The hearing was an anticlimax.

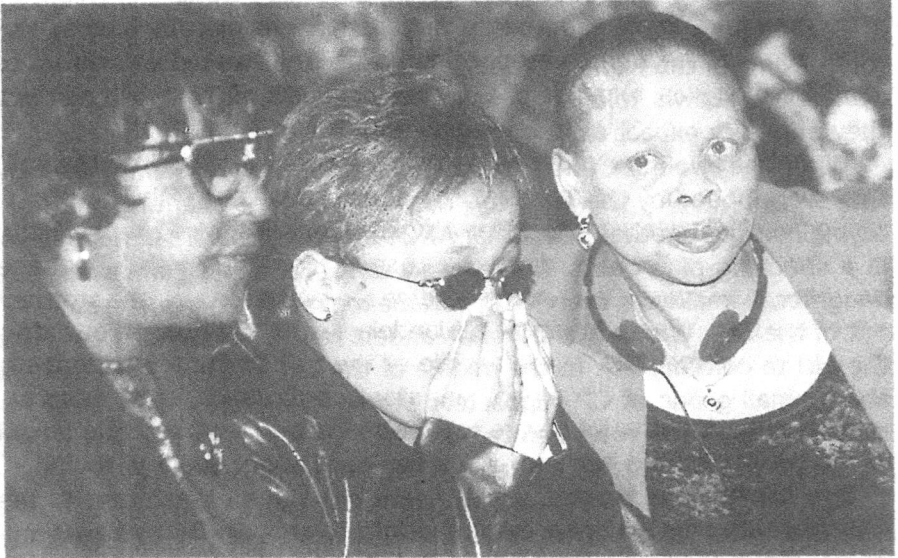

Mrs Winnie Mandela supports Mrs Limpho Hani and her daughter Nomakwezi during the Walus Derby-Lewis amnesty hearing.

Advocate George Bizos who acted for the Hani family and the Communist Party, requested that the case be postponed. Mrs Hani headed a parliamentary committee that was on the point of departing to the United States. There was no way that the visit could be postponed. It was important for Mrs Hani to attend the hearing, Bizos explained. "This is a very difficult part of Mrs Hani's life. She is consumed by inner conflict ... " New information had also been obtained, documents just recently put on the table by the representatives of Derby-Lewis and Walus, which could bring fresh information to light regarding a possible conspiracy. More time was needed to investigate all these things properly.

The legal representative of the two sentenced men, Mr Jan Lubbe, objected. Bizos' arguments did not impress him. For many years they had looked for a wider conspiracy, and nobody could find any. According to him Bizos and his colleagues wanted to delay the case until the Amnesty Committee's term had lapsed.

After prolonged argumentation, Judge Mall postponed the hearing. Tom and I returned to the office without having achieved our objective. He did not even have a chance to introduce me to Winnie Mandela. Not that it mattered much – during the months to come, I would get to deal with her frequently, and would indeed get to know her.

◆ ◆ ◆

The third stage of the trek was over.

The journey had been long and sometimes arduous. Since the Truth Commission had embarked on its road through the history of our country, eighteen months ago, we had achieved a great deal. When the last human rights violations hearing had been finalised at the end of June 1997, in Ladybrand in the Free State, the Truth Commission could already report as follows: more than 11 000 statements from victims had been received and processed, 1 800 victims had testified in public. The hearings, which had been held throughout the country, lasted altogether 180 days. Nearly 8 000 applications for amnesty had been placed on record.

Mary Burton, TRC commissioner from Cape Town, expressed her satisfaction about the distance that we had covered on this trek in an interview with the Johannesburg newspaper *The Star*: "We believe that we, with all the information that has been collected, will be able to paint a clear picture of what had happened during the years of apartheid in South Africa, of the struggle that lies behind us."

The road reached several mountain peaks, pinnacles of success. But the way often led us through deep valleys as well, valleys of pain and sorrow, of frustration and failure. There were numerous legal problems to be solved; legions of organisational problems. Political squabbling sometimes cost the TRC dearly. Appreciation for the work of the TRC was alternated with sharp criticism. The conflict with the National Party had disappointed Tutu during the last weeks of the trek: it had diverted the public attention from the real task of the commission – and from what had already been attained.

But, it was unanimous, the trek had to proceed.

CHAPTER 4

EMBARKING ON
THE JOURNEY INWARD

"Beyers Naudé wants to go to the Truth Commission."

"Naudé, together with five other theologians, wants to confess his personal guilt and omission before the TRC."

"I haven't done enough," the elderly clergyman said to the press.

When the press reports were broadcast early in January 1997, one could sense at once that there was something new in the wind. Before us lay the beginning of the next juncture – a third phase of the TRC trek.

Behind us were the many hearings, held in all parts of the country. Thousands of victims had already told their stories. Many of the perpetrators who applied for amnesty already had their turns. Now the difficult question was: how does one make sense of everything that happened?

Beyers Naudé's statement was one of many which appeared at this time, of persons who were urged by the daily disclosure of atrocities of the past to stand in front of the mirror: how on earth could these things have happened? For some the question was very personal: to what degree had I been involved in all the past events? For others it cut still deeper: which processes that were at work in our country made it possible? Not only individuals, but also various institutions and traditions would have to be scrutinised.

Layer by layer, like peeling an onion, the South African society had to be exposed. The instruction to the Truth Commission was after all not merely to draw up a catalogue of human rights violations, but to attempt to understand, to learn and to make recommendations on how to avoid repeating the same mistakes in future.

This is what awaited the third stretch of the trek:

Firstly Beyers Naudé dared his fellow *church people* to face the mirror. How was it possible, he asked, that while ministers preached the message of reconciliation and peace in Christ from their pulpits every Sunday, gross violations of human rights took place around them, seemingly without affecting them? How was it possible that those who intentionally committed murders and sabotage, could have been sitting in church on Sundays, without it affecting them? "Was there nothing in our preaching, liturgies and sacraments that disturbed the conscience of those who were directly involved in all the evil deeds committed? ... We are guilty of having allowed the rulers (of the country) to execute the ideology of forced separation for the sake of so-called law and order, without offering united resistance as preachers of justice and peace."

Beyers Naudé and his wife Ilse

The guilt of ministers whose lights were supposed to shine brightly, "should be considered as more serious than that of any other person or institution", Beyers Naudé said. "We, who were supposed to be the conscience of the nation, didn't succeed in preventing the most serious forms of abuse of the human conscience."

Oom Bey's statement evoked great reaction. If he, who since the days of Sharpeville and Cottesloe (1960) fought so hard against apartheid, who had to endure years of hardship and abuse, who had been placed under house arrest for seven years for opposing apartheid, felt that he had to confess – what about us then? Several ministers, not only from the NG Kerk, but from many other denominations, had signed the letter. The young, new leader of the Methodist Church in South

Africa, Bishop Mvume Dandala from Johannesburg, declared his support of the letter, and advised his fellow Methodists to consider following his example.

From Windhoek, Nico Horn, pastor of the Apostolic Faith Mission, had published his own confession. Referring to his ministry in South Africa, he wrote:

"I confess my horrible fear in the old days. Fear that the Afrikaners would eventually reject me; fear that the rejection would take my ministry away from me; fear that nobody would listen to me any longer and that my congregation would be going under; fear that my children would be harassed at school and at clubs. I confess that my fear had often forced me to compromise, like the time when two hot-tempered men resigned from Krugersdorp's church council because Joseph and Johannes attended our services. I had promised the church council quite formally that I would not encourage the brothers and sisters of our missionary congregation to attend our services. Though I couldn't sleep for weeks after making this promise, I never withdrew it ... "

Nico Horn proceeded to say that the more "enlightened" members had deterred the others with their pedantry and arrogance. And the white liberals were also not much help! "We understand the struggle", they said, "we are open to black initiatives, etcetera, etcetera ... " – while the black community had long ago given them up as a bad job. "We also failed our black comrades by making them understand that action and violence are synonymous. Now we have a society which is going up in flames."

Not all theologians agreed with Beyers Naudé and his colleagues. The TRC was definitely not the mirror many churchmen wanted to face. Bouke Spoelstra, from the Reformed Churches, joined the debate. This retired emeritus professor from Potchefstroom had serious objections against the TRC and the roles of Tutu and Boraine, he wrote in his topical religion column in *Beeld*. The actions and the composition of the TRC made Spoelstra think of "witch-hunts and the inquisition of the Middle Ages where the Dominican investigators tried to point out the witches and heretics and handed them over to the authorities to be punished or burned to death." Tutu and Boraine and their colleagues on the TRC were, according to him, incompetent and unequipped to undertake the journey to truth and reconciliation. Besides, the process would, according to him, not lead to deep spiritual introspection. On the contrary, the TRC's name was inappropriate: it had little to do with the real truth and reconciliation, as Jesus taught us! In addition,

Spoelstra was uncertain whether he could trust the TRC. Could it be possible that the work of the TRC was part of a shrewdly planned Eastern strategy to break us by means of ju-jitsu? To use the own weight of Christians to finally floor them in their endeavours to truth and reconciliation? How otherwise could the revolution fully succeed'?

During the second half of the year, not only the churches, but also several other institutions – the medical fraternity, legal profession, Defence Force, the media, Correctional Services, the business world, women's organisations – would embark on this journey. For some it would become, as for Beyers Naudé and his friends, a journey of introspection and self-discovery. The country and its people would be able to learn lessons from their journey inward.

Others would, in a manner of speaking, be carried along on the journey, reluctant and demurring, sometimes struggling.

For several the process of the TRC was a negative experience, a confirmation of old fears and prejudices.

For the first of the special hearings, those of the medical profession, we have to retrace our steps to 18 June 1997.

After this date would follow the various stages on the journey inwards, where individuals and groups from all sectors of our society, white, as well as black, had to parade past the mirror of our history.

The journey commenced with the appearance of a group of black students, the murderers of Amy Biehl, who were called before the Amnesty Committee, this time in the presence of the parents of the American student. Then a group of Apla fighters came to testify about the St James massacre. There were moving – and inspiring – scenes. From then on the TRC trek would proceed, to the Old Fort in Johannesburg, to the press offices and studios, to the Defence Force bases and detention barracks, to the court-rooms of our country where judges and advocates heard long rows of defendants, to the once stately Carlton Hotel where the businessmen of South Africa would reflect on their role in the past, eventually to East London were representatives of the religious groupings in South Africa placed themselves under the spotlight.

In between, the Truth Commission had to proceed with all its other activities – the first month or three without Archbishop Tutu, who had to undergo cancer treatment in the United States.

18-19 JUNE 1997: DOCTORS AND PSYCHIATRISTS AND NURSES ON THE EXAMINATION TABLE

There were so many people in the hall that some visitors had to sit on the floor. One and all wanted to hear what the doctors and their colleagues had to say for themselves – and about their actions in the past. Traditionally the health professionals and paramedics were such a closed community that little information on possible human rights violations committed in medical circles ever reached the ears of the outside world.

For two days doctors and psychiatrists, professors and nurses, psychologists and physiotherapists, dentists and many others would gather in Cape Town to talk about the past. Fazel Randera and Wendy Orr, the two medical doctors on the TRC, together with Glenda Wildschut, nurse, and Hlengiwe Mkhize and Mapula Ramashala, the two specialists in the field of mental health, worked hard to make the hearing a reality. "The interest was overwhelming," Wendy Orr reported on the day of the first session. "Several institutions, our colleagues at a great many medical faculties, the Medical and Dental Council, as well as other professional institutions had promised to co-operate, for which we are very grateful." Dr Alex Boraine acted as chairperson on behalf of Archbishop Tutu.

Out of the more than twenty submissions to serve before the TRC, that of the Health and Human Rights Project (HHRP) – drawn up as a joint effort by the Community Health Department at the Medical Faculty, University of Cape Town, and the Cape Town Trauma Centre for Victims of Violence and Abuse – was the bulkiest: a full two hundred pages. Thirty-five doctors, whose names would be connected during these two days with the commission of gross human rights violations, had already been warned before the session commenced.

The HHRP submission used the scalpel without hesitation. Testimonies were given about the conduct of doctors and nurses who, in the past, either failed to object to the unfair apartheid system, or failed to provide adequate medical treatment to patients in their care. One of the doctors who was in the firing line, was Dr Lothar Neethling, former Head Forensic Scientist employed by the state, who was, according to the submission, involved in poisoning political activists and prisoners. Dr Leslie London declared on behalf of the HHRP that not only a few "bad apples" among the doctors were guilty of human rights violations, twenty-eight such cases had already served before the TRC – and this was only the beginning. "We believe that there are hundreds of cases where doctors chose to play a role supporting security forces to commit or cover up human rights violations, which must be investigated."Several members of the medical profession put the interests of security forces above those of their patients, the HHRP report continued. False medical certificates had been issued. In other instances patients had not been treated adequately. Sharp criticism was expressed in regard to health professionals who, while employed by the Defence Force, participated in torturing prisoners, or were involved in the development of bio-chemical weapons. Little would those present be able to guess what shocking facts would crop up exactly a year later, also in Cape Town, when Lothar Neethling and Wouter Basson would testify in more detail about the former government's bio-chemical experiments and projects.

◆ ◆ ◆

A legion of testimonies about misdemeanours committed by health professionals employed by the Defence Force were given at the hearing. According to the HHRP submission, a psychiatrist, former Head of the Psychiatric Unit of 1 Military Hospital, Voortrekkerhoogte, allegedly attempted to "heal" homosexual recruits by treating them with shock therapy and photographs of nude women. The doctor had attached electrodes to the arms of the recruits and then handed them photographs of nude men, instructing them to fantasize freely. Painful shock waves were then sent through their bodies. When they cried out in pain, the power supply would be shut off and they would be given pornographic photographs of women. The psychiatrist would then, in the most imaginative language, tell the recruits what they saw on the photographs. This treatment was continued, twice a day for three or four days in succession. When that particular psychiatrist left the hospital this practice came to an end.

◆ ◆ ◆

During the hearing Sean Callahan, a military medic at the time, told about his struggle against post traumatic stress disorder the past ten years. He and his fellow medics were confronted with one gruesome scene after the other in the former South West Africa and Angola, without any psychological assistance to help them deal with the tragedies that they had witnessed. They often drank heavily or took drugs: "We had unlimited access to Schedule 7 medicine", Callahan testified. Earlier this year Sean came across John Deegan, second in command of the special Koevoet Unit where he worked at that time, who, too, was still suffering from post traumatic stress disorder. "He still wears his camouflage uniform. He has withdrawn from society, takes drugs and is an alcoholic. It all started the day when Koevoet followed the trail of a Swapo political commissar. When they had trapped him in a *kraal*, inside a hut, a Casspir drove right over the hut. They also shot the injured commissar in the arms and legs. He was then handed to me. While I treated him, John interrogated him. I was trying to put up a drip when John became so frustrated that he shot him through the head ... "

Callahan concluded his testimony by telling how he sought help. Eventually the church supported him. "I think I am on the way to recovery. My emotions have returned. I am a good father and husband – but no thanks to the Defence Force." His closing request was that the TRC should provide counselling for people like him. If the TRC couldn't do it, who could? "We are South African men and we do not cry!"

◆ ◆ ◆

The HHRP had recorded a hundred cases of people being ill-treated by doctors, psychologists and nurses while they were detained during the apartheid years.

District surgeons were often involved – by not giving adequate attention to patients who had obviously been tortured. At other times they allowed wounded prisoners to be shackled to the beds, or security staff to abuse them while they were still in the doctor's care.

One exception was our colleague on the TRC. In 1985 Wendy Orr, daughter of the Presbyterian minister Bob Orr, was appointed as a young district surgeon in the Eastern Cape. The things she saw weekly went against the grain. During September 1985 she lodged an urgent application with the Port Elizabeth Supreme Court, for an interdict restraining the police from assaulting detainees. Since the declaration of the state of emergency, Wendy documented 286 cases of detainees, who complained about police assault during questioning. In her affidavit she reported that the police thought they were immune to proceedings against them, and that none of the complaints of torture or assault were ever investigated. She told the court that she felt "morally and professionally" bound to seek legal intervention. As a result of her action, the requested relief was granted. But her duties as a district surgeon were reduced to almost nil. She was barred from seeing detainees and her telephone calls were monitored. She felt ostracised by some of her colleagues. Dr Orr subsequently resigned, to work at the Alexandra Health Centre. After she had left, the SA Police instituted strict security clearances for all district surgeons.

◆ ◆ ◆

The one case everyone was waiting for, was that of Steve Biko, prominent political activist who died in detention. To a great extent he was the focus of the two-day hearing.

During August 1977 Stephen Bantu Biko, the heart and soul of the Black Consciousness Movement, was arrested by Eastern Cape security police and kept at Walmer police station in Port Elizabeth. From there, he was taken regularly to the Head Office of the security police for interrogation. The two district surgeons responsible for his medical care were Drs Benjamin Tucker and Ivor Lang.

On 7 September Steve Biko sustained a head injury during interrogation after which he was unable to communicate properly. The doctors who examined him, naked and manacled to a metal grille, initially disregarded overt signs of neurological injury. They also failed to record his external injuries or to insist that he be kept in a more humane environment, at least be allowed to wear his clothes. When a physician was finally consulted, a lumbar puncture revealing blood-stained cerebrospinal fluid, indicating possible brain damage, was reported as being "normal" and Biko was returned to the police cells.

When he finally lapsed into semi-consciousness, Dr Tucker recommended his transfer to a hospital in Port Elizabeth. The security police refused, and Dr Tucker acquiesced in their wish to transfer Biko to Pretoria Central Prison, 1 200 km from there. He was transported on the floor of a landrover. No medical personnel or records accompanied him. Shortly after he arrived in Pretoria, he was seen by district surgeon Dr A van Zyl, who administered a vitamin injection and asked for an intravenous drip to be started.

A day later, on 12 September, the Black Consciousness leader died on the floor of a cell in Pretoria – naked and alone. The post mortem examination showed brain damage and necrosis, extensive head trauma, renal failure and various other injuries. The medical treatment was subsequently described by a judge of the Supreme Court as having been "callous, lacking any element of compassion, care or humanity".

According to Dr Peter Folb of the University of Cape Town who testified at the Biko hearing, the SA Medical and Dental Council took nearly three years to investigate Biko's death and the accountability of the doctors who had been involved. The Council initiated a preliminary inquiry in which it was found that the doctors could not be held accountable for Biko's death and that they were not guilty of improper conduct. Despite an outcry from doctors both locally and internationally, the SAMDC (as well as the Medical Association of South Africa) adhered to this decision.

The reversal of the SAMDC decision took years, and was the result of the committed efforts of several prominent doctors who took the issue to the Supreme Court. In 1985, eight years after Biko's death, a disciplinary enquiry was held. Dr Tucker was found guilty of improper and disgraceful conduct on three counts and was struck off the roll of medical practitioners – although he was reinstated some years later. Dr Lang, Tucker's colleague, was likewise found guilty and was suspended for three months. However, this suspension was conditionally suspended for two years and so had no impact on Dr Lang's practice of medicine.

It was evident that the Biko case sent shock waves through the medical society. Vehement debates followed. Protesting voices were received from foreign countries. Shortly before the TRC session would commence, the Medical Association fished out from their archives a number of letters received in 1980 from a group of prominent health professionals and academics – which they did not wish to publish as it would embarrass the medical profession in this country. Finally, after seventeen years, the letters were published in the *SA Medical Journal*. "The former hierarchy of this Association intentionally conspired with the SAMJ to keep readers in the dark about the dissatisfaction in our own ranks about Steve Biko," the current editor wrote in the June 1997 issue of the *Journal*.

According to Dr Folb, Biko's death did bring doctors to reflect on their own position and ethical responsibility. Medical students at the University of Cape Town would never again be taught to "put their obligation to the police and the state above their ethical obligation to their patients".

◆ ◆ ◆

It was evident that the doctors experienced some difficulty finding themselves on the examination table. But it was equally true that they also had learned a number of lessons. During the hearing Dr Harm Pretorius, Deputy Director of the Department of Health, apologised for various malpractices of the past. "Where human suffering is concerned, the department has much to account for", he said. It involved more than doctors being negligent or refusing to provide adequate care to detainees. The whole system that was developing, was unfair! The racist distribution of health resources was, according to him, the most important factor in past illness and death for which the department could be held responsible. Four times more money was spent on the treatment of Whites than on Blacks. Although there were great differences in the health patterns of black and white South Africans, the health system was built on that of white people. While the mortality rate of children among Whites during 1980-1994 could be compared to that of developed countries, that of black children corresponded with the mortality rate of under-developed countries. There were also many other injustices: many of the so-called 'family planning services' to black people were only aimed at controlling the number of Blacks in the country. Discrimination also occurred in regard to emergency services, such as ambulances. Several black patients had died because they did not receive treatment swiftly enough.

In addition, Dr Janet Giddy, who was attached to the Bethesda Hospital in KwaZulu-Natal, argued that the unfair practice was still continuing. Black patients in rural areas were not treated adequately. "Black patients often receive an intra-muscular injection, called the *jova*, for an all inclusive fee." Whatever illness the patient is suffering from, "they must get the *jova*". Dr Giddy and her husband, Dr Stephen Reid, testified together about the aspect of maltreatment of patients in rural areas: underfinancing, the immense shortage of doctors and trained staff, unsterile injection needles, misuse of antibiotics, failing to adhere to safety regulations by mining companies and poor medical benefits of mine workers, the need of the disabled in rural areas who live far from hospitals. "The silent pain and suffering of people in rural areas, their premature death as a result of a system which failed them, are not less important because they live in remote corners", Dr Giddy stated.

◆ ◆ ◆

However, not only the medical practitioners made submissions. Also the medical faculties of the various South African universities searched their own hearts. Much attention was focussed on the problems of young black people who wanted to enrol as medical students. Owing to several factors very few black doctors had been trained in comparison to white doctors. To give one example: between 1968 and 1977, 86 percent of all recently qualified doctors were white (which represented less than 20 percent of the population) while 3 percent of the doctors (which represented 71 percent of the population) were black.

The few black students who were given admission to the medical faculties encountered countless problems and frustrations. Dr Ahmed Moosa, who studied at the University of Cape Town, related:

"There were no African students on the UCT campus. The only African people working there were people who were employed as labourers and as assistants maybe in some of the laboratories. All the residences were closed to black students. You couldn't stay on the campus no matter where you lived. All academic or social clubs were closed to non-whites. There were sports facilities, but those were segregated. This lack of integration continued throughout our medical school years. In anatomy, in the second year of study, all the black students were separated into a smaller lab. In third year at the autopsies that we attended, they would only show black bodies if there was a mixed class. If there was a white corpse that had an interesting pathology, these corpses were eviscerated in an ante-room and the organs from these bodies were brought in and displayed to the class. You weren't even allowed to see a white corpse. During our clinical years, the tutorial groups were separated along colour lines. We couldn't work in the white obstetrics wards – the white side of the hospital was a no-go area for students of colour. The separation of doctors continued throughout our internship years. There were separate residences. There were three or four white interns with us – they had a separate dining room. There was obviously the very sore point of differential salaries."

◆ ◆ ◆

After the doctors and professors, several other colleagues, representative of the wide paramedical brotherhood (and sisterhood) came forward. Each had stories to tell, confessions to publicise: nurses, psychologists and psychiatrists, physiotherapists and pharmacists and dentists. The report of the SA Association of Physiotherapists was   quite typical, also those of the other occupations submitted to the TRC:

"As a professional organisation it failed dismally in addressing the needs of all its members during the years of oppression ... we were unwilling to rock the boat and take a firm stand against apartheid health policies and practices ... For the indignities suffered by our members and for our complicity by nature of our silence, we accept blame and apologise unreservedly ... I think it would be ... accurate to apologise for the apathy, the passive way we accepted apartheid by not challenging the *status quo* (in the hospitals) where we worked ... I feel that integrity calls for us to apologise, admit to our blindness and acknowledge the sins of omission. We were wrong and we can learn from that."

8 AND 9 JULY 1997: "LIKE A PACK OF SHARKS THAT SCENTED BLOOD"

"Your attack on Amy was degenerate and cruel. You were like a pack of sharks that scented blood," said Robin Brink. Leading the testimony on behalf of the Amnesty Committee he stared pointedly at the four young black people. Mongezi Manqina and his three companions had been sentenced to eighteen years' imprisonment for the murder of the American exchange student, Amy Biehl. They had applied for amnesty and were asked to appear before Judge Mall and his colleagues in Cape Town. There was huge interest in the hearing: the international media were there in force, armed with tape recorders and television cameras. Among the many visitors at the hearing were the parents of Amy, Peter and Linda Biehl. They kept wiping away their tears as Manqina, the spokesperson, recounted the events on the terrible day in August 1993 when their daughter was stabbed to death in Guguletu.

It was the slogan 'One settler, one bullet' that had inspired them, Manqina said. They were members of Paso, the PAC youth organization, and had been emboldened to the point of mindlessness by the political talk in the township at the time. They wanted, at any price, to make the country ungovernable. "We understood the slogan to mean that we should not miss a shot, as bullets were scarce." He admitted at the hearing for the first time to having inflicted the fatal injury, which probably led to Amy's death. It was he who had pursued the running girl, it was he who had tripped her up and then went to sit in front of her on the ground. Someone in the crowd gave him a knife, he told the audience calmly. He began stabbing her – beginning on the left side of her body. Some of his friends got out their own knives and helped stab her. Others kept throwing stones at her. Shortly afterwards, Amy died in the Guguletu police station.

The four young men apologized to the Biehl family but added that they believed that their action at the time was one of the reasons why South Africa today had a black government. To the question as to how the death of a defenceless and innocent young girl – who had come to South Africa precisely to serve black South Africans – could possibly contribute to black people getting their country back, especially in a time when constitutional changes were fullsteam under way, Mongezi Manqina replied, "We would murder Whites until the government gave in. With the exception of journalists and ambulance drivers no Whites were welcome or safe in black townships." A delegation of the PAC, under the leadership of Johnson Mlambo, the chief of Apla at the time, had already met the Biehl couple the previous day. The PAC had previously distanced itself from the murder, but nevertheless supported the amnesty application.

For the Biehls the events of the day were traumatic. "I must confess, it was very difficult", Mrs Biehl told the reporters at the door. But when the couple addressed the press formally the next day, they declared that they would not oppose the amnesty application. As parents, but also as the representatives of the Amy Biehl foundation which had been established after their daughter's murder, they had committed themselves to remaining involved in South Africa. Various projects, particularly a training project for nurses working in the townships and squatter areas, were already on the agenda. "I don't think I have anything to forgive," Linda Biehl said. "I never truly felt hatred. Our family never really felt anger or hatred, only incredible sadness."

They attended the hearing, added Peter Biehl, because they wanted to know exactly what had happened. "I could imagine that the four young men were terrified during the hearing and that they would be careful about what they said. But I made a point of looking them in the eye when reading them an excerpt from a poem by Victoria West during the hearing." Amy had quoted the poem in a letter she had sent to a Cape Town newspaper:

They told their story to their children,
they taught their vows to their children:
that we shall never do to them
what they did to us.

"We have the greatest respect for the TRC and the entire process of reconciliation," Peter Biehl concluded. "We therefore do not oppose the amnesty application ... But in reality it is South Africa that needs to forgive its own people, based on the tradition of *ubuntu* and the other principles of human dignity. My wife and I came to South Africa, just like Amy did, in a spirit of friendship."

That the people of Cape Town greatly appreciated the Biehl's attitude became obvious soon afterwards. On the front page of the Afrikaans newspaper, *Die Burger*, appeared a photograph of the Biehl couple being handed a painting by Tyron Appollus, a Cape Town artist. Apollus had painted it, bearing the title *A Plea for Peace*, on the very day Amy Biehl had been murdered.

10 JULY 1997: "IT HAD NOT BEEN WRONG TO ATTACK THE CHURCH"

"I did not think that it had been wrong to attack the church" Bassie Mzukisi Mkhumbuzi told the judges the next day, discussing events during the St James massacre. "I have sympathy with the people who died, but we could not stop what was happening. Now there is peace ... "

Mkhumbuzi was one of four Apla members who applied for amnesty for the shocking events of 25 July 1995. During the evening service, armed Apla cadres burst in through the doors of the St James Church in Cape Town and opened fire on the congregation. When the dust settled, eleven parishioners lay dead and fifty-eight were injured. The wounded included many coloured and black Christians, as well as a Russian seaman who lost an arm and both his legs. "We were under the impression that all the people in the church would be Whites, because the church was situated in a white area", he explained. Mkhumbuzi, who had travelled to Cape Town from Kimberley, where he was undergoing training as a member of the new South African National Defence Force, took the story further: "We had to follow instructions blindly, and not ask questions. The Whites, we believed, were using the churches to oppress black people. The main reason why we wanted to attack Whites was because they had taken our land away from us. Apla's aim was to keep on fighting until our land was returned to us – we were the original owners – and until there would be a democracy in South Africa."

Gcinkhaya Makoma, who led the attack, for which he was serving a prison sentence of 23 years, had instructed his accomplices to fetch arms and ammunition from the comrades in the Transkei, thus preparing them for the attack. They returned to Cape Town with two R4 rifles, 365 bullets, three M26 hand-grenades and two hundred rands in cash. Where the attack would take place and whom would be attacked, they did not know. When they arrived at the church they had no idea who was inside, Mkhumbuzi said, but it was clear to him that people would be killed or injured that evening. He expressed his sincere regret about the loss of life: "I was seventeen years old and obeyed orders without questioning them."

In the audience sat Christo Ackerman and Lorenze Smith, both of whom had lost their wives in the massacre. Once the men had testified, Ackerman stood up and looked at the young men who had murdered his wife. With tears in his eyes he began talking: "I forgive you, because I am a Christian ... but in the end God must forgive your sins. That He alone can do!"

11 JULY 1997: MAIL FROM NEW YORK

Desmond Tutu was not there to talk to the Biehls or the victims of the St James massacre. However, the next day a message lay on the desk of every TRC member: The archbishop was in New York to receive further treatment for the prostrate cancer he was suffering from. He had departed reluctantly, not at all keen to travel so far. He was also worried that the fact that he was about to receive treatment overseas would cast South African doctors in a negative light – especially as the medical fraternity was about to make its submission to the TRC in a few days' time. Did South Africa not have good doctors and good hospitals? However, it was on the specific recommendation of his Cape doctors that Tutu had been prevailed upon to undergo the most advanced treatment available. The letter posted from the office of the South African Consul-General, New York, read as follows:

My dear Friends

Thank you very much for your sweet message faxed to me and signed by all of you. I am very, very deeply touched and did not think that I would miss you as much as I do and I know you are all doing a superb job at work. I have seen some of the reports on what is happening at home. Thank you very much again. I have started with the treatment this past Tuesday and it is going quite well and I have a nice secretary and a nice office in the Consulate in New York, a driver and a car – so you can see I am thoroughly spoiled and Leah and I are enjoying ourselves.

Thank you again ...
Much love and God's blessings.

Desmond
ARCH

◆ ◆ ◆

A few days later Johan Holtzapfel, the *Nasionale Pers's* correspondent in Washington, conducted an interview with Tutu, who had been booked for forty-two cancer radiation treatments at the Sloane Kettering cancer centre in New York.

"I am in good hands", Tutu assured him. "The doctors are good to me. The South African consulate's people are looking after me very well. I have much to be grateful for. And it is wonderful to know that the people at home are praying for me. Do thank everybody for their good wishes on my behalf ... The doctors do not seem to be too worried. They tell me not to worry too much either and to continue as normally as possible with my life. Leah and I go for a walk every morning at six along the Hudson River."

With the exception of hot flushes that made him realize what menopausal women felt like and a somewhat fuller face, there had been no side-effects. "I have an office at the consulate and remain informed of developments in the TRC daily; I talk regularly to Dr Alex Boraine. It is possible here, from afar, to reflect on the commission's work and I firmly believe we are on the right road. It's just such a pity that the Whites, in particular, are so suspicious and negative. It makes me sad. They get nostalgic about the past instead of accepting the new dispensation. We are not above criticism ... it is a good thing that we are being criticized. But I am sorry they are so aggrieved. Constructive criticism is essential to carry us through this time and to bring about reconciliation."

But, Holzapfel said, the archbishop was far more interested in talking about rugby on the day of the interview, than about his own illness. He was disappointed that the Springboks had lost the series against

England, even though they had, in fact, won the third test. He was more concerned about the problems in the rugby world, far more, in fact, than about the cancer! Rugby was losing its popularity among Blacks – which had been all the rage during the world cup. Why? Must more not be done for development? "Where was their guts in the composition of the team for the third test? We had by that time already lost the test series. One or two black players in the team could have made a world of difference for the image of the game ... I should like to have a wee discussion with Dr Luyt (president of the SA Rugby Football Union) and tell him how I see things ... "

14 JULY 1997: ARIEL DORFMAN: "YOU WILL SUCCEED, IF ... "

The next Monday we received an interesting visitor in the Johannesburg office, who had his own strong views about the success or failure of the TRC: Ariel Dorfman, the well-known Chilean writer who had to leave his country to go and live as an exile following his criticism of General Augusto Pinochet's rule – who overturned the socialist government of Salvador Allende in a *coup d'état*. Dorfman, whose books are read in more than thirty languages all over the world, travelled to South Africa, among other things because his film *My House is on Fire* was due to be shown at the annual Grahamstown Festival.

How did our Truth Commission compare with the one that had been appointed years ago in Chile?, we wanted to know from Dorfman.

"The Chilean commission was not successful in every respect, was not the ultimate model as is often asserted", he replied – somewhat to our astonishment. "In Chile only the truth about deaths was established: nothing about torture. The victims were not given the opportunity to tell their stories. The military granted themselves amnesty! There was no question of amnesty hearings or confessions. The general population never really found out why people were granted amnesty. The commission consisted of eight jurists: four were well-disposed towards Pinochet and four opposed him."

He had definite ideas about the South African process:

"Every life taken in South Africa, whether on the side of the government or that of the liberation movements, was equally valuable. Nevertheless I cannot see how the actions taken by the liberation forces, can be considered to be of equal value to the deeds of the former government. But this is only my own opinion ...

"The most important thing is that people must tell their stories. In Chile the human rights violations that had taken place officially became part of our history. That was important to us! The victims were also remunerated. This is what is happening in South Africa too. But in contrast to your situation, the Chilean offenders did not show any remorse. That is why the people of Chile were unable to complete the process of reconciliation ...

"Reconciliation is important ... but this can only happen if it is sincere. If Mr F W de Klerk does not want to say that he is sorry, he should not do so. People will then respect his honesty. But his moral stature will be called into question ... However, it is in De Klerk's interest to ask for forgiveness because he did a great thing: he helped prevent a civil war and bring about a democracy.

"By denying the past, you do not simply turn over a new page. It is like a person standing in the door. You try to push the door closed and tell the person: 'Go away!' But he will only go away if you look him in the eye and confess your guilt. Only when Afrikaners do this, will they be able to express criticism about the wrong things that are happening in the country at the moment. It is important for Afrikaners to examine their own past, because the country needs them in so many ways.

"If you ask me whether it is so terrible to listen to too many horror tales of the past, I say that it is a good thing that these stories are coming out. The truth hurts, but it is a good pain. Coexistence is necessary and unavoidable in a democracy. But reconciliation only happens when an offender says, 'Please forgive me. I won't do it again.' When the victim accepts the apology and forgives the offender, then it is an act of love towards that person. But you cannot push around or abuse someone and give him a poor education and then – when that person has taken over the reigns of power in the country – tell him, 'Forget about it, pretend that it never happened!' First tell him that you remember it and that it was wrong – and then you can ask him not to do the same to you.

"Whether reconciliation will in the end be established between victims and offenders, will not depend on the TRC. The commission is merely a structure – it is only ordinary South Africans who will be able to bring about true reconciliation."

15 JULY 1997: THE WET BAG

"Show us how the wet bag method was applied. I want to see it with my own eyes!" Toni Yengeni, ANC Member of Parliament, who had been one of Captain Jeffrey Benzien's victims, insisted that Benzien, who was being heard by the Amnesty Committee in Cape Town, demonstrate the favourite method by means of which he tortured his victims. The judges got up to peer across the table to see what was happening on the floor. Cameras flashed, commentators were groping to find words to describe the spectacle. For the umpteenth time in his life, this time before the eyes of the big, wide world, the brawny policeman squatted on the back of his black victim. Thus the wet bag was drawn over the head. Thus the bag was drawn tight, thus the head bent backward ...

It was a drama-filled day which, in the words of Antjie Samuel, who was reporting on behalf of the SABC, illustrated the double-edged relationship between the torturer and the tortured. Toni Yengeni, polished politician who seldom searched for words in Parliament, began stammering while talking to Benzien.

"Do you remember, Mr Yengeni, that within thirty minutes you betrayed Jennifer Schreiner?", Benzien asked. That's how long he usually needed, Benzien explained later on. Only thirty minutes, and then anybody would talk ...

Ashley Forbes was next on the list. He reminded Benzien that he had tortured him over a long period of time, later on every sixteenth day of the month, to remind him of the date of his arrest. For his part, Benzien could only recall how he had brought the prisoner cowboy books.

Beeld's correspondent noted that Gary Kruser, the head of the Police ministerial protection unit in Pretoria, could not hold back his tears when he asked Benzien about the day, ten years before, when the security police officer had assaulted him with the infamous black bag and had then hung him to the burglar proofing, feet dangling in the air, until his wrists bled. Does Benzien remember how he had hit him repeatedly in the stomach? "I can't remember it now, but in all fairness, if he says I did it, I will concede that I did it."

For three days Jeffrey Benzien sat at the bench. One victim after the other came forward to put their questions. Professional and proper, Benzien answered these questions, provided information, looked worried about Kruser's tears, by this time his senior in the police service.

Antjie Samuel concluded her report in her inimitable way: "Behind

Benzien sit the victims of his torture – in a row chained by friendship and betrayal. Yengeni betrayed Jonas, Jonas pointed out people in albums, Peter Jacobs betrayed Forbes, Forbes pointed out caches, Yassir Henry betrayed Anton Frensch. During the tea break they stand together in the passages with their painful truths of triumph and shame. As everybody is leaving Benzien grabs the hand of Ashley Forbes tightly in both his own – Forbes smiling shyly under his thin moustache."

21-22 JULY 1997: BEHIND BARS IN THE OLD FORT, JOHANNESBURG

It made my hair stand on end to walk through the heavy gate of the Old Fort that morning. It was here that hundreds of South Africans, opponents of apartheid, men and women, old and young, had served their prison sentences. It was here that Mahatma Gandhi had been locked up shortly after the turn of the century. Where Nelson Mandela had been detained, years later. It was here that some of the most shocking events took place that we now had to deal with in the Truth and Reconciliation Commission. It was here that our colleague, Joyce Seroke, was dumped by the police during the Soweto riots.

Hugh Lewin and Tom Manthata, both of whom served prison sentences during the apartheid years – Hugh in the Central Prison, Pretoria and Tom on Robben Island – were jointly responsible for the arrangements for the TRC prison hearing. Not only did many victims of human rights violations give testimony over the past year and a half, about the treatment they had received in the prisons and other places of detention, but the prison setup itself was a microcosm of what had taken place in society at large, in South Africa during the apartheid years. If you wanted to know what was happening in the country, how people acted towards one another, how the law of the land was administered, you had to look through the bars, Hugh and Tom said.

Early on in the planning it had been decided to limit the testimony heard to that of political prisoners, and only those who had been sentenced. It had already become apparent during the human rights hearings what had happened to the detainees who had been arrested for questioning or who were awaiting trial. Conditions in the three big prisons in which political prisoners had been detained, Robben Island (Blacks), Central Prison, Pretoria (Whites) and Barberton (women), would be scrutinized, along with those in the ANC's infamous Quatro prison.

On 21 and 22 July twenty-five witnesses told us what had happened to them personally or to their closest family. Unfortunately the Department of Correctional Services decided not to present a submission, even though many discussions had been held in this regard. Only one warder, who had worked on death row in years gone by, acceded to our request to give testimony. Many issues were raised: the way in which the prisons had been used to remove political opponents from society; how apartheid had ruled, even in the cells; how the prisoners were often tortured; how they had to forgo medical care; how effectively solitary confinement had been used to control or break prisoners. Two prisoners who had been sentenced to death and who had received amnesty at a later stage both, in conjunction with the warder working on death row, made a moving plea that the death sentence be abolished. The conditions in the ANC penal settlement, too, particularly in the notorious Quatro prison, were analysed. Numerous proposals on how prisoners could be treated better, as well as effective rehabilitation programmes, were put forward.

However, it was not the cold facts and the reams of statistics that moved one, there within the stone walls of the fort. It was the voices of people who had themselves been there, who came to tell their own stories, that would haunt one for months to come:

Zarah Narkedien: "I had to go down and live in isolation in the basement for seven months. That was very, very painful. I don't even want to describe what it did to me psychologically. I'll write it down one day but I could never tell you. But it did teach me something, and that is that no human being can live alone for more than I think even one month ... because there's nothing you can do to survive by yourself every single day ... The cells had high walls ... as the months went by I felt that I was going deeper and deeper into the ground ... I became so affected psychologically, that I used to feel that all these cells are coffins ... it was as if I was alive and all these people were dead ... I've been out of prison now for more than seven years but I haven't recovered. And I never will."

Jane Middleton: "Whether solitary confinement should be regarded as severe ill-treatment? The prison authorities themselves know it's ill-treatment, that's why they use it as a punishment. I can't describe its effects on you very well, because you do go slightly crazy, and it's very difficult to describe your own craziness ... I think Colonel Fred van Niekerk of the Special Branch once told the court that prisoners started showing evidence of disorientation within three days."

Murthie Naidoo: "I was kept in solitary confinement for four months. under the 180-day law. It is the worst kind of torture that can be inflicted on a human being. It is far worse than any physical torture."

Harold Strachan: "I got put into solitary confinement for eleven months straight. The cell was as big as four squares on the floor here. I came out of that cell 20 minutes a day to exercise indoors, in total silence. That was for eleven months I didn't speak to anybody. I found I had a very serious disability, very similar to a stammer in speech, and I have it to this day. I get stuck even when reading and I can't break past certain words ... "

Women, it was testified during the hearing, often suffered more under psychological torture than men. If a woman did not want to cooperate, the authorities threatened to harm family members. This was often quite effective.

Zarah Nakardien: "They tortured me for seven days and the only thing that really made me break in the end was when they threatened to go back to my house and kidnap my four-year-old nephew Christopher, to bring him to the 13th floor and drop him out of the window ... At that point I really felt at my weakest. I felt I could risk my life and I could let my body just be handed over to these men to do what they liked. But I couldn't hand over someone else's body ... So at that point I fully cooperated."

Sometimes men were on the receiving end of emotional torture.

Joe Seramane, whose brother had been executed in the ANC's Quatro Camp: "I have seen what it means to be tortured. But when I think of Chief Timothy and compare the way he died to my suffering, my suffering is nothing, and I have decided not to say anything about that. When the system (South African Police) were finished with me, they dumped me in the lap of my people. "There is your rubbish, we are through with it!" But the ANC can't come and dump the bones of my brother and say 'We are through with those bones!' ... My movement can't offer me a piece of paper and show me how they conducted the trial. We still want the truth, otherwise it will be hard to forgive."

Diliza Mtembu held the ANC leadership accountable for what the junior warders did to the prisoners. "As for the young guys working in Quatro, I don't have any grudge, because maybe myself, if I was in their boots, I would do the same. You know sometimes giving very, very young people such great responsibility, is very dangerous."

Ilse Wilson, Bram Fischer's daughter reported about the day her brother died: "The most difficult part of Paul's death was that Bram's brother Gustav came from Bloemfontein to tell him that Paul had died. Bram was called without any prior warning to talk to his unexpected visitor. Bram was not allowed into a private room to talk with his brother. They had to talk to each other through the partitions with the warders on either side of them. By the time the visit was over it was lock-up time and Bram was taken directly to his cell and locked up. So for 14 hours after the news of his son's death, he was left on his own, and he could not talk to anybody."

◆ ◆ ◆

Hugh Lewin, who for a long time had been in prison with Bram Fischer – the well-known Afrikaner who had become the leader of the South African Communist Party – had the greatest admiration for Fischer. "The most Christlike person I've ever met", Hugh liked to say. Hugh could not forget the day Bram heard that his son had died. A day or so after the hearing in the Old Fort, Hugh handed me a copy of a poem he had written in prison. "Do you want to know what it was like, the day Bram got the news?" he asked.

Another day
(For Bram Fischer)

It was like any other day
from un-lock
    breakfast/wash-up/scrub/clean
    garden/lunch
    lock-up
    wash-up/scrub/clean
    shower/4 o'clock supper
lock-up
till un-lock next morning
any day every day
14 hour lock-up
every night,

In the morning
we picked our 11 mielies

10 for us 1 for the boer
which passed half an hour
and another half-hour passed tearing off the husks
excited about our own home-grown mielies
which we sent to be cooked for supper.
In the afternoon
we trimmed the 21 tomato bushes
and were pleased to see
how they were springing up
green with fruitfulness.

It was like any other day
    garden/lunch
    lock-up
    wash/scrub/clean
    shower/4 o'clock supper
but just before supper
he was called unexpectedly
for a visit
which means I said
    either something good
    or something bad
So he missed supper with us
and we took his mielie to his cell
to eat after his visit
    either something good
    or something bad

It was like any other day
supper/lock-up
alone
cell alone
for 14 hours

While we ate
he was in the room
where you peer at your visitors
through a 4-inch strip of perspex
boxed in by wood panels
with sound-boards

to make the tapes clear.
You have the boere on your side
they have the boere on their side.

They call it the visitors room
His brother
peering through the perspex
into the wooden box
told him:
    Your son died this morning.
Through the perspex
into the wooden box
keeping the State secure
    Your son died this morning.

His supper I suppose was cold
by the time he got back to his cell
    alone
    after lock-up
    for the next 14 hours
    like any other day.

◆ ◆ ◆

What did it feel like to be a warder, to participate in the execution of
people? Warrant-officer Johan Steinberg recounted his experiences:
    "It was a good thing that the family members of persons condemned
to death were not allowed to see the bodies. This was not a pleasant
sight ... I know the face of a man who hanged, his expression ... I would
not want my parents to see me if I had been executed ... I think that it
is a good thing that we did not open the coffins for the family members."
    Three days after beginning work at the Pretoria maximum prison he
had to take part in an execution. Seven people were executed that morning. Steinberg had to accompany one of them to the gallows room. It
was deathly quiet in the corridors. The only sound was that of the
hymns and prayers of the condemned. At the gallows room the seven
men had to stand in a queue, their faces turned towards the warders.
The hangman asked each of them, in turn, whether they had a last
request. "Some of them thanked us for their time in prison and said

"God bless'. Then we put on their hoods. On that first day I in fact put on the hood the wrong way round ... I was tense and held tightly on to 'my' prisoner, leading him into the gallows room and letting him stand on the painted rails, as the hangman put the noose around his neck. When the hangman drew the lever, one of the warders slapped my hand away, to prevent me from being pulled downward along with the prisoner.

After the execution the bodies were hoisted up, the rope was untied and the bodies were placed in coffins. The place was then "cleaned and hosed down". The coffins were taken to the chapel where the family members could attend a memorial service. "It did not matter whether they were white or black. We had respect for death – it was almost a holy place. While cleaning up, we did not make any jokes. We were not even allowed to smoke in the gallows room."

For two and a half years Johan Steinberg was involved in executions. "My work became addictive. I wanted to be present at every execution ... At that point I became aggressive. My wife refused to go along when I played rugby because I spent more time in the cooler than on the field ... Alcohol abuse occurred among the warders ... But I do not wish to elaborate on the trauma because it is something with which I have had to make my peace ... Most people have locked it away in their minds and one does not wish to reopen what has been locked away."

The warders did not want to go for psychological counselling, as they feared that they would be discriminated against. "We were men and did not wish to be labelled as *slappies* (weak-kneed). But every execution affected them. The men would not admit it when they were in a group together, but at night, when they went to bed, it was in their hearts."

◆ ◆ ◆

Between 1960 and 1994 some 2 500 people were hanged, an average of a hundred a year. Ninety-five percent of the persons executed were black. All of the judges who convicted them, were white. In one year, 1989, in the Pretoria prison alone, 80 prisoners who had been sentenced for political offences were kept on death row. In one week, the third week of December, 21 people were hanged, seven on the Tuesday, seven on the Wednesday, seven on the Thursday. Later on, people would refer to that week as 'the Christmas rush'.

◆ ◆ ◆

The hearing in the Old Fort brought back many memories; some deeply touching and profoundly human. In the car one night on the way home, it was Joyce Seroke's turn to tell her story.

It was in June 1976, Joyce began her tale, that she and a colleague saw that there was trouble at the entrance to Soweto. Policemen were all over the show. Young people were being loaded into police vans. Before their eyes a young girl whom they knew well — the most innocent of the innocent — was being arrested.

Joyce went to the police officer:

"You are making a mistake. This girl is not an agitator or an activist. I know her parents and can vouch for her."

"Don't poke your nose into our affairs, or else we will simply arrest you as well — for defeating the ends of justice!", was the only answer she got.

Joyce Seroke, general secretary of the Young Women's Christian Association, did not let them frighten her off. Taking her friend with her in the car, she followed the van, right up to John Vorster Square in Johannesburg. When the sergeant in charge did not want to listen to her, she went to the station commander. This man got so annoyed with the two black women that he arrested both of them — on a charge of defeating the ends of justice — and detained them in the Old Fort.

Joyce was to remain in prison for many months, awaiting her trial. Every week her mother came to visit her, with something to eat and news of the children. "My mother was very strong. She never cried, and also encouraged us to remain strong. She was in tears only once, the day when most of the women were released just before Christmas. Together with a few other prisoners, I had to remain in prison!"

Joyce's mother, however, resolved that her daughter and her friends would be able to celebrate a proper Christmas. Bearing a basketful of things to eat, a Christmas pudding and a pristine white starched table cloth, she arrived at the Old Fort on 25 December. By amazing good fortune she was allowed to go the cell where Joyce and a few other women were waiting. To her great embarrassment there was no table in the cell. And how can one present a Christmas dinner without a table?

The warders laughed at her. This was a prison, not a home. And prisoners do not sit down at a table. Go ahead and spread the table-cloth on the floor!

"That will be the day!" one of Joyce's co-prisoners decided on seeing the old mother's embarrassment. She began shouting at the top of her voice. She rattled the bars of the cells, like a spoilt child. "We want to have a table. You must bring us a table. It's Christmas. Don't you have any hearts?" Nobody could get this feisty woman to pipe down – at least, not until the warders did, in the end, have a table fetched.

Then the woman took her place along with Joyce and her mother, and a few others at the table.

"The meal at the table, the white tablecloth – that I will never forget," Joyce Seroke told me that evening in the car. "Nor the woman who kicked up the racket and who had the table fetched. Her name was Winnie Mandela."

23 JULY 1997: SERVICEMEN TELL THEIR TALES

I enjoyed seeing Neels du Plooy again. He and I had been friends as students, sitting together in the lecture halls of the Theological Faculty in Pretoria. He had been a chaplain for many years in the South African Defence Force and would be able to testify about the role of the chaplains, the assistance that they gave the servicemen. Besides Neels, quite a number of people would testify: Professor Anette Seegers and Jannie Gagiano about the political and social context of the seventies and eighties, when thousands of young men had been called up for military service; a few conscientious objectors who wanted to discuss the reasons for their actions – and the treatment they received at the hands of the Defence Force; a number of former commanders about everything that had happened to 'our boys on the border'; and national servicemen who wanted to testify about their experiences in the operational area, which had often been traumatic.

For many years South African society had been deeply affected by the system of national service. Few white families did not at one time or another greet a son who had been called up for national service. Many of the national servicemen and their families regarded their military service as important, and despite the sacrifice and hardships, felt that it was their solemn duty to protect the country's borders. For others, Seegers and Gagiano said in their evidence, it was a growing frustration. For young men who had conscientious objections, who were not prepared, on political or religious grounds, to serve in the South African Defence Force, there were a number of options – each having serious implications, sometimes involving true hardship. Some, such as Professor Johan Hatting, then a captain in the Citizen Force, tried to sound a critical note from within the Defence Force structures and tried to offer passive resistance. Others, like Tim Ledgerwood, bolted, went AWOL – and if they were arrested, had a hard time in detention barracks. There was a third possibility, Laurie Nathan explained in his submission, and that was to go over to the other side, to join up with the exiles, to go and fight with them. In a certain sense the conscientious objectors were the worst off. There was little patience for conscientious objectors who did not want to serve in the SADF for political reasons. For persons like Peter Moll, who refused to take up arms for religious reasons things were not much easier – even though they could put their case before a special Defence Force panel and perform alternative service.

◆ ◆ ◆

When John Deegan, former Koevoet member, began telling his tale, one could hear a pin drop. During the medical hearing, six weeks before, reference had already been made to his case. But now John himself was here to tell us everything that had happened in the eighties, when he was the commander of a Koevoet section in Namibia. He was clearly already under great stress before he began talking. According to his own evidence he suffered from severe post traumatic stress disorder. In his account Deegan took his audience to Oshakati in the operational area, where things were sometimes easy and sometimes very difficult. The men's emotions sometimes ran away with them, and then they did things about which they later hung their heads in shame. Once, during a rocket attack, a number of security policemen, who had been drinking heavily, assaulted a detainee so cruelly, hit him so badly that he later died of his injuries.

On another occasion Deegan and his men were tracking a SWAPO soldier whose name was Congo. One of his comrades had told them where to go and look for him. "His tracks led to a kraal. The elderly headman did not want to talk. I gave instructions that the Casspirs demolish all the huts in the kraal ... I noticed that the old man kept looking nervously at a certain hut. I knew: this was where the SWAPO member had to be."

Deegan gave instructions that the hut had to be crushed by the military vehicles and that the whole section had to fire at the hut. "It was an overkill situation, typical of the Koevoets." During the shooting a section member's rifle became so hot that the barrel bent and exploded. "It sounded like a hand-grenade. I went on shooting as if I had lost my mind. The barrel of my AK 47 became so hot that it burnt my hand. The man in the hut was heavily wounded. I lost my mind and took out my 9 mm pistol. I questioned him, but he refused to respond. He was losing consciousness. I was overcome with rage because he did not want to answer my questions. I went to fetch his comrade. 'Tell us where are your weapons, your cache', I ordered. I then took my pistol and shot him between the eyes. I walked away and told the headman to clean up the mess. It was his problem."

Deegan said during the hearing that he had felt at the time that he had been separated from himself, as if watching the entire scene from above. "I decided that I had had enough. The next day another infiltrator was wounded. I knelt at his side where he lay and interrogated him. The next moment an Ovambo tracker took an R1 and blew off the man's head right in front of me. The whole group saw to it that they were very drunk for the next two days."

Deegan applied for a transfer. But until he resigned from the police service in 1984, he remained a member of the Special Task Force. His experiences in the operational area had destroyed him, John said. He already had two broken marriages behind him. He suffered from various symptoms of post-traumatic stress, including paranoia. "I am giving evidence to the Truth Commission in an attempt to get well ... I have not applied for amnesty, because I believe that the law must take its course." Deegan concluded his evidence by announcing his intention of trying to trace the families of victims in Namibia. If possible, he wanted to do something to try and compensate the families of victims for their suffering. Together with a few of his colleagues he was also working on establishing an organization for veterans of the bush war, people like him who needed help urgently.

◆ ◆ ◆

What did the churches do to assist their members in this period, in the Defence Force and especially in the operational area? In what way did they support their members who had problems, or qualms as far as the Defence Force was concerned?

Not enough, said Neels du Plooy, who had served as a chaplain for fourteen years. Or rather, they did not do the right things. In retrospect there were many questions, he explained: Why did the overwhelming majority of white South African young men – Afrikaans and English-speaking – do their national service without expressing any criticism, and often with great enthusiasm? Why did parents so readily accept it? He felt that the answer lay largely with churches, particularly the Afrikaans churches, which had apparently accepted the government's war effort unconditionally. "It is only now that churchgoers are asking, in retrospect, how it was possible that everything felt so right those days. The church gave us that assurance ... and yet the church is now only prepared to say, 'Sorry, we were wrong to support and justify apartheid'."

Neels du Plooy explained the functioning of the chaplain's services in detail, the nature of the ongoing liaison between the Defence Force and the government and the churches. "The church followed the lead of the National Party government and that of the Defence Council in defence matters. This total involvement was intensified through the now discredited concept of a "total onslaught'. The church had to become involved in winning the hearts and the minds of the people, its main task being the spiritual preparedness of its members. The church was wholly convinced that we had been fighting a just war ... Even when conscripts were expected to do duty in the townships – and some graduate national servicemen were strongly opposed to it – the church never raised a word of protest. Protest was dismissed as disloyalty."

Obviously the church had the solemn duty to minister spiritually to its members in the Defence Force, especially those who were involved on the battle front: "It is true; the churches and the chaplaincy and the cookie-*tannies* (aunties) did a lot to make life easier for the troops. Coffee rooms were established in all camps. The church and other organizations supplied spiritual reading matter. All soldiers were issued with a special edition of the New Testament and the Psalms ... but this Bible had a message bound in from Mr PW Botha, first as Minister of Defence and later as State President. 'This Bible is the most important part of your military equipment.' It was generally accepted that a soldier who believed in Christ was the better soldier. The chaplaincy also accepted the *In Hoc Signo* (in this sign – of the cross – we shall conquer) as their logo and wore it on their uniforms."

Coincidentally, Neels and I had been seated next to each other on the aeroplane earlier that morning, on our way from Johannesburg to Cape Town. "Well", he remarked with his statement in his hand. "I don't

think the church is going to like all of what I am about to say today."
Neels was right. In the weeks following the hearing, many statements
and letters appeared in the press, some of them appreciative, others
highly critical, from the ranks of the Afrikaans churches. It is not true
that the NG Kerk supported the 'apartheid war' uncritically, Rev Freek
Swanepoel, moderator of the General Synod, told reporters. Why did
Rev du Plooy remain in the Defence Force for so long, precisely when
the war was raging at its greatest intensity, while harbouring such
deep-seated reservations, Frits Gaum asked in his editorial column in
Die Kerkbode.

Months later, one morning in my study, I sat talking with another
old friend from my student days, Rev Johan de Witt, Chaplain-General
of the SA National Defence Force. "You know", he said, "one can agree
with many of the things that Neels wrote. In retrospect we probably
should have done some things differently. But it is undoubtedly so that
the church had a real duty to assist its members pastorally in a crisis
situation – and in fact did so. And Neels had not been the only person
who expressed criticism. In the eighties, in particular, there was a lively
debate among the chaplains about church-state relations, about the
legitimacy or not of the war in which we were involved." He added
ruefully, "And PW Botha's message in the New Testament? We removed
that later on – when one of our English colleagues raised serious objections to it."

25 JULY 1997: LYDIA MWALE IS DEAD

The news of Lydia Mwale's death affected all of us deeply. Lydia manned
the telephone exchange in the Johannesburg office – and with her sunny
nature crept deep into our hearts. She knew just about everything about
everybody. During lunch breaks the corridor was filled with laughter,
while she and her friends discussed the things that had been happening to them that day in 'Commissioner Street'. As a single parent she
and her children lived with her mother. She must have had worries, but
Lydia did not really talk about them. We did not know about them. Until
the day Lydia fell ill and was admitted to hospital. She became progres-
sively weaker. Fazel Randera went to visit her regularly, and became
very worried. Neville Arendse, our 'local communist', came into my office one morning. "*Oom* Piet", was his request, "will you come with me
to hospital during lunch? We have to visit Lydia." I was keen to go with

Neville, as I felt that strong bonds had grown between us over the past weeks.

◆ ◆ ◆

Years ago Neville Arendse had left South Africa as a young Coloured student. He lived in various African countries, and tried to do his bit to fight apartheid. In the end, he went to Russia, where he lived for many years – in Kiev and in Moscow. He fell in love, not only with the Communist system, but also with a Russian girl whom he later married. When the major changes occurred in our country, Neville couldn't wait to return. He got a job as a researcher at the Truth Commission. Unfortunately this was only a temporary appointment, and in order to bring his wife with him he needed a permanent job offer. Neville sorely missed his wife. He worried about her and their future together, which impacted on his health so that he fell ill and needed to undergo medical treatment.

Neville was a jolly chap who had never lost his love of a joke – or Afrikaans – while abroad. But one day he turned up in my office, dejected and upset. His plans of bringing his wife home were not coming off. He was worried about both her and his own health. He was often in pain and despite the expensive treatment, the X-rays and sonars, things were not looking up. On the spur of the moment I told Neville, "Don't you think we should pray together? Let's ask the Lord to help you." Our local communist was somewhat flabbergasted, but agreed to this suggestion. I closed the door and entrusted Neville's worries to the Lord.

Neville left my office. In the next week or two we did not see one another. He was busy with his programme – and I with mine.

◆ ◆ ◆

To my astonishment and joy Neville went on, "You must come with me to Lydia to pray for her. I have found out, in the meantime, that prayer helps!" That day a whole group of Truth Commission members stood around Lydia's hospital bed. Alex Boraine, and a few others, talked to her. Lydia was very ill. At times she seemed to hear us, at other times not. I took Lydia's hand. She opened her eyes. "*Oom* Piet, you must pray for me. And for my mother and the children."

We left, on the verge of tears.

Lydia died a few days later. Fazel Randera had decided that we should have a memorial service in the TRC's office. Lydia's women friends saw to the programme: prayers, hymns, eulogies. The hall was full. Many family members and friends also came. Lydia's mother was there, as well as her daughter. Also a formal delegation from the ANC who reported from Shell House, just around the corner. Fazel Randera had to address those present from a Muslim perspective. Yasmin Sooka spoke as a Hindu. I had to deliver the sermon. I read Jesus' own 'funeral service', the one he delivered the evening before his own death: "Do not be worried and upset. Believe in God and believe also in me. There are many rooms in my Father's house, and I am going to prepare a place for you ... I am the way, the truth and the life. No one goes to the Father except by me ... "

After the sermon Neville made a point of coming up to me to thank me. "Jesus' words come close to home", was his comment. I wondered if Lydia, too, would have been grateful that her funeral service had done our local communist some good.

26 JULY 1997: QUESTIONS ABOUT DUMISA NTSEBEZA

Cape Town – The TRC ordered an intensive investigation after Mr Dumisa Ntsebeza, head of the commission's investigating unit, was linked in a police docket with the Heidelberg Tavern massacre which took place in December 1993. Dr Alex Boraine, acting chairman of the TRC, said yesterday that the commission's investigating team had, while preparing for an amnesty hearing, chanced upon a statement mentioning Ntsebeza's name.

In the statement it was alleged that a car that was in Ntsebeza's possession at the time had been used by the attackers as the escape vehicle. The investigating official reported this to Ntsebeza, who gave orders that the investigation continue.

"He immediately met with Dr Desmond Tutu and myself and conveyed this information to us. He indicated that there was no truth in this allegation."

Adv Glen Goosen, director of the investigating unit, led the investigation. "Although various interviews have already been conducted and attempts have been made to find confirmation for the allegations in the statement, no such evidence could be found. According to Boraine none of the applications of three amnesty applicants in prison referred to Ntsebeza's car. "As in all other investigations we shall, irrespective of who is involved, follow up this matter until every possibility has been exhausted."

Ntsebeza, a prominent attorney of Umtata who had in the past worked for persons such as Mr Bantu Holomisa, was nominated by the PAC for his appointment to the TRC. (*Beeld*, 26 July 1997)

28-29 JULY 1997: TOO TERRIBLE FOR THE MEN TO HEAR ...

It was Yasmin Sooka who mentioned it first. When the first year's statistics had been processed, she noticed that most of the statements submitted to the TRC had been made by women. But the vast majority of the stories concerned men – their husbands, their sons or their fathers. "I don't think there were more victims among the men than among the women", Yasmin said. "The explanation must be more deepseated. I think there are many women who suffered hugely under gross human rights violations, but they are not prepared to talk about it. It was too terrible, too traumatic! How can one expect them to shout from the rooftops the most intimate things that happened to them, the greatest humiliation they had to endure?

I understood what Yasmin was talking about. One afternoon, during a human rights violation hearing in Mabopane, north of Pretoria, it had been my turn to question a black woman. She hesitated to make a clean breast of everything, but when I urged her on she began talking. To her embarrassment, equalled only by my own, she gave a detailed account of the day the policeman had torn her clothes from her body bit by bit, and the humiliations she had to endure at his hands as a build-up to her being raped.

There were also other reasons why women, prominent women in particular, were hesitant to testify in public. During a press conference in Johannesburg Ms Cheryl Carolus, acting secretary-general of the ANC, referred to the Benzien hearing and confirmed that she still had to convince herself that everything was OK. But she still experienced irrational moments, a remnant of her days in detention and torture. She had been seriously considering testifying before the TRC but decided against it in the end. She had to ask herself, "Should the stories of ordinary people not be told? I have been fortunate in that I was a prominent person and that they were therefore unable to do to me what was done to others. At one point there were ten thousand people with me in jail – and their stories have not been told." Ms Bridget Mabandla, the Deputy Minister of the Department of Arts, Culture, Science and Technology, too, said during a press interview that she had been tortured in prison, but that she did not intend testifying before the TRC.

For those women who did want to use the opportunity to tell their stories, the TRC decided that special provision had to be made. In Cape Town a hearing was held behind closed doors, at which women only were present. Only women members of the TRC led the evidence. When the Johannesburg women's hearings were due to take place, the ladies on the staff decided that only women would sit on the panel, to reassure the victims – but that men would also be invited to sit in the audience. "You *must* come", Hlengiwe Mkhize said when she ran into Tom and me in the passage, "it will do you good to hear all the things that women had to endure and how they managed to survive. It will also mean a great deal to the women to know that there are men who are interested in their stories."

There were tales of shocking *physical* torture:

Thandi Shezi recounted her experiences in the police cells, "When they raped me I was already torn and injured through electric shocks. The pain was deep inside me. I could not tell anybody. My mother is in the audience today. She is hearing it for the first time ... I am frigid ... If I enter into a relationship with a man I get frightened. I have not told anybody a single word. I don't want their sympathy. I don't want the people to give me all kinds of names ... "

However, it had not only been members of the security forces who had committed gross human rights violations. An outraged Gloria Mahlope came to tell us how the men in the Mshayape hostel, Thokoza, had assaulted, tortured and also raped her daughter Gloria.

Rita Mazibulo then took the stand. Her tale created a storm in the ranks of the ANC. She had undergone military training in Angola and Mozambique before being sent to Swaziland. There she was responsible for working out the routes ANC cadres had to take. At one point, nine of them were caught, and Rita was suspected of being a spy. She was detained in Tanzania and Zambia. For an interminable six months, she said, she had been kept in a hole in the ground. When she refused to have sex with her jailers, they tortured her in various brutal ways, also raping her repeatedly.

Matthews Phosa, the present premier of Mpumalanga, knew Rita and had been told what had happened to her. Jacob Zuma, too, knew all about it and had given her enough money to go to Johannesburg to report her case to the ANC office. In fact, Mr Phosa cautioned her not to testify before the TRC, as he would have to deny her evidence in public. One piece of evidence made everybody sit up straight and later led to a number of press releases and sharp denials: "I fell in love with Chris Hani and gave birth to his son, Simphiwe. He showed the boy to members of his family, but not to his wife. To prevent my husband from divorcing me, I gave the child to my sister-in-law to raise ... "

Sometimes the torture was of a *psychological*, rather than of a physical nature:

Joyce Sikhakhane Ranken, a journalist, was one of seven women arrested by the security police 26 years ago. "You have no idea what kind of things were done to try and destroy our people's intellect! We could not bury our dead. This turned the process of grief into self-recrimination and feelings of guilt. They tried to destroy our family ties through disinformation ... I have flashbacks of being in solitary confinement and remember how it destroyed me. I hate to remember it, but the creators of apartheid understood the long-term effects of their psychological warfare very well. The psychological torture had to destroy women, and foster paranoia. I was taken to my own cell in the Central Prison in Pretoria via death row." She added angrily, "Yes, there was a death cell for women. Women were hanged there!" Ms Ranken had a three-year-old son when she was arrested in 1969. "To break me, they brought a white toddler of three years to me – and then offered me the chance to turn state witness ... Pen and paper was my life. They knew this and took it away from me."

On the second day Deborah Matshoba's testimony began. The audience was riveted by her account:

"When I looked around me, I was astonished at the way in which all of us battled to appear normal, even though all of us were equally broken inside ... The first time I was locked up in the Old Fort, my fellow prisoners included Winnie Madikizela-Mandela, Fatima Meer and Joyce Seroke. This was a strong group! The wardresses knew Winnie by name ... She was very strong. She taught us to stand up for our rights and to make demands. We were livid when we learnt that black women prisoners were not permitted to wear panties. We heard children shouting in the cells one day, and insisted that they be released."

Deborah was later rearrested and detained in Phoenix. "On Saturday they (two security policemen) came for me. 'Yes, Deborah, you say you're ready for us?' They chained me to a heavy iron ball. I had to remain standing there right through the night while they were busy having a *braai* (barbecue). When it was Sunday, they brought me paper on which I had to write my life story. They kept tearing up the paper. My legs became swollen and I began hallucinating. By Tuesday they began hitting me and choking me with a wet towel. I fainted. When I came to I was lying on the ground, wet through. They must have thrown water over me. Roy Otto threw a packet of sanitary towels at me. In the bathroom I found out that I was menstruating. I wondered how he knew.

"The cell was crawling with lice. The blankets were dirty and smelled of urine. I did not know where I was. I shouted and shouted again. I got severe asthma attacks. Yet I was fortunate. An Afrikaner came up to me. His name was Taljaard and I'll never forget him. He said that he had at first thought that I was crazy. I told him that I was a political prisoner. He listened to me and then smuggled in an asthma pump and some pills, and helped me hide them behind the toilet. Every day Roy Otto would walk into the cell and say, 'We don't need to kill you. The asthma will kill you anyway!' But the asthma did not – thanks to Taljaard."

Deborah Matshoba, who was later locked up in the Middelburg prison, shed some light on the extraordinary relationship that sometimes developed between prisoners and warders. "There were two wardresses, Kara Botha and Maryna Harmse. They were supposed to be the meanest of the meanies, but even they flinched when they unlocked my cell in the morning. I could walk around where I wanted to. One day, when I was walking around in the courtyard taking my exercise, I saw Maryna talking to her boyfriend at the gate. She was in tears. When she unlocked my cell door that afternoon, her eyes were red from crying." I asked her, "Why are you crying? 'None of your business', she replied, 'leave me alone!' I told her that I would not leave the cell before she told me. 'I heard your friend say that he was on his way to Katima Mulilo, and that you would not see him for a long time. Against whom will he be fighting there? You see, we are in the same boat. He is going to die on the border – and it will be my brothers and sisters who are going to kill him. Maryna, why do you allow it?' She began crying and opened her heart to me. We began talking ... "

1 AUGUST 1997: HELENA'S LETTER

Helena sent her letter to Chris Louw, the producer of *Radio Sonder Grense*, an Afrikaans radio station. In this long document the farmer's wife from Mpumalanga made one pause at yet another station of the cross along the *via dolorosa* of our country, affording us a glimpse into the life of one of the perpetrators' wives. She aroused pity for the suffering endured not only by the victims but also the perpetrators, and how they themselves had been affected. Angie Kapelianis shortened the letter and prepared it for broadcasting on *Monitor*, an early-morning talkshow. The SABC also broadcast Helena's letter in English.

My story begins in my late teenage years as a farm girl in the Bethlehem district of the Free State.

As an 18-year-old, I met a young man working in a top security structure. It was the beginning of a beautiful relationship. We even spoke about marriage. A bubbly, vivacious man who radiated wild energy. Sharply intelligent. Although he was an Englishman, he was popular with all the Boere Afrikaners. And all my girl friends envied me.

Then one day he said he was going on a "trip". We wouldn't see each other again ... maybe never again. I was torn to pieces. So was he.

An extremely short marriage to someone else failed, all because I married to forget.

More than a year ago, I met my first love again through a good friend. I was to learn for the time that he had been operating overseas and that he was going to ask for amnesty.

I can't explain the pain and bitterness in me when I saw what was left of that beautiful, big, strong person. He had only one desire – that the truth must come out. Amnesty didn't matter. It was only a means to the truth. A need to clean up. In the meantime he has been torn out of our lives in the most gruesome manner possible. Was that the price he had to pay for his dreams?

After my unsuccessful marriage, I met another policeman. Not quite my first love, but an exceptional person. Very special. Once again a bubbly, charming personality. Humorous and grumpy in turn.

Then he says he and three of our friends have been promoted. "We're moving to a special unit. Now, now my darling. We are real policemen now." We were ecstatic. We even celebrated.

He and his friends would visit regularly. They even stayed over for long periods. Suddenly, at strange times, they would become restless. Abruptly mutter the feared word "trip" and drive off.

I ... as a loved one ... knew no other life than that of worry, sleeplessness, anxiety about his safety and where they could be. We simply had to be satisfied with "what you don't know can't hurt you". And all that we as loved ones knew ... was what we saw with our own eyes.

After about three years with the Special Forces, our hell began. He became very quiet. Withdrawn. Sometimes he would just drop his face into his hands and shake uncontrollably. I realized he was drinking too much. Instead of resting at night, he would wander from window to window. He tried to hide his wild, consuming fear, but I saw it. In the early hours of the morning between two and half-past-two I would be jolted from my sleep by his laboured breathing. Tossing and turning in bed. Pale. Ice cold in a sweltering night – sopping wet with sweat. Eyes bewildered, but dull like that of the dead. And the shakes. The terrible convulsions and blood-curdling shrieks of fear and pain from the bottom of his soul. Sometimes he sat motionless, just staring out in front of him.

I never understood. I never knew. Never realized what was being shoved down his throat during 'the trips'. I just went through hell. Praying, pleading. "God, what is happening? What is wrong with him? Could he have changed so much? Is he going mad? I can't handle the man anymore! But I can't get out. He's going to haunt me for the rest of my life if I leave him. Why, God?"

Today I know the answers to all my questions and heartache. I know where everything began. The role of 'those at the top', the 'cliques' and 'our men' who simply had to carry out their bloody orders ... like 'vultures'. And today they all wash their hands of us or revolt against what is being revealed at the Truth Commission.

Yes, I am standing by my 'MURDERER' who allowed me and the old WHITE South Africa to sleep peacefully. Warmly, while 'those at the top' were again targetting the next 'PERMANENT REMOVAL FROM SOCIETY' for the vultures.

I finally understand what the struggle was all about. I would have done the same had I been denied everything. If my life, that of my children and my parents were strangled with legislation. If I had to watch how white people became dissatisfied with the best and still wanted better and got it. I envy and respect the people of the struggle. At least their leaders have the guts to stand by their vultures, to recognize their sacrifices. What do we have? Our leaders are too holy and innocent. And faceless.

I can understand if Mr F W de Klerk says he didn't know, but dammit, there must be a CLIQUE, there must be someone out there who is still alive and who can give a face to 'the orders from above' for all the operations.

What else can this abnormal life that I live be other than a cruel human rights violation? Spiritual murder is more inhumane than a messy, physical murder. At least a murder victim rests.

I wish I had the power to make these poor, wasted people whole again.
I wish I could wipe the old South Africa out of everyone's past.
I end with a few lines my broken, wasted 'vulture' said to me one night:

"THEY CAN GIVE ME AMNESTY A THOUSAND TIMES. EVEN IF GOD AND EVERYONE ELSE FORGIVE ME A THOUSAND TIMES – I HAVE TO LIVE WITH THIS HELL. THE PROBLEM IS IN MY HEAD, MY CONSCIENCE. THERE'S ONLY ONE WAY TO BE FREE OF IT. BLOW MY OWN BRAINS OUT. BECAUSE THAT'S WHERE MY HELL IS."

Helena
P.S. Thank you for your time ... for listening .. for sharing my pain.

1 AUGUST 1997 (CONTINUED): THREE NEWSPAPER REPORTS

Once again the morning paper was filled with news of the Truth Commission. Reflecting the various facets of the TRC's work, *Beeld* reported, among other things, that –

◆ *... two members of the Boere Weerstandsbeweging (BWB) (*Boere Resistance Movement*) had received amnesty.*
Leon Hendrik Froneman (23) and Pieter Johannes Harmse were members of the far-right organization when they set a bomb at a shopping centre frequented by Indians in Bronkhorstspruit. Having received a warning, two policemen went to the centre to investigate. On their arrival the device exploded. Warrant-officer Abraham Labuschagne died instantly and Constable Hendrik Johannes Maree was seriously injured. Harmse was sentenced to eighteen years' imprisonment, Froneman to eight. Froneman explained under cross-examination that he had chosen this target because he believed that "most Indians were Muslims who supported the ANC". He wanted to demonstrate to the government of the day that the BWB were ready to take over South Africa by force. "Based on the evidence we heard and other information before us, we are satisfied that the applicants committed their actions in the belief that it was on the instruction of the BWB, a public organization, and that the act was intended to further the organization's objectives."

◆ *... the TRC had reproached the National Party that it had not been acting in good faith*
The dispute between the TRC and the NP simply did not want to die down. The NP made a semi-urgent application before court, requesting that the TRC be compelled to act impartially. "Why does the NP not, as required by law, lay its objections before Parliament?" was Alex Boraine's reaction. Why does the party not rather answer the questions still hanging in the air, that the TRC put to it? "It is clear that the NP ... expects a final report that will be prejudicial to its interests. This is why the party is already trying to question the potential findings ... The NP did not in this instance act in good faith."

That the NP had its knife into Boraine – the '*Boere* hater', their sworn opponent in the erstwhile Parliament – was obvious. Tutu had to apologize for his comment about FW de Klerk's actions before the TRC, but Boraine was clearly partisan, and had to be called to order. This upset him greatly! The fact that the NP was playing the TRC chairman off against the vice-chairman indicated *mala fides*. He and Tutu spoke as one! Nevertheless, Boraine stressed that neither he nor Tutu harboured any bad feelings towards the NP or any of its office-bearers. The TRC still lived in the hope that the two parties would be able to come to an agreement as far the court interdict was concerned.

Much water had to flow under the bridges before this would happen!

◆ *... three hundred and seventy clerics had signed Beyers Naudé's open letter.*
This was good news! The open letter that Beyers Naudé and his colleagues Cornél du Toit and Nico Smith had drawn up, in which they urgently called the churches to confession and reconciliation, had been traversing the country over the past two months. By 31 July 370 clerics, many of them from the NG Kerk, but also quite a few from other churches in South Africa, openly associated themselves with the letter.

Something was, after all, happening in South Africa – and in the church!

I ticked off the names with my pen: old university friends like Howard du Toit, Neels du Plooy, Joop Lensink, Faure Louw; colleagues and fellow professors, Bernard Combrinck, Jan van Arkel, Etienne de Villiers, Andrie du Toit, Jaap Furstenburg, Daniël Louw, Jaap Durand, Attie van Wijk, Willem Saayman, Klippies Kritzinger, Christina Landman, Hennie Pieterse, Johan Wolfaard, Len Hulley, Louise Kretschmar; the veterans, Professor Ben Marais and Dr D D Rosslee (the former apartheid theologian who stated, at the last synod, that the Lord had led him to arrive at a new insight), Joël Herhold; former students such as Herman Nienaber. Pontie Venter of the Gereformeerde (Reformed) Kerk. From the Anglican and Methodist Churches, the Presbyterians, from the ranks of the Roman Catholic Church, there was a long list of names: Bishops George Irvine, Hansie Mattheus and Peter Storey, Donald Cragg and Tim Atwell, Michael Moore and Terry Sparks, Bishop Denis Hurley and Father Bonaventure Hinwood. Pastor Ray McCauley signed the letter on behalf of the Rhema Church. Long before I had finished going through the list my heart was beating warmly.

4 AUGUST 1997: DIRK COETZEE AND THE MXENGE FAMILY

The Amnesty Commission today decided to grant amnesty to Dirk Coetzee, David Tshikalange and Butana Almons Nofomela for the murder of the Natal advocate, Griffiths Mxenge. The committee expressed blistering criticism of the police chiefs who had planned the assassination, but declared that there was no reason to suspect that the three offenders had any personal reasons for murdering Mxenge. They had done so while carrying out an order received from their commanders. It was clear that they trusted their commanders' judgement in this regard.

The three men, whose case had already been heard in a criminal trial before the court in Durban – and who had been found guilty but not yet sentenced – had every reason to heave a sigh of relief. As far as this charge was concerned, they could go free. The threesome however had further offences on their slate for which they applied for amnesty. And that still had to be decided on.

◆ ◆ ◆

Almost a year before, when Dirk Coetzee was summoned to appear before the Amnesty Committee the first time, I walked towards him standing alone against a wall. Would it be in order to have a brief pastoral discussion with him, I wondered.

"Good morning, *Dominee*", was his friendly greeting. "Do you remember that I used to live in your parish, in Lynnwood Ridge? ... But no, I don't need the church to assist me. To tell the truth, I have lost my trust in church folks. I allowed myself to be led, for years, by people who were, in my opinion, committed Christians. I trusted their advice – and look at me now ... "

◆ ◆ ◆

The Mxenge family was highly upset about the amnesty that had been granted. They felt that justice had not been done. They announced that they were considering appealing to the International Court in The Hague, with a request that the decision be set aside.

12 AUGUST 1997 AND THE FOLLOWING DAYS: "WALUS, IT WASN'T RIGHT WHAT YOU DID."

Limpho Hani sat listening, her face in her hands. Seated next to her was her daughter, tears running down her cheeks.

On that Saturday morning, 10 April 1993, he had wanted to do three things, Janusz Walus said. He wanted to go and exercise in the gymnasium in Johannesburg, he wanted to have a look at Chris Hani's house in Boksburg one last time and, by evening, he wanted to commit the assassination.

The sports centre was closed. On his way to Hani's house he stopped at a gun shop and bought 25 bullets for the Z88 pistol that Derby-Lewis had given him. He loaded the bullets into the pistol and put on his gloves. Near Chris Hani's home he saw a man who looked like Hani come out of the house and get into his car. Walus followed Hani to the shopping centre and watched him getting out of the car. After a few minutes he returned with a newspaper in his hand.

"At that moment I decided that it would perhaps now be the best opportunity, an opportunity that would not present itself again."

At the shopping centre, Walus explained, there had been too many people. Murdering him there would put other people at risk. When he was certain that Chris Hani was on his way home, he drove along another route to the same address. He was there first and sat waiting in his car. Hani stopped and got out of his car. Walus took his revolver, stuck it into his belt and walked towards him.

"I did not want to shoot him in the back. I called, 'Mr Hani!' When Mr Hani turned around I took the pistol out of my belt and fired the first shot into his body. Hani turned around and fell. I then took a second shot at his head. He fell to the ground, and I shot him twice behind the ears."

Once Walus was certain that he had killed the leader of the South African Communist Party he got into his car and drove off.

◆ ◆ ◆

Clive Derby-Lewis, the co-accused, and his wife were drinking tea in their friends, the Venters' garden, when the telephone rang. It was the Venters' son with the news – it had just been reported on the radio:

Chris Hani had been shot and killed in front of his home. For Derby-Lewis, who had not realized then that it had been Walus who had committed the murder, the news came, according to his own evidence, as a great shock.

"I thought something had happened that had saved us. It was no longer necessary for us to do what we were planning to do."

Clive and his wife finished drinking their tea. They got up and went shopping. Although it is true, Clive said, that he and Walus had been planning to kill Hani, he had not planned the assassination to take place over the Easter weekend. "Most people were then at home and in their gardens and I wanted to prevent a dangerous situation in which innocent people could die."

Prior to these events Walus had often spoken to Clive about his experiences in Poland, about the hardships endured by the Poles under the Communist regime. For Walus, who had made for South Africa to escape the Communists, South Africa's "surrender" to the Communists was traumatic. He resolved to made a contribution towards the liberation struggle. Chris Hani, the two men decided, was the real threat to South Africa and the future. After the 1994 election, many right-wing people believed, Hani would "get rid of Mr Mandela" and have himself declared president. That is why they had decided to deal with Hani.

Derby-Lewis made the audience sit up straight when he referred to the list his wife had drawn up "for journalistic purposes", and which contained the names of ten prominent South Africans. He had found Hani's name and address on this list. He had to make out for himself whether his own Christian principles could justify the "war he had been forced to participate in", he said. He had discussed the matter with Dr Andries Treurnicht, the leader of the Conservative Party. The impression he had gained during the conversation was that murder, committed to slay the antichrist, was in certain circumstances permissible.

Clive Derby-Lewis learnt that night that it had, in fact, been Walus who had murdered Hani. He was distraught. "I had terrible thoughts that night. I really felt bad about it." He resolved to request a special meeting of the CP caucus to discuss the events. However, before he could do so, he was arrested.

◆ ◆ ◆

During the amnesty hearing in the Pretoria City Hall, which lasted for more than a week, Janusz Walus declared that he was remorseful about the grief he had caused Mrs Hani and her children. He could not expect the Hani family to forgive him, but hoped that they would understand his position.

"I wanted them to understand that there had never been anything personal in the attempt on Hani's life. Instead, the decision to do so was an indication of his status and how important he was." Eliminating Hani would "realize our objectives – namely to plunge the country into chaos and create a situation in which the rightwing could take over."

Derby-Lewis concurred. He, too, had remorse about the sorrow inflicted on the Hani family. But he also felt bad about the pain he and Walus had inflicted on their own families. "They also suffered. I hope that they understand that we acted the way we did because we had, in our view, a deep obligation towards South Africa."

The Sowetan's comment on the long-drawn-out testimonies heard by the Amnesty Commission

◆ ◆ ◆

There was enough political drama. ANC politicians moved in and out of the hall all week long. Tokyo Sexwale, Jay Naidoo, Winnie Mandela, Sam Shilowa of Cosatu, Jeremy Cronin of the SACP, Cheryl Carolus, all put in an appearance – their supporters at their heels. Impromptu speeches were made. Before the proceedings began the first day, Ferdie Hartzenberg, the leader of the Conservative Party, called together his people: "We'll again be a free nation. We'll have our own country and our own flag will fly over it."

Outside the city hall young people were brandishing posters. Emotion counted for more than spelling: *Jaluz You Are A Looser* read one poster. *Derby Lewis – Julus Waluz You Deserve NO Amnesty*, a second. When the hearing finally adjourned, the chant of the ANC/Cosatu/Communist Party supporters reverberated far outside the doors of the hall: "Walus, it wasn't right what you did ... "

14 AUGUST 1997: A JAPANESE PERSPECTIVE

In London *The Times* (14 August 1997) carried the following report:

A group of Imperial Army Veterans has publicly confessed to wartime atrocities in the hope of counterbalancing moves to sanitize modern Japanese history for the nation's classrooms. As Japan marks the 52nd anniversary of the end of the Pacific War, former soldiers have broken their silence and described their own role in murder, rape and cannibalism in occupied China. "We want to share our raw experiences with young people before we die", said Tsuyoshi Ebato, 84, who heads the Association of Returnees from China, a veterans' group. "There are things that children will not find in government-censored textbooks." The confessions appear in What did Japan do in China?, *a magazine that Mr Ebato's group hopes to publish regularly as a forum for old soldiers troubled by guilt.*

In the first edition, Mr Ebato reveals how soldiers like himself killed civilians using bayonets, how they beat town-dwellers with clubs to get them to reveal the Chinese army's position, and how he personally shot and killed seven elderly people. Women were raped and murdered; because food supplies were short, he made a meal of their flesh. "Terrible things like this happened on a daily basis in our division," says Mr Ebato. "We can no longer remain silent because some historians are now saying that such atrocities never happened." The statements of the five hundred ex-soldiers who spent up to six years in Chinese captivity incensed many in Japan. Other veterans joined up with Japanese nationalists to discredit Mr Ebato and his group, denouncing them as 'masochists'. They are campaigning to purge school textbooks of references to military abuses committed by the Imperial Army.

For years the Education Ministry has ensured that schoolbooks omit or play down shameful events like the building of the Burma Railway at the cost of 16 000 Allied lives. But this year, for the first time, Japanese schoolchildren are being told about the fact that

200 000 women had been forced into prostitution by the Japanese military. This has brought angry protests from a coalition of scholars, business leaders and politicians demanding ... that Japanese children should be taught 'history the Japanese can be proud of'.

Mr Ebato says that as long as Japan tries to cover up its wartime misdeeds it can never enjoy the trust of neighbouring countries. "The Japanese way is to 'keep the lid on the stinking pot'", he said. "But with this magazine we want to lift the lid and reflect on our crimes."

15 AUGUST 1997: HIGH UP IN THE SWISS ALPS

"Caux is actually too good to be true. It does not seem to be part of our ordinary world with all its cares and sorrows", one of the persons sharing our table remarked late one afternoon when we sat down for supper around the table. She was so right. The view through the dining room windows of the *Mountain House* at Caux, high up in the Swiss Alps, was breathtaking. Below us in the valley, on the banks of Lake Geneva, lay the famous conference town Montreaux – and also Clarens, where President Kruger spent the last years of his life. To get to Caux you have to drive by car for half an hour against the mountain slopes, taking one hairpin bend after the other – or you have to load your suitcases on a rack-railway that will bear you through woods up the steep slopes, past fields of flowers and cows sporting alpine bells around the neck. *Mountain House*, the headquarters of the Moral Rearmament movement, seemed to be a fairytale castle, with its turrets and balconies, its elegant conference rooms, its beautiful gardens. And the vista over the lake and mountains, the deep valleys with their picturesque towns, the view that changes every day, every time the suns shines from another angle.

For more than fifty years people from all over the world have come to Caux to reload their spiritual batteries, to talk about the world and its problems, about what people can do to make justice and peace, reconciliation and compassion realities on earth. This year's Caux Lecture, which had to be one of the highlights of a three-month programme in which politicians, academics, journalists, community leaders, theologians, men and women as well as a large contingent of young people from many countries participated, would deal with the subject "Healing the Past, Forging the Future". The obvious choice of the person to present the paper was Desmond Tutu, chairman of the South African Truth and Reconciliation Commission. But the archbishop, who was still undergoing medical treatment, was unable to accept the invitation. A second invitation arrived from Switzerland: would I be prepared to present the lecture? From New York Tutu ordered me: tell them, yes, you're coming!

The hall was packed on the afternoon of my address. Outside guests, politicians from Geneva, and members of the diplomatic corps had driven up to Caux specially for the occasion. The Truth Commission was still world news, and everyone wanted to know what was going on in South Africa. Even more than gaining information on the work of the TRC, people were fascinated by the anecdotes of victims and perpetrators, the personal stories of what had been happening in our country. To conclude my narrative I played a recording in English of a part of Helena's letter, as told by Angie Kapelianis for the SABC. You could hear a pin drop.

There was a constant buzz of conversation that evening at table. Inza and I were seated next to Dame Te Atairangikaahu, the Maori queen, flanked by Joan Bolger, the New Zealand prime minister's wife. "It's not only in South Africa that past injustices have to be righted", the Maori queen explained. "In our country, too, we have had to deal with these things. In 1840 the Maoris entered into a solemn pledge with the British colonial government, in terms of which they would subject themselves to the British crown, on condition that their people, their country and their income would be protected by the British. This did not happen. The Maoris lost virtually everything that was theirs. Two years ago, in 1995, the Maoris decided to institute a claim against the government to reclaim the land that had been misappropriated generations ago. The claim was settled – and the people of Tanui could, after all these years, again call the land of their forefathers their own. This rekindled the hope that, at last, there will be peace and justice in our beautiful country Aotearoa, New Zealand."

"For the people of Tanui it was not easy to stand up for their rights after all these years", Joan Bolger added. "It demanded a great deal of courage." Just as the handful of politicians who associated themselves with their claim needed to demonstrate a measure of courage. But they persevered. Doug Graham, the minister charged with the negotiations, put it succinctly: "It's not that we want to castigate ourselves with guilt feelings all the time. We just want to fix what is wrong."

One person after another at the table began sharing his or her experiences. Rabbi Jeremy Milgrom told us how he and a group of Jewish colleagues had befriended some Palestinians, how they tried to stick together and support one another, despite everything happening in their country. Professor Durdican Fuca of Zagreb told us about Croatians,

Bosnians and Serbians, Christians, Muslims and Jews, who were trying to build bridges to one another. The emir of Kano, Nigeria, Dr Ado Bayero, had a few things to say about the efforts that had been made in West Africa to bring together English-speaking and French-speaking groups, Muslims and Christians. "In the holy Koran", the emir said emphatically, "Allah said, 'I made people different, so that they can come to understand one another'. It is our solemn duty to give effect to this command." Pierre Spoerri, the Moral Rearmament host at the table, told us, later on, when the coffee was already being served, how shocked the Swiss were by the past months' press reports concerning Swiss banks that had been hoarding the possessions of Jewish refugees that they had been entrusted with during the Nazi years. "This unleashed all kinds of emotions among people. We Swiss, too, had to learn how to reach out to the people hurt by our arrogance and blindness. We had to learn, like you in South Africa, to exorcize the ghosts of our own past."

That night at table the world opened up around us. Not only the breathtaking panorama of the setting sun over the Alpine peaks, of the shadows creeping over the valleys and the lake, of towns where a thousand lights began to shine, but that of a wider vista embracing six continents covered in darkness, where billions of people were trying to light the lamp of reconciliation in dark valleys of despair and hope. "You may not fail", one of our table companions, a jurist from Northern Ireland, concluded the conversation, "if the Truth and Reconciliation Commission in South Africa succeeds, this will inspire all of us and encourage us. Go and tell your people: you *must* simply succeed!"

Later that evening, from the balcony, Inza and I could see the sparkling lights of Clarens, in which stands the Villa Kruger. How would the old president have judged our country and our people today? What advice would he have had to give? Take everything out of past that is good and build your future on that – and use the pain and sadness and shame of the past to teach your children the lessons that *you* had to learn?

22 AUGUST 1997: DAWIE DE VILLIERS'S LAST SPEECH IN PARLIAMENT

The journey inwards, the journey to try and understand what went wrong in the past and what share all of us had in it, was not easy. While Inza and I used the opportunity to holiday for a week in the Alps – an unforgettable, rejuvenating few days – Dawie de Villiers, former Spring-bok captain and National Party Cabinet Minister for many years, made his last speech before Parliament in Cape Town. In a few days' time the former minister was due to depart for Madrid, where he was to assume office as Deputy Secretary-General of the World Tourism Organization.

"I cannot distance myself from the fact that the policy of race discrimination and minority government contributed to a climate that created the breeding-ground for the seed of evil to grow." It deeply saddened him that his support of the policy of the old NP made him part of a political structure that had many hidden, dark sides to it. He could only condemn these terrifying deeds in the strongest possible terms. Although he had never, in his political career, been part of – or had any knowledge of – decisions taken in this regard, and had been enormously upset, like many of supporters of the NP had been when he heard of the inhuman behaviour and atrocities perpetrated by persons in the service of the government, he said that he "accepted responsibility" for it. Whatever the good intentions of the past, the fact was that we created a climate for people with distorted ideas to take the law into their own hands.

"South Africa's future may never again provide for race prejudices and an authoritarian government", Dawie de Villiers stressed. "Democracy must be built on transparency and accountability. We must build a sound, strong multiparty democracy." The more he paged through the past, the former minister told his colleagues in the benches, the clearer he understood that apartheid simply could not be reformed. It had to be destroyed completely. That is what the transition to a democratic South Africa had managed to achieve: the destruction of apartheid and the introduction of a democratic foundation for a new, powerful and successful nation.

Over the next weeks a number of Cabinet colleagues would add their voices to that of Dawie de Villiers' confession. More about that, later on.

5 SEPTEMBER 1997: TUTU APOLOGIZES

On the eve of the day on which the case between the National Party and the TRC was due to be heard in Cape Town before the Judge President, Mr Justice Gerald Friedman, Archbishop Tutu, who was still receiving treatment for cancer in the USA, in a dramatic statement tendered his apologies to the NP. According to the statement Tutu said that he did not want to have anything that he had said at the regrettable press conference of 15 May this year stand in the way of unity and reconciliation in our country. "What I said, I said from my heart because I and also the vice-chairman of the TRC, Dr Alex Boraine, believe passionately in reconciliation. I did not want to give offence or create mistrust. I am sorry that the NP feels that it had been treated unfairly by my words."

Boraine associated himself with this statement and pointed out that the TRC had not yet made any findings about the role played by the NP in the past. The NP was on the point of choosing a new leader in the place of Mr FW de Klerk, who had recently resigned. Boraine expressed the hope that when a new leader was appointed, the NP would reconsider its position on the TRC.

Judge President Friedman adjourned the proceedings early that morning and asked the two parties to try and come to an agreement in the course of the day. "Should this case be carried to a finding", was his opinion, "one of the parties will technically be appointed the winner and the other the loser. However, I believe that both will lose. Even worse, the country will be the greatest loser."

Shortly after noon the court resumed, without a settlement having been reached. Advocate G Burger declared on behalf of the NP that they accepted Tutu and Boraine's apology, that they welcomed it, but that the NP nevertheless had no other option but to proceed with the case. "The TRC statement, unfortunately, does not affect the real issues raised, namely the scope and the nature of the work of the TRC as well as the actions of Boraine that necessitated the court proceedings. The serious dispute that exists between the two parties in this regard has not yet been resolved. Unless consensus is reached about an acceptable *modus operandi* for the TRC, these same kinds of difficulties can arise in future and this will inevitably cast a shadow over the TRC's work."

Burger's request that the case be indefinitely postponed so that further discussions can be held with Tutu, who was expected to return in the near future, was granted by a disappointed Judge Friedman. Most people in South Africa shared the judge's feelings.

8 SEPTEMBER 1997: "I CAN'T SEE HOW F W DE KLERK CAN DENY IT ... "

The former security policeman Gideon Nieuwoudt gave evidence during his amnesty application in Port Elizabeth about the work of the now defunct State Security Council (SSC). "I can't see how he (De Klerk) can deny it", Nieuwoudt said with reference to Mr de Klerk's statement before the TRC that he had never, in his years in power, been part of a decision by either the cabinet, the SSC or any other committee ordering the commission of gross human rights violations. An SSC document dated 10 April 1986 contained an express request that stricter security measures be introduced. In an annexure to the document one of the tasks required to restore law and order in South Africa was thus described: "Neutralize/eliminate hostile leaders." The document clearly states that South Africa would "lose the battle for the hearts and minds of the people, and thus seal its own downfall unless the security situation was stabilized immediately, the revolutionaries isolated from the rest of the population to permit the alleviation of socioeconomic problems and clear political guidelines for future political development were presented to the population." However this could not happen without strengthening South Africa's security legislation.

Nieuwoudt explained to the court that he and his buddies believed they had the right, because of the state of emergency in which the country found itself, to assault a person. Should a case ever be made against them, they would be protected. "At that stage, in a state of emergency, we acted above the law ... We believed the Security Police were above the law."

At the same hearing Captain J C Putter explained the implementation of Stratcom (the strategic communication plan) of the former government to the Amnesty Committee. He gave valuable insight into the way sensitive information was dealt with and perceptions created among the country's population. All Stratcom operations, he emphasized, had to be approved by the Minister of Law and Order. Some of the Stratcom operations carried out before 1978 included Operation Playboy, which involved the bribing of the then prime minister of the Seychelles, both to ensure landing rights for South African aircraft, and to make him pass on certain information as to what the Organization for African Unity was planning against South Africa. Following the Information Scandal of 1978 these kinds of operations were stopped. In October 1986 a group of high-ranking persons met to discuss the security position in South Africa. At this meeting it was decided to use Stratcom as yet another instrument to counteract the revolutionary assault on South Africa. "Various departments, including the police, were tasked by the State President to carry out Stratcom."

9 SEPTEMBER 1997: TUTU ON HIS WAY HOME

Just before his return home the chairman of the TRC received the highest tribute of the American National Peace Foundation – a crystal dove – for his "exemplary life, his contribution to social justice, democracy and peace in South Africa, including his share in the work of the TRC."

"I accept the prize on behalf of the people at home who have been nameless for so long, but who were finally responsible for making a miracle happen", was Tutu's reaction.

At his last press conference prior to his and Leah's departure for home, Tutu said that he was feeling well and energetic, even though it was too soon to say whether he had been completely cured. When asked about his apology to De Klerk and the NP – that many black South Africans and an assortment of non-government organizations had taken amiss – Tutu smiled: "Sometimes one must be prepared to lose a battle if you want to win the war. We are prepared to do everything within reasonable limits – sometimes even beyond reasonable limits – to involve everybody in the process, getting at the whole truth, so that a traumatized country can be healed. We are not interested in prosecutions but in the truth. People want to *know*. If they know what happened, they are prepared to forgive."

Two particularly thorny issues that awaited him and the TRC were the amnesty application of the five policemen who requested amnesty for the death of Steve Biko, and the hearing of Winnie Madikizela-Mandela. About these two matters Tutu did not want to say much. "We'll handle it", was all that journalists were able to get out of him.

10 SEPTEMBER 1997: FOUR FILES ON MY DESK

In between all the great events, the Reparation and Rehabilitation Committee began to process the thousands of submissions submitted by victims throughout South Africa. A fixed pattern was followed. The Human Rights Violations Committee handed over all the evidence received from all over the country – the victims who gave evidence in public as well as those whose written submissions sufficed – to the TRC's Investigating Unit. The unit, which had teams of investigators in all four regional offices – Cape Town, Johannesburg, Durban and East London, then checked the statements. Corroborative evidence had to be gathered, from police reports, hospital reports, newspaper reports, television recordings, statements made before the TRC – any reliable source on which they could lay their hands.

As soon as enough corroborative evidence had been found on a particular matter, the Investigating Unit entered the necessary information on the file and passed it on to the Reparation and Rehabilitation Committee, which in turn had to determine the victims' direct needs; this included the requests they had made to the TRC, as well as any medical, psychological, financial and other problems they had to contend with. We had already completed the proposals for reparation that we wished to submit to the government, but the list of recipients now had to be compiled. For days on end the Reparation and Rehabilitation Committee members sat working through heaps of files. It was as though all the pain and heartache, all the past anguish were marching past once again.

On 10 September (according to my notes) I sat with a pile of forms before me on the desk. Of the first four, three were old, well-known cases, the fourth wholly unknown. One was as shocking as the other.

◆ Seipati Mlangeni, who recounted the death of Bheki Godfrey Mlangeni: on 15 February 1991 her husband was blown to smithereens when a bomb concealed in the earphones of a cassette player exploded.
◆ The mother of Hector Sithole Petersen: the first victim of the Soweto uprising in 1976: The photograph of her dying son in the arms of a weeping comrade appeared in virtually every newspaper in the world.
◆ The woman from Soweto who came to tell us how her son Lolo Sono had been murdered by the Mandela United Football Club.
◆ The parents of an unknown girl, killed in a street in Soweto in 1976. Why? She was wearing a T-shirt bearing the words Nkosi Sikelel' iAfrika, the policeman explained.

10-12 SEPTEMBER 1997: THE BIKO STOPOVER

It was inevitable that, on its journey inward, the TRC trek would eventually make a stopover at Steve Biko's death. Twenty years ago Minister Jimmy Kruger was still able to remark, "the death of Steve Biko leaves me cold". In 1997 this was no longer possible. Millions of South Africans regarded Biko not simply as a flagrant example of what had happened to many victims. He was more: a symbol of the injustice and the suffering of the past that had been inflicted on the entire country. For other South Africans, those who had in the past found themselves on the side of the apartheid regime, the Biko case was a persistent indictment, a shadow that kept hanging over the road to the future.

What exactly had happened to Biko, the charismatic black consciousness leader? Evidence had already been led about the role of the doctors who had to treat him during the medical hearing. But what exactly had transpired in the police cells when Biko was arrested?

On 10 September the amnesty hearing of five former security policemen began in Port Elizabeth.

Brigadier Daantjie Siebert, the then deputy commander of Biko's interrogation team, admitted before the Amnesty Committee that they had often in the past blatantly ignored police regulations concerning the detention of prisoners. Torture was an accepted method to gather information. Colonel Piet Goosen, their commander, warned them that Biko was a "difficult customer". When Biko "plonked down on a chair without being asked to do so" once the interrogation had begun, he tended to agree with him.

"I told him to get up. This is our office and we'll tell him when to sit down. The general principle was that we were in control of the interrogation and that we had to have the upper hand."

Siebert and the other officers questioned Biko about the fact that he broke his restriction order, among other things, by undertaking a trip to Cape Town. When Biko alleged that he had undertaken the journey as a result of marital problems, Siebert was dissatisfied. He knew that Biko had actually intended talking to Neville Alexander of the Non-European Unity Movement. Siebert showed a statement that he had obtained previously from Peter Jones who had been arrested along with Biko, confirming this information.

"I could see that Biko knew that I was on to something. I could see in his eyes that he was getting upset ... When Biko again sat down in a chair I became angry and picked him up by his shirt, by his clothes."

Biko then got up again and knocked the chair to Siebert's side, so that he had to use his hand to prevent the chair falling against him. According to Siebert, Biko directed a blow at him; Warrant-officer Jacobus Beneke, who was standing at the door, stormed up to Biko, hitting him in the stomach with his shoulder. They began wrestling; Gideon Nieuwoudt, too, became involved in the fray.

"I was aware of the fact that Detective Sergeant Nieuwoudt on various occasions hit Biko with a hosepipe over the back. All of us then grabbed Biko and we ran with him towards the corner of the room. His head smashed into the wall. He then collapsed and landed on the floor."

Biko, who was "in a state of unconsciousness", his eyes "confused", was led back to his cell where he lay with his back to the wall. Later he was shackled to the gate of the steel door "to break his resistance, when he was unwilling to co-operate". Shortly afterwards Biko was transferred to the Noordeinde Prison.

Colonel Harold Snyman, one of the five, told the amnesty court that he had informed Colonel Goosen what had happened in the office. That was where the cover-up began. On the instructions of Goosen he wrote down, on 8 September, a blatant misrepresentation of the facts in the occurrence book. He stated that Biko had been injured on 7 September, at seven o'clock in the morning – instead of on 6 September, at nine o'clock the morning. This was done because the district surgeon, Dr Ivor Lang, had only been called in on 7 September to examine Biko.

Four days later Biko was loaded into the back of a Landrover. He had to be taken to Pretoria for medical treatment. It was impossible to arrange for an aeroplane flight, they would simply take the road. When they stopped outside Port Elizabeth, at Blouwaterbaai (Blue Water Bay) for a quick bite, Daantjie Siebert noticed that Biko was lying only in his underpants. One of the other policemen explained that Biko was "clumsy and stiff" and that it would be difficult to dress him. They decided to leave him like that.

"I ... did not attempt to dress him and I accept that this was inhumane, but there were a few cell mats and blankets and a cushion. He wasn't naked in public," said Siebert.

The journey, which had begun at about six o'clock the evening, lasted right through the night. They arrived in Pretoria at nine o'clock the next morning. Biko had to be carried in on a stretcher. "Colonel Goosen told me that I should bring it to the people's notice that Biko had feigned illness before and that he practised the art of yoga." Siebert however, asked that Biko should get good medical attention because he was "an important person".

Biko died on 12 September. Goosen called in all the policemen involved in Biko's case. Biko's death was a great embarrassment to the security branch and the government, he said. It could also have a negative effect on South Africa's image abroad. Foreign investments could be affected. An order was given that statements be made that would "adapt and suppress" the facts.

◆ ◆ ◆

Mrs Ntsiki Biko attended the hearing. She was still not certain whether the information that was now being revealed was correct. Was the cover-up not simply continuing, she wondered.

In Parliament a motion recognizing the contribution made by the black consciousness leader in the struggle against apartheid was unanimously accepted. Mr Jaco Maree of the National Party said his party supported the motion: "When these events took place we were all shocked and wondered what the true facts were. We are happy that they are now being revealed, bit by bit ... Biko's death should never have happened. The NP is not simply in favour of the motion, but is emotionally part of it." Mr Douglas Gibson of the DP and Dr Stanley Mogoba of the PAC shared these feelings.

On 12 September, exactly twenty years after the lonely death of Steve Biko in a Pretoria cell, President Nelson Mandela unveiled a bronze statue of the black consciousness leader in East London. More than ten thousand people streamed to the square in front of the city hall to be present at this event. Mandela paid tribute to Biko and asked that his example and the things he stood for be remembered by all South Africans, and that they would continue to inspire them.

The police had their hands full with the crowd which threatened to get out of hand. "Biko, Biko, Biko!" the thousands chanted in unison.

One thing is certain: the bronze statue in the heart of East London will continue to remind future generations of the Biko stopover.

15-17 SEPTEMBER 1997: WHEN THE JOURNALISTS REPORTED ON THEMSELVES ...

For the first time after his return from New York, Desmond Tutu would again assume the chair. The fact that the SABC had invited the Truth Commission to conduct the hearing on the role played by the media during the apartheid years in a large television studio in Johannesburg, afforded me some quiet amusement as I negotiated all the television cables lying on the floor. Not only would the SABC have the opportunity to report directly from "the horse's mouth" about everything being said, it would *itself,* on the very first day, come under the spotlight.

On its journey inward – in its search to find to answers to all the *whys* of the past – South African media workers needed to reflect on their own role. To what extent did the media provide the climate within which the injustices of the past could flourish? To what extent were the radio and television, the various newspapers, the press magnates guilty of distorting the facts? Had there even perhaps been human rights violations in the industry? What had happened to the journalists and newspapers that consistently wished to put across the other side of the coin?

Not everybody felt like – or saw the necessity for – spending time at this stop along the road. In the ranks of the Afrikaans press – especially the *Nasionale Pers* – a lively debate raged. Early in July Hennie van Deventer, group CEO of *Nasionale Koerante* (National Newspapers), wrote in a personal submission to the TRC that the Afrikaans press had not simply been the staunch supporters of the *status quo*, as was often alleged. On the contrary, *Die Volksblad* in Bloemfontein, of which he had been the editor for twelve years, had campaigned for change, often paying a high price for doing so. The newspapers could take a fair deal of the credit for the change of heart undergone by Afrikaners; in the Free State they had voted overwhelmingly "Yes" in the referendum of March 1992. He felt that Afrikaans newspapers and their editors who had been in the political trenches in those years, did not have any reason to be remorseful.

"The *Nasionale Pers* does not regard itself to be guilty of any violation of human rights or other offences and need not make a confession or record an apology", Ton Vosloo, the chief executive officer declared a few weeks later when approached by the TRC for a submission. The press did, however, have a commitment to making a contribution to the process of truth and reconciliation, he added, and that is why they wished to work in close co-operation with the Truth Commission. "If there is an expectation, however, that there were in fact such misdeeds, what use will it have for us to take a stand and then run the risk of our organization's good faith, credibility and integrity being attacked from public platforms, as in fact happened during the TRC's political hearings?"

In Johannesburg, Johan de Wet, the chief editor of *Beeld*, wrote that as his newspaper had quite often advised other bodies to testify before the TRC, this request could certainly also be made of *Beeld*. However, this was easier said than done. *Beeld* would not really be able to report about gross human rights violations in its own ranks. As far as he knew, this did not happen. Personally it would also be difficult for him to talk on behalf of the editors who preceded him. This was a pity, De Wet remarked, "because *Beeld* has an exciting tale to tell – which the new rulers do not generally know about. For example, Schalk Pienaar protested against 'petty apartheid' as far back as 1974; Vosloo had written in *Beeld* as long ago as 1981 that the NP would have to be prepared to enter into discussions with the ANC about a new political dispensation. What about Willem Wepener, who had called for the re-lease of Nelson Mandela in 1983? But *Beeld* would also have to say that it had at times committed errors of judgement; at times it had informed its readers only partially; and it had perhaps contributed to a climate in which human rights violations could have been perpetrated. Of course *Beeld* is terribly sorry about that today. In mitigation it can be said that *Beeld* acted in accordance with the information at its disposal and within the latitude afforded by a government which tried to curtail the press at every turn. We cannot condone omissions. This is in fact noted in our archives. Everything we did, and everything we failed to do."

Tutu was deeply disappointed that an official submission would not be forthcoming from Afrikaans newspapers, and stated this clearly in his opening speech: "Must the silence from those quarters be inter-preted as consent that they had been the servile instruments of the apartheid government? We shall never know unless they talk and give their side of the story." The Afrikaans media would not be able to blame the TRC if it felt that its final report was one-sided. "The Afrikaans media will lose this case by default. It will hamper our work because an important voice will not be heard. We are not partisan. We want to form a full picture. Before this is possible, we need the contributions of all role-players."

Tutu expressed the sincere hope that the Afrikaans media – in some way or another – would go to the trouble of putting their side of the case.

This was about to happen in only a few weeks' time when a hundred and twenty Afrikaans journalists, including senior reporters of *Nasionale Pers* newspapers, did make personal statements before the TRC. But more about that later on.

◆ ◆ ◆

The first to come under the spotlight was the SABC, in other words the old South African Broadcasting Corporation.

It was clear that the SABC had, during the apartheid years, contributed towards the violation of human rights, Johan Pretorius, the former editor of TV News said in his testimony. They had definitely contributed to keeping the policy of apartheid going. But the historical context within which this had happened, should be taken into consideration.

"I do not say that the SABC had not made mistakes ... failed its duty ... I do not try to blame others ... look for excuses ... I am prepared to assume full responsibility for my own decisions or those of my subordinates. However, it was never the deliberate intention to violate human rights."

The SABC had also had successes and helped to bring about changes in South Africa, Pretorius explained. SABC staff were often under enormous pressure from politicians from all parties – but above all from the NP. "Politicians in those days had a wholly naive, simplistic and one-dimensional view of broadcast journalism, particularly of TV journalism. I am sorry to say that some NP politicians were the greatest offenders. They completely confused publicity value with news value and the other way around, if this suited them. They were paranoid about what they considered to be 'exposure to subversive elements' and right-wing opponents. We had to manage both them and the news and often had to take two steps backwards, to be able to take two steps forwards the next day."

The SABC was also constrained by the provisions of the Broadcasting Act. The SABC Board, which had to determine the corporation's policy, was appointed by the State President; the minister responsible for broadcasting had to report to Parliament. Government had a direct hold on broadcasting. During the eighties, in particular, in the time of 'total onslaught', the draconian security legislation made matters very difficult indeed for journalists. There had even been talk of military control over the SABC journalists.

About the role of the Afrikaner Broederbond (AB) in this regard, two former Broederbond members differed sharply. Professor Sampie Terreblanche, who had been a member of the AB for years (1969 to 1989) and who had also served on the SABC Board, believed that the AB wielded great power. For many years Dr Piet Meyer was not only the chairman of the SABC Board, but also the chairman of the Executive Council of the AB. There had been in those years – even after the death of Meyer – a continued battle between the *verligte* (enlightened) and *verkrampte* (conservative) groups in the AB and the SABC Board. He and the other *verligtes*, said Terreblanche, "did not achieve much".

Louis Raubenheimer, who was still attached to the SABC – and who had been head of Actuality Programmes – saw matters differently. He had been a member of the AB from 1990 to 1995, but in his experience the influence of the AB on the SABC had been minimal in those years. Obviously his views had been influenced by the AB discussions he had attended from time to time, but they did not really leave an impression on the work he did every day.

It was not only the AB that had to be taken into account, Professor Terreblanche said on a lighter note. Sometimes it was Mrs Elize Botha, the wife of the State President, who made life difficult for them. At one point a television programme about wildlife in Russia was held on ice because Mrs Botha felt that showing *Durrell in Russia* would be dangerous for the people – part of the 'total onslaught'. When she watched a programme she did not like, she complained to PW, who in turn complained to Pik (Pik Botha, Minister of Foreign Affairs). The programme was then not broadcast. On another occasion she was opposed to a programme that had been announced but had, in fact, never been broadcast. PW, as was his wont, passed on the complaint to Pik. His reply was: "I thought you would not like it, and so I trashed (*opdonne*red) it in advance."

On a more serious note: the most upsetting evidence was led by Zakes Nene of the Media Workers Association (MWASA). Not only did Blacks wait in vain for promotion – during the years in which the various regional services that had to make provision for black listeners were introduced, all the top posts had been assigned to Whites; of 85 senior members of personnel, only six were black – but black workers were sometimes actually physically assaulted. Section 14 determined that any person could be dismissed without any reasons being given. Workers who differed ideologically from the NP lived in constant fear of losing their jobs. Black workers who were unpersuaded *(hardegat)* had a hard time, Nene said. Workers had to endure a talking-to if they dared look at white female colleagues. "People summoned in terms of section 14 had to choose between dismissal and being thrashed with a *sjambok*. Some of them preferred being thrashed with a *sjambok*, although there had not been any proper disciplinary hearing." A list with the names of employees who had been thrashed was handed in by MWASA.

◆ ◆ ◆

On the second day four state agents, John Horak, Craig Williamson, Vic McPherson and Craig Kotze appeared before the commission.

During the apartheid years the government aimed at influencing the top structures of the media organizations in South Africa as well as senior journalists, Williamson said. Journalists were popular targets for both the security forces and the liberation movements. They had access to information and could ask questions. At the time, the government manipulated the media as part of its effort to win the hearts and minds of people. The South African population had to be kept pro-government – or at least neutral. Media organizations had to be infiltrated to achieve this purpose. "We needed various people to play different roles. Some had to plant stories while others had to write them." People at all levels had to be reached, from the cleaners to the editors of the different newspapers.

Many of the 'journalist contacts' did not even realize that they were being used by the police to promote the state's views, Vic McPherson added. According to McPherson, who headed the police unit for covert strategic communication (Stratcom), he had about forty contacts, working for diverse groups such as the Republican Press, BBC News, Reuters, Sapa, the *Sunday Times, The Pretoria News, Beeld, Rapport, The Citizen, The Star, Insig, Huisgenoot and Rooi Rose* (the last three Afrikaans magazines). The forty included two policemen, four informants who were paid from time to time for the information provided, ten 'acquaintances' and twenty journalists who were used by the police without their knowledge.

Information about various Stratcom projects came to light during the hearing. In one case Stratcom falsified information to support the stories told by George da Costa who had crossed over to South Africa from the Mozambique information service. The false information served as the basis for five articles that appeared in *Scope* magazine. Another example was the information about Joe Slovo's involvement in Operation Vula, which was leaked by Stratcom, to the SACP's embarrassment. In 1989 McPherson made a submission about a secret media project to President de Klerk, who had "approved the project in principle". Secret funds of R4,5 million had been earmarked for the 1989-1990 financial year for this purpose. In the end only about half a million rand was used.

John Horak, former police agent who had worked as a journalist for various newspapers for twenty-seven years, said that his task mainly consisted of explaining to the police how press people saw the affairs of the day. In many cases the editors of the newspapers must have known about it. However, this was nothing new – and the practice had not yet stopped either. In his opinion there were more informants at the SABC and the newspapers at the moment than during the apartheid years. Craig Kotze, who was recruited as an agent by the police while working for *The Star*, claimed that the SA Police had now stopped doing this, "but there is no guarantee that political organizations, including foreign intelligence services were not (now) doing the same".

Horak's evidence in particular elicited a sharp response from some sections of the audience, as well as from certain of his journalist colleagues. In his bitter comment on John Horak's submission, the black poet and journalist, Don Mattera, said that if it had not been for the reconciliation that President Mandela had brought about in the country, he himself would have wanted to kill the police agent! Horak's smear campaigns, while working for the then *Rand Daily Mail*, had had terrible consequences for some of his colleagues. "This is the man, if he is a man, who chanced upon me when I was sitting weeping in the toilet about a piece of toilet paper containing the particulars of detainees being tortured which had come into my possession." Mattera was arrested shortly afterwards and assaulted by the police. "Where is the piece of toilet paper?" they wanted to know from him. Over the years 350 raids were conducted on his home and he himself was detained 150 times, Mattera said. The worst was not that Horak had been appointed, but that some of his bosses at the newspaper must have known about his connection with the police – and did nothing about it.

The third and last day belonged to the newspapers. The two English media giants Times Media Limited as well as the Independent Newspapers group (previously the Argus group), were able to present extensive reports about their past. Despite the mistakes made – particularly in that they had not always treated their black colleagues justly, a matter for which they deeply apologised – they said that they had done their best to consistently criticize the government, to ensure that the voice of opposition in South Africa did not die down. Thami Mazwai of the Forum of Black Journalists was fairly outspoken in his criticism of the English newspapers which, in his view, were still stuck in sixties' apartheid thinking. Moegsien Williams reproached the English newspapers for seeing the Afrikaner politicians as their opposition partners – and never thinking about it that the true opposition with whom they had to enter into debate had been incarcerated all those years on Robben Island.

The so-called 'alternative press' also had an opportunity to take the stand. Max du Preez, the editor of the now defunct *Vrye Weekblad*, an Afrikaans dissident newspaper, recounted "one of the blackest moments in our legal history" when his newspaper lost a case on appeal – and had to close down as a result. Legal proceedings had been instituted by Lieutenant-General Lothar Neethling, following reports on actions by the security police that had appeared in the newspaper. As a result of Neethling's perjury – said an outraged Du Preez – his paper closed down. Information subsequently gathered by the TRC, confirmed the veracity of what the *Vrye Weekblad* had been saying about the police's forensics laboratories, namely that they distributed poison intended for political activists. The TRC also came up with evidence corroborating the *Vrye Weekblad's* reports stating that the murdered Anton Lubowski had *not* been a government agent. "I really hope that the TRC can help me bring the man to justice."

Like Tutu, du Preez took umbrage at the fact that the Afrikaans press refused to submit an official statement to the TRC. The newspapers boasted that they had been in favour of reform, that they had been prepared to pay a price for the sake of change. But where was their evidence now? And did they not have things to confess; the dismissal of Johannes Grosskopf, when he began asking difficult questions as the editor of *Beeld*; the cover-up of the army's actions in Angola; the hysteria that had been fuelled when a number of Afrikaners went to Dakar in 1987 to talk to the ANC? The fact that the Afrikaans newspapers did not come to the media hearing made Max du Preez "very, very sad".

◆ ◆ ◆

A few weeks later such a submission did materialize. A hundred and twenty Afrikaans journalists, all of them Naspers people, issued a joint statement in which they expressed their disappointment that the Nasionale Pers had chosen not to testify before the TRC. Many of the journalists added their own comments. At *Beeld* sixty journalists, including the two deputy editors, Tim du Plessis and Arrie Rossouw signed the statement, at *Die Burger* twenty-six. The editor of *Fair Lady*, Roz Wrottesley, the deputy editor of *Die Huisgenoot*, Julia Viljoen, and a senior editor of *Insig*, Tobie Wiese, were also part of the group who had strong feelings on the matter, even though all of them acted in their personal capacity.

In their statement the journalists made it clear that although they had not been personally or directly involved in gross human rights violations, they regarded themselves as morally co-responsible for everything that had been done in the name of apartheid, because they helped maintain a system in which these abuses could take place.

"I was blind and deaf to the political aspirations, anger and suffering of my co-South Africans. I, like many others ... did not fully inform readers about the injustices of apartheid; did not oppose those injustices strongly enough; and where knowledge had been obtained in this regard, too readily accepted the NP's denials and reassurances.

"I offer everybody who suffered as a consequence my sincere apology and undertake to do everything in my power to prevent a repeat of this history."

Ton Vosloo, the CEO of Naspers, was to put it mildly, not impressed by this statement and made this clear in a press release. The journalists' actions were, according to him, a "repudiation of great and honourable names in Naspers' long, rich and proud journalistic tradition, and are to be regretted".

However, Tutu, and everybody on the TRC along with him, were on cloud nine. "I wish to praise them (the journalists) because they allowed themselves to be led by their consciences, in the face of considerable opposition. Their action constitutes a significant contribution to reconciliation and the process of healing in our country."

22 SEPTEMBER 1997: THE TRC AND THE NP BURY THE HATCHET

Good news! The Truth Commission and the National Party decided to bury the hatchet "in the interest of reconciliation in our country". After a meeting in Cape Town between Archbishop Tutu and Mr Marthinus van Schalkwyk, the new leader of the NP, the National Party announced that it was abandoning the legal proceedings that it had instituted against the commission.

Dr Alex Boraine, vice-chairman of the TRC at the same time apologized unconditionally for his criticism of Mr FW de Klerk and the National Party following the party's submission earlier the year. "The TRC admitted and is also deeply under the impression that such public criticism and action shed a negative reflection on the commission's objectiveness and impartiality", the official statement read.

Van Schalkwyk expressed praise for the role played by Archbishop Tutu for the sake of reconciliation in South Africa at a media conference. He welcomed the apology offered by Tutu a few weeks before, on his return from the USA – with regard to his criticism of the National Party and ex-president FW de Klerk. Precisely how the NP and the TRC would strengthen ties in the future and how they would co-operate in future for the sake of reconciliation, would be the subject of further discussions in the coming weeks.

26 SEPTEMBER 1997: WINNIE HAS A BIRTHDAY AT THE TRUTH COMMISSION

"It seems that everybody in South Africa knows that Mrs Madikizela-Mandela has her birthday today, everybody, that is, except the Truth Commission. Why on earth did you call upon my client to appear before the TRC today, of all days?" Advocate Ishmael Semenya began raising objections even before the official *in camera* hearing in Johannesburg began. But meanwhile Mrs Mandela, relaxed and charming in a white suit, was chatting and exchanging jokes with the persons in her entourage. She looked much younger than her 63 years. The eighteen cases about which the TRC wanted to question her – including various murders – did not seem to upset her in the least. She and her legal representatives were unshakable in their demand that they would co-operate with the investigation behind closed doors on condition that a public hearing would take place later in the year at which she could put her case before the entire nation. The TRC had no objection to this: 24 November would be the date.

I was appointed to sit on the panel that had to probe Winnie's activities, on this date and also later on, on 13 October, when the *in camera* investigation continued. Winnie did not say much and left most of the talking to her legal team. However, she kept taking notes, now and then offering advice. Evidently nothing escaped her. During the tea break she warmly embraced me and a few others who had congratulated her on her birthday. Which did not mean that she could not reply brusquely and with irritation to a question, if she felt that the questioner deserved this.

"Just wait for it, something is bound to happen!" I told myself, when I thought about the public hearing scheduled for November. Now that is what I call a prophetic hunch.

27 SEPTEMBER 1997: THE BIBLE IN SOLITARY DETENTION

"No, I don't want to read the Bible with you, particularly not the bits that you are reading. I don't know what it is with you people, you always choose the wrong bits – and then you still read it through Communist spectacles!"

Tom Manthata and I had to travel to Mmabatho to meet the premier and cabinet of the North West Province. Premier Popo Molefe and Tom were old friends who had spent years in detention together. They were together on Robben Island – which naturally meant that our reception was particularly warm.

The meeting concluded, we began talking over lunch, not about the suffering that they had endured but – interestingly enough – about the role the Bible had played in the lives of the prisoners. Most of the anti-apartheid activists who had been detained all over the country, including those who had served their sentences on Robben Island, Tom Manthata explained, were churchgoers. For many of them their faith was a serious matter, the one factor in their lives that kept them going.

"Sometimes we had to wait a long time before receiving a Bible from the warders", he told us, "but when this finally happened, we read the Bible through from cover to cover. We drank in the words! The Bible taught me that it was worthwhile to fight for truth and justice, even if one suffered in the process. I was able to read that there were many people who paid dearly for the sake of these things – and this gave me courage. And, of course, every now and again one does read about occasions when the truth and justice did triumph. This helped me not to lose heart, but to keep hoping."

One day, Tom, deeply impressed by a pericope he had chanced upon in the Bible, invited a warder who had unlocked his cell door, into the cell. But the warder resolutely refused to do Bible study with him – especially not on the "wrong" sections of the Bible. This did not much bother Tom, who had been imprisoned six times between 1974 and 1985, and who had spent long periods in solitary confinement. The prisoners – Tokyo Sexwale, Patrick Lekota, Popo Molefe and all the others – shared the inspiring chapters from the Bible with one another. They also discussed them with visiting clergymen and priests.

"Which segment of the Bible affected you the most, especially dur-

ing the times you were in solitary confinement?" I asked Tom. "Psalms",
was the immediate reply. "In the psalms I could recognize myself. All
my sadness and pain, my frustration, my despair and my hope, my
longing, my faith in the Lord, were recorded in the psalms. It was like
music." On being asked which psalms meant the most of all to him, his
response was immediate: Psalm 91 and Psalm 121. "In the mornings I
could get up with the words 'Lord, you are my defender and protector.'
At night I knelt at my bed: ' I look to the mountains; where will my help
come from? My help will come from the Lord, who made heaven and
earth!'"

Besides Psalms, Paul's letters made for popular reading. Tom and
his colleagues could readily identify with Paul, as he wrote from prison
to people who were themselves enduring their own suffering. But above
all, it was the passion of Christ that fascinated the men in the cells.
Tom told me how he had memorized long sections from the Gospels:
Judas' betrayal, Gethsemane, the trial and the crucifixion of the Lord.
Tom had been brought up a Catholic, and had even studied for a while
at a Catholic seminary. He used this knowledge to mark the fourteen
Stations of the Cross on his cell walls with his spoon. At each of the
Stations of the Cross he knelt daily to repeat the liturgical prayers. "It
took me almost an entire day", Tom remembered with a smile, "but it
gave meaning to every day in solitary confinement. Some mornings I
included the opening liturgy with which the SA Council of Churches
began its work every day – just to retain contact with my Protestant
brothers and sisters!"

The meal was over. It was time to go to the airport. I was especially
touched by Tom's last words at table: "If you think about it the years in
jail were also blessed years. You lived closer to the Lord, were far more
dependent upon Him than is often now the case. Now I am running around
all day long and am busy with all kinds of things. I now have little time
for Bible study, for meditation and prayer. It makes you think ... "

◆ ◆ ◆

July, August, September 1997, the months during which the trek inward would begin, were over. A long list of persons – and also institutions – had come to stand in front of the mirror of history. Like Beyers
Naudé, they acknowledged their guilt, tried to understand it. And confessed it. Other wanted to *know*, and came with their questions and
fears to the hearings. There had been moments of frustration and won-

der. Of bitterness and pain and of reconciliation and joy.

It had been a long line of persons who checked in: Peter and Linda Biehl from the USA; the doctors and medical professors with their stethoscopes and their embarrassment about the past; Janusz Walus, Clive Derby-Lewis, together with Limpho Hani, the widow of the man whom they murdered; the survivors of the St James church massacre; Jeffrey Benzien with his wet bag; the women of the Old Fort; Bram Fischer's two daughters; Helena, the lonely farmer's wife from Mpumalanga; Dirk Coetzee and Gideon Nieuwoudt, the two feared officers; Dawie de Villiers saying what was on his mind during his last speech before Parliament; Craig Williamson and John Horak and the other media spies; the one hundred and twenty seven Afrikaans journalists who could not but look their fellow South Africans in the eye and say, "We are sorry, very sorry"; and last, but not least, my friend Tom with his Bible in his hand.

During the last term of the year the world's interest would once again be fixed on the Truth Commission's work, and many men and women, businessmen, judges and advocates, the 'mother of the nation' and her bodyguard, *dominees* and priests, imams and rabbis would join the queue.

The next chapter will tell their stories.

CHAPTER FIVE

FELLOW-TRAVELLERS

In an Afrikaans poem by the poet Louis Leipoldt, October is called "the loveliest, loveliest month". In that month the Truth Commission – and together with the Commission, the entire country – embarked on the penultimate stretch of the journey. The journey inward – towards a better understanding of everything that had taken place in our country, of everything that had happened to the *people* involved in these things – was not yet over. While it was spring outside, while the trees were covered with blossoms, many old and new travellers reported for the journey: freedom fighters, military officers, police officials, politicians, judges and advocates, business people, members of the Broederbond, religious leaders. Everyone had a story to tell, brought a scrap of information, gave an opinion, an explanation that could serve as a road map.

1 OCTOBER 1997: AMNESTY APPLICATIONS *IN,* SUMMONSES *OUT*

The first day of October was a day not soon to be forgotten.

The IN basket of the TRC was chock-a-block, as was the OUT basket.

At midnight, the previous evening, the amnesty offer had finally expired. This had in fact been due to happen on 10 May, but as a result of delays at the Department of Justice in tabling the necessary legislation before Parliament (in which the cut-off date for acts for which amnesty could be applied was extended from 6 December 1993 to 10 May 1994), procrastinators still had the opportunity to submit their applications up to midnight, 30 September. Telephone calls between the various offices revealed that 99 new applications had been received – the day before alone, 73 applications.

During a press conference interesting facts came to light. The total number of amnesty applications received was 7048, far more than had been expected when the TRC began its work. The last day's applications came from persons affiliated to various parties. The Inkatha Freedom Party provided 14 new applications. From the ranks of the ANC came 13 applications, including those of Deputy President Thabo Mbeki, three ministers, four deputy ministers and four provincial premiers.

From the ranks of the previous government only ex-minister Adriaan Vlok submitted an application. The names of six PAC members and one Azapo member also appeared on the list, together with 25 former policemen and two members of BOSS. A final, surprising application submitted at the last moment, was that of the leader of the AWB, Eugene Terre'blanche. Terre'blance, who had in the past severely criticized the TRC, now said that he was "coming with an open mind (to the TRC) ... I am prepared to say before my God, 'Lord, if I have transgressed, forgive me'". The AWB leader applied for amnesty for two acts: for tarring and feathering Professor Floors van Jaarsveld in 1979 and for his part in the so-called Battle of Ventersdorp in August 1991, when he and his associates had become engaged in a clash with the police during a meeting held by FW de Klerk in the town. Three people died in the fray and many were injured.

"The TRC is grateful for the applications", Richard Lyster said during a press conference. "But the commission had expected more. There are still a group of ANC members who should have presented themselves, as well as a whole lot of ex-Defence Force members who had every reason to submit amnesty applications. Without their evidence many questions will remain unanswered."

Not every application succeeded, he announced at the press conference. Some 2 500 applications did not qualify – the applicants either denied their guilt or it was clear, from the outset, that they did not have any political motive for their deeds. However, a large number of applications had been successful, such as Colonel Jan Nieuwoudt's application; he had learnt only two days before that he had received amnesty for his share in training 200 Inkatha warriors who had been used to assassinate ANC members in KwaZulu-Natal.

"The amnesty process is painful", Fazel Randera conceded during the press conference. "It is not easy to ask for amnesty. One needs to be brave to do so. To appear in such a way before the whole country, to expose, before television cameras, everything that happened and in such great detail, in itself tells its own tale of shame and remorse." "But it is even more difficult for the victims and their families", Khoza Mgojo added. "Some offenders do not even show remorse for what they did; this leads to hopelessness and anger."

Tutu concluded the conference by an ardent appeal to white South Africans to support the work of the TRC. The TRC was not aiming its investigations against one specific group of people in South Africa – and the purpose of the hearings was not at all to ridicule some people or persecute them. "We do want to get to the truth. Black South Africans were hurt, but they do not want to take revenge. Can white South Africans expect people to be more generous than that? May God grant us the eloquence that we can persuade you how much we care for South Africa – and also for you. The only thing we ask of you is to admit the things that you did, that you will understand that you are account- able. That you will say, 'We are sorry!' That will be the end of the mat- ter. Please!"

◆ ◆ ◆

The OUT basket was also full. Overflowing, in fact. On 14 October a special hearing was due to be held on the role of the State Security Council in Johannesburg and a large number of prominent persons were either summoned or asked to testify. The former president PW Botha and various former cabinet members – Ministers Pik Botha, Roelf Meyer, Adriaan Vlok, Leon Wessels and Magnus Malan, had been requested to make submissions. PW Botha, who was recovering from a hip opera- tion, informed the TRC that he would be unable to attend for medical reasons. "This cannot be", Tutu told the press. "President Botha will have to testify. However, we can try to find another date. The possibil- ity is not excluded that such a hearing can be held in George."

Tutu was less happy about the fact that PW Botha had not handed in the answers in writing to the questions put to him the day before.

Members of the present government also received mail. Ministers Mac Maharaj and Joe Modise, together with Deputy Minister Ronnie Kasrils, were invited to a special hearing on the security forces, that had been arranged in Cape Town. They were asked to talk about their role in the war; a key witness would be Mr Aboobaker Ismael, former head of MK's special operations. Five Apla members would also have to appear: Messrs Johnson Mhlambo (former commander in chief), Daniel Mofokeng, Joe Mkwanazi, Lethlapa Mphalele and Vuma Ntikinca.

Two former heads of the SA Defence Force, Generals Constand Viljoen and Jannie Geldenhuys, as well as Major-General Joep Joubert and Vice-Admiral Dries Putter, were summoned to testify about the actions of the Army and the Navy. General George Meiring was also invited to address the TRC. The Police would also be there: Generals Johan van der Merwe and Johann Coetzee (both former commissioners) had been summoned, together with Brigadier Willem Schoon (former head of the Security Police's C Section), Major Craig Williamson (master spy), Brigadier Alfred Oosthuizen and Major Sarel Crafford.

1 OCTOBER 1997 (CONTINUED): EUGENE DE KOCK AND HIS COLLEAGUES

While the regional offices were processing amnesty applications and mailing summonses, a dramatic hearing was under way in Port Elizabeth. Over the past few days, one former security policeman after another had already put in an appearance in the hall. But today the former Vlakplaas commander Eugene de Kock himself would testify. There was great interest in what he had to tell the Amnesty Committee. Two years before, De Kock had been sentenced twice to life imprisonment, plus a further 21 years, after being convicted of 89 charges: six of murder, two of conspiring to murder, in addition to a long list of charges of fraud and other offences. Six of his colleagues appeared with him, all of whom had been involved in various police activities: General Nic van Rensburg, Brigadier Wahl du Toit, Major Gerhard Lotz, Lieutenant-General Kobus Kok, together with three Vlakplaas operatives, Major Marthinus Ras, and Messrs Lionel Snyman and Snor (Moustache) Vermeulen.

The previous week, one amnesty applicant after the next confessed to committing acts involving gross human rights violations. Gideon Nieuwoudt confessed to his share in the murders of two student leaders, Siphiwe Mtimkulu and Topsy Madaka – as well as the fact that he had not in his trial spoken the truth about his involvement in the Motherwell murders, as he thought that he "would get away with it". He also applied for amnesty for his share in the death of Steve Biko, the Motherwell murders, and the murder of the so-called Pepco Three. Nieuwoudt's accounts of how he and his buddies had first drugged the student leaders by putting pills into their coffee before shooting them and later burning their bodies, struck the family members present with horror. The amnesty applicants were waylaid by an angry crowd when they attempted to leave the hall. The attorneys of the victims had to enter into negotiations between the crowd and the police before the armoured vehicle transporting Nieuwoudt and his colleagues was able to leave the premises. Reporters, members of the Amnesty Committee and other TRC employees had to wait inside the hall until peace was finally restored.

Marthinus Ras' account concerned the Motherwell murders. Ras, who had been sentenced to ten years' imprisonment for his share in the murder of three of their own police colleagues and an askari – whom they suspected had crossed over to the ANC – described the gruesome events. After the car bomb had exploded, he had to walk up to the car to ascertain whether his former colleagues were really dead. "Pieces of stuff lay burning everywhere. I almost fell over some body parts in the road. It appeared to be part of a person's spine. I immediately realized that there was no possibility that anybody could have survived the blast."

It was not necessary to use the Makarov pistol in his hand. He, Lionel Snyman and Snor Vermeulen immediately returned to Pretoria, after having completed the "disagreeable job". "It is unfair that we are now being held accountable for an order that came directly from General Nic van Rensburg", Ras complained at the end of his testimony.

Finally Eugene de Kock took up his place behind the microphone. The atmosphere was loaded. He began his evidence by launching a sharp attack on the former government and the police generals under whose command he had acted. "I am prepared to assume responsibility for the deeds of my men, but not for the actions of my commanders. They literally ran away from something for which they had to take responsibility. I am bitter towards the generals and the politicians. I am also disillusioned. One would expect them to have the integrity and backbone to stand up and be answerable to their deeds." The former Vlakplaas commander said that former minister Adriaan Vlok once said that the Police and the Afrikaner would not surrender within a thousand years. "This reminded me of something that somebody said in 1944 during the Second World War", he added, clearly referring to Adolf Hitler. "No member of the National Party – including the former president who has now run away – could go to bed at night knowing that *they* were in control. They were kept in a position of power by the SAP, the Defence Force and the Intelligence Service."

"Many of the people who gave the instructions had themselves never experienced what it was like to pull the trigger. Doing that and then going home – and living a normal life – is extremely difficult", De Kock went on to say. He couldn't talk to his colleagues about these things, as he would then be in danger of losing his life. When he was in detention in 1994, a Vlakplaas colleague told him that the senior generals were distancing themselves from him. "I felt nauseous!"

Eugene de Kock had come to Port Elizabeth not only to ask for amnesty. He also wanted to meet the victims of the Motherwell victims and apologize to them: "For what it's worth – I understand their pain. I am in the same position, although it is not so traumatic that it is beyond the point of no return." Two of the widows, Mrs Dora Mgoduka and Mrs Pearl Faku indicated through their legal representative that they wished to meet De Kock and talk to him.

7 OCTOBER 1997 (AND FOLLOWING DAYS): THE GENERALS ASKED TO EXPLAIN

What role did the security forces as well as the liberation movements play in the past? To what extent were they responsible for gross human rights violations? What were the motives on both sides of the struggle? In order to arrive at a better understanding of everything that had happened in the country it was inevitable that the commanders of both the security forces and the liberation movements should make submissions to the TRC. For this purpose a special hearing was held in Cape Town, which would last for several days.

The first person to take the stand was Brigadier Dan Mofokeng, former Apla commander. There were numerous questions: Why did Apla attack civilian targets – banks and farms, recreation clubs, even a church? What contribution did this make to the struggle? About the attacks of Apla soldiers on all of these targets Dan Mofokeng, who had in the meantime joined the SANDF, made no bones about the way they saw things: Apla, the armed wing of the PAC, had never been involved in armed robberies, but in "revolutionary confiscations". That had been, to tell the truth, Apla's main source of income for a long time. But remember, he emphasized, criminals commit armed robbery – and they had not been criminals. "Since its foundation the PAC has stated categorically that our country and its resources have been taken away from us through force of arms. It had been Apla's responsibility to confiscate that which belonged by law to the oppressed and displaced people of Azania. It is in this context that we admit, openly and proudly, that banks and other financial institutions had been made targets. We remain proud and open about it because these acts fall within the PAC's political and ideological perspective. Consequently we take umbrage at allegations that we were armed robbers." On a question as to whether Apla had exercised control over the money that had been looted, one of the Apla members replied, "I have never met an Apla member who had enriched himself out of the struggle".

What is more, Apla in no way regretted its attacks on civilian targets. Neither will it apologize for them. In the struggle they did not draw any distinction between hard and soft targets. "These terms do not exist in our vocabulary." The entire society was militarized – including the national service and commando systems. In the context of South Africa one could not refer at all to "innocent civilians". Targets were often selected with a view to their potential psychological and political value. The attacks on the St James Church, the King William's Town golf club and the Heidelberg Tavern took place in response to the violence to which black South Africans had been exposed daily – especially through the action of the Third Force. "The Apla leadership accepts full responsibility for these attacks. We are not sorry that such operations did take place, and there is nothing to apologize for." Colonel Mulelo Fihla did acknowledge that the Apla leadership was sometimes shocked about the incidents, but did not discuss these feelings with the operatives.

It was obvious that the Apla delegation were not pleased with the critical questions put to them. Dan Mofokeng accused the TRC of having a political motive and that they just wanted to discredit the PAC and Apla. On being questioned, the man who had apparently given the order for the St James Church massacre, Letlapa Mpahlele, angrily dismissed the TRC as a circus and a farce. Advocate Glen Goosen wanted to know on behalf of the Truth Commission whether the PAC and Apla heeded international conventions concerning the protection of civilians in times of war. Brigadier Mpahlele replied, "When Dingane said 'Kill those who want to take our land', he did not say who they were. The attackers knew! Moshesh knew that all Whites were guilty of taking our land!"

That Apla and the PAC did not relish the thought of dealing with the Truth Commission, was quite evident. As it happened, many of their officers refused to ask for amnesty. Why should they?

◆ ◆ ◆

The ANC, too, was driven into a corner by the questions Glen Goosen put to them. In their first submission the ANC denied that their cadres had ever been involved in the wave of bomb attacks on Wimpy Bars that had taken place during the apartheid years. The ANC dismissed them as 'false flag' operations of the then government forces which had been undertaken to discredit the ANC. But now a number of ANC members had applied for amnesty for precisely these attacks. How can one understand that? Minister Mac Maharaj tried to explain: "When the ANC leadership abroad became aware of the Wimpy attacks, we accepted that it might have been our people's work. In view of further evidence, the suspicion began to arise that it could perhaps rather be the work of the government, the purpose of which was to discredit the ANC's image. However, if applications are submitted that confirm that they could have been involved in the attacks, but remain in good faith of the opinion that they were obeying ANC orders in this way, the ANC would have been prepared to assume responsibility for their deeds."

Minister Maharaj also had to grope for excuses for the action of his members in KwaZulu-Natal. The ANC had previously denied that any of its commanders had ever given an order that IFP members be regarded as legitimate targets and that attacks on them were sanctioned. But from KwaZulu-Natal various amnesty applications were received from ANC members and members of self-protection units, from persons who said that they had taken direct action against IFP members and that they had killed some of them. Mr Ronnie Kasrils conceded in his reply that there were, in fact, people who had not received formal training, who had interpreted the ANC propaganda message incorrectly and had therefore committed misdeeds. Misunderstandings, a lack of clarity about orders and objectives, were the order of the day.

However, Minister Maharaj himself had a story to tell, a story that had a number of senior policemen in the hall shifting around uncomfortably. In 1964 General Johan van der Merwe, who was still a lieutenant at the time, had tortured him – while his fellow police commissioner – General Johann Coetzee, looked on. The security forces did not first, as they alleged, begin torturing people in the eighties when the revolutionary onslaught was at its worst, Mac Maharaj declared. He could vouch for this personally – he and also his wife had been tortured by the Police at this time. One of the methods that they had learnt from the Portuguese was to hit prisoners with a plank of wood in which holes had been bored. If one was hit by one of these planks on the soft parts of one's body, the skin was 'sucked in' by the holes, causing great pain.

◆ ◆ ◆

The next day was the day of the generals. How did it come about that

the Defence Force had been involved in the eighties in murders committed within the borders of South Africa – for example the assassination
of the Ribeiro couple? General Jannie Geldenhuys, the then head of the
Defence Force, and Major-General Joep Joubert, head of the Special
Forces unit, explained: Everything began with a misunderstanding. In
1986 General Geldenhuys gave an order to Joep Joubert to make a plan
in terms of which special forces would assist the police in combating
domestic terrorism. Joubert worked out a strategy on how the special
forces could make a contribution by running secret, covert operations.
He identified three crisis areas: the Northern Transvaal, the Witwatersrand and the Eastern Province.

Joep Joubert gave an account of how he had struggled in getting an
appointment with General Geldenhuys, as he wished to discuss the
plans with him. At last he got the opportunity to explain his strategy to
the general when both of them attended a party. "'That seems to be a
good idea', Geldenhuys said. I interpreted this as approval and put the
plan into operation.'" He did not ask for further approval for individual
actions, as he felt that he had already received the approval of the head
of the Defence Force, who trusted him to carry out his plans. However,
when it was brought to General Geldenhuys's attention that the Defence Force had been involved in the murder of Dr Ribeiro and his wife
Florence, the general immediately intervened. A new procedure for au-
thorizing these kind of operations was introduced. According to Joubert
the police did not, after this incident, request the special forces to help
them.

Major Craig Williamson, former security policeman, had a great deal
to say about the involvement of the State Security Council (SSC) in
secret actions by the security police. If ex-president FW de Klerk alleged
that he, as a member of the SSC, was wholly unaware of the involvement of the security police, his eyes must have been closed. Before
1989 De Klerk was not truly involved in counterinsurgency strategies,
Williamson conceded. "Perhaps he misunderstood our doctrines. However, there was also a large-scale attempt to preserve the appearance
of legitimacy." In fact all 'high-level politicians', including cabinet members, received daily reports of all incidents. No questions were asked,
including questions about mysterious actions against certain politicians.
Incidents that entailed explosions to activists' cars in neighbouring states
were tacitly accepted as part of the government's counterinsurgency
strategy. Some of the politicians and senior officers did go to great
lengths to ensure that they "did not know about certain actions", but

were nevertheless involved in drawing up and voting for budgets that would make the work possible. "The eleventh commandment was well-known: 'you may not be caught!'"

General Johan van der Merwe agreed. Although the SSC had not directly ordered acts grossly violating human rights, they must definitely have known that illegal operations were being conducted. The words "eliminate", "neutralize", "take out" and "remove from society", which were used in an SSC document, elicited a great deal of discussion in the TRC. This is an unfortunate choice of words, the general admitted, but as far as he knew this was never understood to mean "kill". General Johann Coetzee, citing a dictionary of definitions, supported his colleague: "eliminate" does not necessarily mean "kill" – neither did they interpret it that way. At grass roots level, the two generals conceded, it could have happened that people who "faced death every day in ghastly circumstances" did not interpret it this way. More than one security policeman emphasized during the hearing that they definitely read the word "eliminate" to mean "kill".

During the hearing on the State Security Council which was due to be held a few days later in Johannesburg, the debate on the meanings of these terms would be taken a step further.

9 OCTOBER 1997: "THE BRITISH ALSO NEED TO CONFESS", BEYERS NAUDÉ SAID

The British should really, after all these years, express their sincere remorse about the injustice inflicted on the Boers during the Second War of Independence. Would the new Prime Minister, Tony Blair, be the one to take that step? Beyers Naudé travelled to Port Elizabeth, the city where the amnesty hearings were being conducted to read the annual Langenhoven Memorial lecture at the university. "After a hundred years the wounds of the Anglo-Boer War have not yet been healed, despite the brave efforts of somebody like Emily Hobhouse." Would the history of our country not have been completely different, he wanted to know, if the British had confessed their guilt towards the Afrikaners when the Women's Memorial was erected in Bloemfontein, and had underlined their remorse by doing something tangible?

That is to say, would the Afrikaner be generous enough to stand at the Blood River Monument and say to the Zulus: "We never deliberately wanted to kill Zulu warriors; our actions arose from self-defence and a deep conviction that the continued existence of our nation was at stake?" Would we be able to reach out to the Zulu nation in deep sorrow about the pain and suffering we inflicted on them?

Would Afrikaners be able to apologize to the Biko family for the death of the black consciousness leader?

Should a National Day of Reconciliation be introduced – perhaps on 16 December – would it be so far-fetched to hope that Apla would apologize for the murders of white farmers in the Eastern Cape?

The elderly church leader concluded: "White people, especially Afrikaners, would be astonished at the positive response of black, brown and Indian South Africans, if they were to commit themselves to building one true rainbow nation."

President Paul Kruger and Queen Victoria before the TRC (Beeld, 11 October 1997)

13-15 OCTOBER 1997: HOW MUCH DID THE POLITICIANS REALLY KNOW?

"Goodness, it took me a long time to get here from my home in Pretoria. Nowadays I travel much faster to Pietersburg than to the city centre of Johannesburg!" I was able to sympathize with ex-minister Pik Botha in the lobby of the Sanlam Centre, because I myself had also been caught up in the traffic on my way to the Truth Commission. Reaching the tenth floor, I accompanied Pik Botha to the hall where the hearing would begin. Once again we had to wend our way through the 'traffic'. There was great interest in the TRC's special hearing about the role of the State Security Council. The day before, the interpreters and the television crews had already been setting up their equipment. People crowded the corridor and lobby. In the coffee room, next to the hall, Archbishop Tutu waited with a whole contingent of Truth Commission members. The three other former National Party Cabinet members who had indicated that they would testify, Ministers Adriaan Vlok, Leon Wessels and Roelf Meyer, were sipping their coffee.

Although the mood was friendly, the suspense, even tension, was palpable. The million dollar question was: would this hearing proceed differently to the submission of the NP earlier the year? Would Pik and his colleagues shed more light on the actions of the former government? Would they not, at last, be able to explain the inner workings of the State Security Council (SSC), but also, in the end, accept responsibility for gross human rights violations that were committed in the name of the government? Ex-president de Klerk's unwillingness to accept the final responsibility for human rights abuses committed during his administration led to great disappointment and unhappiness. A court case about the TRC's response was averted at the last minute when Tutu and Boraine apologized. Would the next two days proceed differently? Would Ministers Botha, Vlok, Wessels and Meyer set a new example? Would they not be able to help, not only black South Africa, but also their fellow white South Africans to understand the past? To confess our mutual debt – and get it behind us?

The former Minister of Foreign Affairs was sworn in first. In front of him lay a thick statement with many annexures. Pik Botha provided a great deal of factual data, but also talked from the heart: If one looks back at the past, he said, one realizes that the NP would never have been able to succeed in its policy because – this he had learnt at the World Court – if one has lost the moral battle, one does not have a chance of winning the legal battle. "Neither could we win the political battle, not as far as the world or the ANC was concerned, because the policy of the NP did not have any moral basis."

Although he and his colleagues in Cabinet and also in the SSC had never approved the murder of political opponents or given orders that this be done, "not one of us in the previous government can today say that there were not suspicions on our part that members of the South African Police were involved in such irregularities". The decisive question was, however, not whether the Cabinet had approved the murders. "The question is whether we should not have done more to ensure that this would not happen. I deeply regret this neglect. May God forgive me!"

The comment of the Johannesburg newspaper, Beeld, to the politicians' evidence

Like Minister Vlok had already done at a previous occasion, Pik Botha warned the TRC not to make more of the SSC than was necessary. The State Security Council was not such a monster, or even as powerful and influential as was sometimes believed. The National Party had the real power and governed the country through its caucus and Cabinet. Looking back today, one realized that too much power had been placed in the hands of the State President. He was the one who appointed and dismissed people. In contrast the SSC was, for all practical purposes, toothless and all decisions taken, first had to be submitted to the Cabinet for approval. Different ministers were charged with specific tasks. Nevertheless, if one of them had to do something that was, in his opinion, incompatible with any provision of the law, it was his duty to raise this in the Cabinet or to discuss it with the State President. To a question of whether any of his colleagues had been acting illegally, his reply was, "That I really do not know."

◆ ◆ ◆

Ex-minister Botha would himself like to know who exactly were the "people at the top", who had, according to the evidence of many security policemen, ordered illegal actions. He recently visited the former Cabinet minister, Pietie du Plessis, then serving a prison term, Pik Botha said. Opposite his cell was that of the former Vlakplaas commander Eugene de Kock. De Kock made them tea – and used the opportunity to have a long conversation with him. It had often happened, De Kock said, that he and his colleagues received orders from their seniors to commit murders or other illegal acts. He even had to "plant" false documents and diamonds on Pietie du Plessis on one occasion! They sincerely believed that the orders did come from people at "the top" and that these people at "the top" knew very well about everything they were doing. The "top", as Pik understood it, was the Commissioner of Police and in certain instances also the Minister of Police – sometimes also the State Security Council and the Cabinet. But as he had already stated in evidence and what made him wonder about it, was that the SSC never gave this kind of order – even if it was possible that some of the policemen wrongly interpreted SSC decisions, and interpreted the words used differently. To explain what he meant he quoted, in an annexure, a list of words that could be interpreted in various ways: *eliminate, neutralize, exterminate, destroy, stop, combat, remove permanently out of society.* "*Kill*" was not necessarily the meaning of any of these words – said Pik.

Tutu was moved by Pik Botha's evidence. He got up and shook the ex-minister's hand. "I want to emphasize that we have never had such a strong and direct submission from anybody from your community. I hope the people in your community are listening to what you said and take it to heart! These are the people we wish to reach ... Nobody of your political stature, from your community, has ever said that the NP was morally corrupt. It takes one's breath away!"

◆ ◆ ◆

For Minister Adriaan Vlok, too, who presented his evidence in Afrikaans, the chairman of the TRC had great appreciation. Like Pik Botha before him he indicated that the SSC was not the sinister body people made it out to be. But, he conceded, it could definitely have happened that people interpreted the decisions and orders of the SSC far more radically than had been the intention. As the former Minister of Law and Order he had really not been aware of illegal actions – over and above those incidents that he himself had asked amnesty for. But he does accept responsibility, to the degree that subordinates, divisional commanders and police officers working in the field, people who often had to make all kinds of decisions in uncontrollable situations, were in fact guilty of gross human rights violations – in the sincere conviction that they were following orders from above, including those of the State Security Council. "The fact is that our country ... had been plunged into a war psychosis where such words and expressions (such as *eliminate, neutralize, remove*, etc), which were originally used in a military context, became part of the language of the man in the street – just as similar expressions have become part of the language of revolutionaries."

The Truth Commission would probably nowhere find "an unambiguous resolution to act unlawfully" in any minutes of the SSC. The only exceptions, said Vlok, could possibly be a number of Stratcom actions that had in fact been ordered by the SSC, and which could in certain circumstances be regarded as unjust and even illegal.

One of the reasons why he and some of his colleagues were not aware of many of the murders and tortures that were taking place, was probably the custom that only "those who had to know" were informed of certain matters, and others not. For security purposes only the most essential information was passed on to Cabinet members. What is true, Adriaan Vlok conceded, is that he did congratulate hundreds of policemen on their work – and encourage them – without knowing exactly what they had done. In this way he could have condoned illegal actions.

He had visited Vlakplaas on two occasions and encouraged the men in their struggle against terrorism. Not all of them were criminals; many of the men did good work. If he had known about their human rights abuses he would never have tolerated it and would have acted very drastically, Vlok said in evidence.

◆ ◆ ◆

The second day of the hearing belonged to two younger men, Leon Wessels and Roelf Meyer.

Former ministers Leon Wessels and Roelf Meyer before the TRC

"I am both an African and an Afrikaner. I am a liberated Afrikaner. I am also a proud Afrikaner", Leon Wessels began his submission. "Liberated Afrikaners took the reform bit firmly between their teeth when this was necessary. Both our hearts and our minds have been changed. We love this country. We have been liberated from the baggage of an immoral system of government." But the time had now come for Afrikaners to resume their journey, galloping into the future. "I cannot think of any reason why Afrikaans South Africans and their children or any other Afrikaner from days gone by, must bear this burden of apartheid till Kingdom come. Within the framework of the Constitution we'll stand for our place and fight for Afrikaans."

It was right that the book of the past was being opened, but at a stage it would also have to be closed. Apartheid – of this he was now more convinced than before – had been a terrible mistake and a blot on the country. "South Africans did not listen to the laughter or the weeping of others. I am sorry that I had been so hard of hearing for such a long time."

"The political defence of 'I did not know' is not available to me, because in many respects I believe I did not *want* to know ... There were many arguments in Parliament during which it was said that the security men were acting outside the law. We said that this was not true. Yet it was happening right under our noses!"

"The government failed not only the country but also the security forces, because it did not offer a viable constitutional vision to end the conflict," declared the former Deputy Minister of Law and Order. "Moreover, the relationship between the security forces and the National Party politicians in general was not open and transparent. Therefore we did not manage the security forces and intelligence services properly. Although there had never been direct orders to murder political opponents, the (politicians') speeches, among other things, created a climate in which transgressions could become possible."

In his own way, said Leon Wessels, he had his suspicions of things that had caused discomfort in official circles. "Because I did not have the facts to substantiate my suspicions or I had lacked the courage to shout from the rooftops, I have to confess that I only whispered in corridors. That, I believe, is the accusation that people may level at many of us. We did not confront the reports of injustices head-on."

◆ ◆ ◆

Roelf Meyer agreed with Leon Wessels. If blame had to be apportioned about what had happened in the previous dispensation, this must probably be placed on the failure to take stronger steps when the danger signs were evident. "The fact that so many offences had taken place over such a long period was an indication that stronger action was required ... For this failure I assume political responsibility." Like his colleagues he also assumed responsibility for deeds committed by the security forces, who had acted in the sincere belief that they had received orders from above or in any case had approval for what they were doing.

To a question about how many misdeeds of the past could have taken place without the express approval of the government, Roelf answered quite frankly, "Nobody knows! Perhaps things had been developing over a period in such a way that in the end we all became a part of a thought pattern. We all believed that there was an enemy that needed to be destroyed and that there was not a just war on the other side. It was also to protect the (white) minority. Perhaps we were ruled by fear."

In South Africa "we came to a point and a climate developed in which it was no longer the 'in thing' to ask questions". If one receives news daily of people who died as a result of terrorism, that bombs had been planted or that people had been murdered by means of the necklace method, a thought pattern begins to develop in terms of which people stop asking questions. The past must then be judged against this background. "One asks oneself: how the hell is it possible that these things happened? I do not try to excuse myself, but would like to know what had really happened. Some were strong enough to ask questions. Others escaped the mould ... "

◆ ◆ ◆

I listened gratefully – and with satisfaction – to Roelf and Leon. Roelf, who has since left the National Party to become the co-leader of the United Democratic Front, spoke calmly and in an unhurried manner, with great seriousness. Leon acted with deep conviction, with passion, gesturing as he spoke, and introduced variety into his address with his disarming humour. When the TRC prosecutor, Glen Goosen, directed a number of difficult questions at Roelf Meyer, Leon came to his colleague's rescue.

"I know Glen Goosen has now placed me on the reserve bench. I would just like to know whether this is a rugby or a wrestling match. If it is a rugby match, I may not come on to the field now. If it is, however, a wrestling match, may I now come up and help, without the referee's permission. So ... can I come up now?"

Glen Goosen nipped Leon's rescue attempt in the bud: "It's a rugby match!"

Archbishop Tutu said in his response to the evidence of the former Cabinet members that anybody who had been listening to their evidence, would greatly appreciate the fact that the two men had been prepared today to come forward and stand naked in front of the nation. "We regard the events of the past two days, in particular your extraordinary frankness, as something that has not happened anywhere else. One sometimes forgets that you were then the government and that you have come to give account of your lives to us, who in that dispensation were regarded as rubbish, as enemies who had to be neutralized." Tutu concluded, "I hope that you understand that you have helped to pour balm into the wounds of many people."

The hall was perfectly quiet. "Let us pray!" Tutu said.

Once he had said "Amen", Adri Kotze reported the next morning in her report in *Beeld*, only a small piece of the diminutive archbishop's purple robe could be seen as Wessels dwarfed him in an embrace.

◆ ◆ ◆

This hearing had indeed run a different course than that one in May, when F W de Klerk had appeared before the TRC. Reaction streamed in from all quarters. The new NP leader, Marthinus van Schalkwyk praised the four former ministers two days later in an official statement for "their courage and guts" – and expressed his gratitude that they had in fact assumed responsibility for the human rights abuses perpetrated by the NP government's security forces. Quite a few amnesty applicants specially thanked Meyer and Wessels through their legal representatives. The evidence of the past few days had strengthened their cases. Only Azapo remained unconvinced. In a strongly worded statement they accused former ministers Botha and Vlok of still not speaking the truth ...

23 OCTOBER 1997: VICTIMS MUST GET REMUNERATION – BUT CAN THE COUNTRY AFFORD IT?

"Three billion Rands! Where on earth must it come from?"
    "Which people, and how many of them, will be standing in the queue!"
    "How will the money be distributed? Who will supervise?"

"Why money? What about the victims' other needs?"

It was a wonderful day for the Reparation and Rehabilitation Committee when Archbishop Tutu announced to the public the long-awaited proposals concerning remuneration to the victims of human rights violations. After months of planning and research – and meetings lasting days – the Reparation and Rehabilitation Committee was chuffed with their proposals. A significant number of journalists were less impressed. Their questions hung heavily in the air. Hlengiwe Mkhize and her colleagues had to inform and explain, as best they could.

The Reparation and Rehabilitation Committee had been mandated to ascertain victims' needs as closely as possible, to determine under which circumstances they were living, and the most general problems they were encountering. Proposals then had to be formulated on how the government should deal with these cases. It had already become clear within the first months that there were five typical needs among victims and their families – and for these specific needs the TRC wanted to make provision.

Firstly, the most urgent needs of victims who were old, ill or were living in destitution had to be attended to. A scheme was suggested in terms of which these unfortunates – who really could not survive much longer without receiving support, even if this was only to a limited extent – could be given assistance. Since the TRC began its work, smaller amounts of money had already been paid to people requiring urgent medical attention, or those who had to buy a new wheelchair, or who did not have any food or clothes in the home. After the TRC had concluded its work, there would still be many people who would require urgent 'interim reparation'.

Secondly, the TRC suggested, every victim of gross human rights violations, or their survivors, had to be paid a *sum of money.* The payment would serve a double purpose: to give tangible recognition to the victims for the pain and suffering of many years, and to assist these people, of whom the vast majority were living in difficult circumstances, financially. Following the amnesty granted to perpetrators, many victims had lost the possibility of instituting civil claims – which could have helped the widows and children make provision for the future. The government, the TRC argued, had the solemn duty to balance the amnesty benefits to offenders with reparation benefits to the victims.

How much money had to be paid out? Various options were considered. In South Africa the breadline for a family is R15 600 a year. This could be the possible basis for remuneration, but, as one of the TRC members put it: "What do we say by that – that we want to help the victims to barely survive?" A better suggestion was to take the average annual income of a South African family, R21 700, as the basis. In this way the TRC would tell the victims, "We want you to live a fairly normal life." The suggestion was therefore to pay out a sum of between R17 000 and R23 000. Victims living in remote rural areas, far from medical and other facilities, as well as those who had a great many dependents would get more than city folk with smaller families. The TRC also proposed that the amount had to paid annually for six years. If about 22 000 victims were to be helped in this way, it would cost the country an estimated 500 million rands a year – 3 billion rands over six years. This was enough to take away the journalists' breath. "Wait a minute", Wendy Orr, the vice-chairman of the Reparation and Rehabilitation Committee cautioned, "it's not so unreasonably much; it amounts to 0,25 percent of the government's annual budget. And surely the government has this much feeling for the victims? And just think: if we did not make provision in this way for the victims, and the 22 000 victims were to institute lawsuits, how much would *that* not have cost the country? Infinitely more!"

The *third* group of proposals concerned the *improvement of community services*. During many hearings the need was expressed for better and more accessible hospital and clinic services, the erection of schools and other educational institutions in particular communities, the acceleration of housing projects, etc. These needs were discussed with the various provincial governments – who helped formulate a series of practical and feasible projects that would benefit not only the victims, but also the community at large.

The *fourth* group of proposals were made with a view to *symbolic reparation*. Many victims had expressed the wish that their loved ones be reinterred or that tombstones be erected. Others asked that loved ones who had disappeared years ago at last be declared dead, so that their estates could be wound up and legal obligations met. For a large group of persons – persons who had been convicted under apartheid laws – it was of paramount importance that their criminal records be expunged. In addition to all of the above, the TRC tabled a number of proposals about symbolic actions – such as the erection of monuments and memorial plaques, arrangements for reconciliation ceremonies and last, but not least, the announcement of a national day of reconciliation.

Lastly the TRC formulated a number of proposals concerning *institu-*

tional reparation. It was part of the commission's directive to, from the knowledge and insight gained, come up with proposals on how the misdeeds of the past could be prevented in future. For many state departments, semi-state bodies, non-government organizations, educational institutions, faith communities, etc there were proposals to think of – and hopefully to implement.

Who had to implement these proposals? Tutu explained that the TRC had to draw up proposals, but that it would rest with the government to accept and implement these proposals. The Truth Commission hoped that it would be possible to place the 'executive body' in the office of the president – that it would be possible to hold the president himself accountable for implementing them.

27-29 OCTOBER 1997: THE JUDGES DID NOT WANT TO SIT ON THE SINNER'S BENCH

Weeks before the hearing would begin, there were intimations of trouble ahead!

If the other interest groups in the country – the politicians, the doctors, the religious leaders, the media, the generals and the business people – were given the opportunity to testify before the Truth Commission, the same would definitely also apply to the legal community. The judges and the advocates, the lawyers and the state prosecutors, would have to let the nation understand, had to help them make sense of everything that lay behind us. For many years white South Africans had been proud of their legal system. If other organizations in the country were corrupt, we could fortunately still rely upon the integrity and impartiality of our judges. We found it odd that many of our black compatriots were less enthusiastic about the criminal justice system. What would the reason be? Was the legal community truly to be exonerated from all blame? Did they, too, have things to explain and confess?

◆　◆　◆

Yasmin Sooka, who had been given the responsibility of making the arrangements for this particular hearing, was pretty upset when she walked into our office one morning, early in October. Over the past few days many persons in the legal profession had contacted us, promised to come to the hearing and also to make submissions, but look what happened: Five of the most prominent judges in the country had informed her that although they wished to make a statement they would not attend the hearings! These judges, former Chief Justice Michael Corbett, his successor Judge Ismail Mahomed, Judge Arthur Chaskalson, President of the Constitutional Court, as well as the deputies of Mahomed and Chaskalson, Judges Hennie van Heerden and Pius Langa, had informed her that they were hesitant to come. To be questioned in public could create an embarrassment and could call the independence of the bench into question. What is more, their programmes were full!

When this became known, there was a choir of protest. "An untenable situation", the legal experts complained. "If the attorneys-general and a number of advocates are prepared to testify," a member of the bar council demanded, "why not the judges? We had to fight very hard on behalf of black people's rights, in the old Supreme Court. Why cannot judges explain their position and apologize in public for the fact that they often applied apartheid legislation without even thinking about it?"

What a member of the Black Lawyers' Association found difficult to swallow was that Judges Mahomed and Langa had acted in this way. Their experiences in the legal system obviously differed dramatically from those of their white colleagues. They should have known that if the nation did not want to see only PW Botha and F W de Klerk before the TRC, but also Nelson Mandela and Thabo Mbeki, it was important for not only white judges, but also black judges to put their point of view to the commission.

Tutu was just as upset and made this quite clear during a press conference, a week before the hearing was due to begin. He found it unacceptable that members of the legal profession, including judges, claimed for themselves a special status and so decided that it was not necessary for them to testify. It would have had enormous symbolic significance if the judges came, he said. "Not only are they depriving themselves of a wonderful opportunity to examine their *own* past deeds, but also to help us bring closure to past events." Judges are people and do make mistakes. In future, they, like all of us, will again make mistakes. But how would all of us not be strengthened if they were prepared to admit mistakes and to apologize? Although written submissions were received from more than twenty judges, Tutu would have liked to have them personally at the hearing. "I discussed the matter with Chief Justice Mahomed, but was unable to persuade him to appear together with his fellow senior judges. However we are thrilled that he made it clear that other judges are free to appear – and I encourage them to do so."

◆ ◆ ◆

When the hearing at last began in Johannesburg on Monday morning, 27 October, there were many interesting goods on offer.

First of all was that of the chairman himself. Because Tutu went further than to just open the hearing with the usual prayer and word of welcome. It was time for him to tell his own story, Tutu said, of how he and his family had suffered under apartheid laws. And this had to happen here, at the hearing about how the law had been exercised over the past decades in our country.

"Virtually every clash with the law black people had under the old dispensation, was aimed at inculcating in us a contempt for, a hatred of the law. Each one of these clashes was aimed at humiliating the black person, to reduce him to being an animal, because a legal system in which you by definition did not have any share, tended not to be well-disposed towards you." Tutu, who had grown up in Ventersdorp, said he often saw the "location children" scratching around for food in the dustbins of the white primary school's dustbins. "Those who could afford to feed themselves, were on the government's feeding scheme. And those who could not afford to do this, did not have such a scheme. That was the worst logic of a terribly unfair political system, which was entrenched through unjust laws."

The Tutu family later went to the Witwatersrand, where his father was a school principal. Time and again the young Desmond had to see his father being humiliated, having to get out his pass book – in fact his pass exemption. "It did not matter whether you were wearing your school uniform, you had to move when you did not have your blasted paper with you! And all of this happened with us because we were black. And then we were expected to grow up and to honour the law, to become law-abiding adults!" Tutu recounted how their family lived in the Roodepoort location, until it was knocked down to make room for the white suburb Horison. Then they moved to Sophiatown, until in turn that, too, was knocked down to make room for the white suburb, Triomf. Munsieville at Krugersdorp, where the Tutus have a long history, was saved at the last minute through the intervention of Leon Wessels, but the church in which he married Leah no longer exists.

"White South Africans often got angry when we said that unjust laws do not need to be obeyed. They made the mistake to think that what was morally right and what was in accordance with the law, always coincided. Most judges in the apartheid years were appointed because they were believed to be in sympathy with the government and would hardly question its decisions. We regarded it as a big farce. We suspected that the judiciary and the police were often in cahoots. We have in the meantime received proof, that during some trials the police not only received the questions from the bench, but even the answers to the questions that would be put to them!"

◆ ◆ ◆

The fact that no judge turned up for the hearing was soon at issue. Written testimony had been received from many judges, including Judge Mahomed and his colleagues, and also from Judge Harmse and a few others, but this was not good enough, was the general feeling. "The judges were kept for many years on 'pedestals where they were virtually untouchable'", Desmond Tutu said. "They were just about regarded as infallible. But they were not! It would have been of symbolic significance if they had been here today to testify in public, and to tell us about their mistakes, too. From their insight and mistakes we would have been able to learn a great deal, and so be able to build a better dispensation." That they failed to pitch proved that they were still part of the old dispensation.

Which did not mean that the missing judges' statements were not taken seriously.

Since 1984, wrote Judge Mahomed and his colleagues, South Africa in fact had two legal systems – one for Whites and the other for non-Whites. The latter did not meet international standards or respect the rights of individuals – it was instead the means through which the government entrenched apartheid as a policy in South Africa. The apartheid laws were unjust, and to their own embarrassment the judges had to admit that the Supreme Court had done very little in the past to question these laws. The unacceptable and racist slant of the apartheid legislation was seldom mentioned in judgements. Those who did find it unacceptable, evidently felt that the courts were not the place where one should express one's disapproval. When the emergency regulations were accepted in the eighties, this resulted in many human rights violations, but the legal profession's objections were limited and muted.

The advocates representing the General Bar Council endorsed the above view in their submission. Too few judges were publicly sensitive to the injustice of apartheid. The judges were "extremely mechanistic" in their conduct and tried to avoid controversy. "In many cases this approach, coupled with the inherent conservatism and general support for the policy of the day, led to the judiciary being more concerned about the technical points of the law than about human rights issues." The judges could have done far more to soften the effects of the oppressive laws and to promote civilian liberties. Part of the problem, the lawyers felt, could be ascribed to the procedures in terms of which judges had been appointed. In the past, appointments and promotions had been in the hands of the Minister of Justice – and political motives did play a role, to the detriment of the judiciary.

Everything had, however, not been uniformly bleak: according to the advocates the judges did in fact retain a measure of independence. It had been the National Party – and the voters who had brought them to power – who had made the unjust laws. Certain governments knowingly acted outside the law. In contrast, the NP government tabled a totally unjust structure in legislation, without the consent of the majority of the people in the country, and began applying it. According to the Bar Council, the apartheid laws could be divided into two categories: firstly the laws that created a system of racial separation and discrimination and maintained them; and secondly a set of laws that suppressed opposition to the unjust laws. But that did not go much further than appearances. In South Africa the law had been adulterated.

The advocates could not, however, present themselves as being only just and fair. They had a lot to apologize for! The Johannesburg Bar Council, for example, shamefacedly declared that it had thirty years before done Mr Bram Fischer a great injustice when it had him struck off the roll, only two days after he had been convicted as a member of the Communist Party. They did not have enough reason to do so. Even more so: Fischer was faced with a serious moral dilemma, for which his colleagues should have had understanding – and if legislation could be prepared to make this possible, the advocates would welcome this wholeheartedly. The Johannesburg Bar Council assured the Fischer family of its sincere regret.

◆ ◆ ◆

The country's lawyers then took the stand.

In its submission the Association of Law Societies singled out three matters that they wanted to discuss: the Group Areas Act which made it impossible for black lawyers to practise where they wanted to; section 29 of the Criminal Procedure Act that permitted people to be detained without trial; and the fact that access to legal practice had been impeded, which nipped the careers of many persons in the bud. "Paging through the minutes of our society", said Piet Langenhoven, President of the Transvaal Law Society, "it is clear that we could have done far more to fight these injustices. All of this, however, is now history. All that remains is to see what we can learn." Just like the Bar, the Transvaal Law Society also had a skeleton in the cupboard: in the fifties they allowed themselves to be convinced by a senior police officer that Nelson Mandela, who had also been convicted in terms of the Suppression of Communism Act, should be struck from the roll. "To the everlasting glory of the court, the request of the law society was refused", said Piet Langenhoven. "After this event, the society would never again apply for the disbarment of an attorney on political grounds."

There *had been* attorneys who had managed to influence the legal process, those who "tempered the law in the courts, on their feet". But this did not happen a lot. Their deeply inculcated Calvinist convictions kept many Afrikaans attorneys from doing so: the powers that be had to be respected – without the necessary proviso, however, that the government had to earn the respect through its actions. The national aspirations the attorneys shared with many of their fellow Afrikaners also made them keep quiet when they should have spoken out.

◆ ◆ ◆

After the attorneys, the attorneys-general, the persons that decide *who* has to be prosecuted and on *which charge*, were sworn in: Dr Jan d'Oliveira, Attorney-General (AG) in Pretoria, Advocate Niel Rossouw, former AG in the Western Cape, Advocate Les Roberts, Eastern Cape AG and Advocate Christo Nel, AG in the Transkei, Advocate Tim McNally of Natal, as well as the AG of the Witwatersrand, who had just resigned, Advocate Klaus von Lieres und Wilkau. The first four AGs jointly apologized for the apartheid laws that they had to implement, for the injustice and trauma that people often had to suffer as a result of their persecution as a result of these laws. The changes of 1994 and the new constitutional dispensation was "a great relief and a liberation from the parliamentary dispensation in terms of which the law was prescribed to serve sectarian objectives", Jan d'Oliveira stated. "I am now experiencing a greater feeling of freedom – and I am also sorry that I did not

(then) understand the full scope of the degree to which statutory legislation had caused harm, suffering and alienation."

The Witwatersrand AG, Klaus von Lieres und Wilkau did however not
agree that AGs had acted prejudicially and unfairly. "If I'm sorry about
anything I'm sorry that I did not render a better service to the public."
Advocate Tim McNally had everybody sit up straight with his response
to criticism about his handling of the KwaMakutha case – in which
General Magnus Malan was acquitted. McNally got up in an agitated
state and demanded that the lady who had insulted him, be cross-
examined. As befits a good AG!

◆ ◆ ◆

Was the hearing successful? Did new information emerge? In general,
yes. It was a good thing that the legal profession had come to stand in
front of the mirror of history. They, as well as the general public, learnt
valuable lessons. In its response to the three days NADEL (the National
Association of Democratic Lawyers) said, "You succeeded in building a
platform from which various testimonies could be heard. But now we
need to go further. It is not enough for people working in law to understand what went wrong, this must be explained to South Africans who
had little respect for the legal institutions. You let the community down
– and you will have to explain why. You will have to tell them that you
ask South Africans for their forgiveness, but you will also have to convince the community that you are sincere. Only then will you be able to
get the country so far as to respect the law in the new democratic
dispensation. And that will not be so easy."

3 NOVEMBER 1997: THE CHIEF INVESTIGATING OFFICER AND THE GARDENER

Drama upon drama! Bennet Sibaya entered the hall, dragging his feet.
When he saw Dumisa Ntsebeza he embraced him and pleaded, tears
running down his cheeks, "Forgive me!" This nobody had expected – not
the astounded TRC members who saw it all, nor the media people who
quickly grabbed their cameras and their pocketbooks. And definitely not
Dumisa Ntsebeza, chief investigating officer of the Truth Commission.

The past week had been a nightmare for Dumisa.

During the amnesty hearing of the three Apla members who had been involved in an attack on the Heidelberg Tavern in Cape Town on New Year's Eve 1993, an unknown witness presented himself: Bennet Sibaya, a gardener residing in Gugulethu. He was in Gugulethu on the evening of the attack, said Sibaya, when he saw three people loading arms into a white BMW car. They were planning to kill somebody, he said – and when the car drove off he saw and remembered the number: XA 12848. On the ground lay a scrap of paper containing the names "Hartleyvale Stadium" and "Heidelberg". The car belonged to Dumisa Ntsebeza.

To the question: "Would you be able to identify the man whom you saw that night behind the steering wheel of the white BMW", Bennet Sibaya pointed to one of the Amnesty Committee members, Ntsiki Sandi. Laughter filled the hall, and he himself smiled nervously. "Well, it looks like the man." Sibaya then got up and walked straight to the TRC's chief investigating officer, pointing with his finger: "That's him!"

Under cross-examination many questions and inconsistencies emerged. How could Sibaya, who had difficulty repeating his own identity number, remember the car's registration number after four years? Rumours were doing the rounds that he had received a huge payment of R120 000 from the police in 1994. For what services rendered? It transpired that Sibaya, a gardener whose monthly income was R480, had just made an offer to purchase a townhouse costing R217 000. Where did the money come from?

Nevertheless, the Commission was rocked by the allegation made against the senior TRC member. Dumisa, who vehemently denied any involvement in the attack on the tavern, felt it to be a huge embarrassment. For Tutu and his team it was of equal concern. If there was only a shadow of truth to the allegation, it could seriously compromise the work of the chief investigating officer, and of the commission itself. What is more, it had not been the first time that rumours about Dumisa and the white BMW had surfaced. Months ago, already, this matter had been brought to Tutu's notice for the first time, but in the meantime the TRC had not done much to go into the charge. How would Tutu explain this oversight?

Early Monday morning, 3 November, all the commissioners were summoned to an emergency meeting in Cape Town. The reporters who had already turned up and were standing about in little groups, were somewhat surprised when the commissioners entered the room where the press conference was to be held. How come the meeting was over so soon? What would Tutu say? What had the commissioners decided?

Tutu's announcement caught everybody off guard.

Bennet Sibaya was here! He was waiting in Tutu's office. An hour or so before, Sibaya had walked into the TRC office, requesting to talk to Tutu. He confessed that Ntsebeza was innocent. His testimony was a pack of lies. In January 1994 he had been arrested when catching crayfish illegally. The police first tortured him and then forced him to involve Dumisa Ntsebeza in the tavern attack. They gave him a photograph of Dumisa and forced him to remember the BMW's number. But over the past weekend Sibaya's conscience bothered him so much that he could no longer live with the lie. He tried to trace the archbishop over the weekend, but could not. He even went to Bishop's Court, where Tutu had lived when he was still the archbishop of Cape Town.

As a matter of fact, he wanted to spill the beans the previous week when he had to testify in the Apla hearing. But when he saw the sea of white faces in the hall – and at first failed to see Tutu's purple bishop's robe – his courage failed him. He hoped that his mistake in first pointing out an Amnesty Committee member would make it obvious that he was lying. But when forced to look again, he saw Ntsebeza and pointed his finger at him.

Bennet Sibaya could no longer live with himself. He had to talk to Tutu, the truth had to be told. He had to apologize to Dumisa.

The chief investigating officer of the TRC threw his arms around the gardener's shoulders. Everyone in the hall watched in astonishment. Cameras flashed. Afterwards Dumisa told the press that he was relieved and grateful – and that he really wanted to forgive Sibaya. But that he also wanted to know who was behind the plot to discredit him. Years ago the police had already tried to damage his reputation and to involve him in Apla attacks. Was this part of the process?

Tutu had in the meantime announced that the commissioners had decided, before Sibaya had presented himself, that they would refer the entire matter to an independent advocate or judge for his urgent investigation. The plan stood – and Tutu would ask, on that very day, that President Mandela appoint an objective and reliable person to go into the matter. That the TRC – and he personally – had made a mistake in not making immediate work of the allegations against Dumisa, was obvious. He tendered his apologies for this.

◆ ◆ ◆

A month later Judge Richard Goldstone, who had been requested by the president to conduct the investigation, announced his finding. Dumisa Ntsebeza was exonerated from all blame that he had been involved in the attack on the Heidelberg Tavern. There was no truth in the allegations. The TRC was criticized because it had not immediately dealt with the matter when it came up the first time. As far as Bennet Sibaya was concerned – he had to be criminally prosecuted. The Cape Attorney-General ought to consider a charge of perjury.

Collectively the commissioners and committee members of the Truth Commission heaved a sigh of relief.

11-13 NOVEMBER 1997: WHEN THE BUSINESS LEADERS HAD TO SUBMIT THEIR BALANCE SHEETS ...

The swish Carlton Hotel is pretty close to the Sanlam Centre. Just a street block and a half – but it was a totally different world than the one Tom and I had become used to over the past weeks. We walked through the big lobby, up the posh staircase, took the lift up to the top floor where – we were just in time for lunch – the most wonderful delicacies were laid out. It was here that the captains of industry had to submit their balance sheets of the past decades.

We bumped into Professor Sampie Terreblanche. He had just made his submission, creating a bit of a sensation. "Many people want to kill me", he explained. "But I think I have a good idea ... "

The TRC had already, before the hearing that would be devoted specifically to the role of the business community, received fifty submissions – from large companies, business leaders, banks, academics, also from the unions. For three days we would have to talk about the past, about the interface between apartheid and the business world. About who profited unfairly, and who suffered. About affirmative action – and all the other lessons for the future. Some thirty organizations and persons were asked to testify in public. Rembrandt would be there, together with Anglo-American, Armscor, Old Mutual, Sanlam, Eskom, Tongaat-Hullet and Barlow-Rand. They would be followed by the large organizations, Nafcoc, the *Afrikaanse Handelsinstituut* (the Afrikaans Chamber of Business), the South African Banks Board, Sacob and the Chamber of Mines. The Reserve Bank had confirmed that they would attend, as would the Land Bank, after some initial hesitation. The unions couldn't wait: Cosatu, Nactu and Selfsa would not miss a chance like this. Cyril Ramaphosa agreed to address the hearing – as would Chris Ball, Warren Clewlow and the two professors, Nic Wiehann and Sampie Terreblanche.

One of the first persons to lead the discussion, was the Stellenbosch professor. Terreblanche did not hesitate to go for the jugular! White supremacy and racial capitalism, he said, had over the past hundred years enriched the Whites undeservedly and impoverished those of colour, equally undeservedly. By the end of the previous century there had been quite a few wealthy black farmers in South Africa; black farmers together produced more maize than white farmers. Following the introduction of the Glen Grey Act (1894) and the Land Act (1913) they were chased off their farms – and their status was lowered to that of farm labourers or cheap factory workers. Interestingly enough, the professor remarked, one did not read of this in the submissions of the business giants. It was Afrikaans business in particular that had in the past been favoured by the government, be it as far as fishing quotas, mining and liquor concessions and other government contracts were concerned. Various Afrikaner organizations such as Rembrandt, Sanlam, Volkskas and Trust Bank, let alone Nasionale Pers, flourished as a result of the good relationship they enjoyed with government.

It is only right, said Professor Terreblanche, that those who benefited unduly in the past, will have to put their hands deep into their pockets to accommodate those who had been disadvantaged. "Racial capitalism continues to exist, enormous concentrations of economic power and privileges being in a few white hands. The process of reform will remain incomplete as long as the economic power acquired through racial structures remain untouched, as has been the case over the past three and a half years. I agree with Mr Thabo Mbeki that the stability of the new South Africa can be endangered if we do not find satisfactory solutions to inequality and poverty." Sampie Terreblanche's solution was that a levy of 0,5 percent should be used from taxpayers having an asset value of more than R2 million for the upliftment of the poorest 40 percent of the population. Such a levy would be preferable above other forms of taxation. Terreblanche admitted that he was aware of the practical problems in this regard, but that they were not insurmountable – and the symbolic meaning of such a form of restitution was enormous. If necessary, other forms of taxation could be reduced to make way for this form of taxation.

The submission made a definite impact – among others, certainly on the TRC commissioners, who asked virtually every one of the next speakers what they thought of the special 'rich man's tax'. In the course of the next few days Sampie's proposal would reverberate not only in the corridors of the Carlton Hotel, but over the entire country, and even in Parliament.

◆ ◆ ◆

In the meantime one businessman after the other had his say, some humbly, others less apologetically. Some were sharply critical. Nafcoc spoke on behalf of black South African business and severely criticized the white business sector and the former government because they had, over many years, deprived black business people of the opportunity to establish themselves in the market. Mr John Hlongwane, president of Nafcoc added that when all the restrictions that had made it impossible for black business people to compete were finally lifted in 1986, many white retail groups quickly erected large shopping centres close to the black townships, to lay their hands on the shopping power of the black public. Black traders had been hampered in all kinds of bureaucratic ways. In the agricultural and sorghum beer industry, as well as in the taxi and gambling industry, the moneyed interests and assets remained safely in white hands. For many years the large companies – especially in the mining industry – colluded with government. They plundered the environment and even enriched themselves at the expense of the rest of the community.

Things aren't quite so simple, retorted Mr Raymond Parsons of the South African Chamber of Business (Sacob). Over the years various patterns had developed for dealing with the interaction between the races and the business community. Sacob tried to play a proactive role in the past, to try and keep the economic machine going at a time of unrest and strikes, protest marches and mass action. It also did as much as it could to foster better relationships between different communities. To achieve this they had to, of necessity, co-operate with the government – which is now being taken amiss.

Mr Mike Rosholt, former chairman of Barlow Rand, had to answer sharply critical questions about the profitable contracts his company had received from the previous government – as well as allegations that Barlow Rand was trying to suppress the unions. This is incorrect, he explained. His company was one of the first who had signed agreements of co-operation with the unions. It did not serve any purpose to be angry at the large companies, such as Barlow Rand, that they had not disregarded the laws that existed at the time. Of what use would that have been? Instead, they chose to focus on socio-economic reform.

Dr Willem de Kock of Eskom was more prepared to do some soul-searching. His company had done little to improve the fate of Blacks in South Africa, and often discriminated against Blacks as far as appointments were concerned. "Eskom hereby apologizes to all black South Africans in general, and particularly to its employees, that it supported apartheid through our policies. We also apologize to all South Africans that we did not take any active steps to call for the downfall of apartheid." As far as the provision of electricity was concerned Eskom had often served the interests of the white suburbs at the expense of the black areas. Since the late eighties Eskom had been doing its level best to improve matters – but only with mixed success.

Sanlam's executive director, Mr Desmond Smith, also admitted that his company had been greatly advantaged through apartheid. Apartheid was "impracticable and immoral, controversial and repulsive ... and brought in its wake unparalleled destitution, suffering and sorrow for people of colour ... The past cannot be undone, but these events leave us with a feeling of deep sadness and regret. One can only pray that the TRC will, through its activities, succeed in achieving its objective, to heal the deep wounds of the past and to achieve reconciliation and national unity." Sanlam put their cards on the table regarding the cordial relationship with the previous government, but offered a historical explanation: both the government and Sanlam's Afrikaner roots go back a long way – in Sanlam's case to 1918 when the company was established to again empower Afrikaners who had been impoverished through the Anglo-Boer War. Sanlam did in fact get rid of petty apartheid somewhat earlier than others did, but could not identify itself fully with the struggle – on account of the violent nature of the struggle and the policy of nationalization proposed by the liberation movements, with which Sanlam was unable to agree.

Desmond Smith touched on a sore point when he said that as far as human rights violations are concerned, some of the most gross violations are now taking place in our country. "These violations are to be seen in the murders, robberies, hijackings, rapes, assaults, theft, fraud, corruption, etc. We are convinced that the ineffective maintenance of law and order is directly responsible for these gross violations of human rights at corporate and individual levels."

In his submission Mr Bobby Godsell of the Chamber of Mines called for sympathy for the mining industry, which had also been harmed by apartheid. The country's race policy was responsible for the fact that the mining industry was at the moment poorly equipped to compete internationally. He admitted that the wage policy of the past had been extremely unjust, that white workers had been paid much better than black workers – even though it was true that the wages of Blacks had over the past years increased much faster than the wages of Whites.

Bobby Godsell, gifted orator and motivational expert, however, did not succeed on that day to satisfy one and all.

Boraine: "I had really thought that the Chamber of Mines would show greater seriousness in apologizing for its apartheid past, for the harm done by migrant labour to thousands of families in the country, for entire communities that had been torn in two. Your industry played such a pivotal role in the country's economy ... "

Godsell: "It's not difficult today to say that we are sorry. But this is not what is at issue here now. The question is: what can we do now to rectify apartheid's legacy? What solutions are there for us? We are quite prepared to put what happened, the damage, into context. We can do it five times running! But what difference will that make outside? The true challenge is to do something about the legacy of apartheid."

Boraine: "I agree, but you must not underestimate the strong wave of goodwill that will be released in South Africa should the Chamber show remorse about the past."

When Mr Johann Rupert of Rembrandt, son of the well-known Dr Anton Rupert, took his place on the podium, he had a ready audience. Everybody wanted to know what the message of the Ruperts would be. How would the Rembrandt group judge their role in the past? Guilty – or not guilty?

In the end, the answer was a Yes and a No. Yes, it was true that Whites had benefited unfairly from the apartheid period. But no, Rembrandt was not on the list of companies favoured by government. It was true that Rembrandt had been founded by Afrikaners, that only Afrikaners had been prepared to invest in it. "But both my father and I were vociferous opponents of apartheid. Our members of personnel did not benefit from apartheid and neither did our company." The company never got government contracts, "we did not have any sweetheart agreements with government. I can't see, up to this day, how we benefited from apartheid – on the contrary, the state today gets R2,8 billion out of Richmond". Did Rembrandt do enough at the time? "No, but at that time we thought we did ... I believe that apartheid was a waste of scarce resources. We squandered R35 million on gold reserves and so catapulted our children into debt."

Whether all the commissioners were satisfied with Johann Rupert's explanation? Yes and No! A more unambiguous apology would probably have been received better. What was easy on the ear was a surprising snippet of news that the chairman of Rembrandt brought with him. In January 1986 his father, Dr Anton Rupert, wrote a letter to President P W Botha, urging him to get rid of apartheid – which had turned Afrikaner into "lepers" – once and for all. This happened during the serious credit crisis that hit our country when Dr Fritz Leutweiler, who had come to South Africa to act as a broker between the international banks and the South African government, had told Dr Rupert that he was no longer prepared to act as a spokesman for apartheid. "Is apartheid the corner-stone of our survival?" Rupert wrote at the time. "Of course not. I sincerely believe that the misconception that apartheid is promoting the interests of Whites, is no more than a myth. Hence the personal appeal to you. Please confirm that you are relinquishing apartheid. It is crucifying us, it is destroying our language, it is turning a once proud nation of heroes into the lepers of the world. Please remove from their backs the curse of crime against the humanity of our children and grand-children ... "

What was the reaction of the president to Rupert's letter, the re-porters asked. "The reaction? That is private!", Johann Rupert replied.

The *Afrikaanse Handelsinstituut* (AHI) was the only one of the pre-dominantly Afrikaans organizations that was prepared to apologize un-conditionally for its support of apartheid. After a long explanation as to how it happened that the AHI, which had been established in 1942 to promote the economic aspirations of the Afrikaners who had become greatly impoverished since the Anglo-Boer War and the subsequent decades, had uncritically supported the policy of apartheid for years, the AHI confessed. In retrospect it was obvious that the AHI had made great mistakes. Separate development involved social manipulation that exacted a cruel price of people and led to a shocking waste of resources. The AHI should have realized much earlier that apartheid was morally and economically wrong, they should have had far more understanding for the suffering caused in people's lives, and they should have been far more critical *vis-à-vis* the government. The policy of apartheid meant that black people – especially the black business community – had been severely disadvantaged, that the country became poorer. For all of these things the AHI accepted co-responsibility. It acknowledged that fellow South Africans had been seriously disadvantaged through these deeds and omissions and expressed its sincere remorse.

On one point, however – concerning the so-called rich man's tax – the AHI did not agree with Sampie Terreblanche. Mr Theo van Wyk, the former president of the AHI had another, quite creative proposal: why not use the accumulated money of the Sasria fund for remunerating past victims? The fund had been established during the previous dispensation to give cover to people who had suffered as a result of political unrest. The fund had not received or paid out any claims worth mentioning over the past few years. At the moment Sasria had accumulated assets of about R9 billion – the R3 billion required for the remuneration of victims over six years could easily be paid from this fund.

◆ ◆ ◆

The explanations and excuses of white businessmen and business concerns as to the reforms they were undertaking, to ensure that the playing field was being levelled in the business world, did not impress Mr Sam Shilowa, secretary-general of the Congress of South African Trade Unions, Cosatu. On the contrary, "They're lying!" was his comment. He castigated Johann Rupert: "Afrikaners can't come here, telling us that they couldn't do any more. Bram Fischer did more!" Mr Jay Naidoo, Shilowa's predecessor at Cosatu and the present Minister of Post and Telecommunications, had even sharper comment: "There is overwhelming evidence that the business sector and the apartheid government collaborated. I think they should plead for our forgiveness today. None of them can say that they didn't benefit ... what would happen if we put in claims for the wages we lost! ... I held the bodies of persons killed by them. Their blood was on our clothes ... Are Whites prepared to go to the townships to see how they humiliated us? ... The media are just as guilty through the stereotype they have created of the present government as incompetent and corrupt. They also need to learn that the unions are not a bunch of bloodthirsty terrorists. "On the contrary," Naidoo told his audience, "if you want to study truth and reconciliation, you must study the history of the unions in South Africa." It had been, above all, the unions who had created the basis for reform, that had become the largest stabilizing force in the community.

The latter statement was taken with a pinch of salt by many South Africans.

◆　◆　◆

The gathering in the Carlton Centre had its highs and lows. New information and insights did emerge. The fact that everybody who was there had committed themselves to building up the community, was important. But South Africans who had hoped for a national consensus about the country's future would have been quite disappointed after this hearing, one of the Johannesburg newspaper editors remarked. Between the two pillars of the business community – the unions and the business undertakings – the gulf was apparently unbridgeable. In the well-tried South African tradition they blamed one another. Cosatu's irritation with the white businesses that – with a few exceptions, such as the AHI – they had tried to absolve and justify themselves, was understandable. It would have been better if the captains of industry – notably the mining industry – would have confessed their failings and omissions honestly and sincerely. That would in fact have cleared the air.

But Cosatu's emotional and unrestrained language did not help either. One has to ask oneself: why did nobody confront Cosatu with the human rights violations its members had committed themselves? In the eighties old people who refused to go on strike were forced to drink cooking oil and eat soap powder, and so-called collaborators were murdered. What did Cosatu have to say at the time? Humility and shame would not be out of place. It is understandable that Cosatu is angry because business shrank away from open admissions. But if Cosatu had been truly generous, it would have acknowledged the confessions made by business. That could have been the point of common interest for a discussion about national consensus. An opportunity lost – which simply means even harder work for the idealists and those who persevere.

12 NOVEMBER 1997: UNEXPECTED VISITORS: THE AWB PUTS IN AN APPEARANCE

It was an interesting sight. Together with us around the table in the TRC office in Johannesburg sat Mr Eugene Terre'blanche, leader of the *Afrikaner Weerstandsbeweging* (Afrikaner Resistance Movement) and his two lieutenants, Japie Oelofse and Brigadier Dries Kriel. They had called Dr Boraine the previous day to make an appointment. The deputy chairman stopped me in the corridor early that morning: "The AWB is about to visit us. Would you please come along?"

The '*Boer* hater', Boraine, and the '*Boer* of Ventersdorp', Terre'-blanche, had an immediate rapport! This is how it came about: While shaking hands, Boraine smiled at Terre'blanche:

"Mr Terre'blanche, both of us are suffering from the same injustice. The press often quotes us incorrectly and puts labels around our necks, which we do not often deserve ... "

"Only too true, Doctor Boraine", the leader of the AWB replied in his deep bass. And continued: "We realize that the AWB has, as far as violence in South Africa is concerned, reached a dead-end. We have come to the decision that we have only one of two choices: either we have to take the TRC at its word and try to contribute our part to bring about reconciliation, or else we have to return to our days of inciting violence and planting bombs."

The AWB wished to inform the TRC of the perceptions and motives of the right-wing groups in South Africa, Terre'blanche went on to say. They wanted to play their role for the sake of reconciliation and reparation. But they were concerned about two things in particular. *Firstly*: many AWB members who had applied for amnesty, of whom a large number were already serving prison sentences, had already been waiting for months that their cases be heard. Would it not be possible for the TRC to expedite their cases? *Secondly*: the AWB prisoners were living in terrible conditions in prison. Would it not be possible for the TRC to apply to the government, while their cases were pending, that their status be changed to that of political prisoners? This would have many advantages for these prisoners.

Alex Boraine immediately agreed. "Both requests are reasonable. I promise to give immediate attention to these matters, and will liaise as soon as possible with the Amnesty Committee."

I also raised two matters. The TRC also needed the AWB's co-operation. *Firstly*, we were concerned about the fact that many victims from the right wing had not reported at the TRC. We needed their statements to get a full picture of everything that had happened in the past. Could the AWB assist us to encourage them? It would also have many advantages for the victims and their families. They also needed the process of healing. What is more, they would also be able to lay a claim to reparation. And, *secondly*, there was our concern about the process of reconciliation in the country. Would the AWB be able to help with this, even after the TRC had concluded its work?

In turn the three AWB men agreed. "The time has come", the leader said, "that the different communities in the country reach out to one another, that bridges are built between us."

Because both of us lived in Pretoria, it was decided that Dries Kriel and I should remain in contact, and see to it that attention be given to various matters. We parted as good friends. The '*Boer* hater' and the '*Boer*' too.

17-19 NOVEMBER 1997: EAST LONDON – ARE *DOMINEES* AND PRIESTS ALSO SUPPOSED TO CONFESS?

"Probably the best of all the Truth Commission hearings", Desmond Tutu said that afternoon, when we gathered our papers after the last "Amen". I was in full agreement: this specific hearing for representatives of all the faith communities in our country had definitely run another course than the other 'special' hearings.

It all began on the Sunday afternoon of 16 November. Hundreds of believers from various East London congregations, together with the delegates of the various churches who came from all over the country, began to pack the Christian Centre in Abbotsford; it was clear that something interesting was about to happen.

The devotional service was led by a panel of clergymen and pastors. Tutu, who read the sermon, was in his element. Jesus used a little boy's meagre meal of bread and fish to feed five thousand people, he began. That is how God works! He uses the most humble and improbable persons as his co-workers. Jeremiah thought he was too young. Mary couldn't believe that the Lord wanted to make her, a simple young girl living in backward Nazareth, the mother of his Son. In exactly the same way there are many unknown men and women and children in our country today, unsung heroes and heroines, who are being used by the Lord in wonderful ways. The miracles of reconciliation and forgiveness, of ordinary people who reach out to one another, the things that the TRC has been experiencing over the past two years, are deeply moving. In the next few days churches and church leaders, different denominations, will tell their stories, talking about guilt and forgiveness, of love and reconciliation, the archbishop said. At heart it would however be the stories of ordinary people who were appointed by God as His ambassadors in a confused and broken society. After all, if we are not prepared to pass on his love to others, who will?

◆ ◆ ◆

At first it was not certain that a special hearing would be held for South African faith communities. Were the churches and the other groups truly guilty of *gross* human rights violations? Did they have anything to confess? A number of commissioners first had to be convinced. But, ran the counter-argument, the churches and the other communities were so closely involved with everything that had happened in our country – on both sides of the struggle – that one could not imagine the TRC not giving the ministers of religion and the priests, the pastors and imams the opportunity to tell their stories.

Exactly 101 letters were sent to all the different Christian denominations and ecumenical bodies in South Africa, as well as to representatives of the Muslim, Hindu, Jewish, Buddhist and Baha'i communities – also to persons who would be able to speak on behalf of the traditional African religions – with an invitation to make a submission. Depending on the religious leaders' response, the TRC would decide about the desirability of a public hearing. In the meantime the TRC had instructed the ministers of religion in their ranks, Khoza Mgojo, Bongani Finca, Mcibisi Xundu and myself to take the matter further. While some of my colleagues were still debating whether this was a good idea, the archbishop was all fired up. One day, while Tutu was still undergoing treatment for cancer in the USA, I received an e-mail from New York: "I support you with all my heart. Carry on!"

The Salvation Army was the first to bring in its submission. On 2 June Commissioner Paul du Plessis came personally to the TRC offices to deliver it. One after the other the other denominations – in any case, *most* other denominations – followed suit. The Anglicans and Methodists, the Catholics and the Presbyterians, many others, replied. The General Synodical Commission of the NG Kerk at first informed us that they would not be making a submission. However, they were planning on writing a report on the road they took as far as apartheid was concerned – primarily for the sake of their members – but also for other interested South Africans. The Gereformeerde Kerk abided by its Synod decision, earlier the year. They would not come. The Hervormde Kerk did not respond at all, even though I called the administrator's office a number of times. However, the number of submissions sent in – and the quality of most of them – were encouraging. After just more than thirty had been received, the TRC decided: in November a public hearing would be held, not only for the Christian churches, but for all faith communities. East London, where the very first hearing had taken place almost two years before, would be the place where the last of the special hearings would be convened.

To decide which of the many groups who made submissions would be invited to submit in public – and to get all of them in East London – we met for hours. In the course of the three days we wanted to accommodate the full spectrum: the so-called mainline churches, the evangelical groups, the Afrikaans churches, the charismatic and pentecostal churches, ecumenical bodies, as well as the testimonies of the other faith communities. If you don't invite a woman to talk about the role of women in the churches – the women who do most of the work anyway – you are looking for trouble, Joyce Seroke and Brigalia Bam (of the SA Council of Churches) warned us.

It wasn't difficult to get the English mainline churches as well as the charismatic groups to come to East London. They informed us immediately that they were on their way. Dr Izak Burger of the Apostolic Faith Mission called us to say that both he and his co-leader, the Reverend Frank Chikane, would be there. In order to persuade the Zion Christian Church, the largest independent African church, to attend the proceedings Tom Manthata and I, having made numerous telephone calls, finally drove down to Pietersburg to talk to Bishop Barnabas Lekganyane. This clinched the deal. The Afrikaans churches were however a headache. The Gereformeerde Kerk would not be present, but four theologians from the church, Alwyn du Plessis, Bennie van der Walt, Amie van Wyk and Pontie Venter had drawn up their own public confession of guilt, which they would present at East London. The Hervormde Kerk remained silent. And the NG Kerk? I could simply not imagine that the church would not testify and made arrangements that a special place be reserved on the programme for its submission. My faith was rewarded! Early in November the General Synodical Commission unanimously decided that the moderator, Freek Swanepoel, would, after all, have to attend the hearing and that he had to speak on behalf of the church.

Getting the other religious communities to come to East London, also took some doing. The chief rabbi of Johannesburg, Dr Cyril Harris, immediately agreed to attend the hearing. The South African Hindu *Maha Sabha* also informed us, even if at the last minute, that they would make a submission. The *Dharma* centre, representing the Zen Buddhists in the country, responded. Even the Baha'i community requested a turn to speak. But the Muslims had the steering committee in a sweat. I made many calls myself and mailed letters to various Muslim organizations – even, on the verge of despair, resorting to asking Archbishop Tutu and Minister Dullah Omar to help us. At last, a few days before the hearing would begin, Moulana Ibrahim Bham of the *Jamiatul Ulama*, Transvaal, agreed to make a submission at the hearing. The second this was announced in the media, there was an immediate response. Dr Faried Esack, the brilliant Muslim critic, phoned our office with an urgent request: he wanted to make a submission on behalf of the *Call of Islam*. The *Muslim Judicial Council* informed us from Cape Town, when the hearing had just begun, that they were also on their way! In the meantime Moulana Bham of the *Jamiatul Ulama* called to inform us that he was ill and would no longer be able to attend. "That doesn't surprise me", Faried Esack told me. "He doesn't want to be seen on the same stage with me!"

◆ ◆ ◆

When Archbishop Tutu opened the hearing on Monday morning, 17 November, he continued the message of reconciliation he had delivered the previous afternoon in the Christian Centre. "We aren't here to place the churches in the dock. However, we do want to, honestly, with love and humility, look at the past. We want to learn lessons for the future", he stressed. Knowing that many delegates could hardly wait until Wednesday when the NG Kerk – the 'National Party at Prayer' – would be given an opportunity to talk about its past role, Tutu had a friendly and cautionary word.

"It's definitely not easy to admonish somebody you like in public. I can say that I am now making the same mistakes that I used to accuse the leaders of the white NG Kerk of making. We (the other churches) need to confess that we were often arrogant and hard in the way we rejected the NG Kerk, because they did not take on the government about apartheid. They usually responded by saying that they did do so – but behind closed doors. A while ago I was sitting next to President Nelson Mandela, telling him what I thought of a particular matter. Then it dawned on me that I was doing exactly what I had always accused the NG Kerk of doing. It is definitely not easy to take action against somebody who was with you in the struggle and whom you like. I admit that our actions against the NG Kerk could have come across as being self-justifying. Our cause was just ... but we apologize for the way we acted. We hope our apologies will be accepted." Tutu added: "In the past, in a period of protest it was rather easy to know what the church should do. To be the church in South Africa today, is quite a different matter. It's not so simple!"

◆　◆　◆

Admissions of guilt, forgiveness, reconciliation and restitution were the order of the day.

In the very first submission Brigalia Bam, who had just retired as the general secretary of the *SA Council of Churches* spoke about the role of the SACC. She could have said a great deal about what the SACC had done over the past thirty years to counteract injustice, to let a prophetic voice be heard, to care for the victims and the families of exiles and convicted prisoners. She could have said as much about the price this exacted from the SACC and many of its leaders. But the focus of her testimony lay elsewhere: "We could have done far more to help the victims, to act in the name of truth and justice. We failed those who suffered by often acting reactively, instead of proactively."

Bishop Michael Nuttall, who spoke on behalf of the *Anglican Church*, confessed that the church had failed its own Archbishop Tutu. Tutu's support for economic sanctions against South Africa – as a last attempt to bring about change – had been sharply criticized. "Please forgive us for what we did to you and other 'prophets' in the church." He also apologized for his church's unwillingness to speak out when it should have, and for the often arrogant condemnation of those whose ideas and actions differed from those of the Anglican Church.

The following words made us sit up straight: "It was all too easy in the past to pass resolutions or make lofty pronouncements condemning apartheid. It was all too easy to point a morally superior finger at Afrikaner nationalist prejudice and pride. English pride and prejudice was no less real, and it was never very far below the surface of our high-sounding moral pronouncements. The Anglican Lord Milner must be as problematic to Afrikaner Christians as D F Malan, the *dominee*, is to us. In a strange way I think many white Anglicans owe an apology to the Afrikaner community for their attitude of moral superiority. I became aware of this need when, as former Bishop of Pretoria, I got to know such fine Afrikaner Christians as David Bosch and Piet Meiring. Perhaps, Chairperson, I could ask Professor Piet Meiring in his capacity as a member of the TRC kindly to receive this expression of apology from a bishop of *die Engelse kerk* (the English church)".

Above all, Nuttall continued, the Anglican church was guilty before its thousands of black members who in the past – as a result of the church's silence, its hesitant action, even more, the discrimination that was to be seen in the church itself – had suffered greatly. If one looks back today, if you see the large numbers of men, women and children, office bearers and members who had been hurt, one cannot but pray from your heart: "Lord, have mercy. *Nkosi, sihawukele, Morena, re gaugele, Kyrie eleison.* Thank you God for faithful ones, those who were clear-sighted, those who endured against all the odds to the end."

Tutu was moved, and said so. And then turned to me: would I respond, on behalf of the NG Kerk? "Obviously I will pass on the words of the English bishop to the NG Kerk," I said. "That will be a great honour. Your words have moved me, as they will move my brothers and sisters in the church when they hear them. But the NG Kerk also owes you, and many people in the country, an apology. We also failed you. Having said this, thank you that you did not leave us behind in the past and continue without us. Thank you that you kept talking to us and kept challenging us."

Bishop Frank Retief, who spoke on behalf of the *Church of England in South Africa*, told us quite frankly how many members had allowed themselves to be misled by the previous government, how the ideology of apartheid had blinded them to the extent that they had supported such a "cruel and oppressive" system as apartheid. "Like most South African Whites we believed government propaganda telling us that we were involved in a life and death struggle, a struggle to retain Western values and to resist the communist threat endangering us ... The church's effort to remain outside the politics of the country, not to have anything to do with the liberation struggle, was in retrospect a huge error ... In this way we failed the black community – many of our own members."

Bishop Mvume Dandala, head of the *Methodist Church*, expressed both his commendation for and reservations about the work of the TRC. It appreciated what the Commission had already done and achieved, but also expressed its concern: does the act allow enough latitude for true confession, forgiveness and reconciliation? The victims are expected to forgive while many perpetrators show little or no remorse and are not expected to make amends for their role in the past. Is reconciliation possible on this basis? Does this not mean that one would then call out, as did Jeremiah "Peace ... peace" while there is no peace?

However, Bishop Dandala also searched his own heart. Many people in the church suffered greatly, the church itself ran into difficulties as a result of its opposition to apartheid. But there were also large numbers of Methodists who remained silent, who did not want to become involved with the injustice suffered, who hid safely behind the excuse that "religion and politics need to be separated".

Bishop Kevin Dowling, who had at Rustenburg already made a deep impression on the TRC, spoke on behalf of the *Catholic Church*. The tragic assassination of Chris Hani, leader of the Communist Party and the subsequent conviction of Janusz Walus for the crime – while both were members of the Catholic Church – illustrated the complex situation in our country: one part of the church did everything in its power to keep the apartheid dispensation going, while the other part of the church fought tooth and nail to bring apartheid to a fall. Because the church had so many members who felt so differently about so many matters, it was difficult today to report on the role of the church as a whole. It was also difficult from our context to judge the motives and actions of people living forty years ago. Some say the church leaders were pretty moderate and careful in their opposition to apartheid, others say that they were courageous and gave clear guidance! However, it is true that the Catholic Church had, since 1947, clashed repeatedly with the government, to the point that the bishops' conference condemned apartheid as "intrinsically evil". However, the church was hesitant to support the so-called 'defiance campaign' of 1957 and instead called upon their congregants to "maintain order" and "use peaceful means". The continued criticism of apartheid in the years that followed cost the church dearly. Many members left the church. At one point Father Smangaliso Mkhatshwa was arrested and the offices of the Catholic newspaper, *New Nation*, closed. But just as important as it was to look to the past, was the question: What are the churches going to do in the years to come? Bishop Dowling concluded his submission with a passionate plea to the church community, to give one another a hand and co-operate, for the sake of restoring moral values in the country, and also of bringing about reconciliation between all the people of South Africa.

◆ ◆ ◆

The second day was reserved for the representatives of the other faith communities. The chairman, Desmond Tutu, introduced the proceedings, as on the day before, on a serious – and also reconciliatory – note. Most churchgoers had in the past departed from the premise that South Africa was a 'Christian country', where only Christian values and views applied, where laws were made to suit the Christians in the country. And this was the case although adherents of other religions have been living in the community virtually since the arrival of the Dutch in the Cape, three and a half centuries ago. Except for the traditional religions of the San and the Khoi and the black peoples of South Africa, the Muslims settled in the Cape only a few years after the arrival of Van Riebeeck and his party. Jews made South Africa their home in the early 19th century, followed a few decades later by groups of Muslims and Hindus from India. Today virtually all world religions are represented in South Africa, including Buddhists and Baha'is. "I am certain that all my fellow Christians in South Africa will agree with me if I express our deep apologies to you, the members of other faith communities in the country, for the arrogant way in which we as Christians acted – as though ours was the only religion in South Africa, while we have been a multi-religious community from day one."

Dr Faried Esack, the well-known *Muslim* academic, took up from where Tutu left off in his address. If we talk about the past, he explained, we should not only think of apartheid, security legislation and all those things; Christian 'triumphalism' was also an issue. In an avowed 'Christian state', adherents of other religions often ran into difficulties. If you were a Muslim – somebody who was part of the 'Muslim threat' – you were often regarded as an enemy of the state and treated as such. It is ironic, said Faried, that as recently as 1986, the year when the NG Kerk had for the first time begun to take their leave of apartheid, the General Synod still referred to Islam, in one of its decisions, as a "false religion". However, the Muslim community ought not to be too smug, Moulana Esack went on to say. They also had to put their own house in order. There had been times when Muslims, too, had been hesitant to come forward, to do what was right. Where were the Muslim leaders in 1969 when Imam Abdullah Haron was arrested, tortured and, in the end, killed?

Imam Rashied Omar, who later arrived at the hearing from Cape Town, referred to the same matter. "It is not only the NG Kerk leaders who ought to confess their involvement in the apartheid system. Sections of the other important Christian churches, as well as Muslims, Jews and Hindus, were guilty of collaborating with the apartheid regime, often to the definite disadvantage of the liberation struggle. For the sake of rebuilding our country spiritually, it is vitally important that we, as religious leaders, get our people to confess their complicity in apartheid and racism. What is more, those who benefited from the past, ought to put their hands deep into their pockets."

Mr Ashwin Traikamjee, who represented South African *Hindus*, echoed Faried and Imam Omar's sentiments. Among the Hindus there were persons who had suffered and bravely spoke out against the injustice and fought for better things – South Africa was, in fact, the country where Mahatma Gandhi first developed his political philosophy and style – but there were also many leaders who accepted the *status quo*, who had collaborated with the Tricameral Parliament, and who had benefited from the situation in many ways. "We should have got rid of these leaders, but we did not!"

Chief Rabbi Cyril Harris is an accomplished speaker who gave an interesting overview, in Queen's English, of the vicissitudes of the *Jewish* community in South Africa. He said it had been very difficult for Jews to protest against apartheid, in view of their own history of suffering, of the precarious position they often assumed in society. If one looks back today, there had been far more one could have done, he said. But that is only one side of the story, Rabbi Harris said proudly. The other day none other than Minister Kader Asmal had declared that "the South African Jewish community has yielded proportionally more heroes of the struggle than any other so-called white group".

At long last, after the representatives of a number of other groups, including the Baha'i and traditional African communities, as well as the Black Independent Churches had had their say, the day's proceedings were concluded by a remarkable lady, Ms Cathy Makhene. "I am talking on behalf of all the *women* belonging to the various religions", she began. "Over the past few days only men were talking, and this is understandable, as all religions are heavily patriarchal. The fathers rule, while the mothers and the daughters do all the work! Gross human rights violations not only concern apartheid, but also women who are kept away from the pulpit, who may not serve in certain offices, whose full humanity and talents are often not recognized."

Cathy Makhene brought along a new creed. This creed particularly needed to be heard during a session of the Truth Commission. That was how millions of women on earth – many of the women who had told their painful stories during hearings concerning human rights violations over the past year and a half – had understood the most basic truth on earth, the truth of the Gospel. Do you want to know what kept women in prison going, mothers who had buried their children, brides who had to give up their husbands in the struggle, women who were humiliated and raped, who shivered with cold in the winter nights, who tried to feed and clothe their families with great difficulty? Listen!

A CREED

We believe in God
Who created women and men in God's image,
Who created the world and gave both sexes the care of the earth;

We believe in Jesus,
Child of God, chosen by God, born of the woman, Mary,
Who listened to women and stayed in their homes,
Who looked for the Kingdom with them,
Who was followed and supported by women disciples;

We believe in Jesus,
Who discussed theology with a woman at a well,
Who received anointing from a woman at Simon's house
And rebuked the man's guests who scorned her;

We believe in Jesus,
Who healed a woman on the Sabbath,
Who spoke of God as a woman seeking a lost coin,
As a woman who swept, seeking the lost;

We believe in Jesus,
Who thought of pregnancy and birth with reverence;

We believe in Jesus,
Who appeared first to Mary Magdalene
And sent her with the message "Go and tell";

We believe in the wholeness of God
In whom there is neither Jew nor Greek, slave nor free,

Female nor male, for we are one in God;

We believe in the Holy Spirit
As She moves over the waters of creation and over the earth,
The woman spirit of God, who created us and gave us birth
And covers us with her wings. Amen.

◆ ◆ ◆

The last day belonged to the Afrikaans churches. But before they could be given the opportunity to speak, Bishop Barnabas Lekganyane and his entourage – together with two or three other churches – first had to address the TRC. The *Zion Christian Church* had been supposed to make its submission the previous afternoon, but one of their spokesmen who had to bring the manuscripts to be presented to the TRC, had missed his flight from Johannesburg. That morning during breakfast, before the last day's hearing would begin, Brigalia Bam was pessimistic: "You'll see, the ZCC won't come. They've disappointed me too often. When the SACC in the past invited them to conferences or meetings, time and again they balked at the last moment. Bishop Lekganyane has never pitched for an ecumenical event, and I don't think he'll come today. Just you wait and see ... "

Fortunately Brigalia was wrong. When I reached the Christian Centre the bishop, accompanied by busloads of followers, had already arrived. The excited ZCC members formed a guard of honour at the entrance. Tutu, who has an inborn sense of occasion, welcomed the bishop at the door and accompanied him into the hall. The audience seemed somewhat nonplussed when the ZCC delegation announced that Bishop Lekganyane would not himself speak, but that the Rev Thomas Mohape would speak on his behalf. Even Desmond Tutu, who said that many people had come especially to hear his voice, could not persuade Barnabas Lekganyane. The bishop, who was the undisputed leader of the millions of members of his church, and who was regarded as one of the most influential persons in the country, had never granted an interview and does not make public addresses. "If you want to hear him speak, you will have to attend one of his church services", one of his deputies told us. "That's the only place where he will speak. Tom Manthata and I did not find it so odd. A few weeks ago, when we went to see him in Pietersburg, the same thing happened. Before the formal meeting we were exchanging chit-chat over a cup of tea. But when the formal interview began, Lekganyane withdrew. As befitted a traditional captain, Lekganyane spoke only to his advisers, who then passed on the message to the visitors. Neither could Tom and I address the bishop directly, we had to do it via the advisers.

The ZCC in its submission expressed its deep concern about the crime and violence in our country. The Rev Mohape called on the government to reinstate the death penalty. It was a pity, but a necessary evil! "The church feels that those who do not have any respect for the rights of others, can hardly claim that right for themselves. We recognize that the death penalty was abused in the past against Blacks and that many Blacks have sad memories in that regard, but we have to build and protect our democracy. There is no way in which we can look on as women are being raped, children molested and people being murdered by persons who have no feelings." Perhaps it would be possible in a year or ten to abolish the death penalty, but now it was necessary.

Mohape had to answer a number of penetrating questions. For many years the ZCC had strong ties with the government and regularly invited heads of state and military leaders to their annual gatherings. There had also been rumours that Lekganyane trained his own soldiers and received money from foreign organizations. Thomas Mohape vehemently denied the accusations: the ZCC had never been linked to a specific party or quarrelled with other parties. The story about the private army was a classic case of disinformation! And the money? "God does not let Calvin Klein clothing rain from heaven! Our money comes from our members who give their contributions faithfully."

Next on the programme was the congenial and flamboyant pastor, Ray McCauley, who appeared on behalf of the *International Federation of Christian Churches*. He referred to the many charismatic Christians in South Africa, saying, "We often brag about our spirituality, but today we present ourselves in humility, because we have to confess our past shortcomings." Charismatic believers, he explained, often hid behind their so-called spirituality while closing their eyes to the dark events of the apartheid years. "When we had to comfort those in distress and pray for them, we sometimes joined the cheering crowds and gladiators, the remorseless security machine which was always ready to trample the enemy ... We as the white members of the charismatic and pentecostal churches sincerely ask our black colleagues in the church for their forgiveness. Many of these black leaders tried to show us the error of our ways but our pride and our own sense of superiority blinded us." For McCauley it was not difficult to see and confess the collective guilt of Whites who had benefited so long from the apartheid system: "Many South African Christians' guilt is twice as big because the apartheid laws and the violence of the security laws, as well as the action of the police – which sometimes seemed to come from hell itself – were aimed against fellow Christians ... There is hardly a white person in South Africa today who did not benefit from apartheid. All of us, businessmen and the man in the street, have the solemn duty to make contributions to help the victims."

The *Apostolic Faith Mission* began their submission by screening a video. The dramatic events earlier that year, when the black and white divisions of the AFM had united and Dr Izak Burger and Pastor Frank Chikane had embraced one another in front of a cheering crowd, was deeply moving. "It wasn't easy to come here today. Just as there were members who had voted against unification, some members took it amiss that the AFM decided to send its church leaders to the TRC. Some members resigned from the church. Yet the AFM was grateful that they were able to present a truly rainbow submission in which black, coloured and white members jointly accepted responsibility for the past. "We had a look at our own history and found that many of our members had committed offences, that large numbers of them worked for the government – the single largest employer in the country. However one looks at it, we helped maintain the system of apartheid and prolong the agony. We should have been more critical ... We failed terribly."

After Izak Burger and Frank Chikane sat down, Tutu remained quiet for a long time and then spontaneously offered a prayer of thanks. People in the hall got up of their own accord and sang a song, many of them with their hands in the air. "I think we should take off our shoes, because we are now on holy ground. God is good, far better than we ever deserved", Tutu concluded.

At long last it was the turn of the *NG Kerk*. Just after lunch the chairman welcomed the Rev Freek Swanepoel, the moderator of the General Synod, to the microphone. Dr Willie Botha, the director of ecumenical affairs, took his place next to him. "We are very grateful that you are here today", Tutu welcomed the two men. "We would have been very disappointed if this had not been the case. We praise the Lord God who inspired you to present your submission here today."

The Rev Swanepoel began in English but soon switched over to Afrikaans. In his disarmingly honest way the moderator said how grateful he had been for the invitation of the TRC – and also towards the General Synodical Commission of the NG Kerk which had in the end made it possible for him to accept the invitation. It was of the utmost importance for the church to become involved in the process of truth and reconciliation. "This means that we want to listen to other people's stories, that we truly want to see their pain and distress and work together to heal the community and solve problems. We have been called to admit our mistakes and to forgive unconditionally." There had been a time when the church spoke authoritatively in society. That time was over. The church learnt that it would now have to act in the guise of a servant, as did its Lord.

Not everybody in the church was happy that he was standing here today, Freek Swanepoel continued. "I cannot and may not say that I am speaking on behalf of the entire NG Kerk." In the church there were two groups of people: those who supported the church's appearance before the TRC, and those who opposed it. "I believe, however, that the group that have a positive attitude about this matter, are in the majority." The Rev Swanepoel committed himself and his church to working, together with all other South Africans, to build a nation, develop all people, bring about reconciliation and alleviate poverty. But to do this, the church would have to be brave enough to analyse the past honestly – and to approach the future with dedication and realism.

The church had been struggling with the issue of apartheid for a long time before arriving at the point where it rejected it. In 1986 the General Synod said that the church had made a serious mistake in basing apartheid on the Bible. In 1990 the church confessed that it should have distanced itself from the policy long ago. In 1994 the synod went further and gave recognition to the members, office bearers and church meetings that had condemned apartheid in the past.

The role played by the other churches in the NG Kerk family – the coloured and black churches – in showing the NG Kerk the effects of apartheid on South Africa and its people, was gratefully acknowledged. Even though the church had, in the past, often reached out to the poor and the suffering, far more needed to be done. "The lack of understanding of the members and office bearers, reluctance to become involved in alleviating extreme societal conditions and its disobedience were also confessed – they were guilty before the Lord. The NG Kerk asks these people's forgiveness, and admits that its voice of protest and compassion had been too small."

"We dream of a country in which people accept one another and every person makes his or her contribution towards peaceful co-existence. As a church we would like to be guided by God's Word: 'Try to be at peace with everyone' (Heb 12:14)."

A fairly long discussion followed. My colleagues at the table wanted to know many things. Khoza Mgojo asked about the progress of the process of unification in the NG Kerk family. How serious were the churches as far as their discussions were concerned? Bongani Finca, hailing from the turbulent Eastern Cape, wanted to know: was the church truly prepared to co-operate for the sake of truth and reconciliation? Some of the amnesty applicants testified that they had done certain things, among other things, simply because the Afrikaans churches had approved them, even blessed their efforts. Should the church not stand next to them and confess?

After all the questions had been asked and the answers given, Tutu turned to Freek Swanepoel. He, too, spoke in Afrikaans: "I greatly appreciate what you are saying. It is difficult to confess and ask forgiveness. But it is because God is pouring out his grace on us that we can do it. I know about all your efforts to be here today, that you personally wanted to make a submission. We are grateful that you are representing your church here today." He continued in English: "I want to thank the Lord. What happened here today – that you came to say that you are sorry – was truly wonderful! Your church played a very important role in the history of our country; your church affects the lives of many, many people. My prayer is that the Lord will use the NG Kerk in wonderful ways. I always say: Once an Afrikaner has seen the light, he does not turn back again halfway ... we have seen over the past years how the once rejected church has returned, confessed its guilt, admitted to the nation and his own members that it was in error, and that they welcomed back their own prophets who were left out in the cold for years. I feel like telling the devil: 'Just you watch it, the NG Kerk is coming!' It is wonderful having you here with us. Healing has already begun. I am delighted that you are part of the process of reconciliation." Tutu requested Freek Swanepoel to pray – the only time he ever asked this of anybody who had come to make a submission. Then he got up and embraced the moderator of the NG Kerk.

The *Verenigende Gereformeerde Kerk* (URCSA – Uniting Reformed Church of South Africa) had already submitted one of the longest and most comprehensive submissions setting out the history of the church and its relationship with the other churches in the NG Kerk family. In a certain sense the two churches which had united a few years ago – the *NG Sendingkerk* (Dutch Reformed Mission Church) with its coloured membership and the *NG Sendingkerk* (Dutch Reformed Mission Church) with its black members – found themselves in a more difficult position than any of the other churches in the country. While suffering as much as their fellow South Africans did under apartheid, they carried the double burden of many of their compatriots, who took them to task for co-operating with the Afrikaans churches, and who blamed them for being co-responsible for the suffering of the people. The black and coloured *dominees* later recorded their protest, when the two churches drew up their own Belhar Confession condemning apartheid as a sin in no uncertain terms. They then had to suffer harsh criticism from the 'mother church'.

But this was not what the Rev James Buys, the moderator of the URCSA referred to. He wanted to talk about the future, about the role the churches could play in respect of reconciliation. His church listed a number of needs: a programme for the pastoral care of victims as well as offenders; establishing special liturgies of reconciliation which could turn services into opportunities for reconciliation; arranging special days of reconciliation at local, regional and national level; and rehabilitation programmes for offenders.

Late that afternoon Professor Nico Smith submitted to the TRC the *Open Letter* which he and Dr Beyers Naudé had drawn up and distributed. By that time hundreds of ministers of religion and members had already signed the letter – although Nico Smith did feel that many more, especially in the ranks of the NG Kerk, should have done so. As Dr Naudé, affectionately known as *Oom* Bey, was in the Netherlands at the time, Nico had to speak alone on behalf of everyone who had signed the letter. He quoted excerpts from the letter: How is it possible that while ministers of religions had been delivering sermons about justice and peace from hundreds of pulpits year in and year out, so much injustice was the order of the day in the country? Was our preaching so far removed from reality and so powerless? How did we end up in the situation that we were so blinded by the ideology of apartheid that we did not in stronger words admonish the government – our own people – about the things we did see and hear? We are guilty, we have to confess that we had done too little. "We as *dominees* are even more guilty than our members, we should have known better!

Like months ago, when the letter became known for the first time, my overwhelming emotion was: If *Oom* Bey, of all people, said that he suffered fervent remorse – what about me? If he was beseeching his fellow South Africans to forgive him, shouldn't I be doing far more myself? I was convinced that I was not the only person who felt like this.

As he had done on many previous occasions, Professor Smith at this hearing referred to the fatal ties between the NG Kerk and the Afrikaner Broederbond. "When will the leaders of the NG Kerk get rid of the Broederbond millstone that has been hanging around their necks for years?" Freek Swanepoel responded: "I admit that I myself am a member of the Afrikanerbond. I want to stress that I have never concealed this. There are many *dominees* who belong to the movement but I can't tell them whether they should remain members or break their ties. This is a personal matter that everyone has to decide for himself. As far as the church as a whole is concerned, the General Synod is the only structure that can make a statement in this regard. Officially the NG Kerk has, however, never had any links with the Afrikanerbond."

The hearing of three days was concluded with a submission made by the four Gereformeerde theologians – Professors Amie van Wyk, Bennie van der Walt, Pontie Venter and Alwyn du Plessis. Even though the *Gereformeerde Kerk* had officially decided not to come, the voices from the church were more than welcome: "We confess before God and our neighbour that we failed, in our words and deeds, in the church and in society, in private and in public, to witness sufficiently and unambiguously ... against the shaping and execution of the ideology of apartheid, which damaged and impeded, yes, even ruined, the lives of so many of our fellow-believers and fellow-citizens". Their words were a fitting 'Amen' to the many submissions made from Monday morning to Wednesday afternoon in East London.

◆　◆　◆

Were the three days worthwhile? Archbishop Tutu certainly saw to it that it was an inspiring event, that men and women reached out to one another across interdenominational – and also religious – boundaries. People prayed, sang and shed tears. In many respects it was, as the chairman himself said – the best hearing of all. But *was* this so? Did the hearing bring new knowledge, create new understanding? Did it significantly help the TRC trek, on its journey inward, to move forward?

What did become abundantly clear during the three days of the submissions, was that churches and other religious groups had assumed various roles in the past. Each of the roles had something to do with apartheid. Sometimes the religious communities were the *agents* of apartheid, at other times its *victims*. Thirdly, some of the groups acted as *opponents* of apartheid. This happened in different ways. Sometimes the churches had to discover that they had been playing more than one role at the same time!

Most churches and other groups said that they – often against their own deepest religious convictions – had *acted as agents of apartheid*. Not only the Afrikaans churches declared this to be so. The traditionally English churches too, together with Jewish, Muslim and Hindu groups, admitted that they often promoted apartheid, sometimes actively and often passively.

The Afrikaans churches were often reproached for giving *active support to* the former government, not only as far as the implementation of *apartheid* was concerned, but especially by providing a theological basis for apartheid. But, other churches confessed, we were also guilty, we also supported the apartheid government in many ways. The Presbyterian Church told us how many of its members welcomed – and sometimes exploited – the Bantustan policy. Most churches co-operated fairly comfortably with the Defence Force – particularly as far as the chaplains' service was concerned – and so gave the soldiers in the battlefield, and their folks at home, to understand that the cause being fought for was 'our cause', that the struggle was 'fair and just'. Some of the churches and members identified with apartheid to such an extent that they declared people whose views differed from theirs heretics – and sometimes literally persecuted them. One of the most blatant examples was that of Frank Chikane, the former Secretary-General of the SACC and leader of the black arm of the AFM, who was tortured by a police officer, himself a member of the AFM. According to the police officer's testimony, he attended a church service directly after the torture session. Some of the churches humbly confessed that their own structures had been racist, exactly mirroring government structures. The Afrikaans churches had their own 'younger churches' for black, coloured and Indian members, but the same was true of the Lutherans, the AFM, the Baptists and quite a few more. In its submission the Institute for Contextual Theology, their *Kairos document* at hand, accused many believers of openly propagating a 'state theology', aimed at maintaining the unjust *status quo*.

Sometimes it was not acts of commission, but the fact that the churches *failed to do what they had to do*, that ensured their guilt. Some phrases sounded like a refrain in every submission: "We should have seen, but we didn't; we should have spoken, but we remained silent; we should have acted, but we were afraid ... " Tacitly Christians, as well as many Muslims, Hindus and Jews, had given their approval for the way things were going. The *Rustenburg Declaration* put the feelings of many into words: "Our silence can only be described as a sin, and the fact that we failed to struggle against an inhumane political ideology, turned us into accomplices." If one looks back today, more than one group said, we realize that we should have supported the anti-apartheid activists, but we did not. When the *Christian Institute* of Beyers Naudé was declared an 'affected' organization and banned in 1975, even some of the member churches of the SACC, which recorded their official objection, could not individually see their way clear to support the CI financially and morally.

Then there were also churches and religious groups that could only be regarded as *victims of apartheid*. Quite a few submissions mentioned the religious leaders and bodies who came under fire, as a direct result of their opposition to apartheid. Action was taken against people like Beyers Naudé, Frank Chikane, Smangeliso Mkhatshwa, Michael Lapsley and the Muslim Imam Abdullah Haron, but bodies such as the Christian Institute and the SA Council of Churches were also targeted. The most flagrant examples of direct attacks included the bomb explosion at the SACC's Khotso House in Johannesburg and the arson attack on the SACBC's (Catholic Bishops' Conference) Khanya House in Pretoria. Various submissions objected to the closing of church schools and other institutions, mainly as a result of the Group Areas Act and the Bantu Education acts, as a result of which the churches suffered great material damage, but also lost the opportunity to help shape hundreds of thousands of young people.

One of the most serious charges of oppression came from the Muslim and Hindu communities, who recounted how their own religious and moral values had been negated under a 'Christian National system', which did not really grant other religions a place in society but forced their own 'Christian' views and traditions on others. The failure to recognize Hindu and Muslim marriages as being legal, was especially hurtful. Some of the more evangelical churches accused the former government of operating such an efficient propaganda machine that large numbers of their members were misled by its ideology. "We were thus 'assaulted' spiritually and theologically", was their charge.

A third aspect concerned the role of the faith communities as *opponents of apartheid*. It often happened that churches and other groups stood in direct conflict with the government and the *status quo*. One way of expressing one's total revulsion, was to turn one's back on the entire societal system and to establish one's own alternative institutions. This course was followed by the Black Independent Churches. If the 'system' took away black people's history and pride, they would return it to them! A second possibility was to directly approach the government, as did many of the churches – especially the Afrikaans churches – by means of interviews, petitions and private letters, to air their concern. Often churches and ecumenical bodies went even further by taking strong decisions and making them universally known. Many examples were quoted during the hearing, ranging from decisions in which apartheid was condemned and believers called up to take a stand: the *Cottesloe Declaration* (1960), the SACC's *Message to the People of South Africa* (1968), the *Conscientious Objection Campaign* (1974), the *Kairos Declaration* (1985) and many more. Special attention was given to the voices within the NG Kerk which had since 1948 been warning against apartheid and the consequences it would have for the nation and the church. This included the *Reformation Day Testimony* and the *Open Letter of 123 ministers of religion* (1982) and the *Koinonia Declaration* (1977) by persons in the Gereformeerde kerke. The most comprehensive confession drawn up in this regard was the *Belhar Confession* (1982), which was accepted as the official doctrine of the Uniting Reformed Church.

One way in which faith groups and individuals showed their opposition, was to resign from state structures such as the Defence Force and the chaplains' service, and to give open support to conscientious objectors who had come into conflict with the authorities. Or to call on the nation to display civilian disobedience by refusing to obey unjust laws, as in the case of the *Defiance Campaign* and the *Standing for the Truth Campaign*. Now and then church leaders and also groups of Christians went even further out on a limb by assisting the liberation movements, and by going outside the country's borders to negotiate with banned organizations. A similar and also highly contentious action was the campaign for sanctions supported by many church leaders, including Archbishop Tutu – as the last non-violent attempt to bring about political change in the country – but which got little support from the official meetings of the churches.

During the three-day hearing many positive things were placed on record. The role played by the various religious groups, particularly after 1990, in establishing a peaceful transition to democracy was recognized. When the multiparty negotiations were under way, the most important Muslim organizations met to reflect on how they could support the process. The *World Conference of Religion and Peace* (WCRP) convened its members, comprising all religious groups, to reflect about their role in the future. *The South African Council of Churches* and the *Catholic Bishops' Conference* (SACBC) jointly began a National Co-ordinating Committee for the Repatriation of Exiles. And the *Rustenburg Conference* (1990), attended by representatives from many churches, was a precursor to the Truth and Reconciliation Commission, in that many persons at that conference, representing various points of view, came forward to give their testimonies.

On the acceptance of the *National Peace Accord* in 1991 the SACC and the SACBC undertook an extensive programme to prepare people who had never voted for the advent of the democratic dispensation. In those uneasy days, just prior to the 1994 election, when all kinds of rumours of civil war abounded, the *Church Leaders' Conference*, in which the NG Kerk participated, crisscrossed the country in order to meet and encourage political leaders. Leaders who used to have great ideological differences, like the *SA Council of Churches* and the *Bishops' Conference* on the one hand, and Johan Heyns and his fellow-members of the moderature of the NG Kerk, together with the leader of the charismatic churches, Ray McCauley, on the other, formed a united front. The SACC, the SACBC and the WCRP called their own *Panel of Religious Leaders for Electoral Justice*, which played an important monitoring role during the election.

◆ ◆ ◆

The Eastern Cape hearing was indeed a high-water mark. In its own, unique way, it provided pointers to help the TRC trek on its way. With deep seriousness we turned the pages of history, studying the lessons to be learnt. What is even more important, each of the faith groups committed themselves to fighting hardship in society – poverty and unemployment, racism and prejudice, corruption and crime, violence and bloodshed – tooth and nail. In every submission the representatives of the various groups emphasized their resolution to walk the road of reconciliation. The *dominees* and pastors, the priests and the imams had the courage to walk into the future. They were ready to accompany their members on the road ahead.

20 NOVEMBER 1997: BREYTEN BREYTENBACH DOES NOT THINK THE TRC IS NECESSARY

The *Punt* radio station conducted an interview with Breyten Breytenbach. From Paris the well-known Afrikaans poet said that he had considered making a submission before the Truth Commission, but decided against it in the end, because he did not want to upset "the enormous seriousness" with which the process was being driven! It was important that the TRC unearth the truth about the past, about the crimes committed, but it would also be possible to do so in other ways, for example through a public debate or by making films. He would prefer that persons who violated human rights rather be brought to court than for them to ask for amnesty. "They committed the crimes ... They shouldn't be given an opportunity to say that they are sorry and that it concerned political matters. This applies to both our previous and present political masters."

21 NOVEMBER 1997: THE PURPLE CAP ON YOUR HEAD WON'T HELP YOU

A far more acrimonious statement than that of Breyten Breytenbach lay on my table. It was a letter written by a 76-year-old Afrikaner who had sent it to Desmond Tutu while the East London hearing was under way. Janis Grobbelaar of our Research Division placed it there "for your information". I should rather say: for my annoyance, I thought when I started reading! That the TRC had not yet, by a long haul, succeeded in taking all Whites – in this case Afrikaners – with it on its way, was painfully obvious.

The long letter began by dealing with the disappointment about what was happening to the country at the moment. South Africa was rapidly turning into a banana republic, where former good relations between Whites and Blacks were deteriorating daily. The murders on farming folk, who "are being slaughtered like animals, have resulted in my now hating black people ... "

He went on to say:

The actions of the TRC further fuels the hatred because you take great pleasure in the character assassination of all Afrikaners who have, over years, built up our country to a wealthy country on a par with world states, and create the impression that all Blacks are angels from heaven who must be protected in jails where they enjoy life and may not be hurt.

As a Christian I ask you if you and Boraine have ever summoned God to testify before you and to ask amnesty because He allowed you to suffer so heavily under the reign of the atrocious Whites who had done *nothing* in South Africa?

Where is the reconciliation that you preach? That is at odds with the hatred and revulsion that you have towards us! For how long are you going to prolong matters to humiliate even more people so that we taxpayers can labour to pay your fat salaries? Do we also have to pay for your operation in America?

Don't think that your tears and those of the *ousies* (derogatory Afrikaans word for black women) impress us. You are a hypocrite and you will have to confess this before God, if He is the same one I believe in.

Just remember, that purple cap on your head is not a Holy Grail that is going to guarantee your place in heaven – you will have to confess just like anyone of the people who are being humiliated daily by your TRC.

I am not giving my name and address because your ANC Gestapo will arrest me to come and confess before you ANC freeloaders.

Thank God, your day of reckoning will also come.

Gamaliël.
Bloemfontein
18 November 1997

24 NOVEMBER-4 DECEMBER 1997: "WINNIE-GATE"

"Has the moment of truth finally arrived for Ms Winnie Madikizela-Mandela? Or will the 63-year-old icon of black people's struggle against apartheid weather the storms that are now raging over her head? As she did when the apartheid police terrorized her when they dumped her in Brandfort; when the United Democratic Front turned against her in the late eighties; and after she had been charged in the high court for complicity to murder and abduction?" The questions asked by the Afrikaans newspaper *Beeld* that morning, were on the lips of not only many South Africans, but also people from all over the world.

Winnie was a master in the art of political survival – but what would happen over the next few days? Winnie Mandela herself had insisted that she would put her case during a public hearing of the TRC and that she had nothing to conceal. But would she emerge unscathed from the process? In a few weeks' time a new vice-president would be elected for the ANC. Would the hearing conclusively kill off her chances – or strengthen them? There was overwhelming interest in the *Mandela United Football Club* hearing, which was officially called to investigate the charges against the soccer club sponsored by Ms Mandela. Thirty-four witnesses had been called to testify; they included some of the most prominent politicians, clerics and community leaders in South Africa. Journalists converged from all over the world: more than 200 journalists from sixteen countries. Twenty overseas television teams and some hundred news agencies received accreditation. "The most sensational political theatre in South Africa", the "greatest news event in Africa since Mandela's release", the overseas newspapers wrote. "*Winnie-gate* begins", was one person's comment. Like the Watergate hearings that heralded President Nixon's fall from grace, Winnie Mandela's turn had come.

Many wanted to see it happening – *if*, of course, it did. Early the Monday morning there was a throng of officials, journalists, witnesses, victims, legal teams and visitors at the front door of the Johannesburg Institute for Social Sciences in Mayfair. Elderly women, members of the ANC Women's League, brandished posters: *Don't persecute Winnie! God bless Winnie!*

Winnie Mandela's car finally stopped in front of the building. Foreign journalists and cameramen shoved their South African counterparts aside. Winnie's bodyguards roughly pushed the crowd aside to open up a path for her. People rushed into the hall to find a place.

When silence was finally established, Dr Khoza Mgojo, the former president of the SA Council of Churches, began with a prayer: "Lord give us the wisdom of Solomon to distinguish in these days what is true and just." In a few words the chairman, Desmond Tutu explained the brief: this was a hearing aimed at obtaining information, not a trial. Ms Mandela did not apply for amnesty, and so an official finding – guilty or innocent – would not be made. The official findings would, instead, be published in the final report of the TRC.

The witnesses were then sworn in, one after the other. It was soon obvious that this hearing would be of a different nature than the previous ones. Here it was not a matter of *them* (the Whites, the apartheid regime) against *us* (black South Africa, the people of the struggle). The object of the scrutiny would be to establish what had happened to those persons in the struggle itself: ideals that had crumbled, personal ambition, the struggle for control and personal power. Even though one or two Whites would testify during the hearing, this was not their event. This stopover on the trek was meant for black South Africa.

◆ ◆ ◆

Winnie Mandela, dressed in a smart blue and white outfit, sat listening, ostensibly relaxed and unperturbed, her two daughters Zenani and Zinzi behind her. Oddly enough it was not the first witness – who revealed a murder attack by the Soccer Club on a fellow member whom they had regarded as a double-crosser – who revealed the first crack in her armour. It was witness number two, Phumlile Dlamini, whose story – of common assault, in comparison not such a serious charge as those which would follow – who had the Mother of the Nation shifting around uncomfortably. Her reputation as the benefactress of ordinary people was at stake.

Phumlile met Johannes Tau – better known as 'Shakes' – in 1987. Like her brother, Tholi, he was a member of the Mandela Soccer Club. At the time Shakes slept in Winnie Mandela's home; his bed was in the dining room.

"Not long after we fell in love, Shakes told me that Winnie came to him in the middle of the night to his bed and got under the blanket with him." Shakes warned Phumlile to keep quiet about their relationship; if Winnie got wind of it, there would be big trouble. And so it was. A fellow member of the soccer club told Winnie about their relationship. "Winnie then came with Shakes to my house. They pretended that they were looking for my brother Tholi." Shakes tried to reassure Phumlile. "Winnie is actually after me!" Together the two of them went to the minibus, outside the gate, where Winnie was waiting for them. Winnie interrogated her about her relationship with Shakes. "She then slapped me in the face and hit me with her fists all over my body and in my stomach."

A few weeks later Winnie fetched Phumlile at her home, to try and find Shakes who had apparently absconded. Phumlile was wearing a maternity dress. Everyone could see that she was pregnant. "In the car Winnie and members of the soccer club hit me in the face." She was taken to Winnie's house in Diepkloof where Winnie told the members of the soccer club, "Try and see what you can do with this one, because she is not speaking the truth." For five long hours the men assaulted her. They kicked her in the stomach, making her worry: what about my unborn child?" Zinzi pleaded with them to stop, but they replied, "Mummy ordered us to assault her." Zinzi finally managed to stop the men and took Phumlile home.

Phumlile Dlamini wanted to report the matter to the police, but her brother Tholi stopped her from doing so. "If you do that, they will burn down our house", he feared. Tholi subsequently decided to leave the soccer club. The police arrested him to question him about the club. Two days after his release Tholi was shot and killed. Zinzi's friend, Sizwe Sithole and another member of the club, had committed the murder. Sizwe was arrested by the police and died shortly afterwards in detention.

Weeping, Phumlile testified that her baby son, Tsepo, had been born a month prematurely. He was mentally retarded – and she was convinced that this was the direct result of the abuse that she suffered.

The next persons to give evidence was a man and a woman whose son had been murdered – so they said – by Winnie and the soccer club. Shortly after the soccer club had been involved in a shoot-out with the police in 1988, the two young activists, who had at the time been part of the Mandela household, disappeared. They wanted to know what had happened to Lolo Sono and Siboniso Shabalala.

Nichodemus Sono was a businessman from Soweto. He began by telling the TRC how he himself had helped the ANC in the struggle, how he had provided them with a roof over their heads and transport. Following the shoot-out with the police in which one of his own cousins also died, he said, members of the soccer club however began suspecting that his son Lolo had betrayed them. When they arrived with the boy at the Sono's home, his father could see that his son had been badly tortured. "I pleaded with Winnie to let my son go, but she refused. Perhaps he had persuaded them to bring him to me, so that I could save him. But I failed." Lolo Sono was in the back of the minibus, surrounded by members of the soccer club. He had obviously been badly beaten in the face. He was shaking. "Winnie, who was sitting in the front seat, told me that they had brought Lolo to me because he was a spy. She was very aggressive: 'I am taking away this dog. The movement will decide what to do with him!'" Mr Sono never saw his son again.

"I am asking that Winnie return Siboniso to me. I want his bones ... She knows where he is." Mrs Nomsa Shabalala kept looking at Winnie with big eyes. She would never forget that day, 13 November 1988, the day when the Mandela Soccer Club came to fetch her son to, so they said, send him out of the country. This was just after the shoot-out between the police and soccer club had taken place. What worried her was that the men arrived at her house with two names written on a matchbox: Siboniso and Lolo Sono. Lolo was dead, everyone already knew that. But where was her son? She was too frightened at the time to ask Mrs Mandela. The police later turned up with a photograph of her son at their home. They told her that he was dead. "If you want to know more, bring R4 000 to the Pretoria Police Station." She did not do that, because she did not have the money. When the legal representative of Jerry Richardson, the former coach of the club, gave notice that he had asked for amnesty, for the deaths of both Lolo Sono and Siboniso Shabalala, the widow burst into tears.

The name of Stompie Seipei would be heard often the next few days. The death of the young activist, whose dancing figure had appeared on television screens worldwide, was probably the biggest millstone around Winnie Mandela's neck. On Day One John Morgan, Winnie Mandela's chauffeur, was the first person to talk about Stompie. Later other people, including Jerry Richardson, would tell their side of the story.

John Morgan recounted how Mrs Mandela had instructed him to drive with a few members of the soccer club to the Methodist manse of the Rev Paul Verryn in Soweto, to pick up Stompie and three other young activists. He had been present when the four boys had been taken to a room in the Mandela home, "the room next to the jacuzzi", where they were assaulted. "The first person who began assaulting them was Winnie Mandela. She first set on Stompie, and then on the rest. The boys were thrown into the air and dropped, "so that they bounced on the floor". The next day Stompie was "as round as a football. I tried to feed him coffee and some bread as he was not in a position to help himself." On the third day Stompie was in a critical condition. Winnie had Dr Abu-Baker Asvat, who had a practice in Soweto and with whom she had a good understanding, brought to treat Stompie. Dr Asvat refused to treat him there. He said the boy should be taken to hospital immediately.

A day later Winnie told Morgan, "Take the dog away and dump it." He refused – but others did carry out the order, as would be testified later during the hearing. The soccer team had its own disciplinary committee, the driver continued, "and they were rough with one another and were regularly involved in fights". They would undress the young men and squeeze their private parts. Winnie would look in briefly and go away. The soccer club also brought schoolgirls to the Mandela home "and then forced them to do things". In response to these deeds, persons from the community burnt down Winnie's house.

The Mother of the Nation sat listening, her head bent.

◆ ◆ ◆

Winnie came off better the second day. The witnesses who came forward contradicted themselves from time to time. Winnie sat listening, visibly more relaxed, even exchanging pleasantries with her legal representatives.

Pelo Mekgwe was one of the four boys who had been kidnapped on Winnie's instructions by the soccer club. But his evidence was weak and conflicted with previous statements, including those made to the TRC.

When Mrs Xoliswa Falati took her place behind the microphone – a former friend who had in the meantime become her most bitter critic – Winnie Mandela laughed disparagingly. Making screwball motions to her head, she indicated that Xoliswa was a lunatic. Tutu had to call Mrs Falati to order from time to time, as she often wildly digressed and became very emotional in her attack on Winnie. It was for the sake of Winnie that she went to jail, that she had lied in court to protect Winnie, she said. But she would not do so again. "My hands are not dripping with the blood of African children!" she called out, evidently referring to the death of Stompie and the fact that other children had been assaulted. Winnie was guilty of the death of Dr Asvat. What is more: she was the one who orchestrated the commuter massacres on South African trains which nearly wrecked the 1994 election. She knows that Winnie had thrown the bodies of Sono and Siboniso and others into an old mine shaft. She demanded that the TRC retrieve them. From time to time the hall rocked with laughter at the antics of Xoliswa and had to be warned to remain silent. Advocate Ismael Semenya smiled: "Falati showed years ago, when working in Paul Verryn's manse, that she was emotionally unstable." Her evidence needn't be taken seriously.

The evidence of Katiza Cebekhulu, regarded as one of the key witnesses, also largely fell flat. His story, as told by the writer Fred Bridgland in the book *Katiza's Journey*, created a stir when it appeared earlier that year in England and South Africa. In 1991 Winnie Mandela sent him out of the country, much against his will, just before she was about to appear in court on charges relating to Stompie's death, among others. In Zambia he ended up in prison, where the English baroness, Emma Nicholson, found him and took pity on him. She took him to England with the approval of the then prime minister, John Major. Once she had received the assurance that Katiza would be protected in South Africa twenty-four hours of the day, Baroness Nicholson decided to accompany Katiza to Johannesburg. She was sworn in with him and testified along with him.

Katiza stated that he had been present and saw how Winnie herself had stabbed Stompie with a knife. He had not been a police informant, as she alleged. He did however – because Winnie had ordered him to do so – go to sleep in Paul Verryn's bed, in the manse where he lived. He then lied to Mrs Falati and told her that the Methodist clergyman had sodomized him. Katiza maintained under cross-examination that he was not exaggerating Winnie's share in the murder simply because he had been desperate to get out of the Zambian prison. That was only one of the lies Winnie had been spreading.

But under cross-examination Katiza's story was ripped to pieces. His testimony before the TRC differed in quite a few respects from his story in *Katiza's Journey*. When Commissioner Yasmin Sooka remarked that Katiza's book was filled with inaccuracies, the audience applauded.

Winnie and her legal team were smiling broadly when leaving the hall that afternoon.

Late that afternoon Katiza Cebekhulu departed for London by aeroplane. Winnie Mandela had laid a charge of *crimen injuria* against him and Baroness Nicholson feared that he would be arrested.

◆ ◆ ◆

But then the tide began to turn against Winnie.

On the third day two Methodist ministers, Paul Verryn and Peter Storey, moved in behind the microphone. That their testimony would be of a totally different order than that given the previous day soon became obvious.

Paul Verryn, the man whom Winnie originally blamed for all her woes, accusing him of sexually molesting Katiza and the other boys in the church house, recounted the events on the day that Stompie Seipei and his three friends had been abducted from the manse. When he began talking about the events leading to Stompie's murder, the bishop began to weep. He continued in tears: "The thing that has been most difficult for me is that, having heard the allegations against Stompie, I … I … did not remove him from the mission and get him to a place where he could be safe. I think if I had acted in another way he could be alive today … "

He then looked straight at Winnie Madikizela-Mandela. "My feelings about you have taken me in many directions, as you can imagine. I long for reconciliation. I have been profoundly, profoundly affected by some of the things that you have said about me, that have hurt me and cut me to the quick. I find it very difficult to get to the point where I understand, where I can begin to forgive – even though you perhaps don't even want my forgiveness, even though you perhaps feel that I do not deserve to offer my forgiveness to you. I struggle to find a way in which we can be reconciled for the sake of this nation and for the people I believe God loves so deeply."

"The man has spoken from a broken heart. Would you like to respond?" Tutu invited Winnie Mandela. But her legal representative, Ismail Semenya, declined the offer. She would want to talk to the English bishop in private.

Verryn was followed by Bishop Peter Storey, who had, along with a group of other clergyman and community leaders, been directly involved in efforts to rescue the four kidnapped boys. Armed with his diary and accurate notes made at the time, Bishop Storey could give a detailed account of everything that had happened: of how Winnie had misled them as to the whereabouts of the activists, the circumstances in which they had been held, as well as of the futile attempts of many political and community leaders – including Oliver Tambo, with whom they liaised in Zambia – to secure the release of the boys. Storey read a succession of statements by Mrs Mandela in which she accused Verryn of having sodomized the boys, and that they and the church were responsible for the murder of Dr Asvat, to cover up a homosexual scandal.

We went home that evening deeply impressed by the day's dramatic events, especially the young bishop's tears.

◆ ◆ ◆

On the Thursday, the fourth day of the hearing, members of the former United Democratic Front (UDF) and the Winnie Mandela Crisis Committee, took their places.

The *Mail* and *Guardian's* summary of the testimony given against Winnie Mandela

"The Mandela Soccer Club was Winnie's personal gang of lawless thugs. It was unseemly for the honoured Mandela name to be misused in this way." Mr Azhar Cachalia, Secretary of Safety and Security and former UDF leader, did not mince words. In the company of Mr Murphy Morobe, who also used to be a UDF member, he recounted the atrocities committed by the soccer club. And, they maintained, Winnie was equally culpable. They were not only morally disgusted by what had happened, it had greatly harmed the ANC's cause. What is more, the community was convinced that Winnie Mandela had collaborated with the police and that the soccer club had been infiltrated by government agents. One of the most depraved atrocities – except for Stompie's death – occurred when club members abducted two young people to the Mandela house. The letter M was carved into the chest of one of them and *Viva ANC* on the back of the other. Battery acid was then poured into the open wounds. Winnie Mandela did not heed their protests. The assaults continued, and Winnie was part of them. In the end the UDF decided that enough was enough. The UDF, as the domestic wing of the ANC, officially distanced itself from Madikizela-Mandela's actions. "That was one of the proudest moments of my life ... I hope that if I ever have to take a similar decision, I would have the moral courage to do so."

Despite the chairman's call for silence the audience loudly applauded. A number of members of the Winnie Mandela Crisis Committee then each had an opportunity to give evidence: Sydney Mufamadi, Aubrey Mokoena, Frank Chikane and Sister Bernadette Ncube. They recounted that a crisis committee was established to investigate the abduction of the four activists – as well as all the rumours that were flying about. Although they had discussed these matters with Winnie, they could not make any headway.

"Couldn't you have taken stronger steps?" the TRC panel asked repeatedly. "According to Peter Storey's testimony he wanted to ask for a court interdict to have the young activists released. Why didn't you want to co-operate? Hanif Vally wanted to know.

The witnesses were visibly uneasy.

"We did not have a mandate to do so", Mokoena replied.

"We did what we could", Mufamadi added. "In any case, they were released after eighteen days. By that time Stompie was already dead ... There is no way in which we could find out what had really happened. If we had known, we could perhaps have taken stronger action." Mrs Mandela at the time ignored the direct instructions of her husband in the Victor Verster prison, and of Oliver Tambo, to disband the club," Mufamadi added.

"If we wanted to free the children, we would have had to organize our own militia!" Frank Chikane remarked.

"If we did that, we ourselves would have been guilty of abduction", said Mufamadi, the man who would later become the Minister of Safety and Security.

Church leaders did at that time go and talk to Mrs Mandela, said the Rev Otto Mbangula, Winnie's own minister in the Methodist Church in Jabawu, Soweto. He and Father Smangaliso Mkatshwa accompanied Bishop Manas Buthelezi to her home, where Winnie time and again assured them that the boys were safe. She had to take the boys into her custody, she said, because Paul Verryn had molested them sexually. They took her at her word, without asking to see the boys. After the discussion Winnie and her daughter Zinzi prayed with the church leaders before their departure. Stompie, they had to find out later, was by then already dead.

Earlier that day Dr Natho Mothlana, well-known community leader and family friend of the Mandelas, testified that Bishop Storey had requested him to stop Winnie Mandela from making false allegations against Paul Verryn. On another occasion, also at the request of the church leaders, he asked Winnie to release the boys – without success.

At last – on the fourth day – the painful hearing was over. The words of Bishop Storey to Tutu put everything that had been said in a nutshell: "One of the tragedies of life, Sir, is that it's possible to become like that which we hate most ... The primary cancer was the oppression of apartheid, but secondary infections have touched many of apartheid's opponents and eroded their knowledge of good and evil."

◆ ◆ ◆

On Friday, 28 November the police took the stand. From their testimony it was clear that Winnie was not only the offender, but often also the victim; not only the manipulator, but also the person being manipulated.

Paul Erasmus, a former policeman, testified that he and his colleagues had obtained a good deal of information on everything that had been happening at the Mandela house. However, they did not want to take action against her, because they did not want to "upset the political apple-cart". In the eighties the general feeling was that Winnie should be left to her own devices, as she would then cause her own downfall. One of Stratcom's projects during the late eighties, Project Romulus, was aimed at counteracting and eliminating the ANC, the PAC and also the right wing. One method was to disseminate false rumours about Winnie. Her husband, Nelson Mandela, was virtually unassailable. But Winnie was an easy target! They had enough informants to know what was going on the Mandela household. According to their information most of the soccer club members smoked *dagga* (marijuana) and sniffed glue, and could be easily recruited to work for the police. Erasmus himself had spread various rumours about Winnie, namely that she was a nymphomaniac and an alcoholic. To discredit her even further, especially among the revolutionary youth, he began to spread the story that Winnie had a relationship with Chris Ball, the former head of First National Bank. Operation Romulus however, never linked her to criminal activities for which she could be prosecuted. The security police were very satisfied with their work, Paul Erasmus added. And, of course, Mrs Falati's allegation, yesterday, that he himself had had a relationship with Mrs Mandela, was completely false!

Everyone sat up straight at the testimony of George Fivaz, South Africa's police chief, namely that Jerry Richardson, the coach of the Mandela Soccer Club serving life imprisonment for the murder of Stompie Seipei, had in fact been a police informer. What is more, the police paid Jerry R10 000 for information on where the bodies of Lolo Sono, Sibonise Shabalala, and Kuki Zwani were buried. The money was paid to Richardson after he had already been imprisoned, but the bodies were never found, despite an extensive search. Exactly when Jerry was recruited, Fivaz could not say, as his file had disappeared without trace. Earlier on in the hearings Murphy Morobe testified that they had long suspected that Jerry was an informant – especially after the shoot-out at Richardson's house, when Sergeant Pretorius and two MK members were killed. Later Richardson helped murder the two boys, Lolo and Sibonise, who had themselves been accused of being the informers.

Mr Jerry Richardson arrives at the hearing in shackles

Why had the police not done more to try and solve Dr Asvat's murder? the TRC wanted to know. Why, for example, had a statement that Thulani Dlamini made as long ago as 1989 never been handed in, in court? In the statement Dlamini alleged that Mrs Mandela offered him R20 000 to murder Dr Asvat. The police chief had a hard time explaining this. He was very clear about one thing: the allegation that Winnie Mandela had made during her *in camera* hearing, namely that President Mandela had ordered him to "dig up the dirt", which he would then use in the coming divorce case between him and Winnie, was wholly false.

How was it possible for the comrades to sometimes act so heartlessly towards one another, killing people merely suspected of collaborating with the police, the commissioners wanted to know. Murphy Morobe had one answer ready: Winnie's infamous statement of 16 June 1986, namely "our country will be liberated through matches and tyres" had a tremendous effect on the people. Her supporters saw this as a mandate to execute suspects and informants.

Winnie, who showed little emotion during the whole day's revelations, could not keep back the tears during one of the submissions. When Charles Zwane – alleged soccer club member who was serving life imprisonment for nine murders – recounted how he had been tortured by the police, the memory became too much for him. His bowed head between his hands, he began weeping. Winnie took off her pair of spectacles and wiped the tears running down her own cheeks. Zwane said that he had never really been a member of the club, even if he wore the club's track suit. What was true, was that a soccer club member once showed him, in Zinzi's room in the Mandela house, how to use a machine gun.

All of us were grateful that the weekend was about to begin. After everything that had been said, not only Winnie and her team, but all of us in the hall, had to take a breather.

◆ ◆ ◆

That same evening it was announced on the news that the Amnesty Committee had granted amnesty to 37 ANC members, including Deputy President Thabo Mbeki and five senior Cabinet Ministers, Alfred Nzo, Dullah Omar, Joe Modise, Mac Maharaj and Dr Pallo Jordan. Other prominent ANC members included Jackie Modise (wife of Joe Modise and a senior army officer), Matthews Phosa (premier of Mpumalanga), Jacob Zuma (chief secretary of the ANC) and two deputy ministers, Joe

Nhlanhla and Peter Mokaba. It had been possible to complete their separate applications without a hearing as the committee felt that none of the incidents for which they asked amnesty, had really constituted gross human rights violations. They had also already accepted collective responsibility for misdeeds committed by the structures introduced to fight apartheid.

In a separate statement it was declared that Trevor Tutu, the son of the chairman of the TRC, had also received amnesty. He was serving a prison sentence for making a bomb threat at the East London airport, thus seriously disrupting a domestic flight in October 1989.

It had taken my breath away. I was glad for the sake of the Tutu family – as well as for the 37 other families. But had the Amnesty Committee not acted with unseemly haste? What had become of the notion that the process should be transparent? Did the entire country not have the right to know first why the ANC members had asked for amnesty? I could not even begin to guess the storm this decision would raise.

◆ ◆ ◆

On Monday morning the hall was buzzing. Not only about the three convicted murderers who were about to testify, but also about the amnesty granted to Trevor Tutu and the 37 ANC members. There had been an outcry that weekend, from politicians of all parties – except from the ANC which, as was to be expected, welcomed the actions of the Amnesty Committee. The decision of the Amnesty Committee to grant amnesty without explaining the reasons why or revealing all the facts, made a mockery of the law, said Mrs Sheila Camerer of the NP. Granting amnesty to Trevor Tutu, particularly in view of his many attempts to evade the law, stretched the provisions of the amnesty legislation to its limits. Is Tutu giving his son an unfair advantage, was the question I was asked to my face that Saturday and Sunday.

The TRC tried to explain their decision to all and sundry, and even threatened legal proceedings against anybody calling into the question Archbishop Tutu's integrity following the amnesty granted to his son. Alex Boraine told the media that Tutu had not even known that Trevor would ask for amnesty, that he had been in the USA for cancer treatment when Trevor and his lawyer decided to submit an application. In no way had Desmond Tutu tried to influence the Amnesty Committee in this regard, Boraine declared. He had not even enquired about it. Chris de Jager was the chairman of the panel that had dealt with Trevor Tutu's application. He told the press that he was absolutely convinced that the young Tutu had had a political motive for his deed – and that he qualified, according to the law, for amnesty.

There could be no doubt that we would be haunted for a long time by the amnesty that had been granted!

◆ ◆ ◆

Who had been responsible for the death of Dr Abu-Baker Asvat, the benefactor of Soweto? This was the question that had to be answered that Monday.

Winnie Mandela – this the TRC had already heard – had been enraged because Dr Asvat, whom she regarded as a family friend, refused to treat the seriously injured Stompie Seipei at home, but insisted that he be taken to hospital. A few hours before the murder of Dr Asvat, Winnie arrived at his consulting rooms with Katiza Cebekhulu, demanding that Dr Asvat examine him. She wanted to have proof that Paul Verryn had sodomized Katiza. When the doctor once again refused, Winnie exploded! The altercation that ensued was later described by Dr Asvat's brother as "a volcanic eruption".

Winnie had, however, according the testimony given on Monday, already made her plans. She summoned two of her confidants, Zakhele Mbatha and Thulani Dlamini, to her house and offered them R20 000 to murder the doctor. Jerry Richardson, the coach of the soccer club who had to perform all kinds of 'tasks' for Winnie, visited the consulting rooms twice, on 26 January 1989 and again the next day, the day of the assassination. The visits were recorded in the consulting room files, said Dr Ebrahim Asvat, the Soweto doctor's brother. In her statement, the previous week, the former confidant of Winnie Mandela, Xoliswa Falati, also referred to it: Jerry told her about two recces (surveys of the area) that he had made before the murder of Dr Asvat.

What happened next?

The respected Mrs Albertina Sisulu, wife of Walter Sisulu, who worked as a nurse in the consulting rooms, reported as follows:

"On 27 January two young men came to the consulting rooms. They wanted to see Dr Asvat. However, he was not there – and they promised to return. Later that afternoon they turned up again.

"I heard the doctor call out a patient's name and the door of the examination room click open. That was a security door that opened from the inside only if one pressed a button. I don't know what happened inside, but as everything was quiet after the clicking sound, I assumed that the doctor was busy examining a patient. After about ten minutes I heard a report, as of a gun shot. There was no response. I heard a second report, and this time Dr Asvat cried out."

Mrs Sisulu ran out by the back door to look for help.

"When I returned, the doctor was lying face down. Blood was streaming out of the left side of his chest."

For Mrs Sisulu, who regarded Abu-Baker Asvat as a son, the events were traumatic, and never to be forgotten.

Dr Ebrahim Asvat, his brother, was deeply moved by her account. He was in tears when recounting his grievance against the police who had, according to him, not investigated the case properly. When the two murderers, Mbatha and Dlamini, were brought before court, some of the most important evidence – Dlamini's confession that Winnie had hired him and his comrade for R20 000 to kill Dr Asvat, was suppressed. The police "preferred not to use this evidence". The result was that the two were convicted of murder – and that the motive for the murder was stated as being robbery. But, Ebrahim Asvat said in evidence, they had not stolen anything! Following the murder his brother's firearm, and R500 in cash remained in the consulting room – and had not been touched. Whom did the police want to protect? Was it perhaps Winnie, the doctor wanted to know.

◆ ◆ ◆

To be a member of the Mandela Soccer Club was not wholly without danger, especially not if one had had an argument with your fellow club members.

Lerathodi Ikaneng began his testimony on the Tuesday and said that he had twice tried to break his ties with the club. The third time, when caught by his friends, he was stabbed in the neck by them; garden shears were used. They left him for dead in a *vlei* (marsh), among the reeds.

Prior to the attempted murder a number of boys of a high school in Soweto in 1987 raped a girl. The soccer club arrested them and began assaulting them. Later he had to see his friend, Tholi Dlamini, being shot and killed by a fellow club member, Sizwe Sithole. Sizwe used to be Zinzi's boyfriend. When Lerathodi reported the matter to the police, the fat was in the fire!

He was dragged to the Mandela house, where Winnie tore at his clothes and hit him with her open hand and fists. When her former friends wanted to force him into a car he, by the greatest good fortune, had an opportunity to escape. He hid away in Sharpeville for three months.

Once Lerathodi thought it was safe, he returned home. But Jerry Richardson saw him and was lying in wait for him. The soccer club members took him to the reeds at the Mzimhlope *vlei* in Soweto. Richardson attacked him there and stabbed him with the garden shears in the neck. It was Lerathodi Ikaneng's good fortune that the soccer club members thought that he was dead ...

◆ ◆ ◆

Down in the staffroom the commissioners and committee members, together with the other TRC officials, deliberated over the lunch break. I sat next to Leah Tutu that day.

"The *arch* seems tired", I remarked to her. "Are you going to get an opportunity to get away over the Christmas holiday, to relax?"

"It's more difficult than you think. One never really gets away, the people recognize him everywhere. I told Desmond I was going to dye his hair pitch-black so that we could remain anonymous while walking on the beach for once."

"It won't be enough", said the archbishop who sat across from us at the table, listening to the conversation. "Leah will also have to get a plastic surgeon, to do something about my nose and chin!"

◆ ◆ ◆

The second-last day belonged to Jerry Richardson, coach of the Mandela United Football Club and Winnie Mandela's right-hand man. His testimony and the evident pleasure he took in describing the atrocities, had the audience shuddering. At one point he interrupted himself: "The things we did as the Mandela soccer club were terrible, barbarous. I am becoming afraid to recount these things now ... "

But he *did* tell them!

When Jerry Richardson, 48 years old, had to be sworn in, he was every bit the showman. He stood up in his dark suit with red tie and matching red silk handkerchief, a miniature soccer ball in his hand. He refused to raise his right hand, when he had to take the oath. Like

President Mandela during his inauguration, he demanded to put his hand over his heart. His legal representative, Advocate Tony Richard, had to convince him quickly that he was contravening the rules. He then meekly put up his hand. But still the testimony could not begin. His family had not yet arrived, and they had to hear what he had to say! He needed their support as well. Jerry Richardson asked the chairman to adjourn the hearing so that he could go to his home in Soweto and fetch his eldest daughter, Lina. If this did not happen, he would not testify. The chairman *did* adjourn the hearing for a few minutes, to give Richard the opportunity to explain to his client that if he refused to testify before the TRC, he would be guilty of a criminal offence.

"You must remember that I am a soccer star, not a politician", Richardson began at last. Every now and again the chairman had to call him to order: all the detail, the bloody descriptions, were surely not necessary! He defended himself: "You must remember that we are talking about dead people!"

One after the other, the orders given by "Mummy" (he insisted referring to Winnie Mandela in this way) were mentioned. "We did terrible things", he repeated on one occasion, "just like the *Boere* had done terrible things to the freedom fighters ... There is blood on my hands because I had (often) pointed to someone saying 'He is an *impimpi* (traitor) – kill him! ... If anybody was branded in those days as an *impimpi*, there was no turning back. He had to be killed. Mummy gave the orders."

In Soweto there was a complaints book, in which anybody could write down his or her complaints against anyone else. The soccer club investigated the complaints and reported to Jerry. He then discussed the matter with Winnie Mandela, who decided whether the 'guilty' party would have to be fetched and be punished.

But Winnie had testified during her closed hearing that she was not aware of the goings-on of the people of the soccer team living on her premises, that they respected one another's privacy, Advocate Richard remarked. And you want to tell us that she was aware of everything that went on inside and outside the house? Who is correct? "She knew! Nobody living on the premises could come and go as they wanted to," Jerry replied. Only a special group of people – of whom he was one – could do this. Winnie liaised through him with the team, he had to pass on her orders to them.

Jerry Richardson, who was serving life imprisonment for various murders he committed, in fact did have a lot to answer for.

An excerpt from his *curriculum vitae* between the years 1986 and 1989: In January 1986 he joined the soccer club. A year later, in 1987, he became a police informer. He could no longer remember who had been his first murder victim, but there were many of them! In the few weeks between 9 November 1988 and 3 January 1989 the following happened: On 9 November his police handler, Sergeant Pretorius, and two MK members were killed in a shoot-out at his house in Soweto. A week or so later he personally killed the two boys Lolo Sono and Siboniso Shabalala, who had been falsely accused of betraying the two MK members. In December he slit Mrs Kuki Zwane's throat with garden shears and chucked her body away – just because she did not want to carry out "Mummy's" orders. By the end of the month he helped abduct the four boys from the Rev Paul Verryn's manse and tortured them. Four days later he killed Stompie Seipei. On 3 January he stabbed Lerothodi Ikaneng with garden shears and left him for dead among the reeds of the *vlei*.

On 19 February 1989 he was arrested.

Mrs Joyce Seipei shrieked hysterically on two occasions, when he described what he had done to her son. She had to be taken out of the hall to get her feelings under control.

Winnie Mandela ordered him and Slash to take Stompie away and kill him, but as a result of the visits of the Mandela Crisis Committee at the Mandela house they could not do so immediately. When the day finally arrived he ordered the other children in the house to sing freedom songs to cheer up "Mummy", who was somewhat depressed. He and Slash took the hallucinating Stompie to Noordgesig where they killed him. Richardson took pleasure in describing exactly what he had done: "I made him lie on his back and hit the garden shears right through his neck so that the blade came out on the other side." Then, with many more hacking movements he finished off the boy ... "we slaughtered him like a goat!" He and Slash sat waiting in the car until the body was cold – and then assembled the garden shears and put them away neatly in Winnie's garage. "We thought that it had been the perfect crime."

◆ ◆ ◆

It was the last day of the hearing. The hall on the first floor of the Johannesburg Institute for Social Sciences was fuller than ever. On that day Winnie Madikizela-Mandela would have to answer to all the charges laid, all the testimony given.

What would she say?

At the beginning of the first day it was already clear that black South Africa would with this hearing – more than with any other hearing – take a long hard look at themselves. The integrity of the struggle was at stake. For just about two weeks one witness after the other spoke about Winnie Mandela, the soccer club and the people of Soweto. Shocking things were said, things that one would rather have kept quiet about. The "secondary infections" came into sharp focus under the microscope. For how many of them would Winnie accept responsibility?

The week had exacted its toll. It had not been easy to stand in front of the mirror of history. Some of the witnesses barely looked up while talking, and avoided Winnie's eyes. Others spoke defiantly and emotionally, but under cross-examination began to contradict themselves, incoherently and nervously. Some indicated that they felt unsafe, that Winnie's henchmen had intimidated them. Katiza Cebekhulu, one of the key witnesses, was spirited to the airport directly after his appearance, to London. "It's not easy to question such a powerful woman", the Rev Mbungala, Winnie's own minister, testified the previous Thursday. "It's just as bad to *listen* to all of this", Tom Manthata remarked next to me. "To hear how the reputation of the mother of the nation, one of the heroines of the struggle, is being extinguished, is to experience how our reputation, our struggle is being destroyed." Albertina Sisulu also had a hard time getting together all her facts, her testimony against her old friend – and had to return the next day to explain what she had really wanted to say. In the staffroom Tutu remarked to me, following Albertina's first, evasive testimony: "These things make me so tired ... so terribly tired!"

Winnie Mandela sat unperturbed next to her legal representatives when the chairman opened the last hearing. In her navy-blue suit and lime blouse she fielded the questions put to her. Sometimes calmly, a smile on her face. At times aggressively and sarcastically. "I won't allow you to talk to me like that!" she put the TRC cross-examiner in his place. Her colleagues from the ANC who testified against her, received a thrashing. Minister Mufamadi was a "coward", and Frank Chikane and even deputy president Mbeki were "liars". Azhar Cachalia and Murphy Morobe – "Murphy Patel" she taunted him – were "members of an Indian cabal trying to destroy me". The Mandela Crisis Committee's report was in fact a Stratcom document! More than once the chairman had to caution her.

It took Winnie less than an hour to answer to all the accusations brought in about her and the soccer club. Her legal representative, Advocate Semenya, raised the various cases one after the other and asked her response to them. "Ridiculous", "the worst insanity", "hallucinations", "laughable" she dismissed one accusation after the other. "Now why would I do something like that?" she responded to Semenya's question whether she had ever given anybody the order to murder. She did concede that she was sometimes less vigilant than she should have been, but then that happened as a result of "her passion for the pleas of people needing help".

What was her response to the most important allegations against her?

Stompie Seipei and his three friends: It was untrue that the boys were removed by force from the manse of the Rev Verryn. She did not think it necessary to ask the boys herself what happened, or to examine their injuries herself. Neither did she see any of them being assaulted at the Mandela house. However, she let the boys go, after the clergymen came to talk to her. In any case, if it had been so bad for the boys to stay in the house, they could easily have escaped. "I only heard of Stompie's death when the whole thing exploded in the newspapers."

The murder of Dr Asvat: She did not know the two murderers who were supposed to have received R20 000 from her to commit the murder at all. To tell the truth, she met Mbatha and Dlamini for the first time in her life at the TRC hearings. She had been just as deeply shocked as anybody else when she heard of the doctor's death. She had done nothing to influence the investigation and was very upset when she later heard that Minister Mufamadi – without consulting her, as a Cabinet colleague – had asked the police to reopen the investigation.

The deaths of Lolo Sono and Siboniso Shabalala: She did not know Siboniso at all, but Lolo she did, in fact, use as a messenger – and took him to Richardson's house to talk to the two MK soldiers hiding away there. But that was the last she ever saw of him. It was precisely when she was with the boy on her way there that his father saw them together in the combi – and Lolo had not been assaulted or injured at all. "It's ridiculous (to say) that I ordered Sono and Shabalala to be murdered."

The testimony about the disciplinary committee who brought accused persons to her house for punishment: "That is blatantly untrue! I heard about it for the first time ever during the closed hearing of the TRC."

◆ ◆ ◆

The hall was so full and stuffy that I, together with a few colleagues, preferred watching the events of that last afternoon on the large television screen in the staff room. Leah Tutu, who was intensely involved with everything happening in Soweto, followed Winnie's testimony – and her husband's reaction – attentively. Every now and again she would comment, "That's it – tell her!.. Good, ask her. I would like to hear the answer myself ... No, wait, must you really say that?" Most of us chipped in, too.

Until everyone suddenly fell silent. Winnie Mandela made her concluding remarks. She addressed her parting shot to the TRC, which had called her to the hearing so soon before the ANC's national conference – forgetting that she herself had requested this. The archbishop's face appeared on the screen. He looked older and more tired than I had ever seen him. Softly, but with intense emotion, he began talking. Referring to everything that had happened over the past two weeks, all the testimonies, all the charges and excuses, all the half-truths and denials, all the lies, all the pain, he addressed the mother of nation, the nation itself, directly:

"Many of us were dismayed but also refreshed by everything that happened during the hearing. We were dismayed about the conduct of prominent members of the struggle – the moral incompetence they displayed was unexpected and shocking. But there were also shining exceptions! ... It is our duty to show that the new dispensation in which we live, is different, morally speaking. We must be prepared to stand up for goodness, truth and love – not to grovel before the mighty.

"I recognize the place Madikizela-Mandela assumed in the struggle. And yet we need to admit to one another that something went wrong ... horribly, horribly, wrong. What precisely went wrong I do not know! We can really only say: 'There but for the grace of God go I' ... but something did go wrong!"

Tutu looked Winnie Mandela in the eyes.

"There are many, many people who love you. There are many, many who say that you should have taken your position as First Lady of our country ... I am speaking to you as somebody who loves you very, very much ... I want to ask you to get up and say, 'There were things that went wrong' ... , If only you could get yourself so far to say, 'I am sorry, I am sorry for my share in what had happened' ... , I plead with you, I plead with you ... please ... You are a great person. If only you knew how much greater you would be if you would say, 'I am sorry ... things went wrong. Forgive me!'"

Tutu began speaking softly. It was as if he was not talking to the woman in front of him, but to every South African who had gone to stand in front of the mirror.

"I plead with you ... " he whispered for the last time.

In the staff room, in front of the monitor, everybody sat rooted to the spot. What would Winnie Mandela's response be?

Winnie turned to her legal representative and talked to him. Then she switched on her microphone.

"I want to thank you for your wonderful, wise words! This is the father I have always known and I hope that you are still that father. I want to tell Dr Asvat's family that I am deeply sorry. I also want to tell Stompie's mother how sorry I am. It is true, I agree, things did go terribly wrong. About that bit, the bit that went wrong in those years – and we know that there were factors that contributed to it – about those things I am very sorry."

Mrs Winnie Mandela embraces Mrs Joyce Seipei, Stompie's mother

This was another Winnie than the one who had been speaking so confidently earlier the day.

Down in the staff room we stared at one another, at a loss for words. What exactly had happened? Did Winnie in the end confess her guilt? Was her confession sincere or was she simply saying what Tutu expected of her, in fact almost forced her to say? About what, precisely, was she sorry?

Antjie Samuel, the SABC's reporter, was so moved by what she had seen and heard that she stormed into the staff room and embraced Tutu, who had just joined us. Tears streamed down her cheeks. Her feeling was that something quite unusual had happened, that Tutu had taken an enormous gamble ... but that it had paid off.

In the hall there was a commotion. Winnie and Stompie Seipei's mother walked towards one another. Cameras flashed. They took each others' hands and embraced. They made their peace. "Now", Joyce Seipei said, "we can really talk to one another. There are many things that I want to know. We are both women and I know that she also has feelings deep in her heart, but now we must talk ... "

◆ ◆ ◆

In the car, that evening, Tom and I mulled over the events of the day, trying to understand what had really happened. Had Winnie Mandela, the mother of the nation, truly come to see herself in the mirror? Did she see something she had not seen before – or didn't want to see?

The newspapers would analyse the event for weeks to come, and we would talk about it in the office.

When Tom was finally dropped off, his concluding remark was a sober: "There are many things that I'm wondering about. But I know one thing for certain: Winnie didn't win ... "

On the way back to Pretoria the words of Bishop Peter Storey kept coming back to me:

"To dispel the suffocating fog of silence is very important for the future of this country. This tragedy has wounded, it has hurt, it has destroyed people's ability to know the difference between right and wrong. It has shown that it is not enough to become politically liberated, we must also become human."

8 DECEMBER 1997: PW BOTHA SUBMITS HIS REPORT ... AND THE FUR FLIES

Convincing former State President P W Botha to escort the TRC trek to enable all of us to look at the past through his glasses, was not an easy task. He had already from the outset made it clear that he – to put it mildly – did not like the Truth Commission, and that he had no inclination to participate in the "circus". After repeated requests and negotiations, and after the archbishop had personally paid a visit to the former president's home in The Wilderness, it was mutually agreed that P W Botha, aided by a legal team comprising senior lawyers – for which the TRC would pay – would draw up a statement, providing answers to, among other things, the questions the TRC had levelled at him. After the submission of the statement, a date would be set on which the former state president would meet with the TRC to explain his statement and discuss additional questions that might arise.

After months of waiting, the statement was finally ready – and P W Botha's legal representative, Ernst Penzhorn, handed the voluminous document to Tutu. The report, which was also relayed to the media, contained a good deal of interesting – and for some people, distressing – information.

He too, was not entirely satisfied with the way the security forces acted in the past, P W Botha wrote. "The directives I outlined as part of the total strategy against the total onslaught, clearly indicated that violence had to be limited and applied judicially. Everything possible had to be done to gain and retain the good opinion of the nation." However, this was not always the case, as the security legislation and the emergency regulations "had the inherent danger of being misused by law enforcers". One might still justify it in cases where 'terrorists' died, but it is lamentable that civilians were also injured and killed.

If it depended on him, he would not have instituted such drastic emergency regulations, and he would have wanted to lift the state of emergency in the mid 1980s. "The decision, however, did not rest with me. By about 1985 the ANC/SACP/UDF alliance succeeded in putting their so-called people's war in action through horrible bloodshed and terror, the destruction of schools, the burning of houses, damaging property and intimidating people. Total anarchy loomed. It was no longer possible ... to protect the civilians of the country and property, and maintain law and order, by means of regular policing and in terms of the Constitution and the Criminal Procedure Act." In the late nineteen eighties he considered freeing Nelson Mandela, on condition that he renounce the violence and that he and his wife be restricted to one district. However, Mandela refused and he is consequently to blame for the last years he spent in prison.

Not only he and the National Party owe the nation answers, Botha argued further. The ANC themselves have a great deal to answer for, concerning the civilian targets they attacked and the great number of innocent people who died in attacks on schools, hospitals, missionary stations, churches and banks. Who, for instance, decided that innocent men and women, who on 20 May 1983 wanted to catch their buses in Church Street, Pretoria, could be sacrificed for the sake of the struggle against the security forces? The perception exists, the former president said, that the TRC is more eager to investigate the misdeeds of the previous government, than those of the ANC.

Zapiro, following Tutu's visit to P W Botha at his home in The Wilderness earlier this year, in an attempt to convince him to appear before the Truth Commission

In his submission, P W Botha took a few swipes at his former colleagues. His successor, Mr F W de Klerk, had the reputation of being the great initiator of reform in South Africa, but in the Botha cabinet he was a pull-back who opposed numerous reform initiatives. "As the leader of the NP in the Transvaal, he continually raised objections to my reform initiatives, because he feared the Whites' right of self-determination would be jeopardized by the initiatives. Mr de Klerk participated little in the discussions of the State Security Council ... He also seldom delivered comments on the decisions of the SSC. Precisely where and when Mr de Klerk had his 'Damascus road experience', and what it entailed, I do not know ... I suspect it happened towards the end of 1988."

With reference to the appearance of Leon Wessels before the TRC a month or two before, P W Botha wrote: "Wessels says he suspected that gross human rights violations had been committed, and that he, however, did not want to advance the suspicion. If he formed this suspicion after his appointment as deputy minister of law and order, he was in the ideal position to determine the facts. If he had harboured the suspicion before the post was offered to him, one is surprised at his willingness to accept the post."

Wessels was evidently dismayed. "He is rubbing me up the wrong way now ... Mr Botha is conveniently forgetting the four important discussions I personally conducted with him in this regard between 1985 and 1989. I think Botha, through his recalcitrant attitude, is committing an injustice against certain people who are now requesting amnesty. Botha is now fighting for a better past. I am fighting for a better future!"

Former State President Botha also did not spare his minister of Foreign Affairs of many years' standing. In pursuance of Mr Pik Botha's submission to the TRC, he wrote: "If Mr Botha ... informed your commission that he had already in the nineteen seventies come to the realization that the policy of the NP was devoid of moral grounds, he, at all times, hid it from me very carefully. (Then) it is amazing that he, after coming to the realization, continued to fill, and accept the privileges, financial remuneration and status of a minister of the NP government for at least fifteen years. The reason why he did not act in accordance with the courage of his convictions by resigning as minister, is obscure."

"It does not surprise me that former State President Botha now reacts in this way", Pik Botha commented to the press. "It is characteristic of the one-sidedness of particularly the last years of his presidency. I am not eager to say so myself, but in the caucus I was intentionally ousted from posts of leadership as a result of my views on apartheid." On P W Botha's criticism against F W de Klerk, the former minister of Foreign Affairs made the following statement: "In all fairness to Mr P W Botha, he is correct in saying that Mr F W de Klerk was a pull-back when it came to measures of reform – until he (himself) became president. Then the transformation was like a total polar shift. After much toil and sweat Mr Botha repealed certain apartheid laws, but when it came to the cardinal, decisive leap, he was obstinate. He knows it, his colleagues know it, and the nation know it."

Numerous issues concerning P W Botha's submission still had to be resolved. This would take place in the following weeks at an *in camera* session in Cape Town – or so we hoped. Lots of water still had to flow under the bridge, however.

9 DECEMBER 1997: THE AMNESTY GHOST DOES NOT REST

The dissatisfaction that reigned over the amnesty that had been awarded to 37 members of the ANC, would not subside. Not only people and groups from the outside aired serious criticism, but also many TRC members, who asked questions out of concern. The National Party and the Democratic Party announced that they were planning to go to court with the request that the ANC perpetrators' amnesty be declared illegal. Ms Dene Smuts (DP) was very upset, saying, "The way in which the TRC deals with the illegal approval of amnesty for the 37 highly placed members of the ANC is lamentable and undermines the integrity of the process of reconciliation." Within the ranks of the TRC, serious debates were held on the matter. The judges of the Amnesty Committee were adamant: The TRC Act did, in fact, according to their judgement, empower them to award amnesty to applicants in this way also. Ironically, the opponents of the ANC insisted during the negotiation process – out of fear that the ANC would exert too much influence over the Amnesty Committee – that the Amnesty Committee be autonomous. Some of the commissioners wanted the decision to be declared invalid. Others prevented this: The TRC cannot repudiate one of their own committees. Eventually the TRC decided to seek the opinion of senior counsel – Advocate Wim Tengrove. If his finding was that the Amnesty Committee had erred, the Supreme Court would be requested to review the Amnesty Committee's decision to grant amnesty to the 37 ANC members.

10 DECEMBER 1997: THE *BROEDERS* ARE ALSO PENITENT

Another contingent of fellow-travellers arrived. While black South Africa were forced to look in the mirror in the previous weeks, and former State President Botha had to start giving answers to questions about the past, a significant contribution was forthcoming straight from the heart of the Afrikanerdom. The year before, Wynand Malan and I paid a visit to *Die Eike*, the headquarters of the Afrikaner Broederbond (otherwise known by its new name, the Afrikanerbond) to encourage their participation in the work of the Truth Commission. Would they, with their considerable influence over the Afrikaans community, be willing to accompany their fellow-citizens on the road?

Whether our request was instrumental or not, I do not know, but early in December the news arrived: The AB had put their own story – after eighty years of secrecy – in writing. On 10 December the representatives of the AB handed Wynand a copy of the book *Draer van 'n Ideaal*, who, in turn, undertook to give it to Archbishop Tutu. The book was not initially written as a submission to the TRC. It was intended for all interested persons, nationally and internationally, Dr Boet Schoeman, Executive Director of the AB, later declared. The AB did not want to "confess about their past" before the TRC, but they thought it was time to make their view on the past and the future known to the world.

Whether it was a confession or not, the *broeders* deeply searched their hearts. It was true that the AB had supported and promoted the policy of separate development. In the course of time, however, a number of distressing consequences ensued. Instead of a society based on human dignity, a community based on racial aristocracy was born. "The AB cannot deny that their past views and attitudes, as seen from the perspective of the present, at times smacked of insensitivity and a deficient vision. To the extent that conduct of this nature contributed to the injustices of the past, we are sorry. The AB observe the firm resolution to learn from the mistakes of the past."

In the document, the AB stressed that everything was not bad. The principle of separate development represented the honest intentions behind a policy aimed at enabling the development of all population groups, including the Afrikaner, on the basis of self-determination. "This vision was considered as justified and cannot, in principal, be condemned." It also had to be borne in mind that the AB too, had made a contribution to aid transformation in our country. In 1983, for instance, they tried hard to convince the Nationalist government to institute a fourth chamber, for black people, in the then tripartite parliament. In 1987, just before the Dakar deliberation, the former chairman of the

AB, Professor Pieter de Lange, held discussions with ANC officials, including Thabo Mbeki, in New York.

Everyone was not equally impressed by the statement of the AB. "Very little and very late," a colleague remarked at the office. "Why did they wait until all the TRC hearings had been concluded?" "Why did they not go to the TRC and state their case?", another wanted to know. These were valid questions. But I had appreciation for the willingness of the *broeders* to accompany us on the road – on our journey inwards. Their views were important.

15 DECEMBER 1997: CLASH WITHIN THE AWB

The cellphone rang. The summer vacation had already started for me a week before, and Inza and I joined our children in Gansbaai. But our peace was disrupted by the call. "Eugene Terre'blanche has distanced himself from the AWB's submission – or rather, that which we thought was the AWB's submission", the English journalist said. "Who must be believed now – ET, or Kriel, or neither of the two?" According to the journalist, the AWB leader, after a meeting of the "general staff", expressed his dissatisfaction that Mr Kriel had, without their knowledge made a submission to the TRC. As far as they were concerned Kriel had confessed to deeds the hierarchy of the AWB had not committed. Eugene Terre'blanche added that Kriel was summarily suspended from the AWB.

It was a bucket of cold water in my face. During the past few weeks I had conferred with Dries Kriel often, at home or on the telephone. One Saturday morning, Dries and his wife picked me up in their car to meet the AWB prisoners in the Leeuwkop prison, and to answer questions they had about the TRC. We talked at length about the submission that the AWB would make. Just before leaving on holiday I spoke to Dries Kriel again to confirm that he had the approval of all the AWB role players – and that a submission on behalf of all of them would be delivered at the offices of the TRC in Johannesburg.

When I phoned Dries Kriel from Gansbaai he was very upset. He told me what he had also told the media. It was on the evening news: "I don't believe what Terre'blanche told the press. I think he is a coward who is letting his people down." Kriel went on to say that he and "ET" had worked together on the statement the previous Friday, but Terre'blanche had now for some reason lost his nerve and withdrawn from the submission. Dries Kriel – who in his day, had been one of the

AWB's most active members and who had personally applied for amnesty for thirty incidents in which he was personally involved – added, "I worked in cahoots with Terre'blanche in inciting the young men who are now in prison, to take up arms. At night I cannot sleep when I think of their fate in prison."

◆ ◆ ◆

We were already back in Pretoria after the Christmas holidays when Eugene Terre'blanche called me late one evening. There was a crisis in right-wing circles, he said. He urgently wanted to consult with me and Alex Boraine the next morning. Dr Boraine, who was in the Cape, could not be sent for at such short notice. Nevertheless, the next day Ruben Richard and I went to *Meat and Eat*, a popular student restaurant in Hatfield, Pretoria, to meet with Eugene Terre'blanche and his men. Ruben Richard would in the coming weeks handle the submissions from right-wing groups on behalf of the TRC. Both Mr Terre'blanche and Mr Robert van Tonder of the Boerestaat party explained to us that there

Mr Robert van Tonder and Mr Eugene Terre'blanche in conversation with Piet Meiring and Ruben Richard (of the TRC)

were major differences of opinion regarding the TRC in the so-called right-wing groups. Whereas Dries Kriel had already made a submission to the TRC, the AWB and other right-wing organisations were still deciding what they were going to do. Ruben and I undertook to convey their messages to the TRC, at the same time encouraging them to seriously consider the generous amnesty offer.

19 DECEMBER 1997: DRAMA IN CAPE TOWN WHEN P W BOTHA FAILS TO SHOW UP

At five minutes before nine the chairman, the vice-chairman and the leader of the investigative unit of the Truth Commission settled in the chamber of the Cape Town office. The former state president of the country had been subpoenaed to appear before them for the purpose of answering a number of questions – specifically those pertaining to the role of the State Security Council during the term of his presidency. But Archbishop Tutu, Alex Boraine and Dumisa Ntsebeza waited in vain. The seat at the table bearing the name card *P W Botha*, remained empty.

It was not entirely unexpected. The former state president had a long time before, said he would not come. He did not like the "TRC circus" as he called it. And opportunities for escape were available. He opposed his first subpoena on the grounds of having undergone an operation shortly before it was served on him. The particulars on the second subpoena had, fortunately for him, not been fully completed, and could be ignored. But early in December, the third, legal subpoena was delivered to his home in The Wilderness: On 19 December he had to appear before the TRC in Cape Town.

Should he, or should he not? The debate raged for weeks. Calls came from all corners, urging the former president to obey the laws of the country. He had to meet his obligation towards the nation. Others, in turn, took delight in the unruliness of the *Groot Krokodil* (Big Crocodile).

On 8 December President Mandela, after concluding discussions with the members of the moderature of the General Synod of the NG Kerk, told the press he had requested the ministers to talk to Mr Botha in order to seek a solution to the impasse. Nobody was elevated above the law, and if the former president was subpoenaed, he had to obey the laws of the country. And Mandela wanted to prevent Botha from being convicted and punished. The next day, General Constand Viljoen raised objections in earnest and warned the church leaders that they were running a risk – regardless of any good intentions they had – if they allowed the ANC to use them in this manner, and they were repeating the mistakes of the past when the church was too closely aligned with the NP. The Rev Freek Swanepoel, the moderator, nevertheless replied that they would go, not as lackeys of the Government, but to conduct a pastoral discussion with a member of the church who was caught in a crisis. Rev Swanepoel and Professor Pieter Potgieter accompanied the two local ministers of *Die Vleie*, P W Botha's congregation, to *Die Anker* (The Anchor), the former president's house. "Our discussion went well", Freek Swanepoel reported two hours later. "We were warmly received and conducted a good, adequate discussion."

This did not mean that the former president had decided to obey the subpoena. The leadership of the Conservative Party, which had only a few years before been Botha's political arch-enemies, found pleasure in P W Botha's behaviour and declared their total support for him. "If the TRC want to pester a lion with an aching tooth, they must arrest him." Look and see what will happen! was the implication. The TRC was a farce and any Afrikaner who wanted to attempt convincing Botha to appear before the "Tutu Commission", would disgrace his Afrikaner identity.

◆ ◆ ◆

On the road from Gansbaai to the Strand, where we planned to stay for a couple of days, I called Christelle Terreblanche: "If P W Botha appears today, I am first going to Cape Town. I am most interested in hearing what he has to say. But if he does not show up, I will take the turn-off to the Strand." Just as the time signal on the radio indicated it was nine o' clock, my cellphone rang. "Piet", Christelle reported from the TRC office, "you can go to the Strand. Tutu and the others are still waiting in the conference hall, but we received a message from someone in The Wilderness a moment ago that we might just as well adjourn. P W will not be in Cape Town on time. To tell you the truth, he is still standing in the shower ... "

◆ ◆ ◆

When Tutu and Boraine walked down the couple of blocks to the office of the attorney-general of the Western Cape in Queen Victoria Street to lay an official charge against P W Botha for transgressing the TRC Act (section 39), the entire nation knew: Things were taking a serious turn. The former state president could thereby be forced to appear in court, and if he was found guilty, a fine or a prison sentence, or both would be waiting for him. Advocate Frank Kahn, the attorney-general, gave us to understand that he would investigate the merits of the charge and announce his decision on 2 January 1998.

The press descended on Tutu. What would the people of the country, particularly the white people, the Afrikaners, say? We had no option, the Archbishop explained. Nobody is elevated above the law. We must treat everyone in the same way. If we expected Winnie Madikizela-Mandela to deliver her testimony, we cannot excuse P W Botha, just because he does not feel like doing the same.

One of the reporters asked, "But what about the white people? They say the TRC have it in for the former state president. The TRC are solely out to degrade him!"

"You ask me about the feelings of the Whites? Rightly so, I am very concerned about it ... But do you realize that there are other people in this country too, black people, who also have feelings?" Tutu replied.

Ernst Penzhorn, Botha's legal advisor, told the media, "Mr Botha will not make a statement. Leave him in peace so that he can enjoy Christmas. He has had a difficult year. Allow him the opportunity to enjoy his vacation."

◆ ◆ ◆

Not only former State President Botha had earned a vacation.

The stretch that had been completed, was a long and wearisome one – the inner journey to a better understanding of everything that happened to the nation and its people in the past. A great number of fellow-travellers had shown up. Each one contributed to the trek in his or her own way, supplying a piece of the map. The views and the outpourings of the generals and the politicians, the rabbis and the imams, the 'Mother of the Nation' and the *'Groot Krokodil'* were of inestimable value. The pieces of the truth that were presented by everyone, helped complete the picture.

Not only the archbishop and his entourage, but also the nation as a whole deserved to take a rest, I thought while walking on the beach. In less than a week it would be Christmas, and angels would sing in every church: "Glory to God in the highest heavens, and peace on earth to those in whom He takes pleasure."

May it be, I prayed in my heart, that we will experience some of the peace, and the reconciliation between people that was made possible by the Christ child, not only during Christmas, but also in the months that lie beyond the new year.

CHAPTER SIX

THE SECOND LAST LEG OF THE JOURNEY

11-13 JANUARY 1998; ROBBEN ISLAND – WHAT DOES THE LORD WANT TO SAY TO US?

The wind was blowing through our hair, the sun shining warm on our faces. The boat taking us across the blue sea of Table Bay to Robben Island was full: workers, officials, a group of Dutch tourists – and, almost unrecognizable in their holiday garb, the members of the Truth Commission. Archbishop Tutu, who had had the bright idea that we start off the new year on Robben Island, was his jovial self. He felt well, he said, and the doctors were satisfied with his blood count. The cameras of the tourists, who could hardly believe their luck, were clicking away non-stop. Tutu good-naturedly gave them all an opportunity to take a photo.

There was quite some work piling up in those three days. The year's programme had to be finalized. Then there was also the unsolved issue of the amnesty granted to the 37 ANC members. "The TRC is divided!", the newspapers had written the previous week. Dumisa Ntsebeza sided with the amnesty judges; Boraine and a number of colleagues wanted the high court to pass judgment. "Will the TRC split?" the press pondered.

But Tutu did not intend starting work immediately. Robben Island was a living museum – and we first had to go and explore it. The battered bus took us on a long route, past the shipwrecks, the graves, the lime quarries where the prisoners had worked, the humble dwelling where Robert Sobukwe had been detained, completely on his own, without trial for nine years, to the prison where the world's best-known prisoner and his colleagues had been kept for years – Govan Mbeki, Raymond Mhlaba, Ahmed Kathrada, Walter Sisulu, Mac Maharaj, Steve Tswete, Jacob Zuma, Tokyo Sexwale and many others. Between 1963 and 1991 no less than three thousands prisoners were incarcerated – among them my blood-brother Tom Manthata.

On the boat to Robben Island: Alex Boraine, Glenda Wildschut, Desmond Tutu, Fazel Randera

Lionel Davis, who himself was a former prisoner, was waiting for us and accompanied us through the prison. What he had forgotten, Tom filled in. Hugh Lewin, who did his time in the Pretoria Prison, could compare notes with them. We walked through the entrance, past the room where the prisoners were searched, to the square with its brown walls ("the only piece of outside world where we could breathe", the guide said), to cell Number Five, where Nelson Mandela had been detained. In the larger communal cells the former Robben Islanders dished out a hotch-potch of anecdotes. In the big bathroom with its cold-water taps and no privacy, Tutu started talking: "You know that I cry easily. And now the tears are near. We crack jokes and tell stories. But people really suffered here! People suffered here so that we could have a free country today. How do we explain it to our children so that they truly understand?"

Tom was disappointed. The C Section, where he had been locked up in those days, was closed off. Tourists are not allowed there – and he had been promising me for weeks that he would show me his cell.

The following morning, Monday morning, everyone was ready to tackle the serious items on the agenda. Tutu still did not feel like having a meeting. Not yet! After an early breakfast we all went to the conference room where the archbishop was waiting with an open Bible on the table in front of him. "Today is to be a day of silence", he announced. "Today we have to become so quiet that we can hear the Lord speak. We need quiet, and not noise, more than ever before. C S Lewis was right when he said, 'Noise is not of the devil, it is the devil'. Jesus had a need for quietness. He often sought solitude, sometimes He took his disciples with Him." With John 21 open in front of him, the archbishop started telling the story of how the Lord Jesus met Peter. "'Do you really love me?' He asked. 'Then take care of my sheep, feed my sheep!' Peter heard the voice of God – and received a command from him. We, too, must attune ourselves to hear God's voice – then we will also be made aware of his instructions for us." Being the good Anglican priest that he is, Tutu gave us all a lesson in meditation, how to quieten your mind and concentrate, until you hear what God says. "I know that not all of us are Christians", he smiled, looking at Fazel Randera, Yasmin Sooka and Ilan Lax – our Muslim, Hindu and Jewish colleagues. "But it will not do you any harm to listen! In the desert, where everything is quiet, where you are completely alone, one experiences total dependence on your Creator. And this is what we need today!"

With stern instructions to us to go and find a quiet spot where we could focus on the Lord God for the entire day – so as to hear what He wanted to say to us, we dispersed. I found a place next to the sea, in the shelter of a few rocks. The hours slipped by. In silence we went to have lunch and then again returned to our 'desert'. It was a long day ... but an unforgettable one. I could see my colleagues sitting around – under the trees, on the grass. Some were walking peacefully alongside the sea.

At sunset we were back in the conference room. Tutu broke the silence first. "Alex, what did the Lord tell you? Did you hear him speak?" One after the other, the men and women around the table started telling what they had heard that day. "The Lord made me realize how closely knit we as a group have become." "I became aware of how awesome the instructions are that we received to work for truth and reconciliation. They come from the Lord Himself!" "The Lord made me aware of the thousands of people praying for us daily. It gives me courage!" "God made me understand the great responsibility we have towards each other – to support each other and to keep each other on the right path." Virginia Gcabasche: "Next to the sea I could not but think about the thousands of prisoners offloaded here through the years. Some of them came here on the same boat we travelled on yesterday. Did their faith sustain them? What had Christ meant to them?"

Glenda Wildschut, trained as an opera singer, started singing softly:

Were you there when they crucified my Lord?
Have you heard, they accused him of a crime?
... how they shoved him in the lime ...

Tutu, the devout spiritual leader with his feet firmly on the ground, started praying after the last note had died down. And then cheerfully announced, "Now for a rum and Coke!" It was an evening to remember. *Braaivleis* (barbecue), music, good conversation and a lot of laughter. But we still had not got down to our agenda.

On Tuesday we were to return home. The boat was to depart at one o' clock. At nine o' clock we were ready for the meeting. The hot potato of the 37 ANC members who had been granted amnesty was being tabled at last. Should we support the Amnesty Committee – or take it to the high court? Would our newly found unity last? Did we have enough time to think about all the implications and to deal with all the personal feelings? Tutu introduced the matter – and after less than half an hour all agreed: we would request the high court to give a declaratory order. Everyone was happy! The previous day's tranquillity had been worth it, through and through.

◆ ◆ ◆

On the boat back, with the wind still in our hair and the sun still on our faces, I said to myself: The last leg of the trek had started, the trek that would last until the end of June when the Truth Commission would close its doors. When we had anchored and greeted each other, a second thought occurred to me: In actual fact, it was not the last, but the second last leg. Because on the day that the TRC submitted its report to the president – and the nation – the last leg, the journey into the future, would only then really start.

◆ ◆ ◆

The human rights violation hearings had already ended months before.

The institutional hearings were also behind us. The reparation proposals had already been submitted to government. What remained were the numerous amnesty applications that had to be processed. In the months to come they would dominate the main news in the newspapers and on television: the long row of perpetrators who would come forward and tell their stories in the hope of exemption.

That was not all, however. All too soon other problems surfaced ...

22 JANUARY 1998: THE DAY OF THE BIG CROCODILE

Look it up in the Bible. A crocodile does not let anyone mess with it!

"Can you catch a crocodile with a hook and line? Or put a noose around his tongue? ... Will he beg you to desist or try to flatter you from your intentions? ... Can you make a pet of him like a bird ... If you lay your hands upon him, you will long remember the battle that ensues, and you will never try it again!" (Job 41)

P W Botha was – in any case in the eyes of the Truth Commission – as wrong as could be. But when I saw him on television that evening: upright, obstinate, angry, his finger pointing, I could not help but think of Job's words. If you take on a 'big crocodile', you have to know what you are doing.

◆ ◆ ◆

There was drama, even before the court session started: The street in front of the courtroom in George was closed for traffic. Crowds had gathered: ANC supporters waving placards. Staunch right-wing politicians were engaged in heated debate in next to no time. Conservative Party leader Ferdie Hartzenberg, was knocked about. "Boer!", "You dog!", he was mocked – before police intervened.

At nine o' clock the former state president entered the courtroom, straight as a ramrod in his navy blue suit and pristine white shirt, blue tie, handkerchief neatly in his jacket pocket. He took a seat in front *next* to the dock. His supporters, his former companions, were seated in a long row: Daan van der Merwe and Ferdie Hartzenberg, senior Conservative Party members, Lapa Munnik, André van Wyk, Greyling Wentzel, former colleagues in parliament, and the generals, Jannie Geldenhuys and Constand Viljoen. On the opposite side, Philip Dexter and a group of senior ANC men sat down. Between the two groups, Mrs Reinette Te Water Naudé, P W Botha's fiancé, sat watching, smiling.

"All rise in court", the orderly said.

P W Botha nodded slightly in the direction of Mr Victor Lugajo, the regional court president. After the session someone asked him whether he minded appearing before a black magistrate. "Why would I? I grew up on a farm in the Free State where I played with little black boys. I welcome Mandela in my home ... "

The state prosecutor announced: "The state versus P W Botha."

The language was a problem. Magistrate Lugajo did not understand Afrikaans and asked whether the proceedings could be conducted in English. The legal team pointed out that their client was Afrikaans-speaking and that the bulky papers before court they had prepared were in Afrikaans. "Will you be able to understand them?", Advocate Laubscher asked. The magistrate assured Botha and his legal team that he would ask his assessors to help him with the translation. He would also, if necessary, have some of the documentation translated.

The court session lasted barely twenty minutes. After a few technicalities had been dealt with, the court adjourned. Former President Botha was to appear again on 23 February.

After the magistrate had left the courtroom, P W Botha spoke to the press. Challengingly, his forefinger pointing characteristically, he made it clear that nobody, not even the court, would force him to co-operate with the TRC. He would never apologize for what he had done during his term as president.

"God, help me, I cannot do anything else!"

"Hear, hear!" some of his supporters cheered from the back of the courtroom. Botha seemingly enjoyed his interview with the press, but also grabbed the opportunity to reprimand them. When they came too close to him, crowding him, he rebuked them, telling them to come to their senses, otherwise he would not say anything further!

"Are you going to ask to be pardoned for all the people who died in prison or in operations beyond the borders because of your policy?", a journalist wanted to know.

"No, I am praying for them!"

As reluctant as he was to apologize for his initiatives to rid the country of racial discrimination, he was unwilling to apologize for the legal actions of his government in its battle to counter the onslaught on the country, he said. Also not for the principle of peaceful coexistence that he had worked so hard for. After a moment of silence, he added, "I am a religious person who has been saved ... I am not a perfect person. There was only one perfect person and that was Jesus Christ!"

But Botha was worried about the direction the country was moving in and made no bones about it! To tell the truth, he had repeatedly discussed the situation with President Mandela. The humiliation of Afrikaners had to come to an end. What was more, Afrikaners, now than ever before, had to stand together ...

"There's a tiger in every nation. That tiger is found all over the world. Here the tiger is going to fight back! We are busy organizing ... "

Max du Preez, presenter of the television programme *Special Report*, pointedly remarked, "There are no tigers in Africa ... "

"I know", was the quick retort, "but had there been, you would not have been one of them!"

As the conversation began to heat up, Botha's legal team led him from the courtroom. Before the big crocodile said too much. Or went too far ...

18 FEBRUARY 1998: TUTU AND THE AFRIKANERS (1)

On the second last leg of the journey, it was absolutely necessary that everyone in the country came along. In a speech before the parliamentary press gallery in Cape Town, Tutu voiced his disappointment:

"I am appealing to all white people, but especially the Afrikaner. The most atrocious things happened in the past. Most of this was as a result of things that you supported. You now have a chance to admit: Yes, these things happened! You will not get another chance like this one. I sympathize with you ... but if you reject the TRC, you will take the burden to the grave with you and the burden will destroy you. I pray that one day you will understand ... "

Tutu recalled how hard he had tried to accommodate P W Botha, how he had specially gone to the Minister of Justice to obtain legal aid for him. How he had reached out to former President Botha after the death of his wife, Elize. In the black community he was severely criticized "because I had reached out to the white community in this way. But I had to – I want to – do it. But the opportunity may pass ... "

26 FEBRUARY 1998: TUTU AND THE AFRIKANERS (2)

There was immense response to Tutu's words. "The timing is excellent!" Dr Willem de Klerk, political commentator and F W de Klerk's brother, said. But the leaders of the FAK, the Afrikanerbond and other organizations took offence at his words. "Tutu is an absolute enemy of white people and the Afrikaner in particular. The Afrikaner need not bear the burden of the past. Whether or not Tutu wants to know it, the Afrikaner rejects the TRC", Pieter Aucamp, spokesperson for the Conservative Party, stressed.

In an address to the Pretoria Afrikaans Chamber of Commerce, the archbishop elaborated:

"Afrikaners are excellent people! South Africa needs them ... God loves them and will not let them perish ... But you Afrikaners must invest in the transformation process, before you have nothing left to share. As the underprivileged, the poor, the homeless and the unemployed become desperate they will resort to desperate methods. Through the years Afrikaners developed many skills. Help us to progress, like you progressed."

His speech in Cape Town was not at all meant to threaten Afrikaners. "No, it was a cry from my heart, a cry to the people that I as a shepherd and fellow-South African, love you dearly ... it is a call (to you) to turn away from a path that will lead to eternal disaster."

Tutu openly acknowledged that he had made a mistake in Cape Town. "I did not – as I should have – pay homage to the many white people who opposed apartheid ... at their own expense. Also not to the fact that many white people, including Afrikaners, were truly repentant: In the N G Kerk ... and the Afrikaans Chamber of Commerce itself."

8 MARCH 1998: TUTU TALKS ABOUT TUTU

A television interview that Hennie Serfontein conducted with Desmond Tutu on the SABC programme *Issues of Faith*, attracted so much attention that extracts from it were published in the *Sunday Times* (8 March 1998) the next Sunday. Slightly abridged, it reads as follows:

Serfontein: How did you handle the news that something potentially very serious, potentially fatal was wrong with you?

Tutu: The news that it was cancer, was hard – especially after the urologists told me everything was okay. That hit me between the eyes! But eventually you say, well you were given an opportunity. If that turns out to be a terminal thing, incurable, or inoperable ... God has given you a wonderful life. You had many opportunities ... and now you have been given the opportunity to prepare for heaven. It is incredible, the messages I received from people. In South Africa people I never dreamt cared about me sent messages. In the past some of them probably would have said: Finish him off!

Serfontein: How did it affect your faith, your relationship with God? Do you look at things differently now?

Tutu: Absolutely. The cancer helped me to concentrate my mind. There is not enough time to be nasty. Many things that you have taken for granted – the love of your family and friends, lovely moments with your grandchildren, the beauty of God's creation, the flowers – take on a new meaning. Everything is a gift from God: life, the serenity that you experience. There are times that one says: I would not like to die just now. I would like to see my daughter graduate as a doctor. Well, if it must happen, it must! God is so good to me ... People are incredible in their generosity. At the airport, on a bus, a woman gives up her place when I am standing because she heard that I was sick. Some white women even offered to carry my bag!

Serfontein: Is it not human to sometimes say to God: Why me? I am your servant and I still wanted to do so many things?

Tutu: Not really! I think I really could not have been able to work out an ending quite as dramatic. I was around to vote for the first time. Many people who struggled for this were not so privileged. They were not there for the inauguration of our president. But I was able to stand on the balcony of the Cape Town city hall to introduce him to South Africa and the world. When I was awarded the Nobel Peace Prize, the SABC hardly did anything about it. But recently when I retired as archbishop almost the entire service was broadcast live. When I thought that it was all done, I was appointed TRC chairperson. Maybe this is the sum total of my life, to be called to help with the healing process in the country ... with the liberation, not only of the black people, but also the white people!

Serfontein: When you speak to God, do you ask: Please heal me, or help me to deal with what I experience?

Tutu: Of course I pray that I will be healed. I have attended services of healing and people have laid their hands on me. I am receiving medical treatment to restore my health. But I have not had the feeling that I have been hard done by. I can relax ... because I am being prayed for. I threw myself into many areas ...

Serfontein: You have been a pastor for 37 years, giving pastoral advice to others. What advice do you give yourself and Leah when you read the Bible together?

Tutu: I am becoming more aware that I only exist because God exists. Everything I have and am comes from Him. When I pray I often say to myself: "Be still. Relax. You are safe in the hands of Someone who loves you deeply!" I don't get morbid too frequently, because the Bible reassures me that nothing will separate me from God, the church and the people I love so dearly.

Serfontein: Do you think that God has a special purpose with you being confronted with illness at this time of your life? Does he want to teach you something?

Tutu: I think part of it is to keep being reminded that one is wonderful and fragile and that anything can happen to us at any time. In this way one becomes increasingly dependent on God. But the whole process of the Truth Commission has to do with dying and healing, in a special sense. What is happening to me is possibly a parable or a symbol. Our country was diseased, the terrible disease of injustice and oppression nearly killed us. But there is a possibility of healing. Furthermore: In each person there are parts that must die, often shortcomings, maybe unwillingness to forgive. When I was a child I had tuberculosis. One day I bled profusely. I then saw other people bleeding to death. I was convinced that I was also dying, but I experienced wonderful peace. While vomiting blood I said to God, "God, if it means I'm going to die, it's okay. If I'm going to live, it's okay."

Serfontein: You are saying God has given you an extra 55 years?

Tutu: Yes, I have been given an extraordinary kind of reprieve by God. I heard only recently that at the time the doctor called Bishop Trevor Huddleston aside he thought that I was dying. I would not be totally sane if I do not admit that I am scared sometimes. But if you believe in Jesus and his resurrection, you know that a door opens for you, a doorway to the fullness of life. That is why Jesus was resurrected, so we could have eternal life. Death is but a doorway through which we move – from one room to another in a house.

20 MARCH 1998: "TIRO IS HOME AT LAST"

"Finally, twenty fours years after his death, Onkgopotse (Abraham) Tiro is home, laid to rest at the spot his family allocated for him years ago," the newspaper reported. "Thousands of mourners converged on the village of Dinokana to attend the funeral."

Azapo members led the funeral procession. They carried a massive banner: *Azapo remembers Onkgoptse Ramothibi Tiro. Leader, Fighter and Martyr. There is no struggle without casualties.*

The young activist, Tiro, defected to Botswana in 1973. A year later a letter-bomb exploded in his hands at his home in Gaborone. The then Botswana government refused permission for him to be buried near his hometown Zeerust. But after all those years, his remains were now being returned.

It was hoped that the TRC investigation into the activities of the Bureau for State Security (BOSS) would shed new light on the incident. Up to now little progress had been made.

25-26 MARCH 1998: THE FATHER OF THE VICTIM COMFORTS THE MURDERER

Finally the day of the Afrikaner Weerstandbeweging (AWB) dawned. Following numerous delays and also Dries Kriel's threat to sever all ties with the TRC – because the minister of correctional services had refused to comply with the TRC request that the AWB men in prison be granted the status of political prisoners – the first AWB members took their places behind the microphone.

The previous day Corrie Lottering, who hoped to apply for amnesty for murder and for escaping from detention in 1989 and 1990, had wanted to put his case. But Eugene Terre'blanche and Hennie Binneman (a former commander of Lottering) whose testimonies were of central importance in convincing the judges that the deeds were politically motivated, at the last moment refused to appear. Terre'blanche let them know "that he was too busy" preparing for his appeal case that was to come up shortly. Dries Kriel, who had established his *Bond van Boerekrygsgevangenes* (Alliance for Boer prisoners of war) to deal with the applications of former AWB members was very unhappy:

"Terre'blanche's refusal to testify is contrary to his bravado on stage with which he incited young people such as Corrie Lottering to join the resistance struggle."

The two other men, James Wheeler and Corrie Pyper, were ready to testify the next day, 25 March.

Their stories of *braaivleis* and brandy, of politicking and brute force, took the judges back to election day 1994. After they had been partying that day – a barbecue with lots of liquor, in the company of friends – they convinced each other that the time for "the Boere resistance" had come. When Wheeler and Pyper heard on the evening news that bombs had exploded at the Johannesburg airport, they right away decided to become involved in the liberation struggle. They would shoot and kill black people. By so doing they hoped to stop the election and prevent government falling under black rule.

They had received no specific instructions, they testified, but they were convinced that they were promoting the objectives of the Conservative Party and the AWB.

Corrie Pyper's wife had tried to stop them as they left in Wheeler's car. She had even threatened to call the police. Wheeler had ripped out the telephone cable.

James Wheeler related, "While we were driving, I saw a minibus with black passengers in front of us. I cocked my shot-gun and gave it to Corrie. I drove right up to the minibus. Corrie shot at the driver through the open window. I immediately accelerated and sped away." Vuyani Papuyana, a student and part-time taxi driver, was shot dead and his brother, Godfrey Papuyana, wounded. The two Whites were sentenced to fifteen years' imprisonment on charges of murder and attempted murder.

While testifying, Wheeler turned to Vuyani Papuyana's family, saying how deeply he regretted what he had done. "Can you forgive me?", he asked. "I cannot believe I was so shortsighted! I have decided never again to resort to violence to achieve a political objective. I hope that in future, through my actions, I can contribute towards reconciling white and black people who still bear animosity to one another."

The next day the Papuyana family's legal representative read a statement covering the meeting they had held with Corrie Pyper four years earlier. On 4 October 1994, five months after the murder, Corrie had asked the parents of Vuyani Papuyana for forgiveness. Mrs Glenrose Papuyana said that initially she could not look her son's murderer in the eye. Neither could her husband. But, he said, "I immediately knew that it was the best thing I have ever done: to face the man who murdered my son. The meeting helped me to overcome my emotional problems. Before the meeting I was convinced that I would never be able to forgive my son's murderer. In my wildest dreams I did not think that the meeting would become a situation where I would be the one trying to comfort the murderer and his wife. Mrs Pyper was crying so much that she could not really talk. Mr Pyper told me what had happened that night. He said that he still could not explain why he had done such a mindless thing. He repeatedly said that it had been an extremely mindless deed and that he was very sorry."

Corrie Pyper had offered to cover the funeral costs and offered a cheque of R5 200 to the parents. "I at first refused to accept it, but when he insisted I could see that it would relieve his pain if I accepted it. He felt better afterwards." The Papuyanas changed their minds about their initial plan to institute civil proceedings against Wheeler and Pyper in the light of what had happened. They did not want to harm the children of the two murderers.

Why had he committed the murder? Corrie gave two reasons. Firstly, he had been under the impression that the leader of the AWB had instructed them to see to it that "on the day the ANC took over the country, it be taken back by taking up arms". Secondly, he was embittered towards black people, because four black people had shortly before shot and killed his brother with an AK 47.

A strange, wonderful country, ours – I thought – where the father of the murdered son embraces the perpetrator, the murderer, and his wife to comfort them.

◆ ◆ ◆

Three months later, on 30 July, the Amnesty Committee announced that they had granted amnesty to James Wheeler and Cornelius Rudolph Pyper.

9 APRIL 1998: OTHER FELLOW-TRAVELLERS: THE RAPPORTRYERS JOIN THE TREK

In a press statement released at its national conference, the Rapportryers called for a national day of prayer, during which members of the entire community could reach out to each other. It was time to deal with the protracted process of confessions of guilt once and for all, Mr Cas de Jager, the chief secretary of the Rapportryers explained to the press. An appropriate date would be 31 May 1998. They had already written to the Afrikaans churches requesting them to support the initiative.

The church leaders were generally not very positive about the idea. Dr Mike Smuts, the moderator of the Northern Transvaal Synod of the N G Kerk, summed up many of his colleagues' feelings: "I have no problems with the idea of a day of prayer, but the manner in which the Rapportyers want to present it creates a problem. Christians must always be aware of their guilt and *regularly* ask God for forgiveness. Religious people must always remain aware of their dependence on God. The Rapportryers want to cross out the confessions of individual Afrikaners and thereby indicate that all confessions after 31 May would be unnecessary."

Whatever the case may be, it was heartening that the Rapportryers had started to think collectively and join the trek.

14 APRIL 1998: WAS A SETTLEMENT WITH P W BOTHA POSSIBLE?

TRC representatives and P W Botha conferred until late that night. The possibility that the former president would accept an offer by the Truth Commission to answer their questions at an *in camera* session, which would mean that the TRC could withdraw its charge against him, was discussed in depth during the preceding week. The TRC bent over backwards to accommodate P W Botha. "I do not want to be humiliated", he demanded – and he was assured that he would not be. Paul van Zyl, who was to appear on behalf of the TRC, told how Tutu had taken him aside and warned him: "You must be extremely respectful, otherwise you'll be fired!" P W Botha added that he did not want Alex Boraine on the panel – and Boraine, Botha's opponent in the former parliament, agreed. At eight o' clock that night, Botha withdrew from the discussions. He was tired and wanted to go to bed.

The attorney-general of the Western Cape gave the Botha camp until eight o' clock the next morning to settle. Otherwise the court case would continue at nine o' clock. The case, which had been before court for the first time in January, had already been postponed twice. Now justice had to take its course.

On the eight o'clock news Tutu said, "The matter is touch and go. We do not know what the outcome will be."

15 APRIL 1998: "UNTIL THE BITTER END"

The disappointment was tangible. The news was broken early that morning. P W Botha had refused to settle. Against the advice of his legal team, against the advice of Desmond Tutu and even President Mandela who tried to salvage what he could at the eleventh hour, the former state president was adamant. He would not co-operate with the TRC – not in any way!

The trial was to continue.

The charge against P W Botha was twofold: Firstly, there was the charge that he had ignored the summons to appear before the TRC. The alternative charge was that P W Botha had obstructed the TRC in the execution of its work.

"Not guilty, Your Honour!" the former president pleaded.

He had already given his reasons: The TRC had clearly proven that it was prejudiced regarding Botha and his government. What is more, the TRC had acted in bad faith against him. And thirdly, Tutu had earlier on made a verbal agreement that if he answered all the questions put to him in writing, there would be no need for him to appear before the TRC.

During the tea-break the big crocodile spoke to the press, quite spontaneously.

"I will fight to the bitter end. Even if they destroy me, they cannot destroy my soul. They cannot destroy my convictions."

The TRC's Paul van Zyl was sworn in as the first state witness. Firstly, he wanted to respond to P W Botha's objection that the TRC had acted in bad faith. That was not true! The TRC had been negotiating with P W Botha in the best of spirits for months. From his side there had, however, been little co-operation. He, for example, had already in January 1997 received the questions the TRC needed answers for. Only eight months later, in October, had they received the document.

Paul was questioned extensively about the agenda and the *modus operandi* of the TRC and about the testimonies heard regarding the Botha government during the Truth Commission sessions. Responsibility for gross human rights violations, van Zyl explained, could be divided into four categories : *firstly*, persons who had committed the violations; *secondly,* those who had given the orders; *thirdly,* those that helped create a climate in which the violations took place, and, *fourthly,* persons who were guilty *ex post facto* and failed to properly enquire or to take the necessary actions to prevent such violations. No evidence had been found that could implicate the former president as far as the first category of violations was concerned, but the second, third and fourth categories were applicable.

Stating an example, Paul van Zyl mentioned that Botha, according to the testimony of his erstwhile cabinet colleague, Adriaan Vlok, had not only been aware of the bomb explosion at the SACC's Khotso House, but had also ordered it and had congratulated Vlok and his policemen after the explosion.

Paul van Zyl was questioned for three hours, especially about the evidence gathered on the State Security Council (SSC). When Paul was questioned about the list of 'sensitive persons' the SSC had felt action should be taken against, many people strained their ears: Tutu, Boraine, Richard Lyster and Mary Burton! Some time during the trial P W Botha would also have to give his interpretation of the word "eliminate", used so freely by the SSC – and which was frequently brought up at TRC sessions.

Half unexpectedly, at the end of the second day, the case was postponed to 1 June. P W Botha was furious that his legal team had agreed – and he did not care who saw him so angry. How dare they? Paul van Zyl had broadcast many as yet unfounded statements to the world. And he, P W Botha, badly wanted to comment on this.

◆ ◆ ◆

During one of the tea-breaks Botha met with Freek Swart, a *Rapport* journalist, and told him what had happened that morning, while the country was waiting with bated breath to hear whether the TRC and the former president had reached a settlement.

"When the court session started, they came to tell me that Tutu was there and that he wanted to talk to me. Bishop Tutu came to join me. I said to him, 'Good morning, good morning!' He then asked whether he could pray. I said to him, 'You can pray if you wish.' After he had said amen, I said to him, 'You tell me, as one Christian to another, what you are proposing to me.' He then told me that his proposal was that I should come back and testify before the Truth Commission.

"I then said to him, 'Man, you are now asking me to capitulate. That is what you are asking, and you know that I said that I would not appear before you. I added: 'You know that when Christ stood before Herod He refused to answer questions.' He then said: 'Yes, but Christ did answer questions before Pilate.' I answered: 'Yes, but what happened to Pilate?'

"I said, 'I am not Christ, I am his follower.' I added: 'You have the truth at your disposal, and I am telling you now, I am prepared to speak to you and President Nelson Mandela, but you will not force me to appear before the Truth Commission. I refuse to be humiliated and you people want to humiliate me. And at the same time, you also want to humiliate Afrikanes who believe in me just like you have already humiliated others.'

"He then got up and walked away. At that the negotiations failed."

22 APRIL 1998: THE GENERAL WANTED BODIES

After the P W Botha trial, it was the AWB's turn for the limelight again. Nine AWB members had applied for amnesty for "the tough option" they had decided on when, on 12 December 1993, they summarily shot and killed four black people at a roadblock between Krugersdorp and Randfontein. One of them was a child. Deon Martin testified how his commander, Phil Kloppers, had asked him to cut off an ear from one of the bodies. Japie Oelofse, their general, had wanted it to show others how they operated! "I then cut off an ear and put it in a plastic bag in my vehicle."

The nine men were all arrested for a number of offences. But Japie Oelofse had praised them and promised them medals. Some of them were promoted to high ranks in the AWB while in prison.

Deon Martin recounted what happened that day: All cars with black passengers were stopped and the passengers questioned. Those who were not ANC members were allowed to pass. A Honda Ballade and a Cressida were stopped and all ten persons in the cars were forced to get out. They were made to stand against an embankment next to the road, where Martin questioned them. Kloppers "tapped them lightly on the head" when they did not answer satisfactorily. Then Martin fired the first shot – the sign that the others had to follow suit. Four persons died, six survived. Petrus Mothupi – who was shot in the face – survived the shooting, but his face was disfigured for life. He was present at the trial, with Elastoplast covering the part of his face where his nose had been.

What on earth had motivated them, the Amnesty Committee wanted to know. They had hoped that it would be a tinder-box that would explode everywhere in the country. "If everyone had acted in small groups and shot a few people, it would have created havoc. We were unfortunately the only ones that did it!"

All nine men were initially sentenced to death. The sentences were later transmuted to 85 years' imprisonment.

27 APRIL 1998: TERRE'BLANCHE MAKES PEACE WITH HIS MATES

Mr Eugene Terre'blanche, member of the AWB, and Mr Dries Kriel, former 'brigadier' in the organization, last night buried the hatchet.

Kriel, these days secretary-general of the Bond van Krygsgevangenes (association for Boer prisoners of war), said in a statement signed by Terre'blanche, that they would in future co-operate to ensure that 'Boer prisoners of war' and other amnesty applicants would be exempted. All parties confirmed that it meant that they would co-operate with the Amnesty Committee.

Kriel fell into disfavour with the AWB last year when he, according to the AWB, made a submission to the TRC without a mandate, expressing his regret about the human rights violations and deeds of sabotage since the establishment of the AWB in 1973, and conveyed his sympathy to victims.

Last night Terre'blanche did not want to say anything about the split between him and Kriel. Kriel said that they had made peace after a day's discussions which involved 'General' Steyn von Ronge, 'General' Willem Etsebeth and Mr Jannie Smit.

The truce between him and Terre'blanche did not mean that he would again establish ties with the AWB.

(*Beeld*, 27 April 1998)

4 MAY 1998: THE CHURCH STREET BOMB: RECONCILIATION IS NOT THAT EASY

"I forgive you for what you have done. I came to the trial to share my feelings with you. I wanted you to know that I harbour no thoughts of revenge." Neville Clarence, feeling his way around in the square at the Idasa Building in Pretoria, walked over to Aboobaker Ismail and shook his hand – the man who was responsible for the bomb that had almost claimed his life many years ago and had left him totally blind. When the bomb exploded in front of the Air Force headquarters in Church Street, Pretoria, on 20 May 1983, 19 people died and 217 were injured. Ismail was deeply moved. Close to tears, the then head of MK's special operations grasped both hands of the onetime Air Force officer. He started telling Neville about his own friends and colleagues who had lost their lives in the struggle. Neville 'looked' directly at Aboobaker, as if he was able to see him.

"It was a wonderful moment for me", he said later. "One experiences terrible things daily. One is handicapped. Yet it is possible to meet the person responsible for it, without any feelings of revenge." Aboobaker had been a soldier, as he had been, and for that reason he understood, and could respect the MK commanding officer, even though they had been enemies in the past.

The MK officer had a good deal on his slate, indeed. Except for his involvement with the Church Street bomb, he had applied for amnesty for numerous incidents: the bomb explosion at the Krugersdorp magistrate's court (1988), the attack on Magoo's Bar, Durban (1986), the attack on the Witwatersrand command (1987), attacks on Sasol I and Sasol II (1980) and a rocket attack on Voortrekkerhoogte (1981). According to Ismail, 433 people were injured and 29 died in 65 limpet mine explosions, 3 rocket attacks and 4 car bombs detonated under his orders. He applied for amnesty for all these deeds. Two other MK members, Johannes Molefe and Hélèna Passtoors, applied for amnesty with him.

To forgive, however, is not always easy. Marina de Lange (Geldenhuys) also attended the trial. Fifteen years earlier, walking out at the entrance of the Air Force building with her friends on that fateful day, her mind was filled with dreams. She had wanted to become a beautician. But in one dreadful moment everything changed. When she came to her senses later in hospital she found that her hands had been seriously injured and one of her legs was permanently damaged. She had to undergo a number of skin transplants. She still has shrapnel, which could not be removed, lodged in her body. Marina also testified at the first TRC session in Johannesburg two years earlier. At that stage she did have some understanding for the suffering of her black fellow-South Africans. But now, to meet face to face, the man who had been responsible for all her grief and to forgive was not so simple. Marina frankly admitted that she still could "not make peace with the cowardly deeds".

The same applied to Mrs Elizabeth Kok. Her husband, Jacob Ras, died in the blast – and she and her children have never really recovered from the shock. As for Mrs Anita de Wet, who recalled how they had looked for her mother, Stienie Meyer – rushing from one hospital to the next – before receiving the sad news that she had also died, the pain, after all those years, remained as acute. It was difficult to forgive and forget.

In his testimony, Ismail expressed deep regret for the deaths of innocent civilians in the struggle for justice and liberation. "But," he added "in a war situation there is always loss of life and injuries, and deaths among civilians become inevitable ..."

7 MAY 1998: THE FIRST LETTERS OF REPARATION ARE SENT OUT

Thulani Grenville-Grey, our psychologist who had to take over Barbara Watson's position as national organizer of the Reparation and Rehabilitation Committee, was pleased as Punch! Barely able to hide his pride he said, "We have mailed the first letters to victims! From tomorrow the first 700 victims whose testimonies have been verified will be notified by mail that their cases have been dealt with – and that they must forward the necessary documentation, so that a sum of money can be paid out to them." The archbishop was equally pleased. "I am excited", he told the press. "More or less as excited as when we started work two years ago."

Initially only limited funds would be available as part of the urgent interim programme of the TRC: approximately R2 000 per person, just enough to alleviate the most pressing needs. The large payouts that were to take place over a number of years could only be effected once government announced how much it had set aside for the reparation of victims.

Meagre, but a definite start!

8 MAY 1998: THE AMNESTY OF 37 ANC MEMBERS SET ASIDE

Judge Johan Conradie's judgment came as a great relief. Finally the TRC and its Amnesty Committee knew where it stood. For months on end the debate raged about the validity of the amnesty granted to the 37 ANC members. At the beginning of the year, during the TRC's Robben Island session, a unanimous decision was taken that the matter was to be referred to the judicial bench to pass judgment once and for all. Was the Amnesty Committee right in granting amnesty to a group of ANC members without announcing all the facts, or were the rest of the TRC correct in their conviction that the granting of amnesty was invalid?

Judge Conradie ordered the Amnesty Committee to reconsider all the applications. He simultaneously set aside the granting of amnesty to the 37 ANC members. Tutu was grateful that the matter had finally been sorted out.

The ANC, which initially had wanted to contest the matter in court, but later on decided to co-operate with the TRC, was faced with a di-lemma. A total of 37 applicants – leader figures in the ANC – did not request amnesty for specific deeds, but collectively took responsibility for many things that had happened. "It is to be expected that the per-sons will withdraw their amnesty applications", Mr Matthews Phosa, head of the ANC legal division, said. The NP, which also instituted legal proceedings, withdrew its case after the TRC had included certain por-tions of the NP's wording in the TRC court documents. The judge de-termined that the TRC was to pay the NP's legal costs – which made the NP members smile gleefully.

26 MAY 1998: IT IS NOT ONLY SOUTH AFRICA THAT IS SORRY

It is not only South Africans who are preoccupied with the past. There are three places in the world where people stood in front of the mirror of history and repented – all on the same day: 26 May 1998.

Emperor Akihito of *Japan* was on a state visit to England, where he shared his "deep feeling of sadness about the suffering of the Second World War, and the fact that such suffering continues for some people to this day. The war was a great tragedy for mankind and there is tremendous sympathy for those who suffered". On his way to the pal-ace, some veteran soldiers, survivors of Japanese concentration camps, who were standing alongside the streets, turned their backs on the emperor. Others waved to him, welcoming him as a visiting head of state.

In *Australia* the entire country was called upon to participate in a "Sorry Day", a day on which the white Australians asked their Aborigine fellow-countrymen to pardon them for the injustices committed against them in the past. Many of the original inhabitants of the country had been removed from their land and many of them had to watch their children being given to Whites to raise. The Botany Bay National Park should be renamed – given a name referring to reconciliation – the people said to each other. Thousands of people signed their names in a large "Sorry Book".

And in *Switzerland* a commission that was instructed to investigate the illegal enrichment of Swiss citizens who obtained "Nazi gold" during the Second World War acknowledged that the National Bank took delivery of gold obtained from victims in the death camps. According to the report 119,5 kilograms of gold was recovered by melting watches, jewellery and coins belonging to Jewish prisoners. The bank conducted business as usual with Nazis although its officials knew full well what was going on. The bank, which earlier on admitted that it "unknowingly received gold belonging to Nazi victims and in the meantime paid over more van R320 million to humanitarian institutions", will probably have to fork out even more.

JUNE AND JULY 1998: HEARINGS AT VARIOUS PLACES

During June and July – two of the busiest and most important months in the annals of the TRC – a number of hearings and sessions were held at various places, sometimes simultaneously. In those months people such as P W Botha, former Minister Adriaan Vlok, former Police Commissioner Johan van der Merwe, Vlakplaas Commander Eugene de Kok and quite a group of AWB offenders were in the limelight. Most notable of all was the appearance of Wouter Basson, the secretive, taciturn doctor, known for his "chemical and biological projects", before the TRC. And it was the period in which Archbishop Desmond Tutu was received with open arms and embraced tearfully in one of the large N G congregations in our country.

Instead of describing the process chronologically, I will rather tell of a few important events that took place simultaneously at different places in our country.

1-5, 15 JUNE 1998: FURTHER CHAPTERS IN THE P W BOTHA SAGA

"It looks like *Boere* Hollywood", one journalist wrote. The crowds were no longer present to welcome and support P W Botha. Constand Viljoen and Ferdie Hartzenberg, however, were there, two loyal stalwarts. And also two old friends of the president, both men prominent in the world of entertainment: Boet Troskie, the flamboyant millionaire and film magnate, and Nico Carstens, the well-known and popular accordionist.

Boet Troskie had achieved much in his life. Could he act as mediator between P W and the TRC? "Give me a chance", he requested. "If you can persuade P W Botha to come to the TRC, we will ask the magistrate to suspend the hearing – even at this late stage", the archbishop replied. The film magnate tried hard, assisted by the king of the accordion. But he returned home the next day, his attempts unsuccessful.

The hearing had to continue.

During the following days, one witness after the other was summoned. Each one was asked to shed light on one or two aspects of the case.

Bishop Peter Storey, who was on a visit to America, received a return ticket from the TRC. He had to testify about the explosion at Khotso House. "Never in my life had I seen something like that. It was like a scene from hell! The entire façade of the building had been shot away and rubble was scattered everywhere. Strangely enough, a large mural of Christ embracing the whole of South Africa hung intact." Buildings across the road were damaged. People were wandering around dazed, digging in the rubble. The behaviour of the police was somewhat unusual: they were abrupt and quiet. We know, because many testified to that effect – and especially the testimony of former Minister Vlok – that P W Botha had given the orders. Why? What did he want to achieve?"

The following day Eugene de Kock, the Vlakplaas commander – called "Prime Evil" by the press – took his place opposite the accused. He had never met P W Botha personally, but even now he didn't look him straight in the eye. Clad in his green prisoner's uniform, he started testifying about all the projects given to them "from above". The former president was a coward, de Kock said. He had no pride! "My colleagues in the security forces and I are being sold out by cowardly politicians, especially those in the NP!" They want to eat lamb, but never want to see the blood and entrails. It was P W who gave the instructions in 1987 that Cosatu House had to be damaged and that a bomb was to be planted in Khotso House. The same applies to the ANC headquarters in London. For all his successful projects, de Kock not only received a hearty thanks from government, but also a much treasured medal.

"When is P W Botha going to bring home my men locked up in prisons in Zambia?" de Kock asked at one stage in his testimony. "There are three of them and they are dying in prison ..."

Much against his wishes, Tutu himself had to stand in the witness box on day three and day four. Or rather, sit on a bar stool. "It is with much unwillingness that I am seated here ... to testify against my brother", Tutu started. It was not what he wanted. Even at that late stage he pleaded with Botha to "let reason prevail" and to appear before the TRC. The court case could then be stopped immediately.

Responding to P W Botha's defence that Tutu verbally made the undertaking that if he answered all the TRC's questions in writing he would not need to appear personally before the commission, Tutu firmly replied, "This is not the case! It is also not possible for me to grant this kind of exemption to anyone. I do not have the power to do so." Tutu then referred to his empathetic treatment of Botha. "He is my brother! We were created by the same God." Once again he emphasized that the TRC did not want to humiliate the former president, that it went all out to show its good intentions. He had gone to Dullah Omar to ensure that Botha would get adequate legal aid and to Mandela to request that Botha be granted access to all the documentation he required.

Botha's legal representatives, cross-examining Tutu, asked whether he had read and studied all 1 700 pages of P W Botha's submission.

"No", the archbishop answered honestly. P W threw his hands in the air ...

"But that's not my job", Desmond Tutu explained. "I didn't read the entire lengthy ANC submission either. I can't do everything. That's why we divide the work. The Botha submission was given direct to the TRC research division to study and consider."

"Do you not want to apologize for all the pain and suffering your policy caused?", Tutu pleaded for the umpteenth time. It was of great concern to him that P W Botha was starting to use the same argument as F W de Klerk had: that all the atrocities that took place in the past were not government's responsibility. It was the fault of a few 'rotten apples' in the previous government and security forces.

Botha did not want to apologize, neither did he want to change his view about the TRC. Magistrate Victor Lugaju postponed the case for the fifth time: to 15 June 1998.

◆ ◆ ◆

On 15 June the state prosecutor, Advocate Bruce Morrison, launched his attack on for the former president. P W Botha's continued refusal to testify, the moves that he had made, the far-fetched technicalities mentioned, were all but an attempt at "underhand resistance".

According to Morrison, there had been no agreement between Tutu and Botha about the possibility of Botha being exempted from a personal appearance before the TRC should he submit a comprehensive written report. "There was no such agreement, and even if there had been, it would have been unlawful. The TRC Act does not make provision for something like that."

The case was postponed for the sixth time, to 17 August. Then the closing argument for Botha's defence would be heard. The magistrate's findings had to be given the following day.

2 JUNE 1998 (AND THE FOLLOWING DAYS): THE AMNESTY QUEUE GROWS AND GROWS

The Amnesty Committee, which had long been divided into various groups, had a busy programme. Some of the most important cases that attracted public interest were the following:

General Johan van der Merwe and nine colleagues in the security police applied for amnesty for the *death of Stanza Bopape*. The popular Pretoria activist was arrested and taken to Johannesburg to be questioned. Like pieces of a jigsaw puzzle being matched, the testimonies of the police officers painted the picture of what had happened to the respected Mamelodi community leader. On 12 June 1988 General Gerrit Erasmus, the Witwatersrand divisional head, phoned General van der Merwe. A serious problem had cropped up. Bopape "had suddenly and unexpectedly died during questioning, presumably of heart failure following electric shocks".

The generals had decided that a "mock escape plan" would be the best. They did not want to embarrass government by making Bopape's death public. The lie would be told that Bopape escaped from detention *en route* to Vereeniging. In the meantime Captain Leon van Loggerenberg dumped Bopape's body in the crocodile-infested Crocodile River near Komatipoort on the Mozambique border. General Piet du Toit, who was to spread the fabrication that Bopape had fled, even led a few search teams to try and find the activist. The teams went so far as to dig up possible graves pointed out by some people, seemingly in the hope that one would be Bopape's. He kept the truth from his colleagues for years. They were somewhat disturbed when they eventually heard what had happened!

While the testimonies were being given, the shocked family members sat listening, day after day ... They were not sure that they could trust everything being said – especially when evidence was given that the police files on Stanza Bopape had disappeared mysteriously. When the hearing finally came to an end on 9 June, Stanza Bopape's brother, Michael, said the family did not believe that the full truth had been revealed. He did not believe that Stanza's body had been thrown into the Crocodile River. "We think that his body was blown up by the police, as was the case with others."

The hearing of numerous *AWB members* also drew considerable attention. On 5 June four AWB members, Henry Jardine, Martin Christie, Andrew Howell and Christo Brand were granted amnesty for an *attack on the Flagstaff Police Station* in KwaZulu-Natal (5 March 1994) during which one person died and two were injured.

The hearing of nine men who murdered suspected ANC members at a roadblock between Randfontein and Ventersdorp continued. But the men were divided and their testimonies started to differ. The peace between Dries Kriel and Eugene Terre'blanche did not last long either. Kriel accused Terre'blanche, before the Amnesty Commission, that he had betrayed his men. He should have been there on that day to stand by the men who had hung on his lips. Where had he been? "Terre'blanche has the gift of the gab. But as soon as there is any tension or threat, he distances himself", Kriel said.

Meanwhile the hearing of Etienne le Roux, a lieutenant in the AWB's *Ystergarde* (Iron Guard) and nine of his mates who were responsible for a spate of bomb explosions just before the 1994 election, started. Altogether 21 people died and 24 were injured in explosions on the East Rand and West Rand, and in Pretoria and Johannesburg. One of the incidents that caused tremendous dismay was the bomb explosion at Jan Smuts Airport on 26 April 1994. "Loss of life is always tragic", le Roux said, "but I am not at all sorry about the people who died, white or black. We committed urban terrorism to strike fear in the hearts of people – in an attempt at achieving political uprising in the country." Mr Sydney Otong, whose son, Paul, died in one of the explosions, was extremely offended and snarled an insult at le Roux before he and his wife left the room.

One of the men who had planted bombs, Jan de Wet, made those present at one of the sessions sit upright when he stated that he saw no discrepancy between his Christianity and the deeds he had committed – which had claimed the lives of twenty people. "I see it as a Christian deed. We wanted to achieve our objectives. We wanted to prevent the election and try to enforce a *volkstaat* (Afrikaner State). It was war!" Commenting on the bomb, which he had helped plant in Germiston, he reiterated: "I was prepared to die for God, my nation and the fatherland!"

Although they received no direct instructions from Terre'blanche to plant bombs, they were convinced that it carried his approval. His speeches were crammed with suggestions that such things had to happen. If he, for example, said, "If Pink Frikkie (F W de Klerk) does not want to listen, a bomb will go off" sure as anything, a bomb would explode the following day!

Judge Pillay postponed the hearing, after days of testimony, until August.

On 11 June the Amnesty Committee granted amnesty to *three Apla members* who were responsible for the *attack on the St James Church* in Cape Town. Eleven people died and many members of the congregation were injured in the attack. The Amnesty Committee accepted the testimony of the three men, Gcinikhaya Makoma, Bassie Mzukisi and Tobela Mlambisi, that their deeds were politically inspired and that it was part of the military struggle that Apla was conducting on behalf of the PAC. A fourth applicant, Mr Letlape Mphahlele, did not attend the session and his name was struck from the roll.

3 JUNE 1998: FERDIE BARNARD CONVICTED 25 TIMES

The Barnard case did not come up before the TRC. It was a case for the Pretoria High Court. However, the name of Ferdie Barnard, the first, and thus far the only member of the Civil Co-operation Bureau taken to and sentenced by the court, was mentioned so many times at the TRC hearings that his appearance in court was followed with much interest. What would the court do with the man against whom 25 charges had been laid and who was responsible for the assassination of Dr David Webster, the well-known human rights activist?

Ferdie Barnard, who showed great bravado throughout the trial, was pale when he listened to his sentence: a double life sentence for the murder of David Webster (human rights activist) and Mark Frances (drug addict, friend of Ferdie Barnard), seven years for the attempted murder of Dullah Omar, and a further 63 years for the remaining charges.

Maggie Friedman, who at the first hearing on human rights transgressions in Johannesburg, earnestly requested that law and justice be meted out, that the murderer of her friend, David, be exposed, could sleep peacefully at last. Her wish had been fulfilled.

5, 23 JUNE 1998: NEW LIGHT ON TWO AIR DISASTERS

The TRC heard new evidence that helped answer numerous questions in respect of two air disasters that occurred in 1987 and 1989. The TRC recently had been hearing valuable testimonies behind closed doors from a number of people and this shed new light on the Helderberg air disaster. The Helderberg, a South African Airways passenger aircraft, crashed into the sea near Mauritius in 1987. The testimonies also shed light on the accident in which the Mozambique president, Samora Machel, died in 1989. Dumisa Ntsebeza announced at a news conference that the TRC would in its final report to the president in all probability recommend that the investigations into both disasters be reopened.

In testimony heard before the TRC it was alleged that the Helderberg, which crashed into the sea with 159 passengers on board, carried an illegal cargo of highly inflammable chemicals destined for the manufacture of rocket fuel. The aircraft crashed when a devastating fire broke out in its hold.

Ntsebeza continued that the evidence received about the Machel disaster indicated that the findings of Judge Cecil Margot, who was investigating the disaster at the time, were open to doubt. Fresh allegations about a navigation beacon being moved, as well as Defence

Force involvement, called for a new investigation.

A little more than two weeks later, on 23 June, Mrs Graca Machel, appeared before the TRC. Since her husband's death she had kept on investigating the circumstances surrounding the air disaster and she had considerable information to give to the TRC behind closed doors. After all the years she was still convinced that President Machel had been murdered and that more than one country had been involved in the conspiracy.

President Mandela's partner experienced difficulty in giving her testimony. She was deeply moved and burst into tears a few times. After testifying and answering questions for four hours, Graca Machel spoke to the press outside the hall. Her eyes were red from crying. Yet it had been a healing experience for her to testify, she said. She also told the press that she had requested the TRC to not only investigate her husband's death, but also those of the others who had been in the aircraft. She thanked South Africans that the country had taken the initiative to investigate the accident. The entire family owed thanks to the TRC for that.

"Our investigation indicates that elements in the former Defence Force, Military Information and Special Forces were not uninvolved in the accident", Dumisa Ntsebeza said. The TRC was convinced that the case had to be reopened.

8 JUNE 1998 (AND FOLLOWING DAYS): "THE WORMS KEEP ON CRAWLING OUT"

"We are facing the most shocking revelations since the Truth Commission started its work in 1995", Tutu said to the press a day or two after the session started. "I was filled with horror. Today was the worst day in two years! I am trying hard to keep my faith in mankind ..."

Most of the people in the country agreed.

The investigation into Dr Wouter Basson and his colleagues involved in Project Coast – the pseudonym for the Defence Force's secret chemical and biological weapons programme shocked everyone. Not so much because of the huge sums of money it cost taxpayers – between R400 million and R500 million, experts alleged. It was also not because co-workers of the programme enriched themselves unashamedly – one shareholder's input capital of R50 000 gave him a return of R9 million within a few years (if one is to believe the testimony led). It was the absolutely inhumane programme they were conducting that gave many South Africans sleepless nights – the manufacture of enough deadly chemical weapons and biological substances to kill thousands of people, the cruel experimentation on animals (some maintained humans were also used), the development of infertility drugs aimed at effecting birth control among Blacks, and the manufacture of the massive amounts of the drugs Mandrax and Ecstacy, which were sold or distributed who knows where. "Are we so different?" a newspaper editor wrote, "or are we back in the era of the Third Reich of Adolf Hitler and Dr Josef Mengele?"

The story of how Dr Wouter Basson, P W Botha's personal physician and the *Wunderkind* of the SA Defence Force, was asked by the chiefs in the SA Defence Force to start developing a biological and chemical weapons programme, unfolded bit by bit . The idea was – so it is said – to focus almost exclusively on defensive weapons. In actual fact 95 per cent of the time and manpower was, however, spent on the development of offensive weapons and substances. The firm, Delta G, was established in Midrand, and the Roodeplaat Research Laboratories (RRL) to the east of Pretoria. Basson's colleague and friend, Dr Lothar Neethling, head of the SA Police Forensic Laboratories, was his right-hand man. It was testified that initially the management, and in particular the business management, was good. Later on control slackened and the money flowed like water.

At the start, very few people knew about the project, but when Wouter Basson was arrested earlier this year on a charge of possessing a large amount of Ecstacy tablets, the police found a set of documents in a safe expounding all the details of Project Coast. Basson was released on bail of R50 000 – but the curtain had been lifted on the shady world of secret formulas and deadly chemicals, the pills that had to be developed to make black women infertile, poisonous T-shirts, and screwdrivers and umbrellas with poisoned points. Basson's schemes did not only keep him busy locally. He frequently travelled abroad on various shady missions. He closed clandestine transactions and paid millions of rands for business contracts. One British contact, Major Roger Buffham, a key witness, was coming to relate how he had made a fortune of R20 million.

One after the other, Basson's colleagues had a chance to speak.

Dr Schalk van Rensburg, who went to work at RRL as a medical researcher in 1985 told that the possibility of poisoning Nelson Mandela at Pollsmoor Prison was considered. One suggestion was to add thallium to his medicine, which would result in his mental deterioration. Mercifully nothing came of the plans. But, van Rensburg said he wondered whether Steve Biko had not been given thallium. That would explain his irrational behaviour shortly before his death.

Wouter Basson, he testified, had an obsession to develop a deadly poison of which traces would not be detectable in a post mortem. Basson was furious when the attempt to murder Frank Chikane, by putting poison on his clothes, failed. Basson had also approached him to help develop a serum that would make black women infertile. Basson had said that it had been requested by UNITA, which could not afford its female soldiers falling pregnant – but Schalk van Rensburg did not believe that story. It sometimes shocked him to see how much poison was stocked in the laboratories: thallium in beer and whiskey, salmonella in sugar, anthrax or cyanide in chocolates and cyphimurium in deodorant cans. Cholera samples were bottled. Responding to a question about President P W Botha's knowledge of the project, van Rensburg stated that he was absolutely sure that he had known about it.

Next in the witness stand was Dr Johan Koekemoer. According to him, employees at RRL and Delta G referred to Dr Basson as *die Skim* (the Phantom). During 1992 and 1993 Basson asked him to manufacture approximately 1 000 kilograms of Ecstacy tablets. It was allegedly targeted for crowd control experiments. "The entire project, from A to Z, bothered me", Koekemoer said. He knew that Ecstacy tablets could not be used to control crowds. Mandrax, possibly – it was possible to manufacture the tablets in a gas format, for inclusion in grenades to be hurled at people. He was so concerned about the large quantity of drugs he had to manufacture that he refused to continue until the surgeon-general, Dr Neil Knobel, had given him a letter of exemption. However, it was exactly because of these activities that he had been arrested. After the police had arrested Wouter Basson, there was sufficient incriminating evidence for his arrest as well. It took him long to prove his innocence, Johan Koekemoer said.

Dr Mike Odendaal testified about the day the RRL prepared a poisoned shirt that was meant to remove a disloyal policeman. The policeman unwittingly gave the shirt to a friend – who died.

Dr Wynand Swanepoel was a dentist at the time Basson asked him to take over the management of the RRL. He was not aware of everything that was being done in the laboratories as he was only responsible for the RRL's finances and administration. But it was true that various experiments using animals were conducted. Why else would there have been thousands of dog kennels? He also knew that baboons were used to test bullet-proof clothing and rubber bullets.

When it was their turn, General Lothar Neethling and Dr Daan Goosen, Swanepoel's predecessor as the RRL's manager, provided two of the most sensational testimonies of the hearing. The late Minister Louis le Grange had been the first to ask that a chemical weapon against Blacks be developed, Goosen said. It was for this reason that the RRL started experimenting with Mandrax, LSD and *dagga* and how they could be used to control crowds. The idea was to develop a drug that would only affect "pigmented people". Goosen clearly remembered a conversation with Basson, when the latter remarked that government gave the black population figure in our country as 28 million. It was incorrect, however, there were 45 million black people in the country. Something had to be done to find a solution!

The only person who until then had refused to testify was Wouter Basson himself. He refused to answer any questions, using the excuse that a criminal charge had been laid against him and that he would harm his case should he testify. The commissioners were at their wits' end. Threats were like water off a duck's back. On the Thursday, the last day, he did not even attend the trial. He was operating in Pretoria, was all explanation given to the TRC. It was, however, critically important that Basson should testify. What was his comment on all the information furnished by his colleagues? There were also strange events he had to testify about. What, for example, was he doing in Croatia in November 1992, when the civil war there was at its fiercest? Was it true that he was sent there by government to go and purchase 500 kilograms of methacholine (the major ingredient in Mandrax)?

In the meantime the surgeon-general, Dr Neil Knobel, had to provide answers as best he could. Yes, he did know about the baboon foetus that the RRL had supplied and which was thrown into Archbishop Tutu's garden at Bishops Court. No, he could not explain why Basson had to go and buy the Mandrax ingredients overseas. At the time Mandrax was already being manufactured in large quantities in the country. To add to that, General Lothar Neethling at one point had had 200 000 Mandrax tablets placed in Basson's car. The police also undertook to provide him with confiscated drugs. What had Basson wanted to do with them?

Dr Knobel told how President F W de Klerk had put Basson on early pension in December 1992. He was one of the 23 senior officers against whom the president took disciplinary steps – after reading a report by

General Pierre Steyn about alleged malpractices in the Defence Force. In January 1993 the then Minister of Defence, Mr Gene Louw, ordered that all poisonous substances and ingredients used to manufacture drugs be destroyed. Later that month an Air Force aircraft dumped twenty plastic containers in the sea, 130 km south of Agulhas. Basson was in the aircraft. At the end of March 1993 he became a voluntary reservist in the civilian force and was again appointed on Knobel's staff. He continued with his biological and chemical programme. Basson was the only person who was fully informed and when the South African government received letters from the Americans and Britons objecting to its suspected biological and chemical weapons, only he could explain what South Africa was doing.

Rapport comments on all the disclosures

According to Dr Knobel, President Mandela and Deputy President Mbeki were informed about Basson's work and the biological and chemical programmes before and after the 1994 election. The ANC still employed Basson after 1994. He was appointed at a military hospital holding the rank of major-general. When Dumisa Ntsebeza asked, "Did you appoint him because you were scared he would flee the country? Did you want to keep him in check?", Knobel's answer was, "Yes, you summed it up very well, Mr Chairperson."

A question that elicited considerable discussion was: Where are the weapons now? Do they still exist? Who are the two persons who each have one of the two keys to the safe in which the secret formulas are kept? Prior to 1994 the state president and a senior Defence Force officer had the keys. After the election F W de Klerk gave his key to Deputy President Mbeki. Which Defence Force officer has the second key?

◆ ◆ ◆

The journalists who covered the hearing had more than enough to write about. But it was not only about mere facts. The more significant question was: Why? What had motivated the people? "It is like a can of worms that has been opened. More and more crawl out daily," Johan Strydom of *Rapport* wrote.

What was it that drove Basson and his colleagues? Max du Preez, who had to give regular television reports on the hearing – and who was editor of *Vrye Weekblad* some years earlier had crossed swords with Basson's co-worker, General Neethling – had a few tentative answers that he got from the witnesses themselves.

Odendaal said that he had been happy with the deadly bacteria that he had manufactured as it would have protected our country from enemies from outside. Goosen's answer was simple: " I believed that I was doing it for God and my fatherland." Basson did not testify himself, but people who knew him said that he had remarked that he knew a black government in the country was inevitable. But if his daughter asked him one day what he had done to try and prevent it, he would want to have a reply ready. Maybe they had done it for the money, du Preez said. Because money had been in full supply! The men travelled in private jets to watch rugby matches overseas. They stayed in the most expensive hotels. Their investments yielded incredible returns...

◆ ◆ ◆

Eventually the court – to which Basson had appealed – had to order him to appear before the TRC. On 31 July, the day on which the Truth Commission officially finished its work, Wouter Basson, very much against his will, took the stand. Initially he did not want to answer any questions, not even about his age or when he was appointed in the Defence Force. Finally, after it had been pointed out to him numerous times that the TRC had the right to have him arrested for contempt of the law, he did start to talk. The TRC questioned him for no less than twelve hours. Hanif Vally led the discussion on behalf of the TRC. Bassons's denials at the end of the exhaustively protracted hearing, were reminiscent of those of Winnie Madikizela-Mandela on the last day of her hearing. Johan Vosloo of *Rapport* recorded it as follows:

Vally: Why did you lace chocolates with cyanide?

Basson: It was not meant to harm any person or organization. It was for the sake of training, to show people how to be cautious, to be careful about eating sweets placed on their pillows in a hotel room. Anyone can obtain poison. You can buy it at a co-op. Cyanide is readily available. Dettol is also dangerous. A bottle can destroy the Aids virus – but unfortunately also the carrier.

Vally: How about the research on poisonous substances that cannot be detected?

Basson: It is an interesting dream to manufacture a colourless, tasteless, odourless, deadly poison. But it is a myth. We did not give it any priority, because we knew that.

Vally: And the plans to make black women infertile?

Basson: That's absurd! That could only be done with an injection. A million people would have to queue for that.

Vally: How about the alleged plans to get part of the population addicted to drugs?

Basson: That's absurd. You are living on the planet Zero if you think it is possible to cause addiction by launching smoke bombs filled with addictive substances. As things are in the country, people are becoming addicted of their own volition!

Vally: Was it not a great temptation to enrich yourself by means of Mandrax tablets?

Basson: You may as well ask me if the girl sitting behind me (an attorney's clerk) is a temptation. And I must say, she is. Following an objection by a panelist that it was a sexist remark, he added: I withdraw the statement, I will go down on my knees. I should probably say that I am interested in her cooking.

Vally: Were you ever a member of the CCB? Did you supply it with poisonous substances?

Basson: No. I only gave them pain-killers. And gave medical support.

Vally: Did you supply Ferdie Barnard with poison to kill Minister Dullah Omar?

Basson: No.

Vally: What do you think of the Steyn Report, the report that caused you to go on pension at the age of 42?

Basson: The report is not worth the paper it is written on. Eighty percent of the accusations did not hold water.

20 JULY 1998 (AND FOLLOWING DAYS): "IT WAS WORTH IT!" ADRIAAN VLOK SAYS

On the last day of the sensational amnesty trial when the three men about which the press could not write enough during the past two years gave their last answers, I stood talking to them during the lunch break: Former Minister Adriaan Vlok, former Police Commissioner Johan van der Merwe, former Vlakplaas commander Eugene de Kock ...

Adriaan Vlok looked thin and older than when the first TRC hearings had started. The months of preparation, the long days before the Amnesty Commission had taken their toll.

"Tell me, Mr Vlok, was it all worth it?"

"Well, let me answer you as follows: yesterday, when I had to talk about the Khotso House incident for the last time and the SACC representative told the Amnesty Commission that they were satisfied and did not plan to oppose my amnesty application, I closed my eyes. Suddenly I remembered it was exactly on that day a few years ago that my wife died. The Lord indeed led me on strange roads. I thanked the Lord with a lump in my throat. Yes, it was worth it, through and through!"

◆ ◆ ◆

When the amnesty hearing of Vlok, van der Merwe and de Kock – plus more than 30 members of the security forces – started in the Idasa Building on 20 July, three incidents were to be discussed: the attack on Cosatu House (1987), the attack on Khotso House (1988) and the series of bomb explosions at theatres where the film *Cry Freedom* (about the life and death of Steve Biko) was being shown in 1988.

"We were of the opinion that we had reason to attack Cosatu House", General van der Merwe testified. He explained: The ANC/CP alliance had used the building as headquarters and from there many strikes and illegal activities were planned. In April 1987 five railway workers were held captive there. One fled, but the burnt corpses of the other four were found at Kazerne, south of Johannesburg. It was at that stage that P W Botha had ordered him to "make the building accessible to us" – meaning that it had to be damaged to the extent that it could no longer be used for covert activities. Van der Merwe ordered Willem Schoon to deal with it. He and Major-General Gerrit Erasmus then saw to it that Cosatu House was attacked on the nights of 6 and 7 May. Nobody was hurt in the explosion. Schoon testified that he and Eugene de Kock who had planted the bombs had driven through the streets in the dark – not far from Cosatu House – and heard the bombs go off. "It did indeed lead to a decrease in illegal activities", the former police commissioner testified. "Remember, we did everything we could to engage in the revolutionary struggle."

Adriaan Vlok recounted what had happened the night Khotso House was attacked, how P W Botha had told him as far back as 1988 that they, as in the case with Cosatu House, also had to deal with Khotso House, the SACC headquarters. Once again Brigadier Schoon and Eugene de Kock's assistance was required. "Who gave the order?", de Kock wanted to know. "The state president himself", Schoon responded.

Shirley Gunn was seated in the hall. On the first day she recounted in outrage how she had been affected by the Khotso House bombing. She had been an ANC supporter, and an MK member, when she was arrested by police out of the blue, on a charge of being responsible for the bombing at the SACC headquarters. While the police – and, above all, the Minister of Police, Adriaan Vlok – had known that it was a lie, she was detained without trial for two months in 1990. Her 15-month old son was detained with her. Worst of all was that although she was still breastfeeding Harroun, he was taken away from her for more than a week. She was still suffering from the effects of post-traumatic stress and her child suffered anxiety attacks. Shirley Gunn was not at all impressed with the testimonies of the amnesty applicants: they were "spiteful" and made her "feel nauseous".

The prevailing question was: what was the involvement of P W Botha and F W de Klerk? Former President Botha had given the instructions; all the witnesses had agreed on that. But former President de Klerk – had he known? Yes, Mr de Klerk had known since the early 1990s, Vlok testified. He had personally informed him, although F W de Klerk made no mention of it in his TRC submission. In 1994, just before the general that they fought the amnesty legislation right up to the Constitutional Court. Whether the TRC with its reparation measures will succeed in making it clear to everyone that the gracious amnesty offer to perpetrators is balanced by an equally gracious compensation to victims, remains to be seen. The nation will have to be convinced that the process is as "victim-friendly" as it is "perpetrator-friendly".

Too many fish got away! The Sunday Times' comment on the closing of the TRC

And now the most difficult of questions: what about *the broad community*, ordinary South Africans from all walks of life – have they accepted the process?

Generally the experience has been that black and brown South Africans, the people who were mostly on the receiving end of apartheid, were grateful for and satisfied with the work of the TRC. It was often touching to see how men, women and children welcomed the TRC trek when the road led through their communities. The black newspapers, radio and television were usually positive, although critical remarks were aired from time to time. Serious objections were raised in some quarters, especially when Archbishop Tutu, in the opinion of some, bent

Johan van der Merwe had aged noticeably. I reminded him that at his first appearance before the TRC, more than two years ago, we had also been standing talking. At that stage everyone had been grateful that he was present, because he had paved the way for many colleagues and subordinates in the Police Force to also come forward.

I had then asked him, just before he was to testify: "Commissioner, what thoughts are going through your head this morning?"

"Well", he had answered, "there are two things, especially, that I am preoccupied with. In the first place, my colleagues queuing behind me and I are unsure where the TRC is taking us, about what the end of it all will be. And, secondly, we are frustrated – no, furious – because the political leaders of the country, the people who earlier on had appointed us and given us orders, who congratulated us and sometimes gave us medals, have now left us in the lurch."

Commissioner van der Merwe remembered that conversation. With slight amusement, he said, "I still stand by what I said, although I would like to add a *third*, and *fourth* and *fifth* point today ... "

The Vlakplaas commander in his green prison uniform, who had been sentenced for life, remarked, "Do you know what keeps me going in prison, what helps me survive in prison? My faith in Christ. If He was not there, if He could not forgive me ... then I do not know what would become of me."

The following day, when I opened my postbox at home, I found a thick envelope. It contained a neatly bound copy of Adriaan Vlok's testimony to the TRC. On the inside cover he had written:

Dear Prof Piet

Thank you very much for your guidance in this very difficult matter! ... It helped me make the decision to which the Lord was ultimately leading me.

All the best with your task.

God bless you.

Respectfully
Adriaan Vlok

14 JUNE 1998: ARRIVED AT THE DESTINATION? THE DAY THE *DOMINEE* AND THE ARCHBISHOP EMBRACED EACH OTHER

"Piet, tell me quicky, how does one address Desmond Tutu?"

Rev Ockie Raubenheimer, minister of the Lynnwood congregation, had to welcome the archbishop from the pulpit that morning. "Do you say "your grace" or "your holiness" or what?"

I was to preach in Lydenburg but would have given everything to be in Pretoria that morning. When the church council had invited Tutu months before to come and conduct a sermon, most of the people were happy about it. But some weren't! One Sunday night the church council asked me to conduct a discussion on truth and reconciliation during which all those who were unhappy could put their questions. When the church council met shortly afterwards, the enthusiasm about the TRC chairperson's visit was even more overwhelming (137 said 'yes', and 7 'no').

"Don't worry about that, Ockie", I answered, "the archbishop is not concerned about formalities or titles. Just call him "Archbishop" or "Bishop Tutu". You can even try "*Oom* Desmond"!"

◆ ◆ ◆

"As minister in the N G Kerk for 20 years, as one who served for many years as chaplain in the Defence Force, I have to say to you we are truly sorry. For those of us who erred, we have asked God to forgive us."

Tutu and the Rev Raubenheimer embraced each other on the pulpit. The congregation spontaneously started clapping hands and stood up. Some of them wiped their eyes.

Tutu's sermon dealt with the parable of the good shepherd, who left all his sheep to go and look for the one lost one. The parable, he emphasized, tells us about God's eternal and steadfast love for us. We do not deserve his love, nothing that we can do, can make his love less or more. In the days of the struggle he often used that text to convince black people that although they were suffering tremendously, God loved them deeply, Tutu said. In the new dispensation, he realized, white people needed the message as much.

Tutu and the Rev Raubenheimer embrace each other on the pulpit

Afrikaners think that they have only one of two choices left: to be part of the dominant, governing group, or to be powerless, impotent and marginalized. "There is, however, a third option", he said, "and that is to critically, but enthusiastically embrace the new dispensation and to help make a success of it."

The two weeks prior to Tutu's visit to the congregation, was one of the worst times – possibly the worst – in the annals of the Truth Commission. P W Botha's case had been heard, with all the emotions it elicited among white and black South Africans. Shocking facts were revealed in the amnesty applications of a long row of perpetrators. But the most horrifying of all in that period were the testimonies about Wouter Basson and his colleagues, about the biological and chemical weapons that were manufactured, the experiments carried out and the cynical business transactions that ensued.

Tutu had no option but to refer to it in his sermon.

"For me it was the most disturbing testimony that we have had to hear up to now, especially because the plans were so clinical, scientific, cold, cold-blooded and premeditated." Tutu found it diabolical that high officials could meet and discuss the poisoning of President Mandela and how they could make his mind deteriorate. "Thanks be to God. We won. What would have become of the country without Mandela's passion for forgiveness and reconciliation!" Would Robert Sobukwe have died of natural causes? How did Mandela get tuberculosis? One wonders. Tutu made a plea for "a leader who could explain their evil deeds to come forward, to explain how one could digest these things, someone who would ask forgiveness without trying to be clever" ...

After the sermon, Ockie Raubenheimer, addressed the congregation from the pulpit. He related how the Lynnwood ministers had met the previous Wednesday, as usual. They had talked about the revelations of the past week, and about the development of chemical and biological weapons – about the shocking experiments and projects. "We asked each other: 'Where have we failed as ministers of the Gospel?' We did not point a finger at anybody, but asked questions."

He then turned to Archbishop Tutu – and unburdened his heart: "I have to say to you: we are truly sorry ... we have asked the Lord to forgive us!"

With tears in their eyes, the minister and the archbishop, the white man and the black man, held each other. The man who for years had defended apartheid and the man who had spent his life fighting it, comforted each other.

◆ ◆ ◆

What had happened in church that morning resounded in the hearts of many South Africans. There was hope for the country! People could still listen to each other, still reach out to each other and forgive each other. My gnawing concern the past two and a half years, about whether the people of our country – also my own people, the Afrikaners – would be prepared to finish the journey into the future, diminished.

True enough, not everyone was happy. One or two members of the congregation left the church frowning – and later wrote furious letters to the press. One should have expected that. Not all Afrikaners were persuaded.

But Lynnwood gave me hope.

"What happened in the Lynnwood church, is not the beginning of reconciliation. Also not the end in the sense that nothing further need be done. It will, however, be recorded as one of the most important moments in a long and difficult process of reconciliation", someone wrote.

I agreed.

I had courage to take on the long road ahead of us, the journey into the future of South Africa.

◆ ◆ ◆

On Friday 31 July 1998 the Truth Commission officially ended its work. After two years and seven months the doors of the regional offices in Johannesburg, Durban and East London were closed. The large staff corps – investigators, researchers, administrative officers, secretaries, and committee members – said farewell. Their task was completed. Only the commissioners and a core group of researchers, who were responsible for the final report, continued with their work in the Cape office. On 29 October 1998 when the TRC's final report was to be submitted to the president – who, in turn, was to give it to the South African nation – their work would also be complete.

The Amnesty Committee was still far from finished! Hundred of cases still had to be dealt with. Should matters proceed well, the addendum report would be submitted by June 1999, the chairperson, Judge Hassan Mall, said.

The Truth Commission's work was finished.

But the journey was not yet over ...

29 OCTOBER 1998: FINALLY – THE REPORT IS HANDED OVER!

Just after twelve o'clock that afternoon Desmond Tutu rose to present the official report of the Truth and Reconciliation Commission to President Mandela. Millions of South Africans could see on their television screens the archbishop, smiling broadly, pretending to stagger under the weight of the five heavy volumes.

With reason! Not only did the TRC personnel work for months on end, sometimes until late at night, to get the report ready – the report was nearly not handed in that day. The arrangements for the function had been made beforehand. The five volumes, containing more than 3 000 pages, had been printed and were ready to be delivered. But a few days before D-day former President F W de Klerk took the TRC to court and obtained an interdict prohibiting certain information concerning his involvement in human rights violations from being published, before the TRC had replied to some of his objections. And then the final blow: the evening before the report would be handed over, the ANC requested a court interdict to try and stop the report from being issued, as the report, in the ANC's opinion, "criminalized" their role in the struggle. Throughout the night legal teams from both the TRC and the ANC worked on their submissions, as they had to defend their cases before the bench in Cape Town *before* sunrise.

Tutu was devastated by the ANC's action. They had more than one opportunity to record their objections against the findings of the TRC, but disregarded one deadline after the other – and only when it was far too late, they tried to forestall the publication of the report. "How is one supposed to understand it, that the same people who struggled for years on end to establish a free and democratic dispensation in the country, now acted so undemocratically, that they would endanger the freedom of a commission appointed by their own government, and whom they instructed to put its findings honestly on the table? This cannot be!" But it was soon clear that Desmond Tutu and his fellow-commissioners would not allow themselves to be intimidated. The TRC would not allow any party to manipulate or to dictate terms to them.

The presentation would take place in the Sammy Marks Centre, in the city centre of Pretoria. Just across the road, in the foyer of the State Theatre, a large number of journalists were waiting from six o'clock that morning. They would obtain copies of the report before the presentation, to start writing their articles. Now all they could do was to wait patiently. At eight, nine o'clock, the suspense became unbearable: why had the judge in Cape Town not yet delivered judgement? What would he say? Just before ten cheering resounded: the court had rejected the ANC's application, with costs! When a lorry approached, carrying the boxes that contained the reports, South African and foreign journalists crowded to get their copies – to start skimming and writing.

Alex Boraine, Charles Villa Vicencio (who were responsible for compiling the report) and I drew three chairs aside to hold a post-mortem. "An interesting thing happened this morning", the Deputy Chairperson of the TRC said. "On television news this morning, the newsreader asked me what, in my opinion, the ANC was objecting to. 'It is a mystery to me', I answered. 'I myself do not understand the ANC's objections. Every piece of evidence concerning human rights violations that we recorded from their side came from their own submission to us. Just the other day, during the last appearance of the ANC, Deputy President Thabo Mbeki admitted these things.' Dumisa Ntsebeza, who had listened in his room to my interview, immediately grabbed his cellular phone and phoned our legal team in Cape Town. 'Do not restrict yourselves to using only legal-technical terms', was his urgent advice. 'Tell the judge what Alex has just said on television.'" Borraine smiled at us. "I gather it has worked."

At twelve o'clock the ceremony commenced. The auditorium had seats for approximately a hundred people: politicians, TRC members, diplomats, a choir and – in VIP seats – forty-odd victims from all population groups in the country. It was a rare experience: on the podium sat President Mandela, together with the Minister of Justice, the Speaker of the House of Assembly, the Leader of the Council of Provinces, all of them senior ANC members – while hours before the rest of the ANC leadership, with the approval of Deputy President Mbeki, did their utmost to stop the ceremony.

"Your Excellency, Mr President," Tutu's first words were, "I request everybody to rise, to dedicate a moment of silence to the memory of all the victims of our country: in Sharpeville and Boipatong, in Sebokeng and Soweto, Table Mountain and Maritzburg, the KWT Golf Course and Church Street, the St James Church and Bisho and the Heidelberg Tavern, everybody who was tortured and executed in prisons and camps in and outside South Africa, also those who died in vain on the borders of our country."

"Not everybody will be happy with the report", Tutu continued. "Many have already started to discredit it in advance. But even should they succeed, what would they achieve? It will change nothing of the facts: that they killed Stanza Bopape, they blew up Khotso House, they tortured their own people in camps in Tanzania and Angola, that they committed necklace murders. We did not dream up these facts, the perpetrators themselves came to tell them ... "

President Mandela spoke highly of the archbishop and his colleagues. They had performed pioneer work the past three years. Naturally they could not attain everything, either in regard to the truth or the process of reconciliation. "But", he said, "I accept the report as it is, with all its deficiencies, as the TRC's contribution to reconciliation and building a nation."

"Let us approach the future together", Madiba ended his speech.

"Finally we are free, can we accept our calling with responsibility. But to build a better future, we need everybody's hands – your hands, as well as mine."

As if saying "Amen" to that, the choir from Soweto sang – more beautifully than I had heard in a long time, in Xhosa, Afrikaans and English *Nkosi Sikelel' iAfrika*.

That night the report was a buzz-word on the evening news – not to mention the newspapers during the days that followed. There was praise *and* criticism from all sides about the report:

The ANC and the PAC were highly satisfied that apartheid had been found a crime against mankind and that the liberation movements had fought a justified battle against it. However, they were upset that the abuse and murders, the instigation of violence, the 'necklacing' of which they were guilty, were placed on record.

The National Party and the Freedom Front, together with the IFP, were seriously dissatisfied about what was said about them. Former President F W de Klerk went to court, former President P W Botha made his dissatisfaction known far and wide. The IFP undertook to fight tooth and nail to protect the honour of their members. General Viljoen passed the report off as one-sided and incomplete.

The Dutch Reformed Church, who was found co-responsible for apartheid, had decided to appoint a commission to investigate the findings that concerned them.

From overseas, from many countries, praises poured in, from the United States, England, several European countries. The South African experiment with truth and reconciliation had succeeded! For Bosnia, Northern Ireland, for Rwanda and for Israel there was hope – reconciliation could take place, message upon message read.

Tutu and his team could take leave of each other on that Thursday afternoon with a feeling of satisfaction and gratitude. Their work – except that of the Amnesty Committee who still had to hand in an addendum report – was completed. But the Great Trek, the journey of truth and reconciliation, had not yet come to an end. Everybody agreed on that. All of us – every South African – still had to travel a long way on this road into the future.

THE LONGEST JOURNEY – FROM PERSON TO PERSON, VIA THE HEART

With its ambitious commission, South Africa has considerably raised the stakes: if it succeeds, it will set a new standard for such bodies worldwide and we will be in your debt; if it does not, it will be a failure of colossal proportions that will put to risk South Africa's transition to democracy.
José Zalaquett, commissioner of the Chilean Truth Commission

The process is totally one-sided – entire sections of our population are being unfairly stigmatized by these distortions – they are doing great damage to the cause of national reconciliation.
F W de Klerk, former president of South Africa

We are confident that in a generation or two South Africans will look back and give thanks for the process.
Editor, Sunday Independent

The TRC scales are unbalanced.
Editor, Die Kerkbode

It is not the Truth Commission that pulled out the Afrikaner's insides, but members of the security forces, with their admissions on atrocities and senseless killings ...
Louis Nel, former politician

Under the mantle of truth and justice
smooth politicians hide dark secrets.
They have countless uncouth dealings up the sleeve,
and cut the words of people with their sharp tongues,
as if finely chopping up green beans,
in glass cages their remains have been sealed, without any souls.
Cas Vos, theologian

◆　◆　◆

And thus the journey came to an end – for the time being, at least. The trek of two and a half years through the past and present of our country was behind us. It was a long and arduous journey, through dark valleys of pain and suffering, of shame and guilt. It was, however, also an inspiring route over peaks of bravery and generosity, of reconciliation in places where it was least expected. "South Africa will never be the same after the TRC process," more than one commentator wrote – and rightly so. The footsteps of thousands of victims and transgressors, and eventually of the entire South African community who joined in the trek, will stretch across the landscape.

The big question, however remained: Was it worth it? Did the Truth Commission achieve its goals? In January 1996 when the wagons departed, the expectations were noble: to build a historical bridge leading from the pain and suffering and the injustice of the past to a new future of fairness and justice, of unity and reconciliation. Did it did happen – or did it not?

It was an expensive process, not only in terms of money, but especially of manpower and time. During the TRC years 140 hearings took place country-wide, 21 400 victims submitted statements, the names of 27 000 victims were recorded, 7 124 perpetrators applied for amnesty. In addition to the human rights violation hearings numerous sessions were held where political parties, business people, academics, medical doctors, prison officials, members of the media, jurists, spiritual leaders, men, women and children, came to give their perspectives. The TRC was given tremendous power, to investigate and to subpoena, to request generals and commissioners, the president of the country – and his predecessors in the previous dispensation – to take the stand. The process was often contentious. Some applauded, others were less enthusiastic.

What was the result?

José Zalaquett, who played a major role during the Chilean truth commission, had great expectations for the truth and reconciliation process in our country. In one of his documents Zalaquett, however, made the interesting remark, based on the collective wisdom of the nineteen similar commissions held worldwide over the past decade, that three clear *prerequisites for success* had manifested: In the *first* place, the nation has to accept ownership for the process. *Secondly*, government must show political will, not only to appoint and provide the commission with an infrastructure, but also to implement the proposals made by the commission at the end of its course. *Thirdly*, according to Zalaquett, the process must stop! Just as a patient undergoing a critical operation should not stay in theatre too long, a truth commission should know when to call it a day.

It is not difficult to determine whether the first two prerequisites have been met. Whether the government, which set the process in motion at the beginning of 1996 with the support of all the political parties and maintained the infrastructure, will ultimately also be prepared to execute all the proposals – especially those that deal with the reparation and compensation of victims, will be determinable within the following year or two. And regarding the conclusion of the process, well, this *has* finally taken place! Not as soon as everyone wanted – instead of eighteen months it became thirty – but eventually the end came. And the Amnesty Committee? With the appointment of extra judges on the panel and doubling its hearings, it should have its final report addendum tabled within six months.

But to assess the first prerequisite, that the nation should make the process its own, is quite another matter. Historians would be the first to warn that it is far too early to make an assessment. Only in ten or twenty years – possibly only a generation or two later – will it finally be clear whether the TRC achieved its goals. But, albeit preliminary or tentative, a few remarks can still be made.

For the 21 400 *victims* and their families, who sumitted their stories in writing, or told them in public, it was generally a healing experience. Not everyone experienced it positively; there were also those who returned home disappointed and frustrated. But for the great majority it was a cathartic experience, even though it was difficult to take the stand, to relive the past. The tears that flowed freely, were usually tears of healing. The aged Xhosa woman who in East London told the terrible story of her 14-year old child being tortured and killed, spoke on behalf of many others: "Oh, yes, Sir, it was worth the trouble. I think that I will immediately fall asleep tonight, for the first time in sixteen years, and I will not have nightmares."

A nagging worry, however, remains: What about the other victims, the large number of men and women who did *not* come forward? Some – also from the white community – stayed away because of political reasons or because they did not trust the process; others – like many in the war-torn KwaZulu-Natal – for fear of intimidation and retaliation. Then there were also the millions that probably wanted to come forward, but the narrow definition that the Act ascribes to "gross human rights violations" – murder, culpable homicide, kidnapping, rape, serious torture resulting in physical and psychological damage – effectively disqualified them. Millions of South Africans were, however, humiliated

and persecuted over the past decade, arrested for petty apartheid offences and dragged to prison. A total of 3,5 million were forcefully
removed form their homes and 'transferred' to other parts of the country. These people probably have just as much bottled-up frustration
and pain, just as many questions and an equally great need for a process of healing and catharsis. What is to be done for them? Do they not
also have the right to be heard?

For the more than 7 000 *amnesty applicants* the process meant just
as much – in any case for those who were granted amnesty. Initially
most of the applications came from behind bars, from criminals who
did not really qualify, but wanted to put their case to the TRC as a last
resort. When General Johan van der Merwe and his police colleagues
eventually reported, the initially small stream became a river. The fact
that relatively few politicians and Defence Force officers from the former
dispensation came forward, was reason for great concern. When the
TRC closed its doors, it was reported that the final number of amnesty
applications had grown to 7 124. Of them, approximately two thirds,
4 696, had already been dealt with – the majority without the need for
protracted public hearings. In cases where public hearings took place,
75 applicants had already been granted amnesty, while 61 applications
had been turned down. Of the applications being handled, 54 per cent
came from the ANC, 20 per cent from the side of previous government
and its security forces, 12 per cent from the PAC, 9 per cent from the
IFP and 5 per cent from the far right wing.

A great concern was the fact that the Amnesty Committee – because
of the unexpected large number of applications and the lengthy and
reasonably tedious legal procedure required by law – could not finish
its work on time. When the final report was tabled, some 1 200 amnesty applications were still outstanding, and all of them required public hearings. In all probability the Amnesty Committee – which in the
meantime has expanded considerably – will only be finished with its
work by mid 1999.

Was it worth the effort to come forward? The unfortunates who did
not qualify for amnesty, will have one answer. But many others, who
did, have every reason to identify with Adriaan Vlok, "I had a lump in
my throat – and thanked the Lord." For perpetrators who lived under a
cloud for years, the process meant a new life! From the side of some
high-profile families of victims there were serious objections. The Biko,
Mxenge and Goniwe families, from the Eastern Cape, saw the process
as extremely unfair towards the victims. They felt so strongly about it

testimony on the biological and chemical weapon research, the cynical experiments carried out by 'our people', many Afrikaners and English-speaking people were confronted with the harsh reality: Were these things really possible? The moving scene on the pulpit of the Lynnwood congregation was far more than a mere incident in the life of a white minister and a black bishop. It was a symbol of two communities, white and black, reaching out to each other after years of injustice and misunderstanding – embracing, with tears running down their cheeks. The congregation that stood up and clapped hands, did so on behalf of scores of fellow-countrymen in the far corners of South Africa.

◆ ◆ ◆

Did the Truth Commission get to the *truth*? Is the report a comprehensive and fair overview of everything that happened in our country during the years of apartheid? Or is the report, as many feared, a one-sided caricature of reality, aimed at humiliating one sector – the Afrikaners? It was an issue: how to put all the facts that had been dug up together to form one big picture, as fairly and objectively as humanly possible. How could the report reflect the various contexts in which people lived? Tongue in cheek – but with a hint of seriousness – the TRC members on occasion said to each other, "We must be careful! In ten years' time there'll be a Truth Commission about the Truth Commission!"

One thing we did learn during the long journey was that modesty becomes us all. Even when talking about truth, it is often not much more than *your truth, your view* of matters. Michael Ignatief put it exceptionally well: We cannot do everything, we cannot produce perfect truth. "(But) what the Truth Commission can indeed do, is to curtail the number of lies that up to now had free reign in society." The fact that the TRC's report was criticized from *all* sides, that *all* political parties felt their toes had been tread on was, in fact, to the advantage of the process – emphasised its impartiality. The ANC effort to torpedo the report was instrumental in allaying the fears of many Whites, namely that the TRC would become a witch-hunt, with Blacks (especially the ANC) hunting down Whites (especially Afrikaners).

The process of finding the truth has long not been finalized. We will still have to listen to each other's stories a long while. The well-known writer Ellen Kutswayo said, "Africa is a place of story telling. We need more stories, never mind how painful the exercise might be. This is how we learn to love one another. Stories help us to understand, to forgive and to see things through someone else's eyes."

Was it really necessary to battle through the painful process? Yes! Tutu was right: the books had to be opened before they could be properly closed. The *victims* needed to have the truth told: for them the truth was at any time as important as justice. It was a condition for reconciliation. And *regarding the rest of South Africa* – for us it was equally necessary that the ghosts be exposed and dealt with and be exorcized once and for all. It was emphasized at the beginning of the process that the search for truth had to be handled with great sensitivity. Would that *not* be the case, the nation could bleed to death. But if it *did* indeed happen, it would lead to a national catharsis and peace and reconciliation. History will one day be the judge.

One aspect of the search for truth has to do with our need to mourn. Someone once remarked, "Maybe we jumped too far too soon – from the struggle and liberation straight across to joy and celebration. We forgot that there has to be an in-between stage: the stage of remembering and mourning. We need that stage very much, should we wish to understand, should we want to work through our past, should we want to arrive at the point where the truth truly sets us free."

◆ ◆ ◆

And *reconciliation*? What happened to the second leg of the Truth and Reconciliation Commission? Were we naive to believe that once we had welcomed truth at the front door, reconciliation would slip in through the back door of its own accord?

The matter of reconciliation is far more difficult than the issue of truth. Has the process helped to bring people closer to one another – or just the opposite? History will have to make the final judgment on this as well. As was the case with the quest for truth, humility is necessary when we speak of reconciliation. Reconciliation is indeed something wonderful, something fragile, a gift from Above. But it is not something one can arrange or organize. Microwave-oven reconciliation never lasts long!

Sometimes miracles did happen. In some instances it was as if God in all his greatness smiled, and let the rays of reconciliation shine through the clouds: Eric Taylor, Brian Mitchell, Beth Savage, Amy Biehl's parents, Diale and Makgale in Phokeng. To quote Tutu, "Sometimes God knocked your feet out from underneath you when things happened at the most unexpected times and places, and about the mercy and generosity and forgiveness he planted in people's hearts. Our God is a God full of surprises!"

One of the first questions we had to face was, what exactly do we mean when we speak about reconciliation? Lengthy discussions about this were held within the TRC circle. On the one hand there were the jurists and politicians who, with their feet firmly on the ground, warned that we must not expect too much; simply be glad if people let go of one another's throats and stop killing each other. Should the dust settle and the guns be put away, one should be grateful. More than that could not be expected. That is reconciliation. Tutu, and the other pastors – and quite a few TRC members, however – favoured a far more lofty idea of reconciliation: When one talks about justice and forgiveness and especially reconciliation they contended, one is dealing with the deepest principles of our faith. One cannot define reconciliation without referring to 2 Corinthians 5 in your Bible. God reconciled us through Christ, with Himself – and then appointed us ambassadors of reconciliation. We are witnesses of the new creation, the new order on earth that *God* has made possible, of the *shalom*, the peace He brought. In a broken, torn South Africa, signs of his kingdom can and should be erected. Not everyone agreed with this, naturally; indeed, not all TRC members were Christians. But the point was made clear: before future reconciliation can be achieved, we will have to decide about our definitions. We will have to know what type of peace we are striving for.

Another matter that became clear, is that reconciliation is a costly undertaking. Reconciliation cannot be bought at a sale. Ask those who have been through the mill! You cannot, for example, talk about reconciliation without, in the next breath, also mentioning justice, responsibility and restitution. In a country where one part of the population is wealthy and another (large) section do not know where the food on the supper table will come from, you cannot refer to reconciliation, without also talking about poverty – and our responsibility in that regard. And in our day, in our community, it will not be an easy conversation. In the car on the way to a TRC meeting, months ago, a friend put it rather simply, but aptly: "One of the problems of our people – and mine too – is that we want reconciliation. Don't get us wrong. We would like to live in the rainbow country, but as easily and cheaply as possible. Could we live without uncomfortable questions, and not be forced to stand in front of the mirror to reflect on our own privileged positions, we would be glad, thank you very much."

Who is responsible for the process of reconciliation? Of course, every individual, every group, every denomination and religion has a contribution to make. But, I would like to add, especially the Christians in the country!

There are no two ways about it. There are great challenges and opportunities for the churches in the country – and their millions of members. Jorge Heine, the Chilean ambassador to South Africa, mentioned in his assessment of the TRC process how, at many hearings, it touched him deeply to hear Archbishop Tutu pray and Alex Boraine talk to many victims about their faith. In many countries where the division between the church and state is taken seriously, something like that would never have been possible. But in South Africa, the astounded ambassador said, it seems to be working! "The strong underlying Christian text of repentance and forgiveness gets to you time and again." While the Jewish, Muslim, Hindu and Buddhist communities, each with their own traditions and convictions, have much to plough into the process of reconciliation, we will have to pass on to each other the question in Jesus' Sermon on the Mount: What *more* do we have to offer?

Ultimately South Africa does not need reconciliation only. It also needs a new moral order. How can we learn from the lessons of the past? How can we build a new society without repeating the mistakes of the past? These are some of the questions facing us, to which we all must help find answers. South Africa is indeed a broken country. The coming trek must go through the wrecks of the past, and through the valley of crime, corruption and violence where human life has been totally devalued, to a new and better future.

◆ ◆ ◆

The Truth Commission was not the perfect commission. Not in the least. It consisted of people, each with their own history, convictions, dreams, idiosyncrasies and limited understanding. Usually the members of the commission worked together as one big family. Sometimes the sparks flew! The Act in terms of which the TRC worked was not the ideal document. It was an Act of compromise, the result of months and months of negotiations. In places the Act was not clear and the most important sections had to be tested in court. But it was the only Act we had – and things did not go that badly. From time to time the action the commission took was clumsy: the souring of relations with the National Party was not good for anyone. The difference of opinion in the

TRC about the handling of the amnesty application of 37 ANC members was an embarrassment. More could possibly have been done to rectify the perceptions among Whites that the process was one-sided and unfair – although the chairperson did bend over backwards to try and do so. The Reparation and Rehabilitation Committee took too long to finalize its policy and – especially – to make interim assistance available to victims who were sorely in need of it. Administrative red-tape also manifested. Once or twice junior staff members and cleaners went on strike because the Truth Commission of all groups, had, in their opinion, not treated them fairly!

And yet the work continued. The TRC did, with its foibles, warts and all, guide the country on its long journey, its *via dolorosa*. What a privilege to be have been part of the adventure.

We have been wounded but we are being healed. It is possible even with our past of suffering, anguish, alienation and violence to become one people, reconciled, healed, caring, compassionate, and ready to share as we put our past behind us to stride into the glorious future God holds before us as the Rainbow People of God.
– *Desmond Tutu* –

One Sunday evening, just before the TRC's doors finally closed, I was listening to a discussion of Elsa Joubert's work on the car radio. The discussion leader told listeners how the author, who had done so much to introduce her readers to Africa – to teach them what it means to live on our strange, dark, wonderful, challenging continent – loved saying that the last, most difficult trek awaiting us, was the journey from person to person, via the heart.

No-one could say it better. That is where the millions of footprints, on the way to a new future, must be made.

◆   ◆   ◆

My telephone rang one afternoon – it felt much longer than two and a half years later.

"Hello, Piet, Desmond here ... "

I wish I could pass the receiver on to every South African man, woman, child:

"Well, God says you *must* come ... "

Join the trek, the trek to the future. From person to person, via the heart.

REGISTER

1. SESSIONS OF THE TRC

Human Rights Violations Hearings

16-19 April 1996: East London, 22-29
29 April – 3 May 1996: Johannesburg, 29-43
22-26 July 1996: Soweto, 57-60
5 September 1996: Nelspruit, 67-70
15 October 1996: Paarl, 81-86
28-30 October 1996: Alexandra, 92-94
6-8 May 1997: Zeerust, Rustenburg, Mabopane, 133-135
20 May 1997: Athlone (Cape Town), 143-145

Special Hearings

3 September 1996: Political parties (IFP), 65-67
12-13 May 1997: Political parties (ANC), 136-138
14 May 1997: Political parties (National Party), 139-141
16 May 1997: Political parties (Freedom Front), 142-143
12 June 1997: Children, 145-148
18-19 June 1997: Medical (and related) occupation, 160-167
21-22 July 1997: Correctional Services, 175-183
23 July 1997: National servicemen, 183-187
29 July 1997: Women, 190-193
15-17 September 1997: The press, 213-221
26 September 1997: Winnie Madikizela-Mandela (*in camera*), 222
7 October 1997: Liberation movements, security forces, 231-235
13-15 October 1997: State Security Council, 237-244
27-29 October 1997: The legal occupation, 247-253
11-13 November 1997: Business community, 256-263
17-19 November 1997: Faith communities, 265-285
24 November – 4 December 1997: Mandela United Football Club ("Winnie-gate"), 287-310
8 December 1997: P W Botha (written submission), 310-314, cf. 318-320
5, 23 June 1998: Air disasters (Helderberg, Samora Machel), 349-350
8 June 1998 (and days after): Chemical and biological warfare, 350-357

Amnesty Hearings

20-21 May 1996: Phokeng (Diale, Makgale), 43-47
28 April 1997: Cape Town (APLA, Amy Biehl), 130-131
10 May 1997: D-day for amnesty applications, 135-136
23 June 1997: Benoni (Hani, Walus, Derby-Lewis), 152-155
8-9 July 1997: Cape Town (APLA, Amy Biehl), 167-169
10 July 1997: Cape Town (APLA), 169-170
15 July 1997: Cape Town (security forces, Benzien) 174-175
4 August 1997: Amnesty granted – Dirk Coetzee, 198
12 August 1997: Benoni (Hani, Walus, Derby-Lewis), 199-202
8 September 1997: Port Elizabeth (Nieuwoudt, Putter), 207-208
10-12 September 1997 (Biko), 210-213
1 October 1997: New applications, 226-228
1 October 1997: Port Elizabeth (De Kock), 229-231
28 November 1997: Amnesty granted to 37 ANC members, cf. 299-300, 314, 325
25-26 March 1998: Afrikaner Weerstandsbeweging (AWB), 332-334
22 April 1998: Afrikaner Weerstandsbeweging (AWB), 338-339
4 May 1998: Pretoria (MK), 339-341
2 June 1998: Pretoria (Security forces), 346-347
20 July 1998: Pretoria (Security forces, Vlok, Van der Merwe, De Kock), 357-361

Activities/gatherings of the Reparation and Rehabilitation Committee

27 February 1996: Port Shepstone, 18-19
26 October 1996: Mamelodi/Soweto, 90-92
17-19 February 1997: Oudtshoorn, 115-118
10 April 1997: Reinterment, 121
10 September 1997: Johannesburg (four files), 209-210
23 October 1997: Proposals for reparation, 244-247
7 May 1998: First reparation letters sent out, 341

2. BUSH SUMMITS (*BOSBERADE*)

18-19 September 1996: Somerset West, 77-79
20 February 1997: Cape Town, 118-119
11-13 January 1998: Robben Island, 332-336

3. VARIOUS CASES ON THE TRC AGENDA

4. COURT CASES

5. INTERNATIONAL VISITORS/EXPERIENCES

Switzerland, 91-92, 203-205, 343

6. DENOMINATIONS

7. LETTERS/CORRESPONDENCE

8. RECONCILIATION EXPERIENCES

ACKNOWLEDGEMENTS

In writing CHRONICLE OF THE TRUTH COMMISSION, I made ample use of the OFFICIAL REPORT OF THE TRC (Parts 1-5) as well as Antjie Krog's book COUNTRY OF MY SKULL to supplement my own notes and the documents I accumulated during the past three years.

The two poems by Hugh Lewin ALEXANDRA (93) and ANOTHER DAY (178), are published with the author's permission. The data on the hearing of the Faith communities (265-285) was obtained from the report that Steve Martin (University of Cape Town) prepared for the TRC.

For three years the TRC made the headlines in many newspapers. In an effort to give a lively account of the proceedings I quoted liberally from reports published in *Beeld*, *Die Kerkbode*, *Rapport*, *The Citizen*, *The Mail and Guardian*, the *Natal Witness*, *The Star*, *The Sunday Times* and a great number of other newspapers. I relied heavily on especially *Beeld*, whose editor and their Pretoria librarian deserve a special word of gratitude. The photographs in the book (with the exception of the Robben Island photos) are all from the archives of *Beeld* – for which I thank them.

The moving adaptation of "Helena's" letter was done by Angie Kapelianis and was broadcast on the program MONITOR on RADIO SONDER GRENSE. It is used with permission of RSG.

www.ingramcontent.com/pod-product-compliance
Lightning Source LLC
Chambersburg PA
CBHW060135280326
41932CB00012B/1528